*Culture and Economics
in the Global Community*

This book is dedicated to Yukiko, for her utmost patience and support.

Culture and Economics in the Global Community

A Framework for Socioeconomic Development

KENSEI HIWAKI

GOWER

Gower Applied Business Research
Our programme provides leaders, practitioners, scholars and researchers with thought provoking, cutting edge books that combine conceptual insights, interdisciplinary rigour and practical relevance in key areas of business and management.

Published by
Gower Publishing Limited
Wey Court East
Union Road
Farnham
Surrey, GU9 7PT
England

Gower Publishing Company
Suite 420
101 Cherry Street
Burlington,
VT 05401-4405
USA

www.gowerpublishing.com

British Library Cataloguing in Publication Data
Hiwaki, Kensei, 1940-
   Culture and economics in the global community : a framework
   for socioeconomic development. -- (Transformation and
   innovation)
   1. Sustainable development. 2. Sustainable development--
   Social aspects.
   I. Title II. Series
   338.9'27-dc22

   ISBN: 978-1-4094-0412-5 (hbk)
   ISBN: 978-1-4094-0413-2 (ebk)

Library of Congress Cataloging-in-Publication Data
Hiwaki, Kensei, 1940-
   Culture and economics in the global community : a framework for socioeconomic
development / Kensei Hiwaki.
      p. cm. -- (Transformation and innovation)
   Includes index.
   ISBN 978-1-4094-0412-5 (hbk) -- ISBN 978-1-4094-0413-2
(ebook) 1. Economic development--Social aspects. 2. Sustainable development--Social
aspects. 3. Culture. I. Title.

   HD75.H59 2010
   338.9--dc22

                                                                    2010034178

MIX
Paper from
responsible sources
FSC® C018575

Printed and bound in Great Britain by the
MPG Books Group, UK

Contents

List of Figures

Transformation and Innovation Series

Series Editors:
Ronnie Lessem, University of Buckingham, UK
Alexander Schieffer, University of St. Gallen, Switzerland

This series on business transformation and social innovation comprises a range of books informing practitioners, consultants, organization developers, and academics how businesses and other organizations set in the context of whole economies and societies can and will have to be transformed into viable 21st century enterprises. A new kind of R&D, involving social, as well as technological innovation, needs to be supported by integrated, active and participative research in the social sciences. Focusing on new, emerging kinds of public, social and sustainable entrepreneurship originating from all corners of the world and from different cultures, books in this series will help those operating in the area of interface between business and society to mediate between the two in the way that business schools once did until, as is now argued, they lost their way and business leaders came, in many cases, to be seen as at best incompetent and at worst venal and untrustworthy.

Foreword

This outstanding work, entitled *Culture and Economics in the Global Community: A Framework for Socioeconomic Development*, written by Professor Kensei Hiwaki, Vice President and Distinguished Professor at the International Institute for Advanced Studies in Systems Research and Cybernetics, is one of the best books on economics and Sustainable Development that has ever been published. In contrast to other books on economics which influenced the economic reasoning and economic development of the past, Professor Hiwaki's book may be the most influential and refreshing book that will shape the economic development of the world of the future. While many other books of this nature focus mainly on the present situation and offer only short-term solutions, this book offers long-range strategies, the implementation of which may bring a stable, prosperous and humane future for all mankind.

Professor Hiwaki's book reviews relevant literature on the subject, examines the basic premises of the authors from different perspectives and shows why "modern economics" based on these premises failed to deliver on the promises offered. He shows, using several pertinent examples, how the economic thinking of the past failed to take into consideration many important determinants and factors of influence, and how this failure led to serious economic crises and disruptions that affected millions of people around the world. He also shows how the rigid economic thinking of the past has negatively influenced human lives and human development in so many other areas, how it destroyed cultures and how it brought globalized misery to so many around the world.

One of the strongest tenets of Professor Hiwaki's book is his emphasis on identification of a wide variety of relevant variables, factors, actors, determinants, agents of change and other important elements of reasoning that have to be taken into account for the design of effective and humane economic policies and strategies, to ensure Sustainable Development of the present and future generations within their traditional sociocultural context/environment. In addition, Professor Hiwaki shows how important it is to be aware of the mechanism of synergistic interactions of these factors and actors that influence the long-range outcome of Sustainable Development.

This book explores the synergistic interactions of social, economic, technological, cultural, environmental and other factors that influence our trajectory toward a sustainable future. Professor Hiwaki offers a new economic paradigm for balanced socioeconomic development and provides new perspective from which we can satisfactorily solve and resolve many, seemingly intractable, economic (and other) problems. This new paradigm includes thought-frame enhancement, generating creativity and innovation, enhancing maturation process, developing global governance systems for sustainability, insisting on appropriate use of tax revenue, introducing mechanism for social capital accounting and many other important factors.

This book is a must-read for economists, managers, engineers, educators and many others who are concerned with the future of our world and the fate of mankind. The book is like a compass and a road map, helping us to navigate our economies, technologies, politics and human development of the planet Earth through a stormy sea of economic crises, bringing us all to the harbor of peace, tranquility and prosperity.

George Lasker

President and Distinguished Professor, the International Institute
for Advanced Studies in Systems Research and Cybernetics (IIAS)
Conference Chairman, the International Conference on Systems Research,
Informatics and Cybernetics (held annually in Baden-Baden, Germany)

Acknowledgements

Humanity faces a much shrouded future, to say the least. We humans need more light in our minds as well as in our future. The on-going human conditions, however, may indicate no sign of improvement, particularly on the basis of the extremely lopsided value system inherent in the modern material monoculture. Our modern value system, in the midst of increasingly severe constraints on the global environment and resources, may provide no opening to the future or to the human spirit, with its materialism, individualism, progressivism and egotism, all simultaneously driven by the "competitive" antagonism to reinforce one another for a "spiral" vicious circle. In order to rectify the deadlocked conditions, I feel it important to tackle the issue of human viability by an integral approach to balanced human and socioeconomic development in each and every society. For this purpose, we will have to restore and enrich the profound human heritage—our diverse holistic cultures across the world. Such cultural enrichment with our determined *perpetual* collaborations will not only overcome the lopsided value system eventually but also contribute to sound human and socioeconomic development. In my prolonged search for an integral way toward Sustainable Development, I have been indebted to so many great humans with intelligence and kind hearts. Therefore, I take this opportunity as my privilege and pleasure to acknowledge such manifold indebtedness.

I wish to thank Professor Dr George E. Lasker, Founding President of the International Institute for Advanced Studies in Systems Research and Cybernetics (IIAS), who encouraged me to write this book on Sustainable Development and kindly offered many precious opportunities to pursue my integral methodology. He also wrote the Foreword to this book after a thorough read through of my early manuscript whilst suffering enormous pain from injuries sustained in a car accident. Next, I wish to thank Professor Ronnie Lessem of Buckingham University, who, after reading the early manuscript, invited me to publish it as part of Gower Publishing's *Transformation and Innovation Series*. He and his partner at TRAMS4M Geneva, Dr Alexander Schieffer, as the Series Editors, and Mr Martin West, the Commissioning Editor of Gower Publishing, have kindly supported and guided me throughout the publication process.

I wish to thank Professor Ayten Aydin, IIAS, civil engineer/anthropologist and former UN/FAO Senior Advisor, who read the early manuscript chapter by chapter and suggested many improvements. For the development of my ideas and theories on the integral approach to Sustainable Development, I am indebted to my long-standing colleagues and friends at the International Conference on Systems Research, Informatics and Cybernetics (held annually in Baden-Baden, Germany). In particular, I would like to thank Professor William Graham, University of Toronto, Canada, who has shared with me his profound knowledge on Greek philosophy and collaborated with me as a good friend in a variety of activities at the International Conference. Similarly, my sincere thanks go to Professor Greg Andonian, Carlton University, Canada; Dr Steffi Wiesbauer, Anthroplogy Center/IIAS, Austria; Professor Hugh Gash, St Patrick's College, Ireland;

Professor Michele Malatesta, University di Napoli, Italy; Professor Felipe Lara-Rosano, National University of Mexico; Professor Karel Boullart, University of Gent, Belgium; Dr Hiltrud Schinzel, IIAS, Dusseldorf, Germany; Professor John Hiller, University of Sydney, Australia; Professor Vladimir A. Fomichove, Moscow State University, Moscow, Russia; Professor Olga S. Fomichova, State Educational Center, Moscow, Russia; Professor Harry Schwarzlander, Syracuse University, USA; and Dr Toben Larsen, CAST, Southern Danish University, Denmark.

In view of our trans-disciplinary in-depth discussions, I also wish to thank Dr Junie Tong, CEO of J.E. Harrison and Co. Ltd. UK; Professor Debabrata Chatterjee, retired Consultant General Surgeon, National Health Service, UK; Mr Niels Dahlmann, Consul of Latvia, Brussels, Belgium; Lord Sydney, H.ILL.H. Count de Rosielle, France; Professor Roland Benedikter, Stanford University, USA; Professor Viktor Adamkiewicz, Maritime University, Poland; Dr Bernard Teiling, ex-Vice President of Nestle, Switzerland; Professor Brian R. Sinclair, University of Calgary, Canada; Professor Vojko Potocan, University of Maribor, Slovenia; Dr Georgine Lansky, HBLA f. künstlerische Gestaltung, Austria; Professor Jerry L.R. Chandler, George Mason University, USA; Professor Gerard de Zeeuw, University of Amsterdam, the Netherlands; Professor Yang-Taek Lim, Hanyang University, Korea; Professor Akira Ishikawa, Aoyama Gakuin University, Japan; Professor Yukio Ito, Osaka University of Economics, Japan; Professor Masaru Saito, Chuo University, Japan; Professor Joonho Kim, Tokyo International University; and Dr Kazuyuki Ohdaira, Ministry of Foreign Affairs, Japan.

There are so many other colleagues and friends who, also supporting my integral approach, have contributed to the last eleven International Symposia on Sustainable Development: Theories, Strategies and Global Governance Systems; the last seven International Symposia on Personal and Spiritual Development in the World of Cultural Diversity; and the last three International Symposia on Celtic Civilization, all which have been held under the auspices of the International Conference and IIAS mentioned above. Though I cannot mention all their names here, my deep appreciation goes to them nevertheless.

Moreover, my unforgettable thanks must go to my lifelong friend, Mr Seiji Kaku, and his understanding wife Michiko, who have encouraged me and supported me for half a century through the good and bad times. Without them my academic life could not have taken off.

I wish to acknowledge that a substantial idea of the "Credibility Trap" was reprinted from *Human Systems Management*, Volume 25, Kensei Hiwaki and Junie Tong, "Credibility Trap: Japan today and China tomorrow", pp. 31–50 (2006), with permission from IOS Press.

Also, I must thank for the permission from the International Institute for Advanced Studies in Systems Research and Cybernetics (IIAS) for free use of my articles published by IIAS during the period between 1994 and 2009.

Finally, I wish to express my heartfelt thanks to my respected, kind and conscientious Professor Otto E. Rössler, University of Tübingen, Germany, who, after carefully reading my early manuscript, wrote the following deeply illuminating Preface to this book.

Preface

Professor Hiwaki is attempting the impossible with this book: to point a way toward the Sustainable Development of our planet with a long-term perspective. He draws on many areas of knowledge, most strongly on his own international economic and political studies, but also on his profound knowledge-from-within of one particular insular society—the one he lives in—and, equally, on his Celtic transnational and transtemporal research. Apart from these qualities, he is also the most unassuming and constructive thinker on the planet in my view, comparable only to his interdisciplinary friend George E. Lasker. Sustainability of Humanity is the topic of this book in a nutshell—encompassing both meanings of the word "humanity."

This treatise will expand the horizon of any reader. Integrating across boundaries in the vast fields opened up, it is most timely. It hereby represents a natural counterpart to Stephen Hawking's prophetic vision of an insular planet that vitally depends on colonizing other planets in time—to compensate for the statistically unavoidable self-destruction on every planet it touches because total extinction can only be counteracted in this spreading fashion. Hawking's friend and colleague, Martin Rees, in his 2003 book *Our Final Hour* bravely collected all the evidence of how the first (our) planet barely brushed by extinguishing all its higher life forms in the twentieth century—with a single officer on a single submarine deserving the crucial credit for us still being here. This incredible dangerousness of our species is by no means a thing of the past.

Having been granted the undeserved privilege to write the preface to this book, I would like to briefly point to two anthropological constants belonging to the broader background of the field: "smile theory" and "emergency theory." The former theory was developed in cooperation with Konrad Lorenz in 1966, in partial anticipation of Jan van Hooff's empirical comparative-anatomical and comparative-physiological study of 1971 titled "On the phylogeny of laughter and smile": a single species on the planet, moderately advanced and mirror-competent, developed (through evolutionary "ritualization" in the sense of Julian Huxley) an anatomical and physiological convergence up to virtual identity of two innate facial expressions—that of exhilaration and happiness (laughter) and that of bonding (smile). In van Hooff's terms, the "wide open mouth display" in response to sudden tickling and the "silent bared teeth display" when nonaggressive or bonding, converged in the evolution of a single primate species.

In the wake of this event, the whole body of those primates became as hairless as the two cheeks of a happily satiated infant (whose facial expression was evolutionarily adopted as the bonding signal by this species). Hence happiness looks like friendliness in this species. The trend was so powerful that, eventually, two more pairs of hairless cheeks developed on their bodies in "self-mimicry" as it might be called.

This is at first sight a harmless if slightly tactless insight (I apologize). Van Hooff himself was startled when learning that his value-free comparative-anatomical discovery entailed "tangible consequences" and did not want to be part of them back in 1973. This is because an "interactional misunderstanding" is programmed-in as a side effect occurring on the level of two individuals. This epigenetic effect goes so far that a young offspring (toddler) predictably develops the "suspicion of benevolence" toward his caretaker. A positive feedback develops between the mirror-competent toddler on the one hand and his female or male parent on the other. More specifically, the coincidence between a granted satisfaction (when being fed, for example) and the simultaneously felt bonding reward, through the caretaker's displayed joy (laughter) at her successful mothering act, mistaken for a bonding signal (smile), will induce the toddler to make this misattribution to the caretaker—that he cared. Of course, he did care in the direct meaning of the word, as any feeding mammal "cares" by being rewarded by the displayed effects of its activities on the surface of its object of feeding, say, but not by the latter's internal state. Here, however, it is the toddler who makes the misattribution (or not) of the effect on him being intended by the caretaker. Empirically speaking, the toddler will therefore start feeding the adult in a stupid or not so stupid game. This is an otherwise unheard-of trait in biology. "Pongo goneotrophicus" (the parent-feeding ape) is, therefore, the most fitting biological name of that species. No other species on the planet—and presumably the universe—sports this trait. For the latter amounts to a "lethal factor" in the sense of evolutionary biology, being analogous (if opposite in character if not in effect) to "pedophagy"—the eating of progeny by the adults.

The toddler's spontaneously invented suspicion of benevolence being shown to him (no matter whether true or not) amounts to the attribution of a person property—benevolence—and thereby turns the toddler into a person himself. For a person property can only be attributed by a person. The spontaneously invented suspicion of a benevolent other intentionality amounts to an example of creation out of nothing—the only such instance known to science. In the ensuing positive feedback of mutually endorsed benevolence, the toddler's mind gets functionally transformed and so gets the cosmos. When returning to the parlance of evolution theory, the species can be said to have left the main traveled path of evolutionary progress. But at the same time, the two individuals have accomplished evolution's ultimate goal: a jump right into the lap of "point Omega," as Teilhard de Chardin calls the dynamical attractor underlying the cosmos.

This pragmatic scientific theory is very hard to communicate. Only Gregory Bateson fully appreciated it in 1975. It represents an unexpected finding in coincidence with a Buddhist, Jesuan and Rumian tradition. Soeur Emmanuelle's recent book (in French), *Confessions of a Religious Person*, sports a cover photograph of a 99-year-old woman—smiling in an unforgettable way. The picture proves to the eye that this human accomplishment is not intrinsically stupid despite its infinite naiveté. This woman's work with the most underprivileged and their children, in Cairo, is close to the heart of the smile from *behänd* the world which is no misunderstanding at all.

There is a smile in this book. I believe it has to do with the author's father (whom I never met). But the book is maximally serious. The smiling species is at the same time the first to register the total absence of a smile—to come to grips with death. No other animal does as far as we know. Is humanity doomed? There is a saying in the Eastern tradition that we all live in a burning house, but on being told so no one sees a reason for action. This is—to the present reader—the deepest message of Hiwaki's book. Stephen Hawking and I presently disagree on whether the famous atom-smashing "Large Hadron Collider"(LHC) experiment at CERN (European Organization for Nuclear Research) in Switzerland should be ignited or not. It possibly—just possibly—could put the continued existence of our planet in jeopardy if a certain theorem in disproof of Hawking radiation is correct. Otherwise, Hawking radiation will save the planet. The topic of this book—sustainability of humanity—therefore closely touches on "emergency theory." The latter field is bound to become a new academic discipline if everything goes well—perhaps only so because you have read this book, you yourself.

Professor Otto E. Rössler,
University of Tübingen, Germany

Prologue

The time seems to have finally come for me to place on the table a long-term theoretical framework and the relevant discussions conducive to a viable future—the age of Sustainable Development—and also to share with all the conscientious readers worldwide my thoughts, visions, value premises, ideas, basic theoretical constructs, methodology and perspectives for Sustainable Development. The long-term theoretical framework and relevant discussions in this book may largely go against today's mainstream economics that is based on the extremely shaky and lopsided ground of modern civilization. To be candid, I have had a nagging question in my mind from the beginning of my study in economics—it started when I commenced studies at Drew University, New Jersey (USA), as undergraduate student from Japan in 1966—"Can the theories of Economics consistently, adequately and broadly explain human economic behaviors at large across the world?"

The Heavily Slanted Nature of the Economic Discipline

This deep-seated question also refers to the doubt as to whether the basic assumptions/ value premises in economics are appropriate and reasonable in our contemporary world. Such assumptions, if appropriate, should be embedded in the broad characteristics of important and general human values in diverse holistic cultures all over the world. Gradually, I came to see that almost all assumptions of Economics, perhaps, were represented by the value premises firmly embedded only in the modern material monoculture. Some of the important value references in the politico-economic terms using "free," "equal," "rational," "individual," "efficient," and "progressive," indeed, have specific and particular cultural traits that can largely be traced to the modern civilization. This implies that such politico-economic values and concepts primarily based on the assumed "competition"—when translated into non-European languages, cultures and behaviors—may not generally convey the same messages as usually expected in Western societies.

It has been my life-long conviction that *cooperation* is much more productive, effective and desirable in human communities than *competition*, as *fusion* is much more powerful than *fission*. This is one reason why I attempted to prove theoretically (for one thing) in my doctoral dissertation (entitled, "Some Analytical Aspects of the Japanese Lifetime Employment System") at the City University of New York (CUNY) in 1979 that an appropriate *cooperation* between the monopolist and the monopsonist can be more *productive* than the case of the "perfect market competition." Likewise, I feel the misplaced "individual self-interest" (also, the abusive "national interest" of industrially advanced nations) can be extremely destructive to family and community as well as to the entire human world and the global environment.

Further, principles such as "freedom," "equality," and "human rights"—deep-seated in Western cultural roots—when placed in the societies of different cultures, can do much more harm than good. For, "freedom" can be construed as license to naked selfishness, "equality" as incrimination of differences and "human rights" as superseding the existing social codes of morality. Moreover, "rationality" can turn into a dogma that condemns anything short of "perfect rationality," as implicitly assumed in Economics. Likewise, "efficiency," when dogmatically pursued as in Economics, may deny almost all human qualities and characteristics.

When value-laden words such as "efficiency," "individual," "material," "progress," "competition," and "self-interest" are strongly emphasized, as they are in Economics (without providing for their necessary counter-balancing and ameliorating values), they together may mold, over time, extremely lopsided human thoughts, ideas, creativities, attitudes and behaviors which are highly antagonistic, disorderly and destructive forces against humanity, human communities and the global environment. Economics, giving rise to the so-called "market approach" and the lopsided market fundamentalism, has been obliterating the cohesiveness of family, community and nation by destroying their cultural and environmental foundations. Economics and economic globalization have brought about deception, immorality and aggression to inflict an enormous damage on credibility, reliability and viability of humanity in both *intra*-national and *inter*-national transactions and human relations.

By offering my candid thoughts and value premises in this book, I am deeply aware of the risk I run, in our contemporary world with its grossly lopsided value system, of telling the truth and going against the general inculcation. Regardless of the risk, however, it is crucially important now to tackle the *core-value aspects* of the present worldwide predicaments, particularly the drastic degradation of credibility in governance, finance, employment and international trade, among other things. Referring to the *core values*, it is also imperative to view them from a broad and long-term global perspective and orientation, which may go well beyond the Western sphere of academic influences as well as much beyond the confine of the modern times. For that matter, my standpoint and thought-frame in time-space is, perhaps, slightly more advantageous than most of the economists in the Western hemisphere, where there is a strong heritage/bind of the modern civilization, and also most of the Japanese economists who have almost blindly studied and adopted the thoughts, theories and ideas established in the West.

My Academic and Professional Experiences Abroad

I was raised in Japan until the age of 26 and then studied in US universities for nearly 14 years, majoring in Economics (I received a BA from Drew University in 1970, a MA from Duke University in 1972 and a PhD from CUNY in 1980). As a sophomore at Drew University, I participated in the first "Eleanor Roosevelt Workshop for Human Relations" (30 participants from different walks of life in the US and a further 30 participants of different nationalities and different walks of life, lodging together for a week on the campus of Rutgers University, New Jersey) sponsored by the United Nations Association of the United States of America, and I was elected as the first Workshop Alumni President. As a junior at the same university, during the 1969 Spring Semester I had the opportunity of studying at Drew University's "European Community Program" (a consortium of US universities for European Community studies) as one of a group of 15 students in Brussels, Belgium. We received weekly lectures from President Jean Rey (the-then incumbent President of the Commission of the European Community), Professor Jan Tinbergen (Professor of Economics at the Netherlands Economic Hogeschool, later to receive the very first Nobel Prize for Economics in late 1969), and many other distinguished professors.

During my time at Duke University, at the request of the North Carolina Chapter President of the United Nations Association, USA, I organized and presided over the first "Oriental Evening" (presented by well-wishing individuals from China, Philippines, Korea and Japan) introducing the cultures of these nations (demonstrating the tea ceremony, bamboo dance and so on) and representative dishes to the people of North Carolina. As a PhD student at CUNY, in addition to teaching Microeconomics, Macroeconomics, Statistics, Money and Banking, Labor Economics and History of Economic Thought over a period of five years at Brooklyn College (CUNY), I assumed the role of Resident Director General for the Committee on International Campaign for the Northern Territories Problem (supported by about 60 prominent private organizations, leftist-to-rightist, in Japan) for three years. As part of this role I paid visits to the United Nations (UN) representative offices of US, UK, China, France, Soviet Union and other nations, explaining about the Northern Territorial issue to the ambassadors whenever the relevant Japanese delegations came to New York.

At the request of my *alma mater*—Drew University—whilst still studying under the CUNY PhD Program and with their permission to be absent, I assumed (for the Fall Semester in 1976) the position of Resident Director/Visiting Lecturer, supervising the studies of students at the "European Community Program" in Brussels, Belgium. During this time I also had the opportunity to organize a symposium on the "Trilateral Dilemma: US, EC and Japan," represented by the Japanese Ambassador to the European Community (EC), Masahiro Nishibori, and the counterparts of the US Embassy and the EC Commission, coordinated by the Commision's former President, Jean Rey, at the Institute of European Studies/Graduate School of the Free University of Brussels.

Upon completion of my PhD at CUNY, I returned to Japan and in 1980 was appointed by the Prime Minister's Office to head the Japanese youth delegation as National Leader to the "7th Ship of Southeast Asian Youth," traveling through Singapore, Malaysia, Thailand, Indonesia and the Philippines, holding discussions with youth representatives onboard the ship and with the local youth of the respective countries, as well as paying visits to the royal families, heads of governments and cabinet members in these countries and Japan. Also, basing myself at a private university (Tokyo International University) in Japan, I had the opportunity of teaching as Exchange Professor for one semester in 1983 at Willamette University, Oregon, and as Visiting Professor for one year (1990–1991) at the College of Europe (Graduate School of European studies) in Bruges, Belgium, teaching a course on the "Post-war Economy of Japan and Japanese-European Relations."

Toward the end of my guest tenure at the College of Europe, I was invited, together with the Rector Werner Ungerer (among many distinguished political, bureaucratic and academic leaders from all over Europe), by Jacques Delors, the-then President of the EC Commission, to participate in the "First Jacques Dolores Colloqium on Subsidiarity" held for a week in February, 1991 in Maastricht, the Netherlands. The result of the discussions on the "Principle of Subsidiarity" (a new democratic idea of public-role sharing in the European Union (EU)) was later inserted into the Treaty on European Union as one of the most important articles to successfully aid the creation of the EU, at a time when citizens of many European countries were deeply apprehensive and strongly against the prospective strong leadership and control by the so-called "Eurocrats" (EU bureaucrats).

Further, at the invitation in 1994 of Professor George E. Lasker, Founding President of the International Institute for Advanced Studies in Systems Research and Cybernetics (IIAS) (also, Conference Chairman of the International Conference on Systems Research, Informatics and Cybernetics), I presented the basic theoretical construct for Sustainable Development in my paper entitled "General—As Opposed to Orwellian—Socioeconomic Development" at the "2nd Orwellian Symposium" in Karlovy Vary, Czech Republic, and another paper on the long-term theoretical framework entitled "Prelude to the Global Management of Human Systems" at the "7th International Conference on Systems Research, Informatics and Cybernetics" in Baden-Baden, Germany.

I have actively participated as a paper presenter, Board member and Conference Co-Chairman for the last 15 years at the International Conference on Systems Research, Informatics and Cybernetics held annually in Baden-Baden, Germany. Under the auspices of the International Conference, I have had the opportunity to organize and preside over eleven consecutive international symposia on "Sustainable Development: Theories, Strategies and Global Governance Systems" (2000–2010), seven consecutive international symposia on "Personal and Spiritual Development in the World of Cultural Diversity" (2004–2010) and three consecutive international symposia on the "Celtic Civilization" (2001–2003). I am also organizing and chairing the "12th Symposium on Sustainable Development: Theories, Strategies and Global Governance Systems" and the "8th Symposium on Personal and Spiritual Development in the World of Cultural Diversity," to be held in Baden-Baden, in August 2011.

Local Identity and Cultural Diversity in Japan

With regards to my local identity, I was born in a small town, Kumamoto Prefecture, Kyushu Island, Southern Japan, in 1940, when Japan celebrated the 2600th (mythological date) Commemoration of the Founding of the Nation. When I was four years old, my father, a small shopkeeper, was drafted at the age 36 and died in service in March 1945 somewhere in Luzon Island, the Philippines. At the end of the Second World War, I was the only surviving child (out of five children) to my grieving mother. Thus, I amply experienced the misery of the war and the consequential hardship thereafter. At the age of 13, I came to face a "culture shock," moving to the neighboring Kagoshima Prefecture, only about 30 miles from my home town, mainly due to the failure of the family business. The dialect of Kagoshima was like a foreign language, very difficult to learn, understand and speak. As compensation for such difficulty, I was delighted to find a different way of children's fighting—very fair fighting—always one against one (my experience of fighting in my home town was rather unfair—often one against two or more). My experiences in Kagoshima awakened me to the rich and diverse cultures of Japan.

After graduating from a commercial high school (Kagoshima-shiritsu Shogyo Kotogakko) at the age of 18, I took a job with the Kobe Travel Company (Honshu: Mainland), which specialized in overseas travel and, almost simultaneously, I started studying English at a night school (Palmore Institute). After three years at the travel company, I worked for a Norwegian-Japanese Company (AALL and Co. Ltd) also in Kobe, as Assistant Manager of the Oil Division that acted as the sole agents in Japan for Gulf Oil

(USA), Castrol Oil (UK), Antar Oil (France) and Wisula Oil (West Germany) distributing the lubricants for ocean-going ships. Such work experience, along with learning the English language, gave me the opportunity to meet many interesting individuals from a great variety of countries and the chance to visit many seaports in Japan, exposing me further to the cultural diversity.

Extraordinary Lessons in the Way of Flowers

As a young Japanese man, I was very much interested in *Judo*, *Sumo*, *Kendo* (the Way of Sword) and *Kado* (the Way of Flowers). Regarding *Kendo*, I will give a short account of its cultural and spiritual implications for Culture of Peace (in Theoretical Appendix 8). Here, I will briefly take up the important philosophical and spiritual influence the Way of Flowers has had upon me. To practice it may imply dealing symbolically with a microcosm that consists of Heaven (*Ten*), Earth (*Chi*) and Humanity (*Jin*). A few years prior to my studies in the US, I was extremely fortunate to come across, in Kobe, a Maestro of *Kado*, Kusumoto Kaho of *Misho-ryu Anke* School, who was, perhaps, the-then very best *Kado* Maestro in the whole of Japan. Such adistinguished Maestro would usually not accept a beginner as a disciple. He accepted me, however, after I explained that I would like to offer and share with the people in the US something most intrinsic to Japanese culture, otherwise I would be only on the receiving side of scholarship, education and culture there.

The Maestro—a man in his 60s—liked the explanation of my intention and treated me like a friend whenever I visited his modest house for instruction. He ushered me into his tea room (the room for practicing the Way of Tea), leaving all the other disciples (already well-established *Kado* professors/instructors) in his living room where his instruction usually took place, and served me tea (the Maestro was also distinguished teacher in *Sado*—the Way of Tea). While serving tea, he revealed his extraordinary thoughts and ideas about the Way of Flowers in casual and candid conversation.

Some of the extraordinary instructions I received personally from him over time in the tea room and the living room can be summarized, putting the pieces together, into five important lessons. First, all three elements—Heaven, Earth and Human—must always be deemed and treated as dynamic entities. This means that harmony/beauty has to be sought and caught in a dynamic condition. The symbolical elements expressed by flowers/plants, according to the Maestro, change constantly at different speeds and directions, and, thus, require incessant and timely care for rebalancing them with a minimum touch, based on their respective inclinations, to let them grow into their harmonious and holistic glory as one natural and integral entity. Also, all the elements, showing different appearances in the circularity of life (in seasons, for instance), must be arranged in such a way as to imply the past, present and future (focusing on the "present" changing harmony and also reflecting the reminiscence of the "past" and the expectation of the "future").

Second, in order to arrange the three elements harmoniously and integrally, a fourth element (a sort of "invisible hand") must be consciously introduced to form a well-balanced holistic harmony by the well-learned ingenuity through long-term constant practice. Almost all professors/instructors of *Kado* schools routinely emphasize the importance of a balanced "*triangle*" to be arranged with the three elements (symbolically represented by the respective flowers or plants). In that case, according to the Maestro, they are dealing with the balanced view only from the front and the two sides, at best, neglecting the balanced views from the back, from above and from below. Such teaching, being superficial and naïve, does not address the intrinsic balance and holistic beauty, which are sought in the Way of Flowers. This is the reason why you must strive to devise a fourth element, a highly accomplished conscious and responsible hand of the creator that represents the law of nature.

Third, when you arrange flowers, you must not just arrange selected beautiful flowers or plants. According to the Maestro, your arranging responsibility is to *revive, enliven* and *enhance* the beauty of the flowers or plants which you happen to choose. Therefore, it is nonsense to buy already beautiful flowers or plants from florists, or to pick the best possible flowers or plants in gardens and other places where they are already provided with opportunities to show their glory in nature. If you pick such flowers or plants, you are just depriving them the opportunity of expressing themselves. In order to *revive, enliven* and *enhance* flowers or plants, you must find them devoid of such opportunities, being submerged in bushes, for instance.

Fourth, for an intrinsic and earnest practice of the Way of Flowers, you must go beyond the spiritual levels of interior decorators, artisans and artists of flowers, according to the Maestro. This means that you must not practice it for money. It means also that your practice must be in pursuit of a holistic harmony, acquiring appropriate philosophy, world view and mental attitude to life. In the practice of flower arrangement, you are responsible to glorify, to the best of your best ability, the one and only life each of flower and plant. You should not be just an interior decorator, artisan or artist. You must do better and love the flowers more, for they are not just materials for arrangement but have precious life, regardless of how short or long. Finally, and most importantly, you can always practice the Way of Flowers wherever you may go and whatever situation you are in. This means that *you can always arrange flowers in your heart.*

On one occasion I asked the Maestro, almost too frankly, whether it was necessary for me to obtain a teaching license from the head of *Misho-ryu Anke* School in order to teach *Kado* in the US. He said, looking into my eyes straight, "I have never thought of you asking such a silly question. If you think of the question seriously, you could come up with the same answer as I would. My answer is *'Absolutely No!'* As you are well aware, almost all the heads of flower-arranging schools after the Meiji Restoration or the so-called 'modernization', have not been practicing the Way of Flowers in its intrinsic sense. Instead, they have sold their souls and hearts to the 'devil' so to speak, in exchange for various skills to extract as much money as possible from their instructors and students." With such exclusive and extraordinary instructions to enrich my thought-frame, perspective and critical mind, I could always be at ease (not being pretentious) when sharing the enjoyment of flower arrangement at garden clubs and elsewhere in the US.

Japanese Absorption in Modernization

The special instructions I received in my youth helped me establish my identity firmly in the value system of long-endured Japanese culture and helped me gain a rather balanced time-space perspective, which always provided me the critical mind—"second opinions" so to speak—in my studies of Economics and other subject matters. Thus, thinking of

Japan's experiences after the Meiji Restoration, I feel that the Japanese people at large have lost sight of themselves and their excellent heritage, in their anxious and hasty attempt for the "modernization," without adequate chewing, digesting and understanding of the modern civilization and without carefully examining the underlying Japanese culture and nationhood. Such culture and nationhood have been enriched and refined over more than 15 millennia of Neolithic and historical processes on the Japanese Archipelago, encompassing nature-loving aesthetics, mores, knowledge, wisdom, thriftiness, patience and industry, as well as cooperative spirit, versatile skills, practical inclination, keen interest in the things overseas, widespread basic skills, general characteristics of sincerity and trustworthiness, which reflected the very Japanese conditions—mountainous islands deficient of cultivatable land and natural resources.

As a result of the too hasty and too eager "modernization" led by the young revolutionaries, however, Japan blindly followed and imitated the course of the Western great powers, indulging in a rapid industrial and military build-up for an Imperialistic pursuit, against the teaching and warning of the influential thinkers, such as Yokoi Shonan and Saigo Nanshu, who more or less guided the nation toward the Meiji Restoration. Also, with their good insights into and perspectives about the modern civilization, they similarly urged that Japan should enrich the nation and strengthen its force, *not for supremacy but for good and peaceful governance of itself based on the people's good conscience.*

The Japanese, owing mainly to the-then rich heritage, culture-bound diligence, craftsmanship and practical inclination, became rather successful in emulating the West, but successful only to the extent that Japan became "Jack of all trades and Master of none," after Japan gradually degraded the rich, diverse and coherent holistic cultures in its eager and short-sighted "modernization." To achieve an eminent and lasting success in its own right, Japan should have maintained its own rich, dynamic and holistic cultural foundation. After narrowly winning the wars against the-then much weakened China (1895) and Russia (1905), Japan's "modernized/short-sighted/lopsided" military bureaucrats, particularly after gaining power over the Government, became extremely conceited to recklessly force the entire nation to the eventual misery of the Second World War and its subsequent defeat.

Lifetime Employment System: Expected and Unexpected Effects

After the unconditional surrender to the Allied Forces and the humiliating experience of their occupation for some six years, the Japanese people pulled all their remaining capital, manpower, thriftiness, patience and diligence together to rebuiild the country, often narrowly escaping the American vigilance against anything "traditional," "undemocratic" or "anti-American." One ingenious scheme, largely overlooked by the US Government, was that of the culture-bound "industrial relations" instituted among large manufacturers in early 1950s. It was the scheme called the "lifetime employment system" consisting of stable employment with a compulsory retirement age of 55, wage and promotion systems based on seniority, a company-based labor union, bi-annual bonuses and a lump-sum retirement allowance, among other things. It was the holistic scheme/system of employment to *revive* the Japanese cohesive and cooperative spirit within the respective companies (which were somewhat likened as communities similar to *Hans*/clans in the Tokugawa Peace, prior to the Meiji Restoration).

According to my studies and analyses for the afore-mentioned doctoral dissertation, such stable employment brought about one *unexpected* favorable side-effect for the rapid economic development in the latter half of 1950s and throughout the 1960s. Usually *expected* from such an employment system was a productivity growth through cooperation and harmony between the employer and the employee, thus minimizing labor strife. Also *expected* was a greater opportunity for product improvement and refinement on the basis of stability and cooperation conducive to the incessant human-capital formation by means of on-the-job training best fitting the product lines of the respective companies. Thirdly *expected* was the highly probable engineering at each company of the long-term income share in favor of the capital share for rapid investment, on the pretext of reinforcing the competitive edge for continuous corporate growth to improve labor conditions. There were some other *expected* favorable effects, which I omit here in order to discuss the more important outcome—the *unexpected* favorable side-effect.

The *unexpected* favorable effect of the employment system, in my opinion, most important for the post-war development of Japanese economy, was the *strong and lasting* sociopsychological effect of reinforcing the *people's long-term orientation to the future*, which, in turn, accelerated a well-balanced *saving-investment* growth and, consequentially, an *export-import* growth. The almost simultaneous acceleration of *investment* and *export* boosted economic growth and created the decade-long high growth period in the 1960s. Such employment-induced sociopsychological effects also helped lay a good capital foundation, both human and physical, for future development, by accumulating industrial and social infrastructures. Such reinforced *society-general future orientation* helped establish Japan firmly in the international markets as well as helping the Japanese people regain the self-confidence that was shattered by the defeat and occupation.

Cultural Devastation and the Credibility Trap

Japanese people at large, in the absence of supportive education based firmly on the unique and holistic culture and nationhood, became blinded and carried away too soon with too much confidence (a result of unfounded conceit and being devoid of balanced long-term perspectives). This confidence arose as a result of managing and overcoming the first and second oil crises, as well as successfully competing in international markets despite the rapidly rising Yen-value in the aftermath of the collapsed fixed-exchange-rate regime of International Monetary Fund (IMF). Some business leaders even started boasting openly: "There is nothing more to learn from the West." Such unfounded conceit and boasting, perhaps, reflected the emerging and almost totally lopsided Japanese superficial "modernization" (devoid of Japan's intrinsic cultural contents) and/or the new Japanese dogmatism fermented in the close business-government-collaboration scheme for their own mutual benefits.

In the meantime, the people at large also started showing strong tendencies toward a self-seeking attitude, money-hungry mentality and money-talk behaviors ("Money is might that makes right"). These tendencies of business, government and people generally accelerated after the G-5 Plaza Accords of exchange-rate realignment in 1985 (up-valuing Yen and Marks relative to US dollars, as well as more domestic generation of demand), and Japan moved into the period of full-dress "Gamble/Bubble" economy. The "land bubble," in particular, reflected the almost total insanity of Japanese people and the absence of morality in the Japanese superficial "modern culture." At the peak of the "land bubble" toward the end of 1990, they said *plausibly* that, if the entire land of Japan were cashed, the total proceeds could buy the entire United States "four times."

When the "bubble" finally collapsed in the beginning of 1991, the people were exposed to the reality resembling the *"floating way of life"* with no solid cultural foundation to stand firm on, for their holistic culture, particularly the intrinsic social value system, had long been stripped of almost all its contents. The people again lost their self-confidence, but this time they could no longer rely, trust and help each other, unlike the situation that had existed in the immediate post-war period. They had to face the mounting predicaments of an almost totally weakened social morality, gross degradation of corporate ethics, widespread mammon-ism, exhaustion of local communities, dissipating work motivation of youth, anxiety over social security and future living, a demoralized government seeking bureaucratic pay-off, increasingly unsociable individuals, a rise in the atrocious crimes committed by youth, rapid growth in disparity, increasing disintegration of family, rising irresponsibility of youth and an increase in adult, middle-age suicide, and so on.

In short, Japan has fallen into an extreme social lethargy and depression—the Credibility Trap (this concept will be elaborated on in Chapters 2–4). For long-lasting socioeconomic development, particularly for a well-balanced viable development, I surmise, people and society must strive to maintain a solid and reliable cultural foundation—a reasonably sound and holistic society-specific culture. Having allowed the long-endured rich, diverse, dynamic and coherent cultures to be dilapidated by the gross neglect of the people over 140 years after the Meiji Restoration, Japan has been destined to face a serious predicament—an almost bottomless regression/retardation with moralistic, economic and social disorders escalating as they are worldwide. Such has been the rise and fall of "Modern Japan."

The Extraordinary Task Ahead

From both my global perspective and local identity (as described above), in this book, I will attempt to tackle the extraordinary task of offering a long-term theoretical framework for Sustainable Development. This task will be aimed at a viable human future, on the basis of a paradigm shift as well as on perpetual collaborative endeavors of humanity, both local and global, beyond the present worldwide and multi-century-long-fermented disorders arising mainly from the "modern" lopsided value systems.

So far, economic approaches to growth and development, which were built on the historical momentum of the extremely lopsided modern value systems, have emphasized too hasty and "manipulated" growth and development, together with too much and too fast emancipation of all kinds of lusts on the basis of strong profit motives. Thus, such approaches have tended to encourage too hasty, too greedy and very short-sighted industrialization, commercialization and urbanization against the reality of severe constraints on the environment and resources. In addition, the on-going financial crisis and economic predicament on the basis of the extremely unsound "money-breeds-money" approach has very much resembled the rapid multiplication of cancer cells eventually destroying the mother system. Likewise, the present crisis and predicament has deeply affected humanity's integrity, harmony and wholesomeness and severely damaged the human viable future.

One good aspect of the present worldwide financial collapse and economic downfall, however, is their effect in awakening people at large to the danger of the long-left unsound value systems that are detached from reasonably sound diverse cultures all over the world. Now, the whole world expects the healing to start from the bottom-up, hopefully, this time more sensibly and integrally balanced between short and long term, between material and spiritual, between individual and society, between tradition and progress, between self-interest and mutual interest, and between competition and cooperation, by the steady and collaborative endeavors of all individuals and communities across the world.

Strictly Optional Status of Theoretical Appendices

I have debated with myself whether the inclusion of the Theoretical Appendices in this book is crucially important. Owing to the fact that almost all the arguments in the book are solidly based on the new theoretical foundation, I thought it was necessary to include the Theoretical Appendices to support my arguments. Thus, initially, I wanted to insert the Appendices in the respective, relevant chapters. I began to see, however, that it might unnecessarily obstruct the flow of reading to the great majority of readers not particularly interested in the complex theoretical arguments. Thanks to the timely and thoughtful advice of the Series Editor, Professor Ronald Lessem, I have decided to place all the Appendices together at the end of this book. Though highly important to me and, perhaps, to some rigorous readers, I consider the Theoretical Appendices *strictly optional* to all readers.

Introduction

In view of our integral approach to a viable development of the prospective global community, Sustainable Development naturally assumes paramount importance. Sustainable Development is defined by the World Commission on Environment and Development (WCED) in *Our Common Future* (WCED 1987) as follows: "Sustainable Development is development that meets the needs of the present without compromising the ability of future generations to meet their own needs." This definition is complemented with a further clarification of the concept: Sustainable Development is "a process of change in which the exploitation of resources, the direction of investment, the orientation of technological development, and institutional change are made consistent with future as well as present needs." Also, based on the 2002 World Summit on Sustainable Development in Johannesburg, South Africa, the definition is broadened to read as follows: "Sustainable Development is built on three interdependent and mutually reinforcing pillars—economic development, social development and environmental protection—which must be established at local, national, regional and global levels." Interpreted consistently, Sustainable Development is an extra long-term process of balanced local-and-global socioeconomic development harmoniously protecting and enhancing the global environment.

To provide a more concrete definition for the purposes of this book, Sustainable Development is taken here to be a well-balanced personal, spiritual and material thriving of all human descendants in perpetuity on the basis of our socioeconomic activities harmonious with the environment and resource constraints on our insular planet. In this sense, the concept of Sustainable Development addresses squarely the issue of life or death. Yet, the concept of Sustainable Development is not well-known to, or taken seriously by, most of the world population. Perhaps it is due to the lack of a "global community" sharing income, wealth and life commonly and equitably. Also, it may be due to our too heavy reliance on the modern academic inclination to the methodology, relevant to reductionism and pragmatic partial solutions. Such methodology and solutions almost always provide intrinsically contradictory, ambivalent optimistic-pessimistic results. Such an academic bias also detests the insights and analogies even of our contemporary sages, unless they are "scientifically" disguised in terms of reductionism with concrete data of short-run, partial or marginal varieties.

Methodology for Sustainable Development

When we deal with such an unprecedented issue as Sustainable Development, however, it is fundamentally important for us to be open-minded to cherish well-learned, well-wishing and well-reasoned appropriate advice, insights and analogies based on long-term perspectives and long-enduring wisdom. For our scientific knowledge is limited when it comes to the remote future, particularly the long-term future consequences of our contemporary socioeconomic activities. When dealing with a long-term consequence, any short-run, partial or marginal data is, almost always, either misleading or irrelevant. A long-term phenomenon almost always refers to a complex one that can be attributed to a variety of multidimensional, interdisciplinary and short-and-long term causes, involving the environment, culture, history, polity, violence, social characteristics, psychological atmosphere, geopolitical conditions, technological setting, developmental bias, market failure, policy failure, culture failure and so on.

This may mean that Sustainable Development requires, at the very least, an extra-long-term, multifaceted, systemic and analogical approach to closely interacting complex issues. Simultaneously, it may require our firm and unbending will, global-scale public spirit and untiring endeavors based on our keen awareness of the impending predicaments as well as on our appropriate long-term future perspectives resulting from the heritage of diverse society-specific cultures (Culture). We must even be willing to undergo rather drastic changes in our contemporary behaviors and lifestyles for the common good—Sustainable Development—and the relevant issues such as Culture of Peace and Global Humanity. In a broad sense, all such global issues, being not only mutually inseparable but also mutually supportive, may require a coherent and integral approach to their synchronous or systemic realization.

Such complex global-scale problems pose a serious question to the contemporary methodology that favors step-by-step partial and/or patchwork approaches, due mainly to the modern, scientific/academic tendency toward the reductionism and pragmatic "partial" solutions. With only a moment of reflection, we can see through the inherent contradiction and ineffectiveness of such methodology, for the contemporary national and corporate practices are strongly oriented to expansionism (in terms of both power and Gross Domestic Product (GDP)) as well as to local-and-global engagement. Such contemporary national and corporate practices and orientations may point to the necessity of a long-term integral methodology to fit the politico-socioeconomic realities.

Highly contradictory as it is, however, partial and/or patchwork approaches with the collection of quantitative/material evidence are still presumed "surefooted" and "persuasive," perhaps, in view of the vested interests and the limited resources. When confronted with severe criticism, many may just give a gesture of despair or a shrug of the shoulders. Some may even venture to say, "Doing anything is better than doing nothing," while wasting horrendous amounts of resources and, most certainly, worsening the problems over the long term and shifting the accelerated costs en masse to the weak and poor as well as to future generations. Keenly aware of the grave magnitude of human predicament, we cannot easily excuse ourselves by shrugging our shoulders or patching up the situation with a piecemeal approach.

Vested Interests and the Challenges Ahead

What we must keep in mind is the existent intrinsic causes and the historical background of such gigantic and extraordinary challenges. The intrinsic causes include the powerful ideology/dogma of market fundamentalism (abbreviated as "Market") and the logic of the strong or the logic of absolute competition, which together converge on the ideology of "might-makes-right." These causes may stand in the way of our appropriate and successful challenges. The ideology of market fundamentalism and the logic of absolute competition have been strongly backed by contemporary power structure (abbreviated as Big Market) as well as by modern materialism, industrialism, expansionism, rationalism, individualism, liberal democracy, laissez-faire economics and derogatory interpretation of the concept "self-interest." Also, ideology and logic is deep seated in the mind of our contemporary individuals and collectives, resisting against our long-term endeavors for world collaboration.

As a result of such awesome forces behind the global issues we face, the vested interests of individuals and organizations may hinder any attempts to address these challenges. With all odds against our bid, we still need to venture for a paradigm shift, if there seems to be any minuscule chance for it. The paradigm shift in our present argument demands a worldwide enrichment of diverse and holistic society-specific culture ("society-specific cultures abbreviated as "Cultures") that respectively encompass personal and societal experiences, knowledge, skills, wisdom, mores, customs, traditions, expressions and means of communication, among other things. Such a paradigm shift for nurturing the respective soundness of diverse Cultures through constant Cultural enrichment may be conducive to the restoration of humanity, the encouragement of personal character-building, the promotion of human capacity and the enhancement of personal and societal thought-frames.

It can be argued that such comprehensive human development based on conscious and constant enrichment of diverse and holistic Cultures over time may help encourage the enhancement of personal and societal thought-frames and the consequential reinforcement of long-term future orientation, a commonly shared intrinsic code of conduct and humanly harmonious subsistence. In other words, such human development may be conducive to worldwide collaborative endeavors for the common good—Sustainable Development—on the basis of common and intrinsic human spirit, aspiration and survival instinct shared in diverse and reasonably sound cultures ("reasonably sound cultures" abbreviated as "Sound Cultures"). It can also be argued that such comprehensive human development based on Cultural enrichment and soundness relates directly or indirectly to *common personal ethos* for sound, active and fruitful longevity as well as to *common societal ethos* for human improvement/advancement in the spirit, will and value relevant to human continuity, mutuality, solidarity, integrity and harmony. Such Cultural enrichment and soundness can usher in the age of Sustainable Development.

The Classical Paradigm Re-Examined

The paradigm shift for encouraging Cultural enrichment across the world may call for a brief review and re-examination relevant to the classical paradigm that is deeply imbedded in contemporary politico-economic thoughts. Adam Smith's development paradigm consists of the concept of sound market function—invisible hand—and the concept of human nature centering on individual motivation—self-interest—as well as the concept of "division of labor" (Smith 1937). The powerful concept of invisible hand—sound market function—was introduced rather quietly, with only one mention in Smith's book *The Wealth of Nations*. Smith ingeniously made a comparison of invisible hand with free competition of self-interested individuals to the natural order of Newton's universal gravitation (Canterbery 1980).

In defense of such a perfect harmony of individual activities in the market, the Scottish thinker Smith introduced the concept of "natural liberty" and justified laissez-faire, the concept of the *physiocrats* who argued that all that government needed to do was to allow man to follow his own "natural" tendency, implanted by God (Lekachman 1959). Though intentionally ignored by the Marxists and mitigated or tamed somewhat by the Keynesians, the concept of invisible hand seems to have survived the test of historical changes for well over 200 years and has established itself solidly in the world of economy as an important institution, providing useful information to facilitate short-run transactions specific to the monetary market economy.

Even more pervasive in its influence on secularism and gainful motive in the capitalist world has been the classical "self-interest" that indicates the alleged nature of human motivation. Regarding the idea that "self-interest" tends to work for public interest, Smith's indebtedness to Bernard de Mandeville has been often overstated. Smith differed fundamentally from Mandeville as to the very condition, under which self-interest could work favorably for public interest. Mandeville (Hollander 1992) "insisted that private activity ruled by self-interest had desirable social consequences only if under the dexterous management of government." Smith argued that "self-interest" had to be left free for the greatest welfare of society. "Self-interest" did not mean to Smith a sheer selfishness but one that was steeped in the social nature of sentiments, such as reciprocal help and respect, generosity, compassion and humanness (Canterbery 1980).

Smith emphasized the human nature of "public interest" in his first work, *Theory of Moral Sentiments* (1759), and the individual "self-interest" in his more famous second work, *The Wealth of Nations* (1776). He put forward the idea that human statures both of public interest and self-interest would harmonize the individual interest with the interest of general public. According to Smith, the ultimate happiness of humans could be derived from the perfect liberty of self-interested pursuits aroused by their public concern (Canterbery 1980). He seemed to relate confidently or optimistically the self-interest of individuals to the natural harmony of interests in a free politico-economic environment. Also, according to Smith, "self-interest" would motivate individuals to improve occupational skills which lead to a more profound "division of labor" and a greater individual productivity and income, while enriching the whole of society (Smith 1937).

Regardless of the possibility that Smith gave a completely different nuance to the term self-interest as mentioned above, its most derogatory meaning has prevailed as the strong undercurrent in the popular economic thinking. Herman E. Daly and John B. Cobb Jr. deal profoundly with this concern in their outstanding book, entitled *For the Common Good* (1994). In the concluding remark on *"Homo economicus,"* they state that the use of the model based on the narrowly defined human nature "influences actual behavior away from community-regarding patterns toward selfish ones." The derogatory concept of "self-interest" has also served the rich and the strong as a broad license for unreserved pursuit of wealth or "private property." Besides, it has been used as a blanket excuse, albeit implicit, for exploiting fellow humans, not to mention the common and public properties—the diverse Cultures and the Environment (the latter is defined in Chapter 8 to comprise natural, humanitarian and peaceful environments, among others). Further, the derogatory concept of "self-interest" has been used as an excuse for expanding the disparity of income, wealth and socioeconomic amenity among fellow humans and societies, both *intra*-national and *inter*-national.

In the popularized classical paradigm, the famous invisible hand guides "self-interest" to perform the miracle of economic development. In this scheme of things, perhaps, the market function is deemed or assumed to let "self-interest" work for the good of society. To put it differently, the paradigm may mean (or may be misinterpreted to mean) that a society develops without any conscious objective of the social constituents nor with any public direction of the "individual" constituents, who are assumed to pay attention only to the respective "self-interest" for their own fulfillment and satisfaction. Alternatively interpreted, the paradigm may assume either the market as the very guiding hand of God or the market being complemented by a very sound and powerful society-specific culture (sound and powerful Culture). One particular phrase in *The Wealth of Nations* (1937) has been used and abused by both economists and economic layman, as if Smith meant non-existence of public spirit among merchants: "I have never known much good done by those who affected to trade for the public good. It is an affection, indeed, not very common among merchants, and very few words need to be employed in dissuading them from it." This phrase, however, may imply only that their "affectation" may not represent their "true intention."

In a sense, the proposition by Smith is an epoch-making paradigm, and yet it is misleading, to say the least. Interpreted literally (or misled totally), the paradigm excuses the responsibilities of all persons for all possible outcomes, seemingly denying any intentions, concerns and/or public spirit among the social constituents. Furthermore, this popularized paradigm, implying an extremely narrow view of human nature, is even self-defeating over the long duration of time, as far as sound socioeconomic development is concerned. To be sure, individuals are often motivated by greed, ambition, passion for power, or desire to make them superior to others in some way, but many people are also known to be capable of restraining such self-centered motivations for the common good and public interest. The popularized classical paradigm with the derogatory "self-interest," no doubt, spells catastrophe to both the global environment and socioeconomic development in the age of sumptuous mass production, scrap-and-build investment, prodigal consumption, unscrupulous speculation only for profits and wholesale disposal of waste in the environment, accompanied by growing income disparity and exploding global population.

Hence, such a misleading paradigm should no longer be upheld today when we aim for Sustainable Development. The theoretical sphere of Sustainable Development, however, largely constitutes an unexplored domain for economists or any academic on the earth. Therefore, a world simultaneously achieving socioeconomic development and environmental protection militates against the continuing adherence by most economists to the usual dichotomy of "economic development" and "environment protection." Given the plight of the actual world, however, it is absurd to indulge in an easy, fruitless and reductionist approach to the issue, by treating economic development and environmental protection separately and/or by regarding each other as the respective constraint.

The Keynesian Framework Re-Examined

In view of the extra-long-term issue of Sustainable Development, we also need to re-examine the Keynesian framework that is explicitly "short-run" oriented. At this juncture, it is important to differentiate the temporal concepts between the traditional economics and our new proposition. In the traditional expressions, the concepts of "short run" and "long run" refer respectively to the absence and the presence of change in the capital stock of the relevant society/nation. In this new theoretical proposition, the concepts of "short term" and "long term" indicate respectively the absence and the presence of change in the social value system of the relevant society/nation. Since the publication and popularization of *The General Theory* (Keynes 1936), "macroeconomics" has become synonymous with the short-run Keynesian framework. It is discerned, however, that the "short-run" approach has largely lost its validity in our age aiming at Sustainable Development. The framework can offer no viable foundation for theory and policy relevant to such extra-long-term development. The Keynesian framework, purported mainly for managing the aggregate demand for "short-run" purposes, certainly cannot cope with such extra-long-term issue of Sustainable Development. To be sure, Keynes himself did not address the environmental concern in terms of his "short-run" concept of production, consumption, investment and economic growth, nor did he try to explain beyond such "short-run" economic growth.

Economic development goes far beyond economic growth (or "short-run" quantitative expansion of market activities), as discerned from the definition by the Stockholm meeting of experts under the chairmanship of Gunner Myrdal, the 1974 Economic Nobel Prize Winner. H.W. Arndt in his *Economic Development—the History of an Idea* (1987) quotes Benjamin Higgins, Vice-Chairman of the Stockholm Meeting, as saying "When 'development' comes to mean all elements of human life that contributed to human welfare, including nutrition, health, shelter, employment, the physical environment, the sociocultural environment or quality of life, and such matters as participation in the decision-making process, a sense of human dignity, of belonging, etc., standard neoclassical and neo-Keynesian economics has only a limited contribution to make to development policy and planning." Thus interpreted, economic development is a long-term general improvement in social value system, socioeconomic structure, production, consumption, income distribution, knowledge, technology, living standard, lifestyles, institutions and attitudes (Myrdal 1972).

Rather than addressing such socioeconomic phenomenon, the Keynesian framework offers a set of policy tools to the public sector for curing temporary economic ailment, particularly in such an area as severe involuntary unemployment. The Keynesian prescription, accordingly, offers a temporary expedience that is largely inconsistent with the dynamic long-term process of development. An apparent inconsistency, for example, is represented by Keynes' approach to saving and investment, where the "paradox of thrift" plays a crucial role. According to M.H. Spencer in his *Contemporary Economics* (1974), the paradox reads that an increase in saving that is desirable for an individual may be undesirable for all of society because it leads to reductions in income, output and employment.

This paradox allegedly points out a logical fallacy: that is, what is good (meaning "saving") for an individual is not necessarily good for everyone. This may partially contradict the alleged classical paradigm: individual self-interest works for public interest. More importantly, the paradox may indicate a logical fallacy in the long-term context, owing to the fact that a society's ability to save determines largely its ability to invest in the long term for socioeconomic development. This is apparent when the society is taken to mean "global community." In other words, saving and investment not only depend on each other but also change together in the long-term development process, for both saving and investment are driven by the common and the same sociopsychological force—the growing societal orientation to the future—which, though implicitly, aims at inducing better and more meaningful life for people in general.

Long-term socioeconomic phenomena, indeed, are in many ways different from the "short-run" counterparts. Matters that may remain rather stable in the "short run," such as consumer tastes, lifestyles, technology and human capacity, as well as a value system pertaining to worthwhile work and life, tend to vary in the long term. While "quantitative" expansion is the focal point in the "short run," "qualitative" improvement is a vital concern in the long term. Any viable long-term economic framework, no doubt, must deal with changes not only in the economic domain but also in social, cultural, political, psychological, moral, aesthetic, technological and other arenas. It goes without saying that any changes in the latter arenas tend to have an important bearing on the quality of economic activities in the long term.

Thus, any long-term framework must include appropriate variables that may relate meaningfully to the on-going long-term interactions of economic phenomena with social, political, cultural, psychological, technological and institutional ones, among others. Particularly important, the dynamics of society-specific culture (Culture) is, by necessity, related to the future as the foundation of the societal future development. Moreover, a viable framework for Sustainable Development must provide for conditions and directions, which harmoniously accommodate environment protection and enhancement in the development process. This may require a new paradigm or a shift at least of the prevailing development paradigm (see Chapters 14 and 30). In addition, any theoretical framework for Sustainable Development needs to be explicitly based on the long-term future-oriented perspectives and must offer the long-term consistent short-term prescriptions an alternative to the "short-run" macroeconomic framework of John Maynard Keynes.

Major Ideas for Development in the New Perspective

CLASSICAL DEVELOPMENT IDEAS

During the modern process of West European economic development, people may have endeavored to accumulate, almost exclusively, their physical capital in terms of tools, plants, roads, farms, irrigation ditches, public facilities and so on, given the ascendance of the influential thought asserting the *inviolability of private property* as a consequence of the Scottish Enlightenment (see Chapter 8). Whatever human capital accumulated in this process may have been largely to enrich human knowledge/skills for supplementing the physical capital, as well as to serve the capital owners (individuals, firms or public organizations). Given also the economic thought favoring the market system and the social value system upholding "self-interest" as the prime motive for economic activities, such thought and value in favor of the owners of financial capital, land lots, plant facilities and tools may have ushered in the Industrial Revolution and the Modern Capitalism in the industrially advanced nations, often at the cost and sacrifice of the colonies and deprived people all over the world.

The currently prevalent and/or popularized concepts of "market" and "self-interest" (*not* "invisible hand" and "self-interest" ascribed to Adam Smith, which assume a "fair and orderly divine hand" resembling Newton's law of universal gravitation and the prevalence of "socially inclined sentiment," respectively) is apparently devoid of both common interest and public spirit. The prevalent *disorderly* "market" and *raw and crude* "self-interest" relevant to the market fundamentalism (Market) has been somehow socially sanctioned in the modern and contemporary world as the source of economic vitality and development. Then, the economically *stronger* may have a license to exploit and take advantage of the *weaker* in almost all human societies. A domestic consequence of such sanction may have led to the justification and excuse for an extreme income-and-wealth disparity among social constituents. The modern and contemporary sanction of *raw and crude* "self-interest" and the corollary "national interest" in an international context may have provided *a blanket license* for territorial expansion, plunder, exploitation, free trade based on the "law of the jungle," monopolistic control of resources and markets and so on.

Indeed, the market fundamentalism (Market), having emerged as the contemporary reinterpretation and degradation of the theoretical "self-interest" and "invisible hand," may have lent a helping hand to some Western economies (*center*) for their rapid industrialization and economic expansion at the sacrifice of the broadly defined *peripheral* peoples and societies. The success of the *central* economies, therefore, may have largely depended on the sacrifice of the *peripheral* peoples in both *intra*-national and *inter*-national contexts. The same can be said, even if we are persuaded to allow for the "plus-sum world" of international trade. Even then, the existing stock of precious resources in the *peripheral* societies may be traded mostly for the advantage of the *central* economies. Thus, the classicist paradigm under the pervasive Market cannot claim its long-term viability, general applicability or global desirability by basing itself, albeit indirectly, on the *exploitation* of fellow humans (see elaboration in Chapter 5).

SCHUMPETERIAN, MARXIST AND KEYNESIAN IDEAS

The Schumpeterian model cannot claim its long-term viability and general applicability either. According to Joseph Schumpeter, developsment owes to the carrying out of *new combinations* (Schumpeter 1951). The *new combinations* consist of; (1) introduction of a new good, (2) introduction of a new method of production, (3) opening of a new market, (4) conquest of a new source of supply of raw materials or half-manufactured goods, and (5) carrying out of a new organization of any industry. Clearly, the Schumpeterian proposition exclusively relates to a modern "industrial development" that depends strictly on the *entrepreneurs'* creation of new business opportunities. Such model does not question at all whether the *entrepreneur's* new innovation qualifies a "sound creativity" for a viable future (see elaboration on Sound Creativity in Chapter 15). The Schumpeterian model allows only passive roles to the people at large—consumers, workers, savers and taxpayers—while the *entrepreneurs* single-handedly contribute to innovations, discoveries and economic development. Such a development model with a strong slant to the industrial elite cannot possibly bring about balanced socioeconomic development for all social constituents, which is important in the age of Sustainable Development.

Though different in their approaches, the Marxists and the Keynesians perhaps offer similar elitist models. Simply speaking, the Marxists, on the one hand, have been inclined toward the scheme of replacing the invisible hand—the classical market function—by the collective planning of autocratic government bureaucracy that has been heavily biased to strategic production at the cost of the consumer and the general public. On the other hand, the Keynesians have suggested supplementation of the market function by government management of aggregate "effective demand" (or "taming" the market from the demand side by the hands of aristocratic government bureaucracy).

The Marxist model of development might have evolved out of a modern "particular/peculiar interpretation" of history as an incessant and two-tire "class struggle," pointing to an antagonistic strife between two classes respectively united, where the "younger" class eventually topples the "older" one for politico-economic domination supposedly to lead eventually to a "utopian" society of communism (Engels and Marx 1955). This implies that the Marxist politico-economic process demanded the people to involve themselves politically for a constant counter-productive *antagonism and strife* on the way to their "ideal" society, negating both the existing diverse Cultures and the peaceful potentiality of balanced socioeconomic development and comprehensive human development.

As for the Keynesians, their initial short-run macroeconomic theory was introduced against the extraordinary conditions of the Great Depression. Thus, Keynes wanted to rectify the "short-run" extreme conditions by his explicitly "short-run" macroeconomic theory (Keynes 1936), assuming "as given the existing skill and quantity of available labor, the existing quality and quantity of available equipment, the existing technique, the degree of competition, the tastes and habits of the consumer, the disutility of different intensities of labor and of the activities of supervision and organization, as well as the social structure including the forces other than our variables ..., which determine the distribution of the national product."

Thus, the Keynesian approach tended to dodge the important issues of long-term socioeconomic development and environmental concern and to ignore the possible harmful long-term consequences of the "short-run" government policies, particularly the welfare cost of the future generations. In other words, the Keynesian theory had to ignore the inescapable "policy failure" and the consequence thereof. In addition, the Keynesian variation of "division of labor" among *household*, *firm* and *government* sectors tended to divert the respective interests all of households, firms and governments from their *common interests*. This tendency has inevitably left the social common interests almost entirely to the likely long-term misjudgments and distortions, due to the short terms of public offices as well as to the bureaucratic empowerment and sectarian interests.

In the meantime, the Marxists, the Schumpeterians and the Keynesians alike seem to have accepted the classical concept of human nature—"individual self-interest"—for different reasons, even though the concept had been grossly estranged from the original meaning and purpose over time. The Marxists may have suppressed excessively the existing "individual self-interest," while the Schumpeterians and the Keynesians may have belittled the potential danger of the *elitist* "self-interest." It is very difficult to discuss concretely the consequences of excessive suppression of "self-interest" in the great variety of socialist states, but it is, perhaps, more difficult to deny many adverse-and-diverse, personal-and-social, and mental-and-physical consequences over the long duration of time, which might have, albeit partially, prepared the premature fall, disintegration or transformation of many socialistic states.

As regards the Schumpeterian and Keynesian belittling of danger relevant to distorted *elitist* "self-interest," it can be surmised that such "self-interest" being corrupted and twisted by the Market may have gone far to degrade the natural and living environment for the lopsided emphases on "short-run" material growth, not to speak of the devastation of diverse Cultures and the Environment as well as of the rapid expansion of disparities in income and wealth across the world. Perhaps, without any vivid perceptions in their prime, of the devastation of diverse Cultures as well as the impending collapse of the natural environment—the concurrent threat to the very foundation of production and life—they were not in any position to consider the issues of long-term balanced socioeconomic development, comprehensive human development and enrichment of diverse Cultures. Then, none of the "collective planning," "new combinations" and "government management of effective demand" can possibly qualify as a viable approach to a balanced socioeconomic development for all people. Moreover, all these developmental ideas may very well be considered antagonistic to the diverse Cultures and the Environment.

Perroux, Sen and Myrdal for Human Development

THE DEVELOPMENTAL IDEA OF FRANCOIS PERROUX

Francois Perroux was a successor to Schumpeter as well as a pioneer to the school of *Regulation*, according to Professor Jun Nishikawa who once attended one of Perroux's lectures and introduced Perroux's development theory to Japan (Nishikawa 2000). In his theory of development, Perroux emphasizes the "poles" of development, which attract all the necessary factors of production for productive activities. He also emphasizes the "social environment" that must be generated for the spread of development. The *poles* of development are considered to be the centers where the factors of production are concentrated and organized to induce innovations for economic development. The "social environment" in his concept implies social, institutional, political and legal environments for generating the *poles* of development and diffusing the result of development. Also, the "social environment" is supposed to satisfy mental, educational and health-oriented basic needs of social constituents.

Such a "social environment" for the *poles* of development, however, may generate an international imbalance by increasing the *poles'* controlling power over the rest. This indicates a division of the world into the developed and underdeveloped areas. For the two areas to converge and develop together, both the developed and the underdeveloped must change in order to start a dialogue and coordination between them. It takes a *mediator* to "*regulate*" (or adjust) the conflict of interests, so that both the developed and the underdeveloped attempt to nurture the spirit of dialogue and cooperation.

Perroux's idea refers to a "global," "endogenous" and "integral" development. The term "global" indicates a worldwide socioeconomic development. The term "endogenous" means the way of development, in which the society's resources are arranged endogenously and independently, along with the social vitality generated on the basis of its own value system. The term "integral" refers to the integration of various socioeconomic units for development. Perroux depicts the successive processes of economic growth, economic development, individual progress and worldwide progress in order to arrive at the final stage of development—"human development." Perroux's innovative idea, indeed, departs from the prevalent utilitarian, individualistic and profit-maximizing economic thoughts, as seen from his socioeconomic development culminating in "human development." Such an idea implies, perhaps, a quantum leap from the neoclassical economic thoughts as well as from Schumpeter's idea of economic development.

HUMAN DEVELOPMENT ACCORDING TO SEN AND MYRDAL

Perroux's "human development," perhaps, can be contrasted with the "human development as freedom" of Amartya Sen (Sen 1999), since their ideas relevant to "human development" are distinct from each other. Sen's concept of "capabilities" refers to the basic functioning of human beings on the basis of "entitlement" (a combination of goods and services obtainable by the "rights" originally possessed). Sen's concept of "capabilities" implies a value system very much different from that of the "utilitarian" concept as well as from Perroux's "human development." Sen's "capabilities" refers to an expansion of human freedom of choice, whereas the diverse human choices, according to Sen, encompass health, education, income, political freedom, human rights and human dignity, among other things.

Given the "entitlement," "human development" for Sen is the achievement and accomplishment of basic capabilities as well as the expansion of capabilities. Put differently, "human development" indicates simply the expansion of freedom relevant to human choices. Sen's "capabilities" may be extended to his concept of "well-being" respective to areas and social groups, which is based on individual freedom and human rights. Differentiating "human capability" from "human capital," Sen has the following to say: "… the literature on human capital tends to concentrate on the agency of human beings in augmenting production possibilities," while "the perspective of human capability focuses … on the ability—the substantive freedom—of people to lead the lives they have reason to value and to enhance the real choices they have" (Sen 1999).

Thus, Perroux's "human development" as the final goal of development is dissimilar to Sen's "human development as an expansion of human capabilities" and "development as freedom." Yet, a shift of general development idea toward "human development" is more or less a natural course of conceptual evolution, for an ultimate "development" in human world, by necessity, involves "human development" as the most important development. As a third idea, "human development" by Gunner Myrdal can be contrasted with the ideas of Perroux and Sen. Myrdal offers a broad overarching concept that encompasses human and social development. Myrdal's understanding of "development" is an upward shift of all the interrelated social systems that include production, method of production, distribution of products, living standard, institutions and human attitude (Myrdal 1972). Perroux, Myrdal and Sen, indeed, have respectively contributed to the advancement of the ideas in socioeconomic and human development. They, however, have stopped short of the idea relevant to Sustainable Development that may indicate a long-term, perpetual, ultimate development for all individuals and collectives both present and future.

An Alternative Approach and Core Ideas

As a modest theoretical step toward Sustainable Development, therefore, I will offer and discuss a long-term integral framework of Sustainable Development as an appropriate alternative to the presently existing theories and models. In my integral approach, the greatest emphasis will be placed on a new paradigm for the sound enrichment of diverse and holistic society-specific cultures (Cultures) across the world. Such a paradigm is assumed to serve as the main engine for achieving Sustainable Development. This main engine needs to be supplemented by a constantly reinforced future orientation in each and every society as well as by the New Enlightenment across the world. The latter supplement is assumed to aim at emancipating all people from the modern shackles of market fundamentalism and reductionist scientism as well as encouraging the paradigm shift. By means of the main and supplementary engines, a "local virtuous circle" of sound Cultural enrichment, comprehensive human development and balanced socioeconomic development is envisaged to relate to a "global virtuous circle" of Culture of Peace, Global Humanity and Sustainable Development.

By means of the paradigm shift, I will also emphasize the generation of "sound communal value system" in each society, which comprises the mutually reinforcing *human integrity* (spiritual-material value balance), *social solidarity* (individual-social value balance), *societal continuity* (traditional-progressive value balance) and *relational mutuality* (own-other value balance), all of which center on a dynamic *communal harmony*. Such a sound communal value system is argued to rectify the modern lopsided value system of materialism, individualism, progressivism and egotism, all of which center on the antagonistic free competition. All these emphases and others will be theoretically put together with the relevant methodology and guidelines in this book.

Organization of This Book

In order to discuss our long-term integrative framework for Sustainable Development as well as its related ideas, issues, methodology and perspectives, the on-going *unsustainable* contemporary expansion will be examined in Part 1 (Unsustainable Modern Expansion). As an unavoidable issue of the contemporary *underdevelopment* among the vast majority of societies across the world, our introductory discussion will address the Credibility Trap in general, the specific Japanese case of Credibility Trap, and the imminent Credibility Trap in China, which is taken to be a *microcosm* of the contemporary world. I will then take up the controversial issue of the on-going haphazard economic globalization that may be mainly conducive to "market failure," "policy failure," "culture failure" and "human failure" worldwide. Also, I will delve into the nature of market fundamentalism (Market) and relate to the contemporary power structure (Big Market) to compare and contrast with the Orwellian power structure (Big Brother). Further, I will summarily address the contemporary hindrances to Sustainable Development, largely represented by the "disparity-animosity spiral" in the contemporary world of economic globalization.

In Part 2, I will introduce and discuss the present theoretical framework (Theoretical Framework and Ramifications), together with the definitions of pivotal concepts for the ensuing discussions, the important assumptions, value premises and general features of the framework as well as the basic construct of the theoretical framework. Also, I will offer extended discussions on the theoretical ramifications, by explaining society's Value Aspects in terms of the two-way processes on the normative and analogical development path (Optimal Development Path). I will also delve into a new paradigm of socioeconomic development, which relates to People's Own Invisible Hands (that complement the classical invisible hand) with the relevant value renewal based on the dynamic and sound Cultural enrichment. Our mathematical derivation of the theoretical framework as well as the detailed theoretical explanations will be relegated to the Theoretical Appendices 1–8 at the end of the book.

In Part 3 (Cultures and Comprehensive Human Development), the importance of enriching the diverse society-specific cultures (Cultures) across the world will be discussed as the required paradigm shift for accomplishing Sustainable Development. First, the definition of Sound Culture will be offered in view of "sound creativity." Then, the concept of Sound Culture will be related to the "complex wisdom" referring to a *sound communal value system* that is directly relevant to our contemporary insular planet with the severe environment and resource constraints. Further, the enrichment of diverse Cultures will be related to general human development, thought-frame enhancement, innovative education and personal-social maturation of the respective social constituents.

In Part 4 (Methodology for Sustainability), discussions will be concentrated on the institutional and methodological implications relevant to the sustainability of development. To begin with, the relationship between the diverse Cultures and the sustainability will be examined in terms of functional approaches to Sustainable Development. Second, the issue of worldwide "social cost" stabilization will be discussed as a step toward Sustainable Development. Third, "one-rate global value-added tax" will be taken up as a desirable supplementary approach to Sustainable Development. Fourth, a proposal of "Culture-enhancing employment" will be discussed as against the on-going Market-biased employment. Fifth, "Culture-enhancing international trade" will be proposed for the age of Sustainable Development. Finally, the local (society-specific) and worldwide campaigns will be illustrated and explained for the promotion of Sustainable Development.

In Part 5 (Harmonious and Integral Development), the discussion will first take up a new type of democracy ("open democracy") that is required for the community of our insular planet. Second, the contemporary demographic development (Society of Longevity) will be discussed in view of a "happiness triangle." Third, the Value-Real ("spiritual-material") interactions will be briefly explained in terms of the balanced socioeconomic development. Such interactions, then, will be related to dynamic multilateral-value interactions toward a "sound communal value system." Fourth, the mutual and supportive relationship will be discussed regarding major global issues—Sustainable Development, Culture of Peace and Global Humanity—for their simultaneous resolutions. Finally, the proposed paradigm shift is taken up to illustrate the linkage of "local" and "global" trilateral virtuous circles for accomplishing the integral development of the prospective global community.

The above discussions will be summarily drawn together in the Epilogue to clarify the important arguments and conclusions of the book. The Theoretical Appendices 1–8 are intended for optional reading.

PART 1

Unsustainable Modern Expansion

In this part of the book, I will concentrate on the discussion of modern and contemporary predicaments, by referring to some philosophical ideas and thoughts on the modern and contemporary world (Chapter 1). Then, a few examples of *antitheses* to Sustainable Development will be examined in turn. First, the definition, characteristics and framework for the phenomenon called the Credibility Trap will be elaborated as an *antithesis* to Sustainable Development (Chapter 2). Second, the case of Japan today will be dealt with as a concrete example of the Credibility Trap (Chapter 3). Third, the potential Credibility Trap in China will be presented as another concrete example that implies a microcosm and analogy of our contemporary world (Chapter 4). Fourth, the problem of economic globalization—another *antithesis*—will be discussed as a prominent issue of our contemporary world, which makes it extremely difficult for the world population to collaborate on Sustainable Development (Chapter 5). Fifth, the so-called "Big Market" (the contemporary power structure) will be compared with "Big Brother" (the Orwellian power structure) in order to envision a viable alternative (Chapter 6). Finally, a simplified overview of human predicament will be offered as the on-going "disparity-animosity spiral" in the contemporary world (Chapter 7).

1

Introductory Remarks on the Contemporary World

Today, humanity faces its most serious life-and-death question as the consequence of emancipating all sorts of human lusts—the opening of Pandora's box. Given the on-going global expansion of economic activities, sooner or later, we may encounter a sudden human demise, either by resource-entangled warfare worldwide or an environment-triggered global catastrophe. This implies that we must rethink the explosive direction of the modern and contemporary world, which has encouraged the extremely self-centered and lopsided social and politico-economic values relevant to the concepts/phenomena, such as "individual," "progress," "growth," "competition," "avarice," "acquisitiveness," "extravagance" and "aggressiveness," among others. Our contemporary world has also excessively emphasized the "individual persons" over and above the "society," the "material," over and above the "spiritual," the "private property" over and above the "common property," the "social progress" over and above the long-endured "social tradition," and interests of "one's own society" over and above interests of "all the other societies," destroying everywhere the integral, holistic and harmonious balances that may be embedded in a sound society-specific culture ("Sound Culture" to be defined and elaborated in Chapters 15 and 16).

Consequently, our contemporary world seems to deny the sound Cultural function for maintaining the *social solidarity* that represents a dynamic, harmonious and integral balance between "individual" values and "collective" values; the *human integrity*—that represents a dynamic, harmonious and integral balance between "material" values and "spiritual" values; the *societal continuity* that represents a dynamic, harmonious and integral balance between "progressive" values and "traditional" values; and the *relational mutuality* that represents a dynamic, harmonious and integral balance between the "*own* personal and societal" values and the "*other*'s personal and societal" values. Perhaps, the existing cultural and communal degradation nowadays is largely attributable to the pervasion of the market fundamentalism (Market) and the modern ideology of social progress and economic growth with the free market competition (the "law of the jungle") and the survival of the fittest (the "might-makes-right" ideology).

Such distortions may also amount to the excessive encouragement of "economic growth" over and above *human integrity*, "competition" over and above *cooperation*, "avarice" over and above *modesty* and "aggressiveness" over and above *decency*, while the study of viable human life on our Insular Planet (Planet Earth with the ever severely limited resources and the devastated natural environment) points to the importance of human integrity, cooperation, modesty and decency (Hiwaki 2007b). In the world of "insularized" natural environment and resources together with the growing human population, we can neither afford nor accept the explosive implication of economic and digital "globalization," based on the materialistic ideology of "self-interest" and "insatiable want." Carrying on our daily life and business, we should be aware of the "bottleneck" that cannot be changed instantaneously by a "magic wand" or technological innovation. This bottleneck in our contemporary life is the "insularity" of resources and environment.

If we continue to ignore the insular nature of our bottleneck and seek an endless expansion of "lusts" and "insatiable wants" under both the economic-and-digital globalization and the population explosion, we will most probably have to face an irreversible conflict and disaster sooner or later, in one way or another. In the process of such economic globalization, there seems to be an escalating "perception gap" between the trans-national business actors of advanced nations and the local ones of developing and underdeveloped nations, as well as an accelerating disparity between the overall human wants and the available resources, to say nothing of the accelerated disparity of wealth, income and amenity among fellow humans. These discrepancies may prepare and induce a manifold clash course among people and societies. For survival and subsistence, we humans should comprehend our physical world as an insular planet and act accordingly. In this book, I will offer, among other things, an argument against the pervasive "global and expansionary" perception of our contemporary world. Planet Earth has already turned into nothing but an Insular Planet, as far as the constraints on the environment, resources and humanities are concerned.

Put differently, the on-going economic globalization as well as the communicational revolution has not only made our world "global" in terms of economic activities but also "insular" in terms of the environment and resources, not to mention our inner world turned into "desert." In an insular society, people must share whatever is available for the sake of life and peace in a viable manner. For general subsistence and well-being, the insular society must encourage cooperation and modesty, discouraging excessive competition and avarice. For spiritual contentment and peaceful co-existence, the insular society must favor polytheism and symbiosis, abhorring monotheism and exclusion. For viable socioeconomic development, the insular society must reward thrift and long-enduring wisdom, despising waste and transient sharpness.

It is about the time we humans comprehend our world as an "insular society." The "insularity" of constraints on the environment and resources has been revealing itself, due to the rampant globalization of economic activities particularly in the recent decades. Living in the age of insular constraints, we must change gradually but steadily our priority of values toward cooperation, modesty, polytheism, symbiosis, thrift and long-enduring wisdom, away from the modern excesses of competition, avarice, monotheism, exclusion, waste and transient sharpness. Such redirection and renewal of values may favor the emphasis on some decent and constructive values common among diverse society-specific cultures ("Cultures" to be defined and discussed in Chapter 8 and elsewhere) across the world as well as the worldwide enrichment of respective Cultures toward sound and viable ones. This comprehension of reality and the necessary redirection of our contemporary values, when shared by the peoples particular to all the modern, "modernized" and "modernizing" societies and nations, may usher us into a just and viable future.

The modern mind that is largely based on monotheism, individualism and independence of the self may correspond to the modern characteristics of analytical methodology and reductionism, as well as of ethnic ideology (nationalism) and religious antagonism (fundamentalism). Such modern methodology, reductionism, nationalism and religious fundamentalism may encourage the innate exclusionism and the ideologies of "chosen" and "might-makes-right." The modern mind, coupled with the modern economic idealism (nothing but ideology and dogma, in reality) of free competition, free market and free trade, which is based on the extremely contradictory assumption of "self-help individual humans" is in turn based on the definition of "autonomous and self-sufficient individuals" (Graham 2005). Such economic idealism, which has been promoted dogmatically by the International Monetary Fund (IMF), the World Bank and the World Trade Organization (WTO), along with the leading governments of "advanced" nations, has naturally induced and produced the growing disparity of income, wealth and amenity among individual persons, peoples and societies across the world, as well as the accelerated degradation of the global environment and the diverse Cultures.

The modern mind and the economic idealism, together, have induced and encouraged the scramble for colonies and the "law of the jungle" to reduce the militarily weaker societies to the colonial subjugation, on the one hand, and consigned the economically weaker individual persons, peoples and societies to inescapable poverty and misery, on the other. In the age of economic and digital globalization, the modern mind and the economic idealism have also accelerated the depletion of natural resources and the degradation of the global environment ("Environment" to be defined and discussed in Chapter 8), by mobilizing a growing proportion of what little remaining resources there are toward the production of goods and services for the "insatiable and avaricious" individuals of the contemporary world. Under the conditions of overt economic disparity among individual persons, peoples and societies, the economic idealism of free competition, free market and free trade, together with the ideologies of "self-interest," "national interest" and "might-makes-right," has exaggerated the disparity and the suffering of weak and poor. Such idealism has encouraged the accelerated fluctuation of "monetized economies" and the rapid and incessant alteration and invalidation of products, technologies, skills and employment to increase the uncertainty and insecurity of weak and poor individual persons, peoples and societies.

Thus, the self-seeking and lopsided tendency of social and politico-economic values in the modern and contemporary world of alleged "democracy" ("closed democracy") is highly question-begging (Hiwaki 2006c). Why is the "greed" of one person more important than the "life" of another in "democracy?" How can "competition" contribute to the peaceful coexistence of humanity as well as to the harmonious human-and-environment symbiosis in the world of exploding freedom and disparity? Whose "benefit" is envisioned in the emphases on "growth," "development," "progress," "competition," "acquisitiveness," "aggressiveness" and "avarice"? Why is the ideology of "might-makes-right" as well as the related practice of the "law of the jungle" so powerful a guideline in our "civilized" and "democratic" world? Why is "free competition" pursued with aggressiveness and acquisitiveness being considered as the propelling force for "human evolution" and "social progress?" What is behind the seeming obsession with "economic expansion" that is borne on the shoulders of devastated humanity and environment? All these are but examples of questions intrinsic to viable life on our Insular Planet with the limited resources and the collapsing environment.

Values, Philosophies and Concepts

In his insightful discourse on European identity and traditions, Greg Andonian, Professor of Architecture at Carlton University, Canada, takes up the millennium life cycle of "three caves" models relevant to the human dwelling experiences (Andonian 2001). Such experiences are characterized respectively by the "reflective and critical thinking" during the first millennium (fifth century BC—fifth century AD); by the "imaginative and projective spirituality" during the second millennium (fifth century—fifteenth century); and by the "innovative and creative vision" in the third millennium (fifteenth century—today, the halfway point). Alternatively, he summarizes the experiences, respectively, as attempts for creating the "perfect intellectual man," the "perfect spiritual man" and the "perfect hi-tech man" and offers a skeptical view about the future of humanity. "If man's history will continue to be a history of selfish competition, inflicting suffering and cruelty on masses, the social, economic and ethnic conflicts will propagate further global tension." Moreover, Professor Andonian suspects that man's tool of advancement will become "tools of utter disintegration, subjugation and manipulation." Projecting further into the future, he offers a sad prediction: "Then, man will question, in his final moments of reflection, whether he has ever learned anything from the three 'caves' experiences."

Also discussing European traditions from somewhat different angle, William Graham, Professor of Philosophy at the University of Toronto, points out that the prevalent European characterization of "individual" refers to the concept of "self-sufficient and autonomous individual," which goes back to Permenides of Elea who flourished about 500 BC (Graham 2005). Asserting that "rationality, autonomy and transcendence" belong to such individuals, Professor Graham relates to the idea of John Locke (1632–1704) who characterized such individuals as having a "natural, rational and inalienable right to property." These individuals, according to Professor Graham, are also to "maximize their interests through competition and conflicts," for "rational and autonomous individuals are ends in themselves, and all the other things are 'tools' for their own fulfillment and satisfaction," thus, leaving "little room for sympathy, empathy or compassion." Then, the alternative and more realistic concept of individual or "relational, dependent and incomplete individual," must replace that of "self-sufficient and autonomous individual." He argues that "collaborative consciousness of relational, dependent and incomplete individuals" is "a necessary precondition for the possibility for creating and maintaining a sustainable society."

George E. Lasker, Professor of Computer Science at the University of Windsor and Founding President of the International Institute for Advanced Studies in Systems Research and Cybernetics (IIAS) (which has sponsored the International Conference on Systems Research, Informatics and Cybernetics for 30 years mainly in Baden-Baden, Germany), emphasizes also the importance of "collaborative consciousness" for generating a cooperative spirit and an amicable dialogue of civilizations in the Third Millennium (Lasker 1998). "The collaborative consciousness is characterized by a propensity of an individual to relate to other humans and to cooperate with them in order to survive, to meet his needs and to build a better future for himself, for his family and for society." Regarding the contemporary conditions with "socio-political institutions and many of unenlightened, ignorant, malevolent and sometimes downright corrupt political leaders and corporate managers," Professor Lasker offers a candid view of them (Lasker 2002) as producing conditions and generating "contingencies that reward destructive, immoral and corrupt actions and practices." "Those in control of the socio-political affairs of the world are bent on building, developing, and perpetuating the Culture of War and Violence, and Culture of Misery and Death." Professor Lasker also expresses his own skepticism regarding "democracy," asserting that it is "fashioned by special interests group into a tool that in many instances is used to polarize, fragment, divide, control, brainwash and manipulate the electorate/society in such a manner that ensures the election and re-election of those politicians who usually represent the 'entrenched interests' of the people/electorate."

Discussing the contemporary issue relevant to human evolution, Jerzy A. Wojiciechowski, Professor of Philosophy at the University of Ottawa, asserts (Wojciechowski 2003): "The evolutionary system of mankind is an evolution producing devices." The system "forces human to evolve toward higher levels of humanness, and toward a more rational, conscious, self-directing and synergistic, globalized humanity." However, "rational activity makes the human phenomenon more and more complex." "The more humans think, the more problematic they become for themselves." On this evolutionary premise, he argues that "intellectual knowledge" is distinct from "knowers," for the former, not the capacity of the latter, can become limitless owing to writing, printing and electronic means of communication and storage of knowledge. Intellectual knowledge in terms of "knowledge construct," as it becomes more and more complex, distances itself from the "knowers" and develops independent of the "knowers." Due to the widening gap between the "knowledge construct" and the "knowers," therefore, "knowledge produces ignorance." Then, Professor Wojciechowski declares that our future is in "the realm of values" or realm of value judgment, since "by and large, the human race is not a collective candidate for suicide," implying that in order to survive humans will refrain from their heavy reliance on rationality and scientism.

In his Keynote Address to the 1995 IIAS Conference held in Carlsbad, Czech Republic, entitled "Does Democratization help economic development?" (Yushkiavitshus 1995) the-then Assistant Director-General of UNESCO, Dr Henrikas Yushkiavitshus stated:

> If we consider economic growth only as percentage figures of Gross National Product, Gross Domestic Product or other statistics that provide national profiles in economic terms, the world record may seem to be impressive. If we analyze the data further, however, to see how these gains have been shared with the populations, how they have participated in GNP in terms of employment, buying power, consumerism, literacy and education, fuller sharing in the social and cultural fruits of society, in a word, how economic growth itself has been democratized, the eventual picture may be disappointing.

Depicting the "Cup of Shame" based on the World Bank statistics that shows the grossly distorted distribution among peoples of global Gross National Product (GNP), Dr Yushkiavitshus goes on to assert that "in many cases economic growth has created disparities, leading to what is today called exclusion, a term that covers everything from exploitation to poverty, plain and simple."

Evolution Hypothesis and Social Progress

A HISTORICAL SWING FROM ONE EXTREME TO ANOTHER

All the above discussions may illuminate human failings that might have originated in the extreme characterizations and assumptions, namely, too much idealization, too much sanctification, too much dehumanization, too much polarization, and too much manipulation of humans, human institutions and human concepts. The concepts that have been too much manipulated and deployed are ones such as "freedom," "individual," "rationality," "democracy," "competition," "evolution," "progress" and "free market," among others. The discussions above may also suggest the historical dynamics of extremism, which, once the momentum accumulated, may move from one extreme to another to cause unexpected, far-reaching and drastic consequences over a long duration of time. Further, the discussions may imply an extreme difficulty for respective societies to escape from their traps of the "complex bias" and "entrenched interest" embedded in self-centered thoughts, institutions and lifestyles, as well as inextricably enmeshed through history in their respective traditions.

Thus, those individuals and peoples, who gained wealth and power through their accustomed favorite tricks, without a broader perspective, may fall into the self-righteous preoccupation with their own polity, religion and lifestyle, as well as on their own method of acquiring wealth and power, despite the existing diverse Cultures across the world. Our modern "self-centered" and "lopsided" cultural and politico-economic values continue to reflect the "drastic and explosive" series of West European reactions, such as Renaissance, Reformation, Enlightenment, Industrial Revolution, Imperialism and Economic Globalization, to the extremely tight, repressive and oppressive *medieval binds* of Catholicism and despotism upon human freedom, lifestyles, thoughts and ethics, which lasted for as long as a millennium. Such explosive reactions and the consequential swing of the pendulum toward the opposite extreme culminated in the dogmatic pursuit of rationalism, individualism, materialism, liberalism, scientism, reductionism, industrialism, colonialism, progressivism, expansionism and the present-day Market-driven globalism. Such a continuous swing to the extreme, justified on the basis of repeated military and economic victory for centuries, gained momentum and progressed even further.

EVOLUTIONARY THOUGHTS FAVORING CAPITALISM

The swing to the extreme was also encouraged by the manipulation of the evolutionary hypothesis in nineteenth century Europe and America. "Social progress" on the evolutionary premise gained popularity through the writings particularly of Herbert Spencer (1820–1903), Graham Sumner (1840–1910) and Lester F. Ward (1841–1913), whose thoughts largely accommodated the Christian faith and strongly supported the system of natural liberty with its competition, which had been advocated by the classical economists, such as Adam Smith and David Ricardo (Ellwood 1938).

According to Spencer (Ellwood 1938), evolution is construed as "a process in a relatively straight line toward increasing definiteness, coherence, and heterogeneity" and as "a straight-upward trend of greater complexity and better adjustment." Sumner, an ardent admirer of Spencer, approached the issue of social progress from the standpoint of economics rather than from Spencer's standpoint of a general theory of evolution. Sumner asserted (Ellwood 1938) that a system of laissez-faire or natural liberty would be "the surest way to insure social progress." In Sumner's view, capital accumulation owes to austerity, and, thus, capitalists are virtuous men. Progress, according to Ward (Ellwood 1938), meant the increase of happiness in human society. "Human happiness is the ultimate end of effort, and progress is a direct means of happiness."

All these advocates of social progress, as being staunch supporters of the laissez-faire economics, overlooked the corrupt, mean and monopolistic practices of their contemporary capitalist tycoons (White 1911, Holbrook 1953, Canterbery 1980). They also influenced American Protestant leaders who, as being very often teachers and advocates of the classical economics, taught and preached that God established the natural law over both material and human worlds to protect the right to private property and its accumulation, even going all the way to defend the love of profits as the best of human motivations (Canterbery 1980); practically fanning, either intended or unintended, the crude, corrupt, cruel, greedy, extravagant and aggressive tendencies of the rich and strong. Thus, social evolutionists, classical economists and Protestant leaders, not to mention business and government leaders and also mass-media in the Western World, may have sanctioned and sanctified social progress and economic growth as the almost imperative aim of humanity. Now, for the sake of social progress, the love of profits or avarice was seemingly sanctified in Church as the best of human motivations, for it was deemed to promote social progress.

The system of natural liberty with its competition was explained as the surest way to social progress, where the "survival of the fittest" could easily find the way to emphasizing the "might-makes-right" ideology. Also, the powerful capitalists, in the setting of laissez-faire with its free competition, were now further reinforced to reign over all humankind on the pretext of "peaceful coexistence" of humanity under the market fundamentalism ("Market" to be defined and discussed in Chapter 8). Even the extravagance of the rich was sanctioned as demonstration of the "American Dream" that propagandized material prosperity as the most important goal. Economic growth was often understood as embodiment or incarnation of social progress, and, moreover, social progress was considered as the direct means of human happiness. Eventually, the terms such as "human evolution," "social progress" and "economic growth," being used interchangeably, have been made an ideology and inculcated generally, albeit vaguely and cunningly, by means of the "modern" education and mass-media, so that they are to be taken together as one and something imperative to pursue in our contemporary world.

INCULCATION OF PEOPLE BY EVOLUTIONARY THOUGHTS

By and large, our contemporary fellow humans have been made "progress proponent" on the premise of the evolution hypothesis, as well as in terms of manipulation by secular and holy leaders who have knowingly or unknowingly served the modern power structure ("hidden controllers/entrenched interests"—"Big Market"—to be discussed in Chapter 6) that benefited most from such "social progress" or a rapid expansion of economic activities. An actual economic growth, as deemed to represent the ideological "social progress," has been related to human progress and happiness, which are in turn related to the political ideal of "democracy" with freedom and equality, as well as to the economic ideal of the laissez-faire market with competition and efficiency.

The "ideal democracy," however, is nothing but an empty fiction where most or all the human inhabitants are deemed "self-sufficient and autonomous individuals." Likewise, the "ideal market" is an extreme fiction, where all the participants are deemed equal and perfectly rational to represent the "self-sufficient and autonomous individuals." Despite the fictitious existence of idealized democracy and market, their respective dogmas and ideologies have now settled deeply in the consciousness of the general public to be justified or tolerated without much doubt. Any related phenomena and behaviors, such as excessive competition, profit motive, self-interest, disparity, extravagance, aggressiveness, and exclusion, may also have been inculcated on the convenient pretexts of "progress," "democracy" and "market."

Such justification and tolerance have, as a matter of course, encouraged the extremely biased politico-economic institutions and ideologies as well as the lopsided value systems. With such institutions, ideologies and value systems, the concept such as the "survival of the fittest" on the pretext of "social progress" has favored and encouraged the powerful and malevolent "individuals" with avarice, extravagance, aggressiveness, exclusion and cruelty. The worldwide frantic pursuit of "social progress" or "economic growth" has now come to endanger the human continuity, by devastating the ecological system and the diverse society-specific cultures (Cultures). Pursuing "social progress and economic growth" further, sooner or later, may result in the sudden end to life or the drastic change, at least, in the condition for human subsistence.

Under the circumstances, we may question how we can possibly work for personal, spiritual and intellectual development of all individual persons and peoples, as well as for Cultural enrichment, resource conservation, environmental protection and Sustainable Development. We can easily imagine the confusion of people and societies who have adopted the strange ideologies of "progress," "democracy" and "market" without knowing intrinsically the assumed fictitious "individuals" and without the historical and spiritual experiences similar to that of Westerners. In particular, the general public in such societies is now extremely confused with the socially enmeshed contradictory values, both domestic and alien, both old and new, to degrade the humanities inevitably by imitating the superficial and civilized behaviors of the advanced nations. However, viable, personal, spiritual and intellectual developments (or a comprehensive human development) can *only* be pursued and accomplished on the premise of *social integrity and solidarity*, as well as on the basis of a well-coordinated and harmoniously integrated value system firmly embedded in the specific Culture. This is to emphasize the importance of holistic and sound culture specific to each society ("Sound Culture" to be defined and elaborated in Chapters 15 and 16) for comprehensive human development, as well as for viable life on our Insular Planet with limited resources.

The Impending Credibility Trap

The mainstream and/or major studies of economics, including those of classical, Marxian, neoclassical, historical and Keynesian schools, seem to have largely avoided the phenomenon of long-term social lethargy as well as the real issue of underdevelopment that shrouds the greater part of the contemporary world. Perhaps, this is mainly because of its implied scope exceeding the "alleged" framework of economics. "Credibility Trap" is a term newly coined by the author of this book to explain the state of serious social lethargy that has occurred as a result of the devastation of the relevant society-specific culture (Culture). Credibility Trap refers to the social condition of devastation as regards the mutual trust among the social constituents, as well as the centripetal force of the society. It is the state in which no short-term government initiative can invigorate the people and society, due to such a devastated Cultural condition.

It is quite likely that many science-oriented and/or quasi-science-inclined economists, resorting to reductionism, have devoted to the "scientifically observable and/or provable" phenomena to derive the "partial and temporary" results by mainly dealing with the "marginal," "partial" and/or "short-run" issues. It is also likely that many history-oriented economists, dealing with extra-long-term economic phenomena, have abstracted some "stages of development" almost solely from the European/American experiences, paying little attention to the forced contributions and sacrifices of other peoples and societies to the development of the modern Western/advanced nations. Further, it is easily understandable that many popular economic thinkers, having been brought up in the modern and industrially advanced societies, have intentionally avoided the *incrimination* of their own people and societies. Because, the very people and societies who, in the course of their modern aggrandizement, have inflicted devastating damage upon many people and diverse Cultures of the presently "underdeveloped" and "developing" world.

It is obvious, however, that such narrowly confined "scientific approaches," such a neglect of the long-term comprehensive approach and/or such avoidance of the self-incrimination can offer an extremely limited explanation, if any, of human economic behaviors, particularly of their influences on their own and other societies over the long duration of time. Such explanation may leave out the complex interactions of human economic behaviors with a wide variety of other human activities, as well as with their long-term broader and global consequences. Such economic studies, therefore, offer not only biased but also wrong policies and solutions for today's issues of global importance, such as persistence of underdevelopment, population explosion, deepening poverty, and growing disparities in income, wealth and amenity. Even worse, we economists may learn little from our past and present mistakes and, as a result, we may be totally incapacitated to pave the way for our meaningful future, particularly for Sustainable Development.

It goes without saying that there are numerous examples of the Credibility Trap in our world, which have not been recognized as such, due mainly to the lack of appropriate concept and explanatory framework to associate severe long-term social lethargy with Cultural devastation/dilapidation. More precisely, the collapse of mutual trust, as well as the evaporation of societal centripetal force due to the devastation/liquidation of the relevant Cultures by one drastic cause or another, might have ushered the societies into the Credibility Trap. Such a severe social malady might have been witnessed worldwide in history as a by-product, for instance, of a massive tribal movement, an ambition for empire building and an Imperialistic scramble for colonies.

Such a by-product may have implied unfortunate miseries on the side of the victimized people, who happened to be caught in such movement, ambition and/or warfare. As a consequence, the victimized people were very often deprived of their own life, resources, personalities, identities, humanities and respective Cultures. This kind of process, however, has not been the only avenue to the Credibility Trap. A much more prevalent avenue today, though essentially related to the past colonialism, Imperialism and "might-makes-right" idealism is the economic globalization driven by the market fundamentalism

(Market). This book will address mainly the latter avenue—the unfavorable worldwide consequences of the Market—as the one that distorts and destroys the diverse Cultures, leading to a prolonged malady as characterized by the term "Credibility Trap" that is an *antithesis* to Sustainable Development.

Concluding Remarks: An Alternative Course

Today, it is crucially important to advance both global and grassroots endeavors for holistic Cultural enrichment and diversity, as well as for the emancipation of all people from the shackles of the Market in an attempt to resolve the global issue of Sustainable Development. In view of such crucial issue, however, there are many closely related global issues to be resolved simultaneously. Among them are a Culture-enriching education, humanity-oriented fair employment system, fair and viable environment for international trade, humanity-and-nature-favoring cluster of technological innovation, harmonious global governance systems, democracy appropriate to Insular Planet, Culture of Peace, Global Humanity and so on. In other words, potential solutions and resolutions of all such issues may commonly hinge on our full-fledged endeavors to revive and enrich the diverse holistic Cultures across the world, for human wisdom, capacity, morality and value system tend to root in the solid foundation of respective Cultures. This blanket emphasis on the holistic Cultural enrichment and diversity, indeed, calls for not only a long-term orientation to the future but also global-and-grassroots endeavors to enhance human values, human development and humanity-directed solidarity ("New Enlightenment" to be defined in Chapter 8).

Such long-term, future-oriented and humanity-enhancing endeavors can naturally enrich the Cultures directly, on the one hand, and encourage a global consensus on intrinsic human values, on the other hand. Such human values may indicate the *personal human ethos* that favors a sound, active and fruitful longevity, as well as the *societal human ethos* that favors a comprehensive human development for survival, subsistence, continuity, solidarity, peace and well-being. An augmented endeavor for enhancing such human values in our respective societies may help prepare a favorable atmosphere for Global Humanity and Culture of Peace. Also, an augmented endeavor for enhancing comprehensive human development may help pave the way for Sustainable Development. Furthermore, an augmented endeavor for enhancing humanity-directed solidarity and well-being may help cultivate global Culture of Peace, Global Humanity and Sustainable Development (see, definitions and discussions in Chapter 8). All these endeavors may enrich our respective Cultures and enhance our thought-frames—personal and societal scopes of thought in time and space.

The resultant enrichment of diverse Cultures, as well as the enhancement of personal and societal thought-frames, can counter-balance the awesome and pervasive force of the Market and deal effectively with the important global issues. The holistic Cultural enrichment and the thought-frame enhancement, no doubt, can stimulate a comprehensive human development that may largely comprise personal and spiritual development and human capacity augmentation. Such human development can, in turn, stimulate a balanced socioeconomic development. This is the reason why it is important to induce and produce a synergistic process of *trilateral virtuous circle* among Holistic Culture Enrichment, Comprehensive Human Development and Balanced Socioeconomic Development (see discussions in Chapters 8 and 30), as a viable process toward Sustainable Development.

2 *The Credibility Trap in Our Contemporary World*

In this chapter I will take up the concept of the "Credibility Trap" that indicates a consequence of devastated society-specific culture (Culture), in particular, a consequence of liquidation and degeneration of the mutual trust among social constituents as well as of the centripetal force of society (Hiwaki and Tong 2006a). I will also discuss the relevance of the Credibility Trap to modern colonialism and the consequential degradation or underdevelopment of many colonized societies. Further, the Credibility Trap will be attributed to the market fundamentalism (Market) that has devastated the diverse society-specific cultures (Cultures) in our contemporary world. For simplicity here, the term "Culture" represents the holistic culture specific to a society, while the term "Market" indicates the acquisitiveness-oriented aggressive "alter ego" of modern civilization. (More detailed definitions of both "Culture" and "Market" will be presented in Chapter 8.) Finally, a few examples that represent the lack of mutual trust in the economic domain will be discussed as ones potentially leading to the Credibility Trap.

The Credibility Trap and Cultural Implications

Credibility Trap is the newly coined term to explain the state of serious social lethargy caused by the devastation of the Cultural foundation. It is the state so devastated, both culturally and politico-economically, that no short-term government initiative can invigorate the people and society. To concretely discuss Japan and China in terms of the Credibility Trap may require a little further elaboration of the concept that may relate not only to the Japanese and the Chinese situations but also to more general ones in the contemporary world. The Credibility Trap mentioned briefly in our Introductory Remarks (Chapter 1) refers to the systemic malfunction of society as well as to the drastic degradation of humanities, attributable to the serious impairment of the relevant Culture. As also implied there, the Credibility Trap may emerge when the respective Cultures suffer devastation to the extent that they lose the function of dynamic and coherent syntheses pertaining to the social constituents, organizations, institutions, traditions, values, mores and newly acquired knowledge, among other things.

Thus, the Credibility Trap refers to the devastated state of societal vitality, due mainly to the heavy damage inflicted on mutual trust in personal and social interactions as a result of the Cultural liquidation. The Cultural function of social integration largely refers to the centripetal force of society, which, in turn, rests on the mutual trust in general among the social constituents consisting of both natural and legal persons. A reasonably sound society-specific culture ("Sound Culture" to be defined and explained in

Chapters 15 and 16) is assumed here to maintain a particular variety of mutual trust, which acknowledges the tacit complementary relationship, for example, between the general public and the government, the employer and the employee, the producer and the consumer, the lender and the borrower, the young and the old and so on. Such mutual trust is largely a Culture-based social sentiment arising from long-term harmonious and consistent interactions of the social constituents in general.

In his famous passage, Adam Smith emphasized the importance of the existing Cultural foundation, implying that individual constituents of society were inevitably bound by the inherited holistic Culture when it comes to the most advantageous employment of their own resources in the long course of time (Smith 1937). "Every individual is continuously exerting himself to find out the most advantageous employment for whatever capital he can command. It is his own advantage, indeed, and not that of the society, which he has in view. But the study of his own advantage naturally, or rather necessarily leads him to prefer that employment which is most advantageous to the society."

Once the Culture—the common social property and identity of the social constituents—suffers devastation, caused by severe damage to the Culture-based mutual trust and centripetal force, it is quite natural that the people in general begin to assume an extremely self-centered, defensive, defiant and/or disorderly attitude for a lengthy period of time. Such an attitude may lead to a general behavior that tends to nullify any short-term remedial initiatives of the government, particularly its usual makeshift politico-economic measures. Also, the devastated Culture may condition the society to suffer from a long-lasting serious lethargy and/or a continuous moral, spiritual and intellectual downfall. This, in turn, may lead to a socioeconomic state characteristic of the Credibility Trap.

The Credibility Trap and Underdevelopment

It goes without saying that there are numerous examples of the Credibility Trap in history which have not been recognized as such, due mainly to the lack of *appropriate concept and explanatory framework* to associate a severe long-term societal lethargy with a Cultural degeneration and/or liquidation. Modern history alone saw plenty of such examples of the Credibility Trap, as a consequence of Spanish-Portuguese conquests for the spoils of many societies with the ensuing colonization and the Imperialistic scramble for colonies by major powers of the eighteenth and nineteenth centuries, particularly after the Industrial Revolution. We may justifiably add to the list the sixteenth to nineteenth-century colonization by Russia of neighboring societies and the twentieth century "Sovietization" by Russia of an even greater area. Not only the useful resources, both human and material, but also the vitality of the victimized societies were exploited and or exhausted by the colonial powers for their own socioeconomic development and power-hungry military build-up.

In a sense, the then aggressive Modern Powers might have taken for granted the ideologies of "free competition" and "might-makes-right" to have other peoples subjugated to the Imperialist purposes without self-reproach. The modern Imperialist powers, such as Spanish, Portugal, the Netherlands, England, France, Russia, United States of America, Germany, Italy and Japan, among others, imposed their own languages, religions and value systems on the victimized peoples and societies, draining their most important resources, both human and material, at the same time. In the process, they destroyed intentionally the native tongue, human capital, integrity and identity of each country, in such a way as to deprive the peoples and societies of their respective long-accumulated Cultures, upon which their knowledge, wisdom, value systems, aesthetic sentiments, means of communication, skills, mores, motivations, vitality and lifestyles had been firmly structured.

It is quite important to note here that a cursory glance of historical events or phenomena as delineated above have been often interpreted much differently or only superficially. A standard argument and/or stereotyped opinion has associated the victimized societies' *underdevelopment* with the resource exploitation or deprivation by the colonial powers. More far-fetched, some have argued for the simplistic association of *barbarous* societies (ones not civilized in the manner of the Western societies) with their *underdevelopment*. The matter cannot be so simple. These associations and the implied scenarios may only scratch the surface of the phenomenon of contemporary *underdevelopment*, totally ignoring the systemic collapse of the victimized societies, as a result of the *Cultural destruction* by the colonial suzerains. *Underdevelopment* due to the systematic destruction by force of the relevant holistic Cultures, however, has not been the only avenue to the Credibility Trap in our contemporary world.

A much more prevalent avenue today, though essentially related to the past colonialism and Imperialism as well as to the ideologies of "free competition" and "might-makes-right," is the economic and digital globalization driven by the market fundamentalism (Market). In our contemporary world, the Market has distorted and destroyed the diverse Cultures across the world to lead, sooner or later, many societies to a prolonged malady characteristic of the Credibility Trap. It is obvious from the above discussion that the Credibility Trap refers to the socioeconomic state that dwarfs the Keynesian "Liquidity Trap," despite the similarity of expressions. The latter indicates an economic state where a variety of expansionary monetary policies of "short-run" nature are deemed totally ineffective (Dornbusch and Fisher 1978). Such an economic state, however, does not negate or exclude the choice that remains in the "short run"—a fiscal variety of expansionary policies—which is supposed to stimulate and invigorate economic activities, according to the Keynesian hypothesis in the *General Theory of Employment, Interest and Money* (Keynes 1936). In other words, the Liquidity Trap refers to an extreme predicament as far as the "short-run" monetary policy is concerned: nothing more and nothing less.

When it comes to the Credibility Trap, no "short-run" economic initiative of the government can be deemed to alleviate the seriously weakened vitality of the society, which is attributable to the Cultural devastation. Such a socioeconomic predicament may arise as a result of devastating damage to the society's centripetal force as well as to the long-cultivated mutual trust among the social constituents. Such mutual trust, together with the centripetal force, is usually considered essential to sound personal and social relations and socioeconomic activities within a society. In the event of serious damage to the mutual trust and centripetal force, the only useful measure, perhaps, is a long-enduring, society-wide, full-fledged and whole-hearted endeavor to reconstruct a vast variety of mutual trust and sound human relations among the social constituents, institutions and organizations. In other words, revitalizing the society may require untiring personal and societal endeavors for restoring and enriching the Culture over many generations.

Lack of Mutual Trust and Reliability

LENDERS AND BORROWERS

The absence of mutual trust and centripetal force, implying a collapse of the framework for interdependence of the social constituents, tends to increase personal and social costs, both obvious and hidden, of almost all the socioeconomic relations and activities, both tangible and intangible. For an obvious instance, first, both lenders and borrowers of financial credits may, in the absence of mutual trust, plant doubts in their respective minds about the reliability of the other party. This entails a much greater risk and cost than otherwise to both the lenders and borrowers. The former may feel unable to rely on the latter's faithful repayment of the principal and interest in due time, while the latter may feel unable to trust the former for a supply of credit when needed.

The lenders, under such circumstances, may demand a much higher rate of interest and/or collateral of greater value than otherwise on whatever credit is to be supplied. Also, the borrowers, under the circumstances, may search for a more reliable lender as well as for lower-cost credit without avail, ending up with a greater search cost and repeated disappointment. The absence of mutual trust entails a much higher average "interest cost" broadly defined, as well as the relevant "psychic/emotional cost" of anxiety. The negative effect does not end there. A variety of future-oriented plans, projects and activities tend to be profoundly discouraged and the economic vitality likewise damaged, not only in the present but also in the future. This economic predicament, no doubt, negatively influences all sorts of socioeconomic planning and activities, devastating the societal vitality for a prolonged duration of time. This may imply a likely path leading to the Credibility Trap.

EMPLOYERS AND EMPLOYEES

As a second example, employers and employees, in the absence of mutual trust, may polarize their respective interests, negating the chance of their long-term cooperation, collaboration and solidarity for mutual benefit. The polarization of interests can, no doubt, increase the cost of industrial relations with an accompanying rise in the average rate of labor turnover, as well as in the frequency of conflicts between the employers and the employees. The employer-employee relationship may degenerate into temporality and fluidity, which may invite leaks of important ideas, plans, skills and know-how, entailing heavy extra costs of corporate operation, not to mention a great production loss.

The lack of a long-term relationship may discourage their mutual and positive orientation to the future, which is highly important for new plant investment, as well as for the relevant human-capital formation on and off the job, not to mention the growth of their productive activities. The absence of mutual trust between the employers and the employees may also increase personal and social costs, both obvious and hidden, through their temporary and unstable relationship that includes strike, strife and other production disturbances. Such a relationship in the vital activities of "winning bread" for all tends to discourage the long-term future orientation of the general public. This means that the social constituents may become inclined to aim at only their respective self-seeking interests of a temporary nature, such as an immediate satisfaction, selfish lifestyle and insolent behavior.

Such derogative self-interest may also lead to a "cut-throat" competition for income and goods, banning the society's efficient allocation of scarce resources, as well as its fair distribution of income for reasonable satisfaction of the social constituents at large. It also means that the society's public good or common property—the Culture—that has incorporated the long-accumulated experiences, knowledge, wisdom, mores, and so on, may inevitably face a further degeneration to nullify the value so dear and indispensable to society as a whole. Under these circumstances, the great majority of social constituents tend to be left discontented and unhappy. The resulting instability that accelerates the uncertainty of occupation, earning and living may entail a heavy loss to the society's vitality and productivity, as well as its future continuity and development. Such instability, uncertainty and insecurity tend to damage the society-wide peace and order to increase the "social cost" of security and the "psychic/emotional cost" of personal anxiety, leading to serious damage to the societal vitality as well as to the remaining mutual trust.

PRODUCERS AND CONSUMERS

As a third example, producers and consumers, in the absence of mutual trust, may question their mutual reliability and invite the proliferation of instability and disruption in production and consumption. The producers, in their day-to-day competition among themselves, may try constantly to entice the consumers overtly or covertly with deceptive and/or exaggerated advertisement of product quality, function, safety, durability and so on, leading the consumers as a whole to a high "search cost" as well as to a high "psychic/emotional cost" of incessant disappointment. The consumers for their part may send contradictory, sporadic, transient and capricious signals of changing needs and tastes, leading the producers to a high cost of marketing and inventory adjustments as well as to a high extra cost of constant trial-and-error approaches in search of potential long-sellers and popular products.

In other words, the lack of mutual trust between the producers and the consumers tends to deprive them both of the otherwise reliable and steady relationship for mutual benefits. In addition, the lack of mutual trust, which accompanies the endless process of futile and mistaken explorations of output and consumption, may entail irreversible resource wastes and heavy "social costs," by excessively exploiting the scarce resources, as well as deteriorating the natural and human environments. This indicates a never-ending "win-or-lose" competition among the producers as well as among the consumers, leaving eventually a small and shrinking minority of winners and a great majority of losers, respectively, who are highly antagonistic to each other and also to the society. Naturally, this entails an endless growth of personal, psychic/emotional, social and environmental costs, which diminish the socioeconomic activities and devastate the societal vitality over time.

It is almost self-evident that the lack of mutual trust entails such heavy complex costs as well as formidable and negative effects on the future vitality of the people and society concerned. Such socioeconomic consequences attributable to the collapse of mutual trust may feed back to the market fundamentalism (Market) to accelerate instability, uncertainty, disparity, insecurity and cruelty in everyday market activities. Also, there is a long list of important human interactions that require mutual trust in many domains other than the economic one. Several important examples refer to the relationship between the voter and the politician, the taxpayer and the government, the ethnic majority and the minority, the learned and the learning, the healthy and the sick, the young and the elder, doctors and patients, parents and children, husbands and wives, and so on. Compounded with the lack of mutual trust in all thinkable domains, a society must face over time a variety of ever-rising risks and costs that accompany the long-term diminishing public spirit and socioeconomic activities and, hence, leading to the collapse of societal vitality—the Credibility Trap.

Concluding Remarks

One main cause of such devastated vitality in "peace time" can be largely traced to the Market in our contemporary world. As implied above, the Market has a strong tendency to trample on the diverse society-specific cultures (Cultures), though the Market cannot survive without the intrinsic value system that nurtures mutual trust. The Market-driven economic globalization has now been devastating the diverse Cultures across the world to the detriment of mutual trust and centripetal force in the respective societies. The economic globalization has not only effected the Market-inflicted deprivation of mutual trust and centripetal force but also led many a society to a prolonged severe malady, characteristic of the Credibility Trap that may usually refer to the state of persistent socioeconomic and human *underdevelopment*. Such a devastated state of societal vitality, due mainly to the ever growing abrasive force of the Market, may represent broadly the "dying" catalysis and synthesis of the respective Cultures in our age of economic and digital globalization.

3 *Japan in the Credibility Trap*

In this chapter I will discuss the lasting and even deepening lethargy of Japan in terms of the Credibility Trap, relating it to the country's Cultural devastation, as well as alluding to the socioeconomic-and-systemic malfunctions and personal-spiritual-intellectual degeneration. After the Meiji Restoration in 1868, Japan hastily adapted to modern civilization as self-protection from Western colonialism, neglecting its Cultural foundation as a result. After defeat in the Second World War, Japan immersed itself in Western capitalistic values; a result of forced adaptation to the American-style liberal democracy and market economy as well as the accompanying ideology of "might-makes-right." Further, Japan's hasty and reckless growth policy of "catch-up-with the West" can be said to have resulted in almost total sacrifice of the country's long-accumulated, invaluable Cultural foundation. In a sense, Japan's long-enduring insular Culture has been sacrificed for short-sighted industrialism and market fundamentalism (Market).

Hasty and Half-Boiled Modernization

Discussing the "Japanese modernization," it is rather customary to refer to the "great success" of emulating the Western models, which culminated in the much-applauded "Oriental Miracle." The story, however, is not so simple nor does it imply a happy ending. One can easily penetrate the glorious façade of Modern Japan to see the real struggle, confusion and dehumanization of the Japanese people. To begin with, the people in general have suffered from the chronic indigestion of Western philosophies, thoughts, ideologies and lifestyles, in addition to suffering from the rapid centralization and industrialization as well as from the miseries of repeated Imperialistic warfare. The people of Japan have also suffered from the compounded confusion of Japan's "modernization" in view of their originally coherent *insular-and-diverse* society-specific cultures (Cultures).

The rapid centralization of the existent social systems, governmental functions and military-industry institutions, as well as the imitation of the Western models of nation state and industrial society, have steadily eroded the long-cherished Japanese personality, morality, spirituality and other Cultural characteristics. Japan's economic, intellectual and political emulation of the modern civilization after the Meiji Restoration of 1868 and, more significantly, the country's politico-economic and intellectual commitment and subjugation to the US after defeat in the Second World War, have dilapidated the different but coherent national and local Cultures in Japan to the detriment of personal, spiritual, moral and intellectual continuity.

One may find a variety of triggers for the Japanese modernization. One trigger may be found in Dutch studies (*Rangaku*) that attracted a group of young Japanese scholars interested in the Western medicine, mathematics, astronomy, chemistry and military strategy after the early eighteenth century. Another trigger may refer to the Japanese reaction to Dutch studies—the feverish studies of ancient Japanese thoughts and traditions (*Kokugaku*). Simultaneously, the Japanese also reacted to the earlier influences of foreign origins (such as *Buddhism* and *Confucianism*). Moreover, Japan had a more immediate trigger in the violent reactions to the American "battleship" diplomacy in the mid-nineteenth century. As a consequence, disputes arose over "opening" and "exclusion" with regards to the Japanese stance toward all Westerners. Also, there were divided and futile arguments between the sovereignty of the "State" and that of the "people."

In addition, there were furious struggles for the realignment of beliefs and thoughts combining Buddhism, Confucianism, Shintoism and, later, Protestantism, without any coherent results (Nishibe 2000). To complicate matters further, the political and military struggles began to surface between the existing regime of Tokugawa tycoon and the anti-Tokugawa alliance of Southwestern clans. The latter wanted to restore the Emperor to Head of State, which would be accompanied by sovereign political status. With such a variety of roots and the related manifold vortex, a social revolution—the Meiji Restoration—was started by the the lower but educated echelon of *samurai* who belonged mostly to the Southwestern clans.

Those who held the reins of government as a result of the Meiji Restoration might have been somewhat confident in their strategy to "fight evil with evil:" that is, the "poison" (the Western aggression against Japan) could be checked by the same "poison" (the Westernization of industry and army on the basis of "Japanese spirit and Western knowledge"). Thus, they encouraged the massive inflow to the Japanese society of the Western knowledge and thoughts, albeit superficially, together with the Western political, legal, educational, industrial and military systems, despite the lack of corresponding or similar traditions, spirituality and values in Japan. Furthermore, throughout the pre-war period, the "self-righteous and modernized" Japanese bureaucrats guided the people to adapt themselves to the Western thoughts, manners and lifestyles through the centralized education system that combined the French model of centralized education with the American model of utilitarian education (Encyclopedia 1983). Additionally, the compulsory uniform education that contradicted the diverse Cultures and the versatile educational traditions in Japan was instituted with the aim of producing a docile standardized people, as well as a "modern" industrial workforce.

Being more or less forced to adapt to the modern civilization by the new central Government that imitated, only superficially, the Western model of the nation state and "democratic" government, the generations after the Meiji Restoration began to disregard the intrinsic "Japanese spirit" and gave their mind and soul to "Western thoughts and knowledge." In other words, they often evaded and discarded the Japanese traditions and Cultural foundation in favor of a rapid "Westernization of Japan," without successfully incorporating the historical, philosophical and spiritual complex of Western civilization into the life and knowledge of the Japanese at large. Such "Westernization" naturally resulted in a typical case of "going for wool and coming back shorn." Japan herself became a late-come Imperialist power and ended up as a troublemaker in Asia. Naturally, the country lost the confidence of the other Asians, as well as its own self-confidence after defeat in the Second World War.

Post-War Negation of Japan's Culture

The post-war Constitution of Japan and the Fundamental Law of Education, both of which were largely dictated in terms of Western ideals and ideologies by the General Headquarters of the Allied Occupation (or the American Armed Occupation), generally negated or banned the Japanese traditions and Cultural foundation, insinuating them as "undemocratic," "warlike" and "barbaric." These important legal canons, therefore, encouraged and urged the Japanese people to create a sort of "brand-new" Culture on the basis of Anglo-American ideals and ideologies, which were largely alien to the Japanese people and beyond their clear grasp. These ideals and ideologies appeared to them as nothing other than the symbolic images of Japan's total defeat and elusive post-war optimism. On top of such legal canons, Japan's inevitable acceptance of US military protection or the "nuclear umbrella," as a result of the US-Japan Security Pact of 1951 (and its revision in 1960) has, over time, worked to rob the people, particularly the youth, of their will to defend their fellow people and motherland, as well as their clear sense of national sovereignty and identity.

The post-war Western condescending praise of Japan's economic achievement as an "Oriental Miracle"—referring to the rapid economic development under the slogan of "Catch up with the West"—induced the misguided adaptation of the people to the Anglo-American "individualistic" values, money-hungry selfish pursuits and competition-oriented aggressive behaviors. Such praise also encouraged the people to devote themselves to their respective occupations of "modern inculcation," often ignoring the *insular heritage* of cooperation, understanding, mutual concern and mutual help among people, as well as slighting the hitherto strong attachment to family, community and hometown. In the meantime, such incoherent and misguided values, attitudes, behaviors and lifestyles have grossly undermined the coherent heritage of diverse national and local Cultures in Japan. Such incoherence and misguidance also resulted in the personal, moral, spiritual and intellectual degradation by the nonchalant neglect of the long-accumulated and multi-layered complex heritage, as well as the light-hearted attitude of "going-with-the-tide" or "sitting-on-the-fence."

No one disputes the fact that the Japanese people as a whole have gained much materially by "modernization" and industrialization. The gain, perhaps, has been at the long-term cost of their morality, personality, spirituality and identity, as well as of their stability, confidence and solidarity. Nowadays, the Japanese face ever-increasing deceit, fraud, cover-up and outright crimes committed by individuals, firms, government agencies and political machines, along with the rapid destruction of important Cultural values. A further consequence of modernization has been the rapid break down in mutual trust among the social constituents. Personal, societal and general reliabilities of both natural and legal persons have seriously suffered without the general awareness of what is happening society-wide. Accordingly, the centripetal force of the society seems to have vanished like an illusion. After all, such a materialistic "rat-race" has created a gaping hole in people's minds, making them excessively selfish, closed, lonely, insatiable and unhappy.

With all of the above taking place, Japanese mainstreamers in politics, journalism, business and economics have regarded the on-going societal lethargy as a serious issue limited only to the economic domain, particularly to its structural adjustment problem in the age of economic globalization. Thus, the policy makers and the law makers, with short-sighted advice provided by popular and opportunistic mainstream economists, have attempted to resort to varying mixes of fiscal, monetary and structural policies only to repeat expensive mistakes. These are nothing short of crimes against the people—at the cost of other societal priorities—most importantly, the reproduction and enrichment of diverse Cultures within Japan, not to mention the obvious cost to taxpayers both in the present and future.

The leaders of Japanese business organizations, who think of nothing but catching up with Western trends, particularly those of the US, have been mindful only of profitability, rationality, efficiency, competition and American-global standards, disregarding the interest of the people at large. Such leaders have eagerly tackled the task of rationalizing production, and have been enthusiastic in replacing their domestic employees and facilities with cheaper labor in the developing nations and direct investment overseas, respectively. Along with political and business leaders, mainstream economists and journalists have eagerly advocated the so-called "market approach" and the dogmatic trinity of freedom (free competition, free market and free trade) as the golden rule, paying very little attention to what such approach and freedom may bring to people and society without an appropriate and stable Cultural and moral foundation. These mainstream, self-styled "conscientious" leaders, who have been inculcated in Western ideals and ideologies, often seem to have despised their own Cultural heritage and ignored their more intrinsic duties to the people and society.

The misguided Japanese general public, unaware of what "modern liberal democracy" really means, have long assumed, naively and/or passively, that their post-war "democratic" Government would lead them to a safe and prosperous future, as long as they minded their own businesses. Now, they have come to realize that, despite the altruistic stance and avowal, public officials with their "half-boiled" knowledge and spirit of the modern civilization, as well as their naive detachment to the Japanese insular Culture, have actually been working only for their own benefit. They have augmented their power, security and comfort, paying almost no attention to the predicament of individual fellow citizens, particularly the weak and victimized. Officals of the Japanese National Government have even taken to treating the local communities as if they were their colonies. The attitude of condescension and lack of compassion of public officials toward the fellow people has resulted in the neglect of their responsibilities. An example of this is the cut-and-dried legalistic approach toward the victims of the domestic Arm terrorism (the sarin attacks by the Aum cult in 1994–1995) and the Awaji-Hanshin earthquake in 1995. A slow, uncoordinated response was also shown to victims of subsequent earthquakes.

Statistical Indications of Social Lethargy

The recently disclosed blatant neglect, massive cover-up and widespread embezzlement and appropriation by the Japanese bureaucracy of the national pension-plan eloquently tell the story of the so-called "democratic" Japanese Government. By now, most Japanese people have become highly skeptical, negative or dissociated toward their politicians, bureaucrats and political machines. The economic condition after the collapse of the "bubble economy" in the early 1990s shows a long unprecedented stagnation, very close to a zero or minute rate of annual income growth on average, in view of the Japan's experience of economic expansion in the late 1950s and throughout the 1960s. The

Government, prior to the US economy-rooted financial-and-economic predicaments in recent years, was deceptively glossing over Japan's minute and uncertain economic recovery as an "unexpected continuous growth" longer than the *Izanagi* boom in the latter part of 1960s, which was a four-year long rapid economic expansion with the average real growth rate of over 10 percent.

In the meantime, the Government's outstanding debts (according to official announcements) have amounted to more than 900 trillion Yen (about US$80,000 per capita) or about 200 percent of nominal Gross Domestic Product (GDP). It has often been suggested that the total debts (both exposed and hidden) of national and local governments may go well over 1,500 trillion Yen (about three times the current Japanese GDP or approximately US$15 trillion, equivalent to US$130,000 per capita (at 100 yen/US$1)). One cannot dismiss such profoundly "atrocious" public management in peace time simply as "policy failure." It is nothing short of a "huge crime" against the people, committed by the one-party rule of the Liberal-Democratic Party, together with the arrogant, condescending and demure Japanese bureaucracy. They have not only wastefully expended the fruit of the hardworking people but they also inevitably make the people at large suffer undeserved hardship by robbing their present and future income and vitality in favor of the rich minority of natural and legal persons.

Such atrocious "governmental crime against the people" has also had the consequence of accelerating an unprecedented income disparity in recent decades as a consequence of the largely imitated Anglo-American capitalistic ideology of new liberalism and "might-makes-right." The mounting income disparity, also attributable to the Government encouragement of and involvement in the market fundamentalism (Market), has also accelerated anxiety, uncertainty, instability and insecurity among the people. The resulting distrust of politicians and bureaucrats at large and the political apathy can be discerned from the abrupt decline of voting percentages in the national elections after the early 1990s. In the elections for the House of Representatives, the voting percentages oscillated up and down within the range between 75.4 (highest) and 68.1 (lowest) during the period of 1976–1993, but the oscillation changed to the range between 62.9 (highest) and 60.2 (lowest) during the period of 1996–2004. The younger the age group, the more extreme the drop of voting percentages. For the youngest group of voters (aged 20–24), the percentages in 1996–2004 declined from 56 to 38.2.

A sudden rise in the voting percentage in the national elections of 2005 may have reflected the people's desperate bid to escape from the Credibility Trap by "clutching at straws" under the then popular Premier Koizumi, who, subsequently, stepped down without providing any hope for Japan's future. After the serious and repeated disappointment of the 60-year regime of the Liberal Democratic Party, the people gave the Democratic Party a landslide victory over the Liberal Democratic Party in September 2009, hoping for a "once-for-all" change in the politico-economic atmosphere in favor of the people in general.

The younger generation, in particular, has often become transient, present-oriented, apathetic, indifferent, inactive, passive and/or antisocial, as they face the widespread socioeconomic predicaments of accelerated uncertainty, instability and insecurity. Given the growing uncertainty about the future, the young have become increasingly skeptical about the nation's welfare policy which implicates a transfer of income from the young to the old, when the demographic share of the young is rapidly declining. Moreover, many of them have started to ignore the welfare system, in which they are inclined to see only their own immediate costs, lacking trust in the corrupt Government as well as being indifferent to their society. The recent rapid drop in the premium collection rate of the semi-compulsory National Pension Plan (*Kokumin Nenkin*) from 96.1 percent in 1980 to 70.9 percent in 2001, and then to 65.8 percent in 2004, with the continuous downward trend has been often attributed to the negative attitude mainly of the younger generation toward the credibility of the Pension Plan and their indifference to and/or pessimism about the future prospects of society.

It is known well in the Japanese educational world that the average achievements in all levels of formal education have rapidly deteriorated and polarized in recent years, not to mention the devastated state of home and community education. When it comes to the achievement of the average 15-year-old Japanese youth, a recent investigation by the Organisation for Economic Co-operation and Development (OECD) reveals a rapid degradation (Nihon Keizai Shinbun 2004b). Results showing compulsory education achievements in 41 countries and areas indicated that Japanese youth stepped down to the 14th position in 2003 from the 8th position in 2000, in terms of the ability to correctly comprehend writing in the national language. More drastically, perhaps, the Japanese ability to apply mathematics went down to the 6th position in 2003 from the top position in 2000, being overtaken by the respective youth of Hong Kong, Finland, South Korea, Holland and Liechtenstein. At the same time, Japanese higher education is crumbling at its foundation as a result of the rapidly degenerating motivation of college students at large, as well as to the rigidity and mannerism of the educational system.

The Japanese people have come to sense the gross distortion of their society, now amounting to the regime of "Market sovereignty" biased to the transient and materialistic values that encourage the immediate satisfaction of individual self-interest, greed and convenience. Such "Market sovereignty" has accelerated the income disparity and contributed generally to the advantage of dishonesty, trickery, fraud and bribery. Accordingly, most households have become either opportunistic or extremely pessimistic about their future. The half-century trend in the household-saving rate may tell the story of changing orientation. The saving rate grew rapidly from 11.9 percent in 1955 to 23.2 percent in 1976, indicating a steadily growing future orientation, among other things. After the peak rate in 1976, it declined to 13.4 percent in 1998, 6.7 percent in 2002 and 2.2 percent in 2007, implying a rapidly rising orientation to the present, among other things. Within only a decade, from 1998 to 2007, the same saving rate was drastically reduced from 13.4 percent to 2.2 percent. The mythology of "Japanese thrift and long timeframe" has been largely contradicted by the recent household-saving behavior.

An equally noteworthy fact is the rapid drop in the Japanese birth rate. In 1952, there were 23.5 births for every 1,000 population, but the rate declined drastically to 9.3 by 2001 and 8.9 by 2004. The decline was equally drastic in the number of births per woman, from 2.98 births in 1952 to 1.29 in 2003 and to 1.25 in 2005 (Nihon Keizai Shinbun 2004a, 2008). The latter figure is much smaller than the 2.08 births per woman that is required to maintain the present size of the Japanese population. Many plausible interpretations regarding the causes of decline have been presented, such as greater freedom of choice based on the rapid increase in household income, greater and longer participation of women in the workforce, greater opportunity and longer period of education for women, higher cost of child-raising and education, and so on.

Loss of Social Vitality

Getting down to the bedrock, however, the Japanese people as a whole apparently have come to evade their adequate reproduction of themselves, slighting their Cultural and biological continuities. This may imply an increasingly short-sighted, self-centered and closed attitude of the people, as well as an increasing detachment from their familial, social, Cultural and national identities. It is likely that most of the Japanese people have been retiring to their self-centered transient pleasure, cutting themselves off from the past and the future. The Japanese at large now seem to ignore or slight their ties with their own families, neighbors and fellow citizens, not to mention the international community and the global environment. After all, they have been largely negating their Cultural values in favor of the transient market values, behaving crudely in accordance with the market fundamentalism (Market).

Such a tendency, together with the rapidly deteriorating social order with the rise of atrocious and/or unsolved crimes, is a symptom of the people being badly infected by the epidemic of the Market and the aggrandizement of "scientific potentials" (namely, the ideology of science as panacea), which can be deemed as the "twin alter egos" of the modern civilization. The Japanese people at large may have fallen victim to such twin alter egos by following or misinterpreting the modern thoughts, values, methods and lifestyles. In the meantime, they have been inculcated by the centralized lopsided education as well as by the highly biased mass-media to place human above nature, individual above community, material above mind, competition above cooperation, change above continuity, liberty above security, greed above life, quantity above quality, present above past and future, flow above stock, exploitation above conservation, and so on. As a consequence, they have gradually come to trifle their long-cherished inclinations toward nature, mind, cooperation, continuity, family, hometown, and so on.

The post-war Japanese Constitution, despite being an ideal Anglo-American legal canon, may have been extremely hazardous to the vastly different national inclination, nationality or nationhood of Japan. The Constitution stresses superficially the principles of "freedom," "equality," "private property" and "human rights." Such ideal principles of the modern civilization require a clear and appropriate grasp of their intended meanings: that is, their origin, history, thought, spirit, mores and philosophies have to be understood profoundly by the general public in order to be effective. Otherwise, these principles may act like a *hurricane* that rampages around in conflict with the existing mentality and background, when the principles are not only severed from the relevant historical processes and Cultural roots but also transplanted in the settings of totally different traditions, values and mores.

Put more severely, such principles have been acting like *cancer cells* that expand ferociously, eventually destroying the mother system. In the given Japanese settings, these "principles" have been turned into lopsided "principles" or "dogmas." "Freedom" has been largely construed as a license for naked selfishness, particularly by naïve and/or maliciously-inclined individuals; "equality" has been used indiscreetly to incriminate all sorts of differences; "private property" has been claimed, for example, by misguided persons heaping up garbage, rubbish and waste on their property causing trouble and annoyance for their neighbors; and "human rights," together with the lopsided "freedom," "equality" and "private property," have been expanded endlessly to topple the existing social value system, social order and environmental concerns. Accordingly, the Constitution may have devastated the long-cherished human relations, mutual trust, mores and reliability incorporated in the coherent diverse local and national Cultures, by disregarding the familial, communal and insular traditions of Japan. If so, the Constitution is, indeed, working to mass-produce a misguided, apologetic, frustrated and unhappy population, instead of contributing to an equitable and reasonable life for the Japanese people.

The Japanese Constitution, without roots in Japanese traditions, can be viewed as a legal institution contrived to destroy the inherited diverse Cultures that represent the accumulated endeavors for knowledge, creativity and wisdom of the Japanese forebears (see Chapter 16). As a result, the Constitution may have degraded and degenerated the existing mutual trust, mutual understanding, confidence and continuity, which are an essential source of vitality today and in the future. It can also be perceived ironically that the most important legal canon has contributed over time to the degradation of Japanese personality, morality, spirituality, identity and nationhood, as well as to the general confusion, social disarray and the Credibility Trap. Of course, there are other factors, such as the Fundamental Law of Education, US-Japan Security Pacts and the alter egos of the modern civilization, which have all contributed to the destruction of Japanese traditions, wisdom and identity, and hence, to the devastation of the coherent diverse local and national Cultures that have an integrative and cumulative history over some fifteen millennia.

Concluding Remarks

The greatest damage to the Cultural foundation, however, has come from the Japanese people's nonchalant neglect and light-hearted attitude of "going with the tide," as well as from the Market-inflicted corrupt and conspiring triangle—business, government and mass-media—of the post-war Japanese society. No wonder Japan has come to suffer from the destruction of her centripetal force and has fallen into the Credibility Trap after the collapse of the bubble economy in the early 1990s. With penetrating insight into Japan's history, people and society, Susumu Nishibe in his *Kokumin no Dotoku* (literally, *Morality of the Nation*) aptly describes the modern and contemporary behaviors of the Japanese people, as follows (Nishibe 2000):

> To speak of the Japanese with favor, the people without any consorted principles and systems had to run for opportunism by compulsion. Knowing the circumstances well, however, we must still recognize such an opportunistic adaptation entirely to the circumstances as nothing but a pathological case (this quotation was translated into English by the present author).

This self-inflicted pathological case may entail an exorbitant remedial cost in the long duration of time in order for the society to survive and continue despite the devastated Cultural foundation and identity. The nation is now in great need of finding itself and rebuilding its integrity by revitalizing its diverse Cultures, starting with the rehabilitation of its devastated home and community education. This could be based, perhaps, on the wisdom complex of Prince Shotoku's "Seventeen Article Constitution" (see Chapter 16).

4 *The Imminent Credibility Trap in China*

In this chapter I will turn to China and examine the plausibility of this country falling into the Credibility Trap in the near future, despite the seemingly impressive economic growth after the open-door policy instituted in 1978. The fast-changing polities, policies, thoughts and activities in the last hundred years, implicating the degradation of mutual trust and centripetal force, will be discussed together with the rapid polarization of income and wealth, the forced demographic change, the widespread unemployment, the rampant corruption and the ethnic-geographic-occupational variety of growing disparity, among other important factors. Also, the changing treatment of the farming majority will be considered as an important factor that may swing the sociopolitical climate, reflecting a drastic damage to mutual trust among the very diverse social constituents. This discussion will directly refer to the Chinese example, but it is intended to suggest the case as microcosm of the contemporary world at large. China with its huge population, 56 ethnic groups and their respective Cultures, as well as the rapidly growing income-and-wealth disparity among individuals, occupations and districts, may very well represent our contemporary world.

The Rise of Communist China and the Cultural Revolution

The Chino-Japanese War, particularly the defeat of China by its small neighboring county, Japan, was perceived as an absolute humiliation to the Chinese. This defeat triggered the very first patriotism of the people, which resulted in political, social, economic and philosophical changes. Such patriotism also contributed to the desires of intellectuals, thinkers and scholars to reform, unify, modernize and strengthen China. A firm believer of "bourgeois democracy," Dr Sun Yat-sen—the "Father of the Chinese Nation"—led over ten revolutionary struggles and finally overthrew the Qing Dynasty in the Wuchang Uprising in October 1911. After the collapse of the Qing Dynasty (1616–1912), the Chinese society has undergone nearly 100 years of many twists and turns. Dr Sun Yat-sen pursued a new polity and political aim on the basis of equality among people, independence from Western imperialistic powers and equitable land distribution. In other words, he was exploring the principles of people's nationalism, democracy and livelihood. Soon, however, this exploration was disrupted by the struggle between the National Party and the Communist Party. Additionally, the Japanese intrusion with the puppet emperor in Manchuria and the ensuing Second World War complicated the founding of the Chinese nation.

The careful and undaunted revolutionary endeavors of Dr Sun influenced Mao Zedong to join the revolutionary army. Mao shaped the direction of China after 1949, particularly of the Chinese Communist Party which had been formed in 1921. Born and raised in a peasant family like Dr Sun, Mao was sympathetic and empathetic with the poor peasants and workers who comprised the great majority of the Chinese population. In 1949, the population in China was estimated as 541.7 million, of which 484.02 million (89.4 percent of the total population) belonged to the peasantry. Mao had a deep understanding of the importance of providing the poor peasants with a better life and fought for the benefits of the poor majority. No doubt, such majority support for the Communist Party was the most important reason for the victory over the better-armed-and-equipped *Kuonmingtang*—the Nationalist army.

Over the course of half a century, after the founding of the People's Republic of China, the country has discarded its local identity by adopting a thoroughgoing communist ideology and, after 1978, by assuming a *raw capitalist ideology* that corresponds largely with the market fundamentalism (Market). Thus, the country generally, and the business specifically, has had to face the "value renewal," thereby fusing together local Chinese spirit (or traditional social values and philosophy) with global technique (or contemporary business management and technology). The century-long process of value renewal has caused confusion for the Chinese people, especially given the diverse ethnic groups with their respective Cultures.

From 1949 to 1976 (the year of Mao's death), there prevailed equality and fairness among the people, although every Chinese person was very poor during the period. Mao set the goal for the Chinese Communist Party that the party members had to work whole-heartedly for the benefit of the people and against corrupted concepts and ideas of bourgeois. Thus, the Chinese people did not have to undergo the suffering of unemployment or worry about the cost of retirement, medical care and children's education. Mao, however, was always an idealist and, much worse, an idealist dictator. Many decisions he made ended up in failure or even in disaster and atrocity, such as the cases of the People's Commune, the Big Leap Forward and the Cultural Revolution. His most disastrous attempt at the Cultural Revolution had underlying reasons: he wanted to rebuild his idealistic world by pushing the high-class and intellectual people, as well as the bureaucratic officials, into farming villages in order to have their minds reinvigorated for the reform of China. Mao had an idealistic desire to create a steady, independent and powerful China.

Open-Door Policy and Raw Capitalism

Following the ten-year attempt at the idealistic and atrocious Cultural Revolution, the death of Mao Zedong gave an opportunity for Den Shaoping to gain the control of the Communist Party. In view of the then backward and poor China, in 1978 Den commenced the "open door" policy or the "economic reform." This economic reform was accompanied by a policy to abolish the socialistic system of the People's Communes by returning the private plots of land to the peasants and encouraging them to engage in sideline businesses. The new policies provided incentives to the peasants, resulting in the best period (1978–1984) of the agricultural development since 1949.

In the meantime a new system was worked out in terms of "household contract responsibility with remuneration linked to output." Den's policy of economic development brought an improved standard of living to many Chinese but also accelerated the disparity in income, wealth and amenity, particularly after 1985. The income disparity between the rural and urban population was first diminished from 1:2.4 in 1978 to 1:1.7 in 1985, and then rapidly increased to 1:3.09 in 2002 or to 1:5.9 if the various kinds of social benefits to the urban population are accounted for (China (Hainan) Reform Development Research Center 2003, Li 1998). Moreover, the foreign capital invited by Den's "open door" policy brought with it Western democracy, freedom and liberty as well as raw capitalism, which were alien to the Chinese society and resulted in the Tiananmen Massacre in 1989.

Despite a rapid growth of aggregate economic activities after the "economic reform," the excess rural labor, the laid-off urban workers and the growing population have created a serious unemployment situation. The officially released data of unemployment of 3 percent in recent years, however, grossly understates the actual situation, perhaps, beyond the reasonable argument for the official definition of unemployment. The official data refers only to the urban registered workforce, which constitutes a fraction of the total labor force. Most of the current Chinese unemployment may have been unnoticed (or ignored) in the official statistics of the Government (Hu 2002, China (Hainan) Reform Development Research Center 2000) and the actual unemployment today, calculated in terms of the Western definition of unemployment, may very well amount to 30–35 percent of the total workforce on the basis of various evidence (Chinese Academy of Science 1998, Yang 1997, Wu 2002, Hiwaki and Tong 2006a). As a result of the recent US-originated financial and economic crises, the total number and the proportion to the population of the unemployed might have increased significantly, mainly as a result of severe export loss.

Corruption has been a very serious economic and social issue, particularly the Government initiative to sell many national assets by the piece as well as by the block, with the pretext of stimulating economic activities. Following the official enclosure of national common land, many land plots have been undervalued and subsequently transferred to the private assets of individuals capable of bribing Government authorities. Rising public and private corruption, as well as the escalated cost of bribery, triggered an all-out land speculation in the industrial cities, resulting in a bubble economy, increasing the living costs of poor peasants and workers, not to mention the unemployed.

Disparity and the Predicament of the Farming Majority

Following the "economic reform" of 1978, in addition to the rapidly growing disparity in income and wealth, huge unemployment and widespread corruption, the policy of social welfare has become drastically skewed in favor of urban residents at the cost of the rural population. Furthermore, the demographic and psychological changes that have resulted from another of Den's policies—the "single-child" policy—may also have affected the Government welfare policy against the interest of the rural agricultural population. It is highly important to be aware of China's instability and situation, for China today aptly represents the microcosm of the instable and divergent global world with its gigantic population (over 1.3 billion), diverse ethnic groups and Cultures, as well as with its vast income-and-wealth disparity and environment differential.

The following quotation regarding the 2,000 Gross National Income (GNI) per capita, using the World Atlas calculation method, eloquently describes the current Chinese predicament that divides the nations into vastly different geographical areas (Hu 2002) to the detriment of mutual trust and centripetal force:

In view of GNI per capita measurement of the World Bank, China can be divided into "four worlds". Shengzhen and Shanghai have already reached the higher-income (above US$9,076) economies and become "1st world", equivalent to about 2.2 percent of the total population. Coastal cities such as Guangdong, Liaoning, Jiansu, which is equivalent to 21.8 percent of the total population, have reached the upper-middle income (US$2,936–US$9,075) level. 26 percent of the total population has reached the lower-middle income (US$736–US$2,935) level, located in the North-East, the North and the Central China. Finally, 50 percent of the total population has remained in the low income (US$735 or less) level.

What we can surmise from the above is the underlying fate of the Chinese peasants, as rural dwellers and the great majority of the total population, who have been tossed back and forth within the time span of a century. Their resentment and distrust of the Government authorities may have become accumulative and deep-seated. They once experienced fair and equal treatment under the regime of Mao Zedong, and their memory of this time may have created strong antagonism against the current Government. China's economic success story over the past quarter of a century is at the cost of the Chinese peasants in both farmlands and cities and as a result of the increasing disparity in income, wealth and amenities. The predicament of the peasants and their resulting resentment has been caused by the polices that have downgraded their economic, political, social, cultural and psychological conditions. These predicament and resentment may, thus, lead to the peasants' self-protection as well as their self-centered unsafe production particularly of foodstuff by excessive use of poisonous herbicide and pesticide, especially when the young having been drained to large industrial cities. This situation may result in the consequential degradation of agriculture as well as discrimination against the peasant farmers.

These phenomena in a long course of time may have given heavy "body-blows" to the rather fragile unity and solidarity of the diverse population divided into as many as 56 ethnic groups and the long-term credibility and reliability of the current Chinese Communist Party, as well as to the increasingly liquid social integrity and Cultural identity. The new Communist Party, which commenced its leadership in 2003, has implemented some policies aimed at lowering the tax burdens of peasants, but this has had little effect on the income disparity. If the degradation of agriculture continues in the future, China may face a growing shortage of foodstuffs (in particular, safe foodstuffs), as well as the accelerated shortage of natural resources (the majority of China's oil consumption is now imported). In the meantime, serious corruption, very poor corporate governance and heavy unemployment have tended to sacrifice further the interest of the rural farming communities.

Economic Expansion and Uncertainty

It is, however, not realistic to think that, as a result of the problems outlined above, as divisive as they are, China will immediately fall into the state of the Credibility Trap. The nation still seems to have a strong historical momentum to grow and pursue its aggrandizement economically, politically and militarily. This national motive to grow strong may continue for some time, regardless of socialistic or capitalistic aggrandizement, so long as the US, the only super power in today's world, provides an outrageous threat of Americanization or standardization of the world. Economically speaking, China's immediate aim is, perhaps, to maintain over 8 percent growth of Gross Domestic Product (GDP) to maintain the current level of employment, in an attempt to weather the current worldwide economic crisis. Politically, China may aim to excel the European Union (EU), at least in voice, and may hope similarly to match the US, speaking for itself as a nation, as well as for the Far East and South East Asia. The Chinese people, with their impressive history of four millennia, may want to assert themselves Culturally, economically, politically, technologically and demographically, as much as possible.

As long as such China's motive, aim and self-assertion are shared largely among the population, however divergent they may be, China's historical momentum will continue to be fed by the mutually reinforcing economic growth, political stability, Cultural reassertion and technological development to compensate partially for the increasing income and wealth disparity, as well as for the rising resentment against, and distrust of, the current regime. Put differently, so long as the people at large feel that their standard of living is improving, there seems to be no immediate threat to the Communist Party or the Government. As a result, the present policy emphasis on economic growth in perpetuity may serve the purpose of the Communist regime, at least for the time being.

Such growth policy, however, requires a rapidly growing import of energy, other resources and even foodstuffs, in view of the massive population of some 1.3 billion. This may pose a threat to the rest of the world, particularly an imminent threat of worldwide scramble under the "law of the jungle" for the remaining, dwindling global resources. Such a worldwide scramble will, no doubt, create environmental and political stresses among peoples, both in industrially advanced and developing countries, and lead to unexpectedly severe and antagonistic diplomatic and trade relations to check the Chinese economic growth sooner or later. Even worse, it may lead to a more direct political and armed conflict with the advanced nations, as the new Communist regime is going to be compelled to resort to a more aggressive growth policy for the management of its domestic predicament and for the survival of the Communist Party.

Concluding Remarks: China as a Microcosm of the World

China today is, no doubt, facing growing instability, uncertainty and insecurity, with the narrowing range of choice for socioeconomic development, given the growing scarcity of Chinese and global resources as well as the alarming deterioration of the global environment. Some symptoms of the "one-child policy" have been felt worldwide, such as Chinese illegal migration and underworld activities in large cities. China is suffering from a manifold societal turbulence and disorder with the mounting number of drifting people without employment; the drastically skewed welfare benefits; the explosive "disparity-animosity spiral" among the diverse social constituents; public resentment and personal grudges against the rampant corruption of the Government and the Communist Party; the conflicting demarcations of areas, ethnics and occupations; and the eerie existence of huge unaccounted number of sons and daughters as result of the "one-child policy." All these factors have already seriously damaged mutual trust among the social constituents and devastated the society's centripetal force. As reported in recent years, over 100,000 local riots and revolts a year have been taking place in China. Such a large number of social disturbances may sound ominous, especially in view of their possible development into a unified front against the regime and the Communist Party.

In addition to the riots and revolts, and the rural predicament and resentment, there is growing urban discontentment, particularly among the newly unemployed, as well as among the huge drifting urban jobless and discriminated-against population who originally came from farming villages. To add to this discontentment, the negative legacy of "one-child policy"—the profoundly "spoiled" younger generation as well as the huge non-registered underworld population—may swing the direction and fate of China into social upheaval for one pretext or another against the very contradictory Communist Government. Thus, the issue of the Credibility Trap in China cannot be dismissed in the near future. Serious political infighting within the Communist Party and/or within the military complex, or even a casual mistake in the Government handling of the huge and widely distributed military forces may immediately trigger an oscillation of the societal undercurrent, stimulating the advent of the Credibility Trap.

If China were to make wrong judgments and create policies inconvenient to North Korea (with its A-bomb issue and other self-seeking behaviors), the ensuing results may rock the whole nation. If, for example, there were to be mass migration from North Korea, as a result of possible US intervention, the resulting impact on China could be huge as the countries share a border. Severe inflation or stagflation, a sudden collapse of the on-going construction and stock "bubbles," a widespread plague, a deepening worldwide economic crisis or a large-scale man-made disaster may also ferment an uprising to trigger a "hard landing," ushering in the Credibility Trap. This could happen as a result of the repeated man-made oscillation that has degenerated the Chinese mutual trust and centripetal force as well as changed the fates of the farming majority for a century. Moreover, the instable, uncertain and dashing China, heading for the Credibility Trap on a tight rope, may sound a knell to the world.

The reality is that China, with its 56 ethnic groups; the population of 1.3 billion; devastation of its diverse society-specific cultures; its extremely lopsided distribution in income, wealth and amenity; rapid growth of greed-and-selfish orientation among people; and escalation of "diversity-animosity spiral," all resembling and representing the reality of our contemporary world, may indicate a microcosm of the world that is now heading unknowingly for the Credibility Trap.

5 *Economic Globalization and Sustainability*

In this chapter I will discuss the incalculable cost of the often-glorified economic globalization, as well as the fallacy of the usual neoclassical proposition that economic globalization, along with free trade, contributes to efficient allocation of resources (Hiwaki 2007a). In reality, the endless money-and-material expansion through financial and economic globalization has induced an accelerated disparity between fellow humans, destroyed the respective Cultural integrity of human societies and discriminated heavily against human resources as a whole—by far the most important assets for human survival. In this chapter, I will argue that global economic expansion, driven by the well-established world power structure (Big Market), imposing upon humanity such uncanny facilitation, destruction and exclusion, has strongly discouraged worldwide human collaboration for the common good—Sustainable Development. The thrust of this discussion will be that the market-centered argument, given all the modern and contemporary distortions, offers little validity of efficient resource allocation and overall alleviation of human suffering. Moreover, economic globalization is the force manipulated by the Big Market to increase the suffering of fellow humans, destroying the diverse legacies of Cultures and value systems as well as accelerating the inhuman distribution of power, income, wealth and amenity.

Market Failure Broadly Defined and Interpreted

A usual neoclassical proposition may go as follows: economic globalization with free trade contributes to efficient allocation of resources. This "theoretical" proposition naturally misrepresents the global reality that we witness. Such a misleading proposition by mainstream neoclassical economists is largely based on the classical tenet of Adam Smith, which presumes the automatic adjustment mechanism of the free and competitive market (perhaps, justifiable to some extent in the age of Adam Smith). In the classical argument, such a market automatically brings about efficient resource allocation and equitable income distribution.

Our contemporary mainstream neoclassical economics—the neoclassical synthesis with the Keynesian economics—already recognizing the phenomenon of "market failure," asserts and pushes to the front the so-called "market effect of efficient resource allocation," while becoming skeptical about the market function for "equitable income distribution." Some mainstream economists today, though skeptical of "efficient income distribution," still believe in the intuitive and global "trickle-down effects" and suggest the importance of economic growth through financial and economic globalization, particularly in view of the "assistance" to the stagnant developing nations.

With some knowledge of "market failure," however, it is easy to arrive at the idea of long-term consequences diametrically opposite to the above neoclassical proposition if we broaden our scope to what goes on in our global economic affairs. Our proposition, therefore, asserts, as follows: economic globalization with free trade grossly distorts resource allocation to the detriment of human survival, among other problems. Before dealing with this actual and truthful proposition, we may briefly review the broad definition of "market failure" by Herman E. Daly and John B. Cobb, Jr. in their book entitled *For the Common Good* (1994). Their three categories of the broadly defined "market failure" are: (1) the tendency for competition to be self-eliminating; (2) the corrosiveness of self-interest on the moral context of community that is presupposed by the market; and (3) the existence/presence of public goods and externalities.

Category (1) of "market failure" indicates that, as competition involves winning and losing, the winners constantly eliminate the losers from the market to increase the monopoly power over time, eventually eliminating the "competition" itself. Similarly, Category (2) indicates that, for its effective functioning, the market depends on common social values such as honesty, freedom, thrift, collaboration, initiative and other virtues, all of which tend to be depleted over time by "self-interest" sanctioned by the very same market. These two categories of the "market failure" tend to destroy the economic and cultural contexts required by market for its own function and survival. Even if we dismiss the above two categories of the "market failure," assuming the competitive structure and the basic sociocultural values to be intact, the market still cannot effectively deal with massive externalities and public goods in Category (3) that represents a narrow definition of "market failure."

An externality—external *economy* or external *diseconomy*—occurs when production or consumption by one person affects the welfare of another, where the effect is not mediated by market. "Spillover effects" offer an image of externalities (Daly and Cobb 1994) that is, "the effect of one person's acts on another's welfare are generally channeled through markets, but occasionally spill over the levee of the market channel so that third parties 'get wet'." An "external *economy*" can be seen, for instance, if some people are vaccinated against polio. In this case, those who are not vaccinated also benefit ("free riders"), owing to the reduction of their probability of catching the disease. A standard example of "external *diseconomy*" is the case of a factory whose effluent into a river spoils fishing downstream. A localized externality, such as the case of effluent can be dealt with "theoretically" to some extent by "internalization" of the relevant cost by the factory. A pervasive externality, such as global warming, is general in scope and requires major institutional changes.

Public goods, having the property that their use by one person does not exclude use by others, refer to national defense, scientific knowledge, lighthouses and so on. A holistic society-specific culture (Culture) in particular is a good example, for use of it by one social constituent is at no cost to others. This means that the "use price" of the Culture should be zero, although the cost of generating and accumulating the Culture over the long duration of time is enormous and incalculable. Thus, there is no market incentive to "supply" the Culture (not to mention to "enrich" the Culture) free of charge, even if it is highly beneficial and wanted by the individual social constituents. Thus, public goods cannot be adjusted to market or transacted in market and, therefore, need to be "supplied," "maintained" and "enriched" by the general public and/or the government.

Economic Globalization and Market Failure

The "market failure" may have been proliferated almost *infinitely* as a result of the economic (financial and industrial) globalization that has distorted almost everything on the earth, particularly belittling humanity and human resources in an effort to expand profit and capital for the benefit of the rich and powerful across the world, namely, the well-established world power structure (Big Market). When a modern society starts "trading freely" with a "non-modernized" society, it is quite *doubtful* that the so-called "free market competition" can suddenly emerge for whatever transaction between them, given the difference or the inequity in modern knowledge, technology, capital and experience, not to mention the difference in their social value systems.

The former (a modern society) may very well and quickly *subjugate* the latter economically and politically. The so-called "free trade" between the modern advanced societies and the "non-modernized" societies may imply simply a *politico-economic subjugation*, given the "might-makes-right" ideology of the former that introduces the convenient interpretation of "free market competition" to patch things up for the moment. In reality, such international transaction amounts to the *absence* or *elimination* of "free market competition." Such *absence* or *elimination* of the "free market competition" through *politico-economic subjugation* may constitute the "market failure" broadly defined.

Actually, economic globalization in the contemporary world was initiated by the modern advanced countries, establishing their international agencies, such as the International Monetary Fund (IMF), World Bank and the General Agreements on Tariffs and Trade (GATT)/World Trade Organization (WTO), to force or "persuade" all "non-modernized societies" into opening up their economies for international "free market competition." Such "free market competition" was an excuse or euphemism to gloss over the real intention of international *politico-economic subjugation* by the modern rich-and-powerful leaders (Big Market). Then, the so-called "free trade" was naturally intended for the "self-interest" of the Big Market and/or the "national interest" of the rich countries.

As soon as the so-called "free trade" was introduced or forced worldwide through the rhetoric of "free market competition," the social value systems of the *subjugated* countries started being ignored or replaced by the pervasive and derogatory "self-interest" and "self-interested competition" of the market fundamentalism (Market) that prevails in the modern advanced nations. Therefore, the Market in service for the Big Market has been forcing all the *subjugated* to start degrading their respective social value systems embedded in the respective society-specific cultures (Cultures), to the detriment of the relevant social values that are necessary for the market function. This constitutes another "market failure"— depletion of important social values by "self-interest" (and "national interest").

It is quite clear from the above reasoning that, by means of economic globalization, the Big Market has opened up for itself a huge source of "external *economies,*" both domestic and abroad, by standardizing and forcing their convenient "market rules" to be adopted by all nations and individuals all over the world. That is, all sorts of resources of the "non-modernized societies," human resources in particular, have become accessible at almost "free" or "minute" cost in comparison to the cost of human resources available in the advanced countries. A variety of such exploitation of the *immediate* "external *economies,*" however, has resulted in a variety of *long-term* "external *diseconomies,*" such as quick depletion of natural resources, human degradation, environmental devastation, population explosion, social disturbances, civil wars, terrorism and more atrocious warfare, which has increased almost all supply costs across the world. Such "external *diseconomies*" has also increased, particularly, the cost of public goods such as national defense, security, peace and order all over the world.

It is important to be aware, therefore, that the so-called "market failure" has prevailed generally in the international economic transactions between the rich and the poor. Accordingly, economic globalization for the benefit of the world power structure (Big Market) is almost synonymous with the "market failure." Economic globalization has created the *immediate* "external economies" to the Big Market and the *long-term* "external diseconomies" to the rest, as well as the greater public cost (including defense cost) worldwide, which would be eventually to the benefit of the Big Market. In other words, through economic globalization, the Big Market has *grabbed* huge profits quickly and *left* all the resulting personal, social, environment and defense costs to the others that include the future generations. Such *long-term* costs, outrageous and incalculable, have amounted to more than the latter could shoulder. Those who have been forced to bear the *long-term* "external diseconomies" all over the world have been severely impoverished in the meantime. Also, they might have been influenced and inculcated by the greed, immorality and irresponsibility of the modern rich and powerful leaders (Big Market) and, as a result, would have left such "external diseconomies" largely unattended or neglected to invite severe poverty, human degradation, Cultural impoverishment and environmental devastation worldwide.

Allocation Failure and Human Resources

The above examples as consequences of economic globalization may indicate the *failure* of "efficient global resource allocation" as well as of "equitable global income distribution"—the *failure* of Modern Economics. Economic globalization at the outset flourished on the exploitation of the prevailing Cultural differences that represent largely the historical, political, geographical, climatic, socioeconomic and technological legacies of the different societies based on their available resources as well as on the respective Cultures. Economic globalization may, however, end up with a total denial of the legacies of the respective societies, leading to the destruction of peace and order as well as of the Environment—the very foundation of human existence—under the pretension/fiction of "free market competition." Naturally, economic globalization has disregarded the efficient allocation of all resources in order to produce the *immediate* "external economies"—a huge incessant bonanza to the Big Market.

Such "market failure" or total disregards to efficient allocation of natural and human resources implies nothing but a bankruptcy or a "practical denial" of the theoretical foundation of neoclassical economics that is supposed to have thrived particularly on the very principle of "efficient allocation." Also, such proliferation of the "market failure" reveals the most serious problem of economic globalization, coupled with the "modern liberal democracy" that has been totally incapable to stop such subtle politico-economic *subjugation—new colonialism*. In spite of the fanfare for universal application, both the "modern liberal democracy" and the "efficiency principle" of the mainstream Economics may have staggered at the borders of the modern societies (if they are somewhat successful within their respective borders), leaving almost everything either to their respective "national self-interest" ("*national interest*") or to the proliferation of "market failure."

Such *failures,* both of the democracy and the Economics of the modern civilization, have provided a vast maneuvering scope for the Big Market that has operated the pervasive forces of multinational/global corporations, financiers and IT enterprises, and dictated underhandedly their mother-country politicians and governments and their international agencies, such as IMF, World Bank and GATT/WTO. Global and multinational corporations, often dislocating the labor market in their mother countries, have advanced into the developing nations to exploit the human resources under the pretense of offering job opportunities and technology transfer. Like the slave traders in the past, they may have suffered no pangs of conscience by taking advantage of poor and weak societies, and by using their human resources at the lowest possible wages in order to increase their own profits and "private property" under the given sanction by the neoclassical Economics (that is, "Firms are to maximize their profits"). In other words, multinational/global corporations, financiers and IT enterprises, being inculcated by the Market and manipulated by the Big Market have heavily discriminated against human resources through economic globalization to expand the capital share of income at the sacrifice of the labor share across the world.

They have vastly increased the use of the cheapest possible workers in the developing nations at the sacrifice of the employment with the hard-won working conditions in the modern advanced countries. Through such uncanny and widespread *employment reshuffle,* they have applied a rapid downward pressure to the worldwide wage rates to reduce the overall labor costs of their operations for the growth of benefits to the Big Market. This may indicate that, completely ignoring the principle of "equal pay to equal work," they have come naturally to "suck the workers to the bone" in both the developing and the advanced nations. Even if such workers were treated worse than "slaves" according to the conditions and standards once prevailed in the advanced nations, no governments, including the ones of their mother countries, would dare to protest against it. Every government and international public agency, democratically run or not, has entrenched itself in the so-sanctioned *"national interest,"* given the *failure* of the "modern liberal democracy" and the *pervasive control* by the faceless Big Market over politicians and governments.

Concluding Remarks

Economic globalization, therefore, has brought to light all the *profound* "market failure," "allocation failure" and "democracy failure." These *failures,* due to the lust-emancipating Economics, the law of the jungle-based Market and the liberty-propagandizing politics, all together, have enriched and strengthened the Big Market. Accordingly, both local and global income distributions have become extremely skewed in favor of the rich and powerful, as clearly revealed even by the conservative data of United Nations Development Program (UNDP) (1994, 1999, 2005) to be briefly discussed in Chapter 7. This reality also corresponds to the destruction of diverse Cultures worldwide and the simultaneous liquidation of human social values and ties. Such destruction and liquidation of human achievements and human virtues (diverse Cultures) have been reducing humans to isolated animals/robots devoid of public spirit and responsibility, subjugated to money and power of the Big Market.

Without much awareness of the logical consequences of the financial and industrial globalization, therefore, contemporary humans as a whole have been made busy changing nature into debris, exchanging virtues with vices, and replacing the long-strived human achievements—diverse Cultures—by the constantly-changing *market signals*. Then, under the on-going process of economic globalization, driven by the Market and manipulated by the faceless Big Market, it seems to have become almost impossible for us humans to collaborate together for the common good—Sustainable Development. It is now the time to generate a positive impulse by enlivening the healthy seeds still alive within this on-going and deepening socioeconomic crisis, from which the livelihood of the grassroots are at a great risk and from where new small but real life-signs can start sparkling.

6 *The Big Market versus Sustainability*

George Orwell's book, *1984*, creates a "negative" utopia, in which the material and mental lives of all Party members and the general public are controlled, negating their personalities and human-like existences (Orwell 1949). This imaginary or prophetic Orwellian World can be compared and contrasted with the factual development of the world based on the Market—the world of the "modern material monoculture" established on the ideology of "might-makes-right" or "the logic of the strong." The latter world, simplified as the World of Big Market, fanatically asserts the deceptive trinity of "free competition," "free market" and "free trade," by imposing on all humans a particular and lopsided value system (including greed, competition, efficiency, progress, extravagance and aggressiveness) that may be intrinsically alien to almost all societies. It also forces all humans into an ever-escalating perpetual competition—"battle royal"—that results only in the uncertainty, instability and insecurity of human life and living, except for the small minority of "the haves," as well as the world power structure of modern capitalism—the Big Market. In this chapter, I will examine four prototypal worlds and discuss our appropriate choice for a viable future.

A Framework for Classified World Prototypes

Our contemporary world is increasingly based on the Market and this has been driving all people and societies into a "rat race," chasing endlessly after, and competing perpetually for, newly marketed goods and services. This has only served to quicken the collapse of both Environmental and Cultural foundations. The choice between the Big Brother controlled state of the Orwellian World and helplessly driven state of the Market in perpetual competition in the World of Big Market is a bleak one. The Orwellian World, with the slogans *"War is Peace, Freedom is Slavery, Ignorance is Strength"* (Orwell 1949) and the World of Big Market, with the likely slogans *"Greed is Virtue, Efficiency is Felicity, Competition is Equity"* (Hiwaki 2004c), do not seem to constitute a viable proposition for the future of humanity. We are now faced with the encroaching radical force of the Market, which has rapidly degraded humanity, the human environment and the human future under its lopsided value system. An alternative and viable human world be explored in this chapter.

Our aim in this chapter is to explore a concrete and viable world of decent life for all. To begin with, a broad framework is required for comparing and contrasting Orwell's negative utopia with other important alternatives of conceptual prototypes. The other prototypes to be compared and contrasted with the world of negative utopia (World D) include the world of positive utopia (World B), the world based on the Market (World C), and the world favoring sound and diverse Cultures (World A). Thus, for the convenience of comparison and contrast, an intuitive framework is devised here as shown in Figure 1.1 (Hiwaki 2004c). The top right quadrant of the diagram indicates the world favoring sound and diverse Cultures—World A—with "Collective" on the horizontal axis and "Human-Personal" on the vertical axis. The top left quadrant shows the world of positive utopia—World B—with "Individual" on the horizontal axis and "Human-Personal" on the vertical axis. The bottom left quadrant represents the world based on the Market—World C—with "Individual" on the horizontal axis and "Inhuman-Material" on the vertical axis. Finally, the bottom right quadrant refers to the world of Orwell's *1984*—World D—with "Collective" on the horizontal axis and "Inhuman-Material" on the vertical axis.

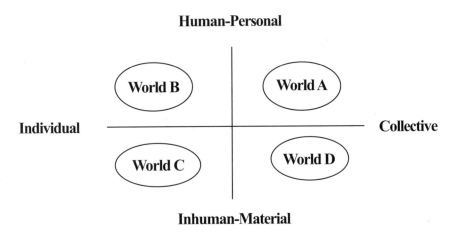

Figure 6.1   Conceptual world prototypes

To begin with, World A (World of Sound Cultures) and World B (World of Modern Utopia) are assumed to be similar to each other in their common "Human-Personal" emphases. They, however, differ from each other in their "Collective" and "Individual" emphases, respectively. For, the world favoring the sound and diverse society-specific Cultures—World of Sound Cultures—encourages all societies to enrich their respective Cultures over time, with the attendant respective value systems that, in general, emphasize community, harmony, integrity, solidarity, mutual trust, cooperation and Cultural identity, among other things. In contrast, the world of positive utopia—World of Modern Utopia—upholds a unitary Culture with its attendant standardized value system that emphasizes individuality, independence, rationality, justice, equality, liberty and fraternity, among other things.

Second, World B (World of Modern Utopia) and World C (World of Big Market) are assumed to be similar to each other in their common "Individual" emphases, but they differ from each other in their "Human-Personal" and "Inhuman-Material" emphases, respectively. The world based on the market fundamentalism—World of Big Market—encourages a greed-propelled material monoculture that emphasizes egotistic self-interest, acquisitiveness, individual identity and inviolable private property, among other things. Also, the World of Big Market has a strong "Inhuman-Material" view of the social constituents in terms of rationality, efficiency, aggressiveness, perpetual competition, and expendability of humans and/or human labor.

Third, World C (World of Big Market) and World D (World of Big Brother) are assumed to be similar to each other in their common "Inhuman-Material" views of their people, but they differ from each other in their "Individual" and "Collective" emphases, respectively. Similar to the case of the World of Big Market, the World of Big Brother (the world of Orwell's *1984*) assigns the "Inhuman-Material" roles to all social constituents. The World of Big Brother allows no deviation whatsoever from the Party line or no exercise of individual freedom, even in terms of mental exercise and, thus, is capable of extreme cruelty both mentally and physically. The "Collective" Party or the Big Brother, being sovereign and almighty, possesses all properties within its world and controls the entire thought, attitude, behavior and lifestyle of the people.

Finally, World A (World of Sound Cultures) and World D (World of Big Brother) are assumed to have similar "Collective" emphases, but the similarity ends in the nomenclature of the horizontal axis. The Orwellian World—World of Big Brother—has the "Collective" emphasis that refers specifically to the Party and its power to control the mental and material/physical lives of the people in general. In contrast, the world favoring diverse and sound Cultures—World of Sound Cultures—has the "Collective" emphasis mainly on the cooperation-propelled human development and socioeconomic development as well as the enrichment of respective community-interested and common-property-centered diverse Cultures. It goes without saying that the World of Sound Cultures is diametrically opposed to the World of Big Market, while the World of Big Brother is diametrically opposed to the World of Modern Utopia.

Market Fundamentalism versus Holistic Culture

A further rise of the Orwellian World—World of Big Brother—in our time cannot be entirely dismissed, but the imminent threat today is the *factual* development of the world based on the Market—World of Big Market—which is more subtle and as hideous as the World of Big Brother. Thus, we now briefly comment on the characteristics of market fundamentalism (Market) in order to contrast with those of society-specific cultures (Cultures). The Market caters to the contemporary power structure of the world (Big Market). The Big Market campaigns for the strictly "Market-sovereign" ideas and values to be adopted anywhere and everywhere, compelling all people and societies to behave according to what the Market asserts. In a sense, the Market is the ideology to solidify and eternalize the power of the Big Market, as the institution of omnipresent telescreen-and-spy network is for the Big Brother. The Market favors and facilitates large established producers and financiers to take full advantage of global business operations to control the world economy and standardize the global political environment in favor of the Big Market. Thus, the Big Market, both faceless and merciless, can be compared with the Big Brother in the Orwellian World.

Also, the Market asserts the lopsided "free-market" ideology of "level-ground competition" or "absolute" competition, disregarding the differences in sizes and capacities of competing entities as well as the differences in societal characteristics, which have resulted from different historical processes and different climatic and geographical environments. Such disregard of differences is the rule except when the Big Market can take advantage of any differences. This kind of politico-economic ideology and tool (Market) encourages individuals to resort to utterly self-centered lifestyles and avaricious behaviors and, hence, to crave for material abundance and convenience without end, in spite of the existing global constraints on the environment, material resources and humanities. The Market maintains the ethos that is individuality interested, short-term engaged, competition propelled, outward/centrifugal directed, product-flow-oriented and private-property-centered (see Chapter 8 for a detailed definition).

With this ethos, the Market has exploited aggressively and excessively the diverse Cultures and the global environment (Environment). Such Cultures maintain the ethos that is community interested, long-term engaged, cooperation propelled, inward/centripetal directed, accumulation-oriented and common-property centered. The Environment is a broadly defined concept that consists of natural, cultural, humanitarian and peaceful environments, and maintains the ethos that is global-community interested, extra-long-term engaged, continuity-accumulation-oriented and common-property centered. The near-sighted Market has been antagonistic to the diverse Cultures that interact intimately and harmoniously with the Environment. Accordingly, the Market has exploited both the Cultures and the Environment as "free goods" without any pangs of conscience with devastating consequences.

Diametrically opposite to the Market, the concept of Culture indicates a long-accumulated whole of experiences, knowledge, skills, wisdom, values, mores, customs, traditions, modes of communication and expressions, among other things, positive as well as constructive to the particular people that constitutes the relevant society (see Chapter 8 for a detailed definition). Put differently, such a Culture is the holistic product of long-term dynamic and synergistic interactions within the society and with the constructive influence of the neighboring societies, as well as with the relevant geographical location, surroundings, climate, resources and environment. Such long-term interactions in the process of generating and enriching the holistic Culture must have had the general purpose of securing integrity, continuity, subsistence, peace, identity and well-being for the social constituents and society.

Such a Culture, including a variety of both tangible and intangible, as well as both visible and invisible elements, refers to the holistic common property that represents the cumulative endeavors of the people in numerous generations to weave together a great variety of moral, spiritual, intellectual, physical, material, social and environmental fabrics in time and space. Also, such a Culture provides the particular society a centripetal force and relates both horizontally and vertically the social constituents that consist of all individuals, families, firms, non-profit organizations and government entities. Accordingly, the Culture facilitates multilateral interactions for *intra*-generation coordination, *inter*-generation solidarity, *inter*-society amity and person-society-environment synergy in the process of socioeconomic development. After all, such a Culture as holistic common property of the particular society accommodates as well as encourages the *general personal ethos* that favors a sound, active and fruitful longevity.

World of Sound Cultures versus World of Big Market

The world favoring diverse and sound Cultures (World of Sound Cultures) can also be postulated as against the world based on the pervasive market fundamentalism (World of Big Market). Given the escalated thrust of the Market into our diverse Cultures, without providing any meaningful light for the future of all humanity, it is crucially important for us all to take a hard look at the modern capitalism with its strong emphasis on the "law of the jungle" (absolute competition), asserting the ideology of "might-makes-right." Such competition embodied in the Market, indeed, indicates "red in tooth and claw" of predators. Thus, it is highly important for us humans to start collaborative endeavors for restoring and enriching our diverse Cultures across the world for more humane, wholesome, flexible and viable ways of future life.

With its inhuman and materialistic inclinations, the World of Big Market always introduces a hasty and radical change in all aspects of human life and implants instabilities in socioeconomic relations and activities, uncertainty in future prospects, anxieties over income, employment and living, as well as helpless feelings about the way things turn out and fade away. As a result, almost all people in the World of Big Market may inevitably suffer from the consequence of the explosive "disparity-animosity spiral" that has been produced by an escalated inequality in income, wealth and amenity, as well as by an accelerated degradation of the diverse Cultures with their respective value systems. With all the suffering it imposes on humanity, however, the World of Big Market may only be interested in accumulation of wealth and power of the merciless Big Market.

Put differently, the World of Big Market may indicate an incarnation of Pax Americana, harnessing the power of multinational corporations, global financiers, mass-media and IT enterprises, as well as the might of the International Monetary Fund (IMF), the World Bank and the World Trade Organization (WTO). This enforces the value system of the Big Market, including the ideology of "might-makes-right," and helps to uphold the Market as a tool and institution as well as thought and lifestyle. The influence of the Big Market under *Pax Americana* has become so strong and compulsive that almost all the societies in the world might have voluntarily or involuntarily acceded and succumbed to the compelling force of the pervasive Market, letting their respective Cultures degenerate and lose their respective integral functions.

This implies that these societies' attendant value systems have been largely replaced by the peculiar and lopsided value system of the Market to result in a drastic value renewal and confusion across the world, only encouraging the merciless and crude "law of the jungle." Such value systems include, among other things, the dogmatic trinity of deceptive "free competition," "free market" and "free trade," the emancipation of insatiable wants and warped self-interest. Also, it includes the characteristics of short-run engagement, flow orientation, outward aggressiveness, perpetual "battle royal," "might-makes-right" ideology, expendability of human labor and inviolability of private property, among other things. All these Market values put together may mercilessly liquidate the diverse Cultures accumulated by the extra-long-term endeavors of our predecessors and, thus, deprived of the most essential Cultural foundations, leave no hope for any viable human future.

Concluding Remarks

Earnest grassroots and local endeavors for restoring and enriching the world's diverse Cultures are, indeed, indispensable for countervailing the avaricious, dehumanizing and destructive force of the Market. A global movement of the New Enlightenment for enriching diverse Cultures may also be imperative in order to coordinate and support the local endeavors over an extra-long duration of time. Not only for preventing a further process toward the World of Big Market but also for guiding each and every society to take part in the World of Sound Cultures, the New Enlightenment must assert itself with two major aims. The first aim is to free all persons, peoples and societies from the shackles of politico-economic ideology that fanatically assert the Market and its lopsided value system. The second is to enhance moral, intellectual, personal, spiritual, common-and-mutual values, as well as to bring out the common and constructive Cultural traits of all societies to find simultaneous and consorted long-term solutions to the closely interrelated global issues—Sustainable Development, Culture of Peace and Global Humanity. To begin with, however, the New Enlightenment must bring to light the "doubletalk" in the World of Big Market as well as the "doublethink" in the World of Big Brother.

7 *Overview of the Contemporary World*

In relation to the discussion in Chapter 6 of market fundamentalism (Market) under the Big Market, in this chapter I will first discuss the growing disparity between the rich and the poor in our contemporary world and indicate the current human predicament. Then, I will offer a diagrammatic framework in which to examine the simplified contemporary setting of the human world in terms of the "disparity-animosity spiral" as well as the contemporary interactions of conflicting interests. This latter discussion, centering on interactions between the industrially advanced societies (West) and the developing/underdeveloped societies (Non-West), will examine the interactions of the modern civilization (Civilization), market fundamentalism (Market) and the diverse society-specific cultures (Cultures). This discussion will also characterize the nature of interactions between and among the Civilization, the Market and the Cultures. Finally, an allusion to a viable world will be made in view of its important characteristics.

Predicaments under Market Fundamentalism

The market fundamentalism (Market) seems to embody an extreme bias toward a particular value system of contemporary global capitalism. The pervasive and standardizing forces of the Market—a modern alter ego—have been based mainly on the modern civilization (Civilization), in particular, the "modern material monoculture." Such pervasive and standardizing forces based on their peculiar and lopsided value system may have led humans to the accelerated predicaments of instability, uncertainty and insecurity. Before examining this delicate issue, we need to be aware of the characteristics and actual conditions provided by the Market, which have developed rapidly during the past 25 years as the very driving force of the on-going economic globalization accompanied by the IT revolution.

To begin with, we need to clearly differentiate the market fundamentalism (Market) from the classical concept of "market" as a pure theoretical concept of modern Economics founded by Adam Smith. The Market seems to work for a "topsy-turvy" and paradoxical global expansion of economic activities by means of the fundamentalist dogmas that uphold the fictitious concepts of "free market," "free trade" and "free competition," as well as the deceptive idea of the "greatest happiness for the greatest number" (the political slogan of the nineteenth century utilitarian Jeremy Bentham). What actually happened behind the impressive expansion of global output was an appalling disparity between rich and poor, among other human predicaments.

According to the *Human Development Report* of the United Nations (UNDP 1994), the income share of the top 20 percent of the world population increased from 70 percent to 85 percent in the 30-year period from 1960 to 1991, while the income share of the bottom 20 percent of the world population decreased from 2.3 percent to 1.4 percent during the same period. As a result, the ratio of incomes between the top 20 percent and the bottom 20 percent expanded from 30 times in 1960 to 61 times in 1991. Also, the same *Report* informs that the total net assets of the 358 richest persons in the world were equivalent in value to the total annual incomes of 2.3 billion poor people, amounting to 45 percent of the world population in the beginning of 1990s. Five years later, the *Report* (UNDP 1999) indicates that 1.3 billion people in the world were necessitated to live under less than one US dollar per day (adjusted to the 1987 Purchasing Power Parity (PPP)). The 2001 Nobel laureate Joseph E. Stigliz laments in his *Globalization and its Discontents* (Stigliz 2002) that the people living under less than two US dollars per day amount to as many as 45 percent of the world population. This data, as a matter of fact, represented those who still lived, of course, escaping the death of starvation and illness. In a rapid expansion of the global output, the number of the population in absolute poverty (living on less than one US dollar per day) has been on the rise.

As well as exploiting and depriving a growing number and proportion of human population, the Market seeks privatization of all sorts of properties (including the so-called "intellectual properties") and demands the strictest protection or the inviolability of "private properties." The Market, in its eagerness to privatize and protect properties, also exploits all the common and public properties—the diverse Cultures and the global environment, in particular—with no arrangement for their maintenance and conservation. As a result, the Market is narrowing the choice of people (now and in the future) by limiting it only to "marketable" goods and services, and destroying those that are not amenable to "market transactions." Moreover, the Market is committed to the "Market sovereignty" (much different from either the "producer sovereignty" or the "consumer sovereignty") strictly favoring the market winners, upholding the idea of profit maximization. Accordingly, the Market is intrinsically devoid of social responsibilities for human subsistence, security, stability, welfare, education, social order and global peace.

In other words, the Market caters to the "law of the jungle" and the ideology of "might-makes-right," both of which favor only the winners in the market. Thus, without providing any alternatives for survival, subsistence, employment and income, the Market demands that the losers fade away with good grace. The world power structure—the Big Market—armed with the market fundamentalism (Market) may seek to control the world, without offering any long-term vision for the future of people and societies, The Big Market is only interested in carrying on with constantly repeated short-run momentum to spread and grow with its inherent profit motive. As an offspring of the modern civilization and instrument of the Big Market, the pervasive Market imposes on people at large the one-sided ideas of freedom, individualism, democracy, human rights and private property, which happen to be only in favor of the rich and strong. These ideas, reflecting a particular value system, have meanings and nuances peculiar to modern capitalism. They are, therefore, very often strange and confusing to people outside the modern civilization.

Serving only the modern capitalism and its beneficiary, the Market naturally and constantly acquires the strong support of those who belong to the Big Market. It may include business leaders of multinational corporations, global financiers, mass-media, political leaders of Western societies and bureaucratic leaders of Western governments and international agencies, among others. Also, the Western people and the so-called "modernized" people at large, being inculcated through "modern education" and driven by the insatiable wants and lusts for transient freedom, comfort and convenience, may support the Market to expand the reigning territory of the Big Market. Indeed, it is the people and societies, inappropriately inculcated and driven by the Market, that have been directly destroying diverse society-specific cultures (Cultures) and the global environment (Environment). In the meantime, the Market has prescribed no viable future for humanity. It has provided only a deceptive and contradictory propaganda of the "greatest happiness for the greatest number," as if the Market could solve everything for the benefit of all humans. It is deceptive and contradictory because the Market has been accelerating the "disparity-animosity spiral" for greater misery across the world.

It is very important to note here that the naive human desires for "freedom," "individualism," "competition," "convenience," "acquisitiveness" and "aggressiveness," which are all inculcated by "modern education" as well as by opportunistic mass-media, do not seem to know any moderation or include any stoppers in themselves. Such explosive and fanatic forces, as naive as they are, seem to back up and cater to the Big Market, escalating the human mental desolation, the Cultural failure and the Environmental devastation all over the world, at the same time. As a result, the market fundamentalism (Market) may deprive all present and future generations of the chance for Sustainable Development, Culture of Peace and Global Humanity, all of which are, perhaps, the most important issues of the twenty-first century. Put differently, economic colonization, value standardization or hard-sell power politics cannot constitute an alternative world that is either acceptable to the vast majority of humans on earth or useful for solving the impending global issues. The one-sided and lopsided ideology of the Market has been largely responsible for our accelerated predicaments that necessitate our tireless endeavors for Sustainable Development and other closely related global issues.

Interactions of Conflicting Interests

As indicated above, our contemporary world can be characterized by an increasing disparity in income, wealth and amenity among individuals and collectives. Accordingly, our contemporary world may have accumulated the feeling of exclusion and resentment over time, often, without knowing whom to blame. For a simplified analysis of the contemporary world, a simple diagram is now devised to show the inequitable and explosive conditions, as shown in Figure 7.1 (Hiwaki 2004c). At the center of the diagram, there is the circle relevant to the contemporary international interactions (Interactions) showing the dynamic relationship between the modern societies and the other ones, which interacts positively or negatively with the three circles around. The latter circles refer to the respective *dynamics* of the modern civilization (Civilization), the market fundamentalism (Market) and the diverse society-specific cultures (Cultures). These circles also mutually interact with the neighboring ones either positively or negatively, influencing one another to reinforce or weaken the relevant *dynamics*, respectively.

The modern societies or the industrially advanced ones (West) in our contemporary world are "justifiably" assumed *dominant* in their interactions with other societies that consist mostly of the deprived and handicapped societies (Non-West). This is mainly a result of the past and present *subjugation* by the modern nations. For survival in the contemporary world, the *subjugated* have been forced by the respective *suzerains* to imitate their Cultures that gave birth to the modern civilization. This assumed reality of

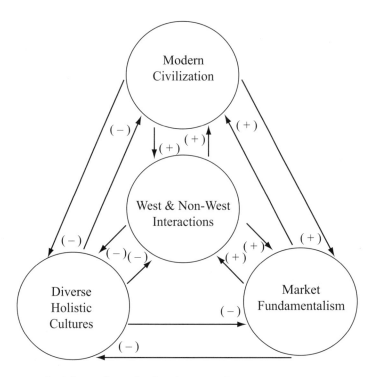

Figure 7.1   Inequitable and explosive interactions

dominant-subjugated relations augments the power of the modern civilization (Civilization) and favors its application worldwide, as indicated by the positive sign (+) that means the continuous reinforcement of the power of the Civilization. This reinforcement now feeds back to the *dominant-subjugated interactions*, by reinforcing the inequitable interactions (Interactions), as shown by the positive sign (+).

Likewise, such *dominant-subjugated interactions* invigorate the Market (alter ego of the modern civilization) to control more of the world economy, as shown by the positive sign (+). The invigorated Market now feeds back to the Interactions for reinforcing inequitable resource allocation and income distribution between the *dominant* and the *subjugated* to exaggerate the inequities/inequalities in favor of the dominant, as shown by the positive sign (+). When it comes to the relationship of the international interactions (Interactions) with the diverse society-specific cultures (Cultures), however, the *dominant-subjugated interactions* have worked against the Cultural diversity and dilapidate/destroy the Cultures of the *subjugated*, as shown by the negative sign (-). This indicates the continuous degradation of the existing diverse Cultures. Such unfavorable effects on the diverse Cultures, in turn, feed back to exaggerate the conflicts and antagonism in the international interactions between the modern societies (West) and the rest (Non-West), as shown by the negative sign (-).

Further, the augmented Civilization and the invigorated Market naturally reinforce the positive and amicable support to each other for their consistent and expanded influences on the world affairs in favor of the West, as shown by the two-way positive signs (+). Much differently, the interactions between the Civilization and the diverse Cultures, however, are highly hostile to each other and exaggerate the mutual animosity over the Civilization's pervasive ideas and values for the worldwide application and standardization. The high-handedness of the Civilization in dealing with international affairs in particular, often, demands the one-sided cost of the diverse Cultures that, figuratively speaking, inflate the grudges against the Civilization, as shown by the two-way negative signs (-). Similarly or more drastically, the interactions between the Market and the diverse Cultures are antagonistic, as shown by the two-way negative signs (-), and the former is determined to undermine and destroy the diverse Cultures to standardize worldwide the value system favorable to the Market.

In Search of a Viable World

The dominant modern societies, spear-headed by the power structure (Big Market), are mobilizing the formidable force of market fundamentalism (Market) to have their own way against all reasons. For, such dominant societies cherish, on the one hand, their common and accustomed Cultural foundations of the modern civilization and, on the other hand, ignore and degrade the other diverse society-specific cultures (Cultures) across the world. Such an attitude relevant to the World of Big Market has been reflected in the historical relationship between the Western (*dominant*) and the Non-Western (*subjugated*) societies, in which the former have continuously taken advantage of the human and material resources of the latter, on one pretext or another. Also, modern Western societies have devastated the diverse Cultures of other societies to stifle their societal vitality and nip their development in the bud. All such inequitable and Culture-destroying interactions have worked for the polarization and destabilization of the world, only in favor of the Big Market, without providing any light of viable future for humanity overall.

In order to prevent a further lopsided aggrandizement of the destructive force inherent in the World of Big Market, therefore, all humankind must resolve to have appropriate long-term strategies for replacing the existing negative and antagonistic conditions in Figure 7.1 with the positive and collaborative ones in the global relationship. Put differently, all the negative signs (-) have to be replaced by the positive ones (+) in the diagram, eliminating the *"dominant-subjugated interactions"* between the advanced and the developing/underdeveloped societies, paying respect to the diverse Cultures in their own right, and moderating the aggressive, acquisitive, self-centered and insatiable forces of the Market. One reasonable approach, to begin with, is to take a hard look at the global reality of the explosive *"disparity-animosity spiral,"* which is clear evidence of the World of Big Market. This reality may suggest the necessity of a countervailing force against the Market. Such a force can only come, perhaps, from the earnest and tenacious endeavors to reorient the manifold education (home, communal, formal and virtual education) for the restoration and sound enrichment of diverse Cultures across the world.

Once the importance of Cultural enrichment and diversity is firmly recognized throughout the world, there may emerge a worldwide pressure or a rising global opinion against the current inequitable and explosive relationship between the advanced and the developing/underdeveloped societies. Such a global climate may demand the former to take the initiative of amelioration in the inequitable resource allocation and income distribution. This pressure of global opinion needs to be more sharply applied to transnational/multinational corporations, global financiers and IT enterprises to alter their self-seeking practices in employment, production, trade and finance. In pursuance of this new direction or worldwide movement of the New Enlightenment (to be elaborated in Chapter 8), the modern civilization must evolve over time to be more respectful and accommodating to all the diverse Cultures in the world.

With such an evolution of the modern civilization, the world power structure (Big Market) may gradually sense the advantage of Cultural enrichment and diversity for viable augmentation and invigoration of worldwide market activities and exchanges in a more amicable environment. When this happens, the existing hostility between the modern civilization and the diverse Cultures may be gradually ameliorated, transformed and developed into a positive and mutually beneficial relationship in collaboration for the purpose of Sustainable Development. Such a positive turn of events may stimulate everywhere an endeavor for encouraging Comprehensive Human Development and Balanced Socioeconomic Development (to be defined in Chapter 8), by means of enriching all diverse Cultures for the benefit of all people and societies.

Concluding Remarks

The World of Sound Cultures represents a viable and constructive social amalgamation and integration, in which the pragmatism of Cultural enrichment and diversity matches the idealism of Comprehensive Human Development and Balanced Socioeconomic Development. Earnest grassroots and local endeavors for restoring and enriching the diverse Cultures all over the world, indeed, are indispensable for countervailing the avaricious and destructive force of the Market. A global movement, such as the New Enlightenment, is also imperative in order to encourage and support the local endeavors over a long duration of time for enriching diverse Cultures as well as for freeing all people from the shackles of the Market. Such a global movement, indeed, is essential for rectifying the currently inequitable and, often, antagonistic interactions among the advanced, developing and underdeveloped nations. Moreover, the New Enlightenment is necessary not only for preventing further progress toward the World of Big Market but also for guiding each and every society into developing the World of Sound Cultures.

In view of the New Enlightenment that contrasts with the seventeenth to eighteenth century Enlightenment, I would like to clarify the so-called "modern civilization" or "Modernity." Being the off-spring of the Modern Age, Modernity is heavily based on the mechanistic and industrial advancement that has taken place since the seventeenth century and, therefore, has a considerably obliging slant and foundation for the present Market-driven economic system. Modernity represents all the vices of the capitalistic system with no human face. Modernity strongly asserts a lopsided idea: "Money is might that makes right." Thus, it largely ignores deep human values and their cultural varieties. Modernity is uniformly imposed on all societies regardless of their different phases of development and their different Cultural foundations. Modernity is one of the culprits of present day problems, the collapse of humanity, human communities and the Environment. In dealing with a balanced value system of Sound Culture (see Chapters 15 and 16), Modernity that gave birth to the Market needs to be replaced gradually by "Sustainability" (Sustainable Development) with sound and balanced values, thoughts, plans and actions. Such "Sustainability" is worthy of support by the New Enlightenment that arises from sound residues or healthy and harmonious living still existing on our Insular Planet. The Age of Sustainable Development must replace the Modern Age to safeguard the well-being of humanity and the sustainability of the prospective global community.

2 *Theoretical Framework and Ramifications*

Many of the new concepts and ideas introduced in Part 1 may require further elaboration for clarification. Thus, I will define and discuss the pivotal concepts, such as Sustainable Development, holistic society-specific culture (Culture), market fundamentalism (Market) and other related concepts (Chapter 8), prior to the discussion of the theoretical framework for Sustainable Development. Next, value premises, assumptions and general features of the theoretical framework will be taken up to clarify the idea relevant to the basic construct of the theoretical framework (Chapters 9 and 10). In order to supplement the introduction of our theoretical framework, I will relegate to the appendices (optional reading) the mathematical derivations of the theoretical construct, the elaboration on the important variables, human-capital accounting, the interactions of society's Value Aspects and Real Aspects, the necessary and sufficient conditions for a balanced socioeconomic development and the diagrammatic expressions of balanced socioeconomic development, among other things (see Theoretical Appendices 1 to 8 at the end of the book).

In Part 2 I will also introduce the diagrammatic expression of the Optimal Development Path (ODP) with its application in mind (Chapter 11), but the elaboration on the four theoretical processes (Growth, Maturation, Retrogression and Breakdown) will be relegated to an appendix at the end of the book (Theoretical Appendix 4). Also, based on the ODP that may indicate an *interest theory of development*, I will examine diagrammatically the changing "gap" that implies the changing profitability in the normative processes of development (Chapter 12). After this, I will discuss in detail the concepts of both the People's Own Invisible Hands (Own Hands) and the thought-frame enhancement for Sustainable Development (Chapter 13). Finally, a developmental concept—"sunny-side proposition"—will be discussed in terms of Balanced Socioeconomic Development, relating to the new paradigm appropriate for the age of Sustainable Development (Chapter 14).

8 *Pivotal Concepts: Definitions and Elaborations*

As the beginning of the theoretical part of this book (Part 2), this chapter will deal with the definitions of important concepts, including Sustainable Development, Culture of Peace, Global Humanity, holistic society-specific culture (Culture), market fundamentalism (Market), Balanced Socioeconomic Development, Comprehensive Human Development and New Enlightenment, among other important concepts. All these pivotal concepts are introduced to examine the broad actual and analogical relationship of important factors, values, behaviors, institutions and phenomena encompassing human past, present and future, particularly in the modern setting of the world. The diverse Cultures and the Market, both *dynamic* factors, may contrast with one another to reveal in their simplification the respective inclinations *for* and *against* Sustainable Development. A holistic Cultural enrichment may largely facilitate dynamic and harmonious spiritual-material, personal-societal, traditional-progressive and own-other value balances in life and living, while the Market in the process of its propagation may represent the one-sided value system for the material aspect of lifestyle. Thus, our theoretical framework for a Balanced Socioeconomic Development—a local precondition toward Sustainable Development—emphasizes the important role of holistic society-specific culture (Culture).

Sustainable Development

It is well known that the World Commission on Environment and Development (WCED), chaired by Gro Harlem Brundtland (former Prime Minister of Norway), was inaugurated in late 1983 by the General Assembly of the United Nations to deal with the task of Common Future. After some three years of hard work, the Brundtland Commission came up with its report entitled *Our Common Future* (WCED 1987), which provided the definition of Sustainable Development as follows: "Sustainable Development is development that meets the needs of the present without compromising the ability of future generations to meet their own needs."

Defining the concept of Sustainable Development, the Commission believed that widespread poverty in the world was "no longer inevitable" and argued that sustainable global development requires those who are more affluent to "adopt life-styles within the planet's ecological means." The Commission added to the concept of Sustainable Development an explanatory sentence: "It is not a fixed state of harmony, but rather a process of change in which the exploitation of resources, the direction of investments, the orientation of technological development, and institutional change are made consistent with future as well as present needs."

Thus defined, Sustainable Development was the main issue at the 1992 United Nations Conference on Environment and Development, the so-called "Earth Summit," held in Rio de Janeiro, Brazil. The Earth Summit adopted the action plan known as "Agenda 21." Unfortunately, the action plan was not based on any integral theoretical framework for Sustainable Development and, thus, failed to provide for clear and coherent priority, direction and process. This action plan was to suggest only that "economic, social and environmental considerations were intertwined with issues of poverty, equity, quality of life, and global environmental protection." After the Earth Summit, the idea of Sustainable Development evolved through the 1993 World Conference on Human Rights, the 1994 International Conference on Population and Development, the 1995 World Summit for Social Development, the Fourth World Conference on Women (1995), the 1996 Conference on Human Settlements and the 1996 World Food Summit.

The 2002 World Summit on Sustainable Development (WSSD) in Johannesburg, South Africa, in particular, broadened and strengthened the definition of Sustainable Development. The definition now reads: "Sustainable Development is built on three interdependent and mutually reinforcing pillars—economic development, social development and environmental protection—which must be established at local, national, regional and global levels" (Political Declaration, Para. 5). The definition now recognizes the complexity and interrelationship of critical issues such as poverty, wasteful consumption, environmental degradation, urban decay, population growth, gender inequality, health, conflict and the violation of human rights. Thus, the Johannesburg Summit resulted in the broadened commitments of human communities to expanding access to safe water, proper sanitation and modern, clean energy services, as well as to reversing the decline of ecosystems.

As a result of the 2002 WSSD, the definition of Sustainable Development has become broadened as well as blurred in an effort to cover a wide variety of issues within the concept of Sustainable Development. The concept now, to a great extent, addresses to a real issue of *life and death* as well as a philosophical one of human subsistence. Moreover, it has come to refer to the issue of personal and socioeconomic transformation away from the mental and behavioral characteristics in the modern civilization, particularly from the Western idea and method of development. After all, Sustainable Development is the issue that rose to the surface as a "hounded-down" recognition of the *modern politico-economic failure*, due to the reckless expansionism on the basis of strongly material-individual-liberty biased politics and Economics.

In our age of excessive exploitation of resources as well as of drastic environmental degradation, not to mention the devastation of diverse Cultures across the world, we must face the global reality squarely to recognize the Planet Earth as an "Insular Planet" with its severe constraints on the environment and resources. Thus, we should not waste any more time just glossing over the issue of Sustainable Development that demands our *mental and behavioral transformation* to engage in the inevitable task of human-ecological symbiosis and survival. With this in mind, I will use in this book a simple working definition of Sustainable Development as "globally balanced socioeconomic development harmonious with the global environment."

Other Concepts Relevant to Sustainable Development

Sustainable Development can be interpreted as a logical and global process consequential to a *perpetual* "local virtuous circle" among Balanced Socioeconomic Development, Holistic Culture Enrichment and Comprehensive Human Development in each and every society. A Balanced Socioeconomic Development here is meant to conduce to the reasonable balances in terms of social-and-economic, material-and-spiritual, short-and-long-term, individual-and-collective, and own societal-and-other societal needs. In other words, such a Balanced Socioeconomic Development indicates a socioeconomic development harmonious with the Environment on the basis of reasonably sound Culture (Sound Culture) that harmonizes integrally the short-and-long-term human needs relevant to material-spiritual, personal-societal, traditional-progressive and own-other-societal value balances. Thus, such a Balanced Socioeconomic Development must interact constantly in a "virtuous circle" with Holistic Culture Enrichment and Comprehensive Human Development.

A Holistic Culture Enrichment here roughly represents the continuous improvement in the accumulated whole of personal and societal experiences, knowledge, skills, wisdom, values, mores, customs, traditions, expressions and means of communication, among other things, in the relevant society. Such a Holistic Culture Enrichment, including the dynamic improvement of personal-spiritual-intellectual aspects in particular of the social constituents, may have strong ramifications for a Comprehensive Human Development and vice versa.

A Comprehensive Human Development implies an accommodation of *personal long-term common ethos*—sound, active and fruitful longevity—and represents a general improvement in thought-frame, personality, spirituality and capacity of social constituents (both individual and collective), based primarily on the dynamism relevant to the Culture. Also, such a Comprehensive Human Development may generally proceed together with a Balanced Socioeconomic Development in each society, since the former may stimulate the latter and vice versa. In view of the existing divergent conditions relevant to different societies, each society must strive to bring about its own Balanced Socioeconomic Development in order to promote Sustainable Development in the prospective global community.

Holistic Society-Specific Culture

The terms of "holistic society-specific culture" (Culture) and of "market fundamentalism" (Market) constitute the two important vehicles in the present discussion of Sustainable Development and its antitheses—the world of the Credibility Trap (see Chapters 2 to 4) the World of Big Market and the World of Big Brother (see Chapter 6). The capitalized term "Culture" here, as briefly introduced above, means a long accumulated whole of personal and societal experiences, knowledge, skills, wisdom, values, mores, customs, traditions, linguistic and other means of communication, among other things, which are positive as well as constructive to the relevant people and society concerned. Put differently, such a Culture is a *holistic* product of extra-long-term dynamic and synergistic interactions within the specific society and with its neighboring societies and their Cultures, as well as with the relevant geographical location, surroundings, resources, climate and environment.

Thus, the diverse Cultures are closely intertwined with the global environment (Environment) that largely consist of natural, cultural, technological, humanitarian and peaceful environments. For, such Environment may maintain the ethos that is global-community interested, extra-long-term engaged, continuity/accumulation-oriented and common-property centered. Given the long-term complex interactions with the Environment in its process of generation and enrichment, such a holistic Culture must have the general long-term purpose of securing integrity, subsistence, peace and well-being for the particular people and society. The Culture as such must include a variety of both tangible and intangible as well as both visible and invisible elements. Further, such a Culture must be the holistic common property of the relevant society and must represent the cumulative endeavors of the people in numerous generations to weave together a great variety of spiritual, intellectual, physical, material, social and environmental fabrics in time and space for its general purpose.

Further still, such a Culture must provide a centripetal force for the society and nurture a general reliability and trust among the social constituents. It must relate, both horizontally and vertically, the social constituents that consist of all natural persons, families, firms, non-profit organizations and government entities. Similarly, such a Culture must facilitate a variety of interactions for *intra*-generation coordination, *inter*-generation solidarity and symbiotic person-society-environment synergy in the processes of general socioeconomic development and comprehensive human development. Thus, it must shape the commonly shared characteristics of the people as well as their distinctive features among all the people in the world. Moreover, such a Culture may not only facilitate the means and ways for integrity, subsistence, peace and well-being of the people, but also contribute to the cultivation of the ensuing generations for their future integrity, subsistence, peace and well-being along with all people in the world.

Therefore, the Culture offers an identity to the people, encourages them to nurture mutual trust as well as reliability, and facilitates the people with smooth as well as harmonious interactions among themselves. Put figuratively, the Culture provides the people with the *social glue and lubricant* for their mutual relations and collaborations. Likewise, the Culture works as the *immune system* of society, encouraging adoption of appropriate foreign influences and rejection of undesirable ones. After all, such a holistic Culture, providing the above meaning, purposes and functions as the *integral common property* of the particular people, accommodates as well as encourages a *general personal ethos* that favors a sound, active, fruitful longevity. Such a Culture may also maintain its *own ethos* that is community interested, long-term engaged, cooperation/collaboration propelled, inward/centripetal directed, continuity/accumulation-oriented and common-property centered. An ideal Culture—"Sound Culture"—that provides a "constant sound communal" value system, among other things, will be taken up and elaborated in Chapters 15 and 16.

Market Fundamentalism and the Big Market

Contrasting with the concept of holistic society-specific culture (Culture), we have an almost diametrically opposite concept of market fundamentalism (Market), particular to our age of hard-sell "economic globalization" with "liberal democracy." The Market, for our present purpose, represents the profit-seeking aggressive force of the modern capitalism, the free-market ideology of "level-ground" absolute competition and the ideology of "might-makes-right," all favoring the Big Market (the contemporary world power structure). The Market may not only ignore humanities but also take advantage of different peoples and/or the different sizes and capacities of societies, consequential to the different historical and socioeconomic processes. The Market, asserting the ideology of "might-makes-right" based on the "law of the jungle," upholds the maximization of both corporate profits and consumer utilities as well as the strict market-centered value system of short-run nature, for the "alleged" efficient allocation of global resources. Such a Market may not only encourage but also justify individual persons to devote themselves only to self-seeking purposes and may condition them to crave for insatiable wants, material abundance, convenience and private property, in spite of the severe constraints on resources and the alarming state of the Environment devastation.

Put differently, the Market caters to the contemporary power structure of the world (Big Market), which campaigns for the Market-centered ideas and values to be adopted anywhere and everywhere, compelling all individuals and societies to behave according to what the Market asserts. Thus, the Market encourages and facilitates large established producers and financiers, mainly of the industrially advanced nations, to take advantage of the global operation of businesses for profit maximization at the sacrifice of the native peoples and, perhaps, for the control of the world economy, as well as for the standardization of global political environment and value system in favor of the Big Market. In a sense, therefore, the Market is the "*instrument*" to benefit and consolidate the Big Market in our contemporary world, similar to the "*omnipresent telescreen-and-spy network*" is for the Big Brother in the Orwellian world.

Thus, the concept of Market has the characteristics that contrast almost diametrically with those of the diverse Cultures. The Market maintains the *ethos* that is individuality interested, short-term engaged, competition propelled, outward/centrifugal directed, expanding product-flow-oriented and private-property-centered. With this ethos, the Market has aggressively exploited (without proper compensation or remedies) the diverse Cultures and the Environment for "perpetual short-run" purposes. The Environment, as stated already, refers to a broad concept that consists largely of natural, cultural, technological, humanitarian and peaceful environments. Such Environment maintains the *ethos* that is global-community interested, extra-long-term engaged, continuity/accumulation-oriented and common-property centered. The near-sighted avaricious Market has been antagonistic to the ethos of diverse Cultures, which interact intimately and harmoniously with the ethos of the Environment. Thus, the Market has exploited both the Cultures and the Environment as "free goods" and has devastated both of them over time. Perhaps, the most important aspect of the Market is the fact that its power and influence reinforced by both *Pax Britannica* and *Pax Americana* have become extremely dangerous, even to the very human survival.

Cultures, Market and the Contemporary Human Mindset

Now, it is important to stress that both the Cultures and the Market represent simultaneously the *working* of very humanity as well as the human *mindset* in our contemporary world. The Cultures may largely reflect the long-term accumulation of personal and societal endeavors for integrity, subsistence, peace and well-being of the respective peoples as well as their craving for harmony, intimacy and identity. The Market may indicate roughly the "short-run" individualistic desires for the satisfaction of daily needs and wants as well as their craving for immediate satisfaction and convenience. Thus, the author argues against the simplistic *either-or* choice between the Cultures and the Market. Instead, the author argues for *reasonable and harmonious long-term balances* between short-term and long-term needs, material and spiritual needs, and social and economic developments. Also, the author argues for the importance of "*sound and fair*" *market function* that caters to the enrichment of diverse Cultures and encourages the alleviation, particularly, of the crude, inhuman, hideous, cruel, exclusive, aggressive, greedy and extravagant aspects of the Market.

More importantly, the author argues for the intrinsic function of the "classical market" (or "invisible hand") for facilitation of fair and viable exchanges of resources, goods and services on the basis of the reasonably sound Cultures, as well as for such market activities to expand together with the enrichment of diverse Cultures across the world. Moreover, the author considers it important for both the Cultural enrichment and the augmentation of fair market activities to promote personal-character building, human-capital formation, thought-frame enhancement and well-balanced socioeconomic development in each and every society. A holistic enrichment of diverse Cultures (Holistic Culture Enrichment), therefore, is viewed imperative not only to countervail the currently pervasive and abrasive Market but also to let the civil humanity develop soundly, by shunning the crudest aspects of the Market, such as cruelty, rapacity, greed and the "might-makes-right" ideology, among other things.

The intrinsic and fair market function harmonious with the holistic enrichment of diverse Cultures may inevitably enhance the importance of "sound-and-fair" market activities, and the expansion of such sound-and-fair market, in turn, may take care of the constantly upgraded human needs and to help enrich the diverse Cultures across the world. Alternatively stated, the diverse Cultures that represent the respective extra-long-term human endeavors for securing integrity, subsistence, peace and well-being in harmony with the Environment must not be sacrificed for the capricious and short-sighted Market that encourages only "short-run," self-seeking and material-biased efforts for the aggrandizement of individual wealth and power at the cost of both the diverse Cultures and the Environment, not to speak of the sacrifice of human future.

Culture of Peace

The term "Culture of Peace" here refers to a worldwide cultural foundation for the pursuit of peace in national and international communities. "A culture of peace consists of values, attitudes and behaviors that reflect and inspire social interaction and sharing, based on the principles of freedom, justice and democracy, all human rights, tolerance and solidarity, that reject violence, endeavor to prevent conflicts by tackling their root causes to solve problems through dialogue and negotiation and that guarantee the full exercise of all rights and the means to participate fully in the development process of their society." This interpretation of Culture of Peace was offered in the introduction of Culture of Peace by Dr Federico Mayor, Director General of UNESCO, in his "Toward a Culture of Peace" (written on the basis of "The Human Right to Peace"). The UNESCO declaration was submitted in July, 1998, by the Secretary-General of the United Nations to the 53rd session of the General Assembly.

Peace has always been threatened by the "logic of the strong" or the ideology of "might-makes-right" that caters to the Big Market as well as the modern civilization. Such ideology encourages the "free market competition" or the "law of the jungle" for the individuality-interested, private-property-centered and profit-maximizing activities, which always produce the insolence of the winner and the resentment of the loser. Such a civilization-sanctioned ideology of "might-makes-right" goes directly against the Culture of Peace, for peace must be cultivated constantly with unflagging endeavor, enthusiasm and fair spirits through dynamic and harmonious interactions among individuals, peoples and societies. No lasting peace can be achieved without the totally committed endeavor to enhance our own thought-frames, as well as to make our own minds balanced and harmonious. Both our thought-frames and minds can be effectively enhanced only if they are solidly based on our own reasonably sound Cultures. With this understanding, I may offer a tentative definition of Culture of Peace as a worldwide common cultural foundation that encourages and supports all personal, societal, national and international peace-making and peace-keeping endeavors, as well as all endeavors for human harmonious co-existence.

The interactive possibilities among Culture of Peace, Sustainable Development and Global Humanity may suggest the relationship of mutually supportive prerequisites. Sustainable Development that requires the encouragement of endeavors for worldwide collaboration as well as for the viable socioeconomic development of our global world is an essential prerequisite for both Culture of Peace and Global Humanity. Culture of Peace that conduces to both internal harmony and external amity of our respective societies is an essential prerequisite for both Sustainable Development and Global Humanity. Global Humanity that conduces to the accommodation of all humans with minimum human needs of subsistence, health and education is an essential prerequisite for both Culture of Peace and Sustainable Development. Thus, all these global issues relate closely with one another, conducing to their mutual enhancement.

Global Humanity

Global Humanity, for our purpose, refers to a future-oriented global principle that prevents future human miseries, frustration and mental desolation, as well as social disorder and man-made catastrophe worldwide. Also, Global Humanity suggests a long-term socioeconomic policy based on such a principle. In a sense, Global Humanity is a future-oriented *sound globalism* that asserts a general idea that *prevention is better than cure*. Gunnar Myrdal, Swedish Nobel laureate of 1974, once proposed a half century ago the concept of "welfare world" in his *Beyond the Welfare State* (1960) as *preventive policy* with the argument that every person born on the earth has a right to enjoy a minimum level of guaranteed subsistence. The idea of "welfare world" is said to involve an ethical motive and the process of globalization (Okada 1997). The ethical motive, according to Okada, is equated to "social conscience" of William Beveridge in his *Voluntary Action* (1948), which refers to "the feeling which makes men who are materially comfortable, mentally uncomfortable so long as their neighbors are materially uncomfortable." As to the process of globalization, Okada refers to Ralf Dahrendorf's "Preserving Prosperity" in the *New Statemen* (1955), where the latter associates the economic globalization with the new inequality or "the increasing divergence of those near the top and those near the bottom."

The acceleration of Market-driven globalization in the last half century has destabilized almost all the lives on the earth and dehumanized the living and working conditions at the same time, leading to the "vicious circle" or "rat race" of the unending waste chasing after the insatiable wants and extravagance of the rich minority. The economic globalization has also caused unprecedented miseries worldwide, shifting income, wealth, resources and amenity from poor to rich. The economic globalization, thus, has amounted to the *moral bankruptcy* of humanity. In view of all such abuses by means of market fundamentalism (Market), I feel it imperative to strive for a future-oriented socioeconomic policy of prevention. Thus, the present definition of Global Humanity emphasizes the *preventive trinity* of minimum human needs that includes subsistence, health and education, as well as favoring positive and viable human prospects. Global Humanity, therefore, means here the future-oriented global socioeconomic policy for our common future to secure for all humans the preventive trinity of minimum human needs on the basis of worldwide collaborative endeavors. Such global endeavors must involve all persons, natural and legal, and all levels of governments for a guaranteed accommodation of all humans on the earth with the minimum human needs of subsistence, health and education.

To advance Global Humanity, by which every person on the earth can enjoy the preventive trinity of human needs, may necessitate worldwide peace-keeping and peace-making endeavors—Culture of Peace—as well as global and local endeavors for a balanced socioeconomic development harmonious with the environment—Sustainable Development. Likewise, to promote Sustainable Development may require Culture of Peace and Global Humanity. Simultaneously, Culture of Peace may require Sustainable Development and Global Humanity. Thus, Global Humanity, Sustainable Development and Culture of Peace, being mutually supportive, interactive and integrative, must be promoted together. In addition to these mutual relations, all such global issues assert, by necessity, a common value that upholds a global endeavor for the *general societal ethos* encouraging personal, spiritual and intellectual advancement and humanities-directed solidarity, as well as the *general personal ethos* favoring sound, active and fruitful longevity.

Further, these global issues commonly require both the *conceptual space* encompassing the entire world and the *conceptual time* encompassing the past, present and future in the continuous human history. Accordingly, these major global issues are closely related to our diverse society-specific cultures (Cultures) that have endured the twists and turns in their respective processes of long-term dynamic accumulation. Since our diverse Cultures link the human past, present and future, the constant holistic enrichment of respective Cultures provides the foundation and direction to grope for the unknown future. Also, such long-enduring Cultures, if enriched constantly, may naturally accommodate the humanities-oriented endeavors for the future and the longevity-favoring personal ethos, both of which are intrinsically involved for dealing with the Global Humanity, among all the contemporary global issues.

New Enlightenment

The Enlightenment of the seventeenth and eighteenth centuries in Western Europe attempted to emancipate the subjugated, irrational and uncritical human consciousness that had been prepossessed with feudal authority, religious dogmas and social prejudice.

The Enlightenment also attempted to guide the ignorant and unenlightened people to the thinking of all phenomena in the light of autonomy and rationality. In other words, the central thought of the Enlightenment insisted on the equality and homogeneity of all humans as rational beings and denied the born inequality and dependency on the existing order that had been inculcated by the feudal societies. Thus, for self-assertion of the modern citizens, the Enlightenment featured the proposition relevant to the principles of civil life. Although the Enlightenment took different forms and emphases in different nations, the common features among nations were social reforms, respect for education, scientific rationalism and progressivism, as well as critical attitude toward religious prepossession.

One important case is the Scottish Enlightenment that distinguished itself by the inquiry into the historical, moral and institutional frameworks of economic activities (Eatwell, Milgate and Newman 1991). This inquiry gave rise to the idea of a healthy and coherent *market* (the classical "invisible hand") as well as to the historical authenticity of *private property*. The Scottish Enlightenment practically ushered in modern capitalism on the basis of private property and the theoretical framework of development, which consisted of the classical "invisible hand" and "self-interest." The framework of development also included the concepts of division of labor and laissez-faire with competition. The classical idea produced under the Scottish Enlightenment was excessively simplified and distorted over the long duration of time to lead to a blind faith in the "free and competitive market" that had different meanings to different persons. Consequentially, there emerged the market fundamentalism (Market) that presupposes, among other things, the perfect market function to equate the demand and supply in all goods and services, and even in all sorts of human labor.

Against the devastating forces of the Market in our contemporary world, it is highly important to bring about a new global movement—New Enlightenment—aiming at promoting Sustainable Development. Such New Enlightenment must, for one thing, encourage the emancipation of all persons and societies across the world from the shackles of politico-economic dogmas that justify and even uphold individuality-interested, short-term-oriented, private-property-centered and strictly material-biased lifestyles, despite the global constraints of overall scarcity. Such emancipation must aim at an acceleration of well-balanced human development (Comprehensive Human Development) and enrichment of diverse Cultures (Holistic Culture Enrichment) to nurture long-term broad perspectives and future-oriented ways of harmonious individual and social life at each and all societies.

In other words, the New Enlightenment is meant to encourage a continuous cultivation of overall human capacities and community-interested sentiments and humanities-respecting values for long-term, constructive and harmonious human endeavors for Sustainable Development. The New Enlightenment is also conceived here as the new enrichment of humanity through reinforcement of the *general personal ethos* favoring sound, active and fruitful longevity to promote a well-balanced integral personal-spiritual-intellectual advancement (Comprehensive Human Development) on the basis of the reasonably sound diverse Cultures (Sound Cultures).

Emphasizing the importance of sound Cultural enrichment in respective societies, the New Enlightenment may encourage a balanced and viable socioeconomic development in harmony with the Environment (Balanced Socioeconomic Development locally and Sustainable Development globally). It may also encourage a Culture of Peace that is nurtured by decent and harmonious global human solidarity. Simultaneously, the New Enlightenment may promote the atmosphere favorable for the diverse-Culture-respecting global endeavor for "non-exclusive" human well-being that conduces to the Global Humanity. Then, the New Enlightenment may help usher in the new age that encourages, simultaneously, Sustainable Development, Culture of Peace and Global Humanity, well supported by the respective local endeavors for the *trilateral virtuous circle* among Balanced Socioeconomic Development, Holistic Culture Enrichment and Comprehensive Human Development across the world.

9 *Balanced Development and Strategic Environments*

After the discussion of pivotal concepts in Chapter 8, the stage is now set for the description of images of human-global interactions, general features and ideas relevant to our broad, integral and open-ended theoretical framework for a Balanced Socioeconomic Development. As a general assumption, I will depict diagrammatically the expanding interactions of economy with society, global community and global environment. Also, I will explain the diagrammatical assumption of systemic interactions among the physical-biological super-system, the human social system and the politico-economic sub-system. Further, I will deal diagrammatically with the interactions of socioeconomic development and environment enhancement. Finally, I will refer to the essential factors for the theoretical framework as well as the essential strategies for Sustainable Development.

Circles of Expanding Interactions

Our long-term theoretical framework offers an integral and general approach to the issue of Sustainable Development, accompanied by the "virtuous circle" among Balanced Socioeconomic Development, Comprehensive Human Development and Holistic Culture Enrichment. The virtuous circle we have in mind is not just a repeated circle but expands continuously to cover an ever greater space (and also time) along with the growing general societal orientation to the future, as depicted in Figure 9.1 (Hiwaki 1998a). Loop (1) represents the "society-economy" interaction (indicating the "Value-Real" interaction) based on the society-specific culture (Culture). This socioeconomic interaction is limited by the national boundary. Thus, this loop represents the combined motion in the early stage of self-motivated socioeconomic development with a rapidly growing future orientation.

Loop (2) indicates a broader "society-economy" interaction that goes beyond the national boundary to take into consideration the global community with its diverse Cultures. It refers to the development of a highly industrialized society with a growing general orientation to the future as well as a broadening perspective and improving thought-frame of the general public. This development also involves a dynamic Cultural enrichment. Loop (3) illustrates the sustainable "society-economy" interaction that expands to take into account the global environment (Environment) and diverse Cultures. This last loop implies a Balanced Socioeconomic Development of a highly mature society with a steadily growing future orientation and long-term perspective, as well as with the

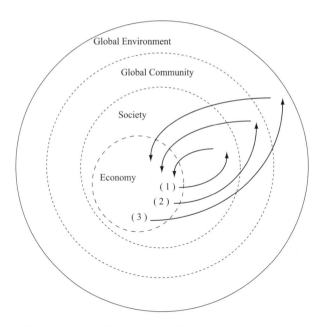

Figure 9.1   Expanding circles of economic interactions

matching responsibility for the full account of the Environment, resources and Culture. Such a socioeconomic development depicted by Loop (3), we believe, represents the societal view of viable development process toward Sustainable Development.

Simplified Systemic Interactions

Alternatively, we may envision a simplified interaction of the human-social system with the physical-biological super-system and the politico-economic sub-system. In this scheme, the politico-economic sub-system (PES) interacts with the societal human system (SHS) and the physical-biological super-system (PBS), as seen in Figures 9.2 and 9.3 (Hiwaki 1998c). Such a perspective of long-term interactions among different systemic levels shown in Figure 9.2 is redefined as a short-hand expression in Figure 9.3. The two diagrams indicate respectively three bilateral interactions, as shown by the two-way arrows and their corresponding numbers. These interactions, being different both in level and nature, tend to produce different mutual effects. To begin with, Interaction (1) pertains to relatively natural interactions between mankind and the physical-biological environment for tangible (physical, biological, chemical, climatic) and intangible (cultural, aesthetic, philosophical, religious) effects.

Interaction (2) indicates the mutual relationship between the society-general activities and the more specific politico-economic activities. This interaction may influence the nature of the socioeconomic value system, lead to a variety of personal and societal endeavors for socioeconomic development, and influence the availability of societal and natural resources. The interaction may also influence the socioeconomic values, attitudes and behaviors as regards such various resources, in terms of conservation, maintenance, enrichment, resource extraction, waste disposal, and so on. Interaction (3) suggests, on the one hand, politico-economic judgment for utilizing the physical-biological environments

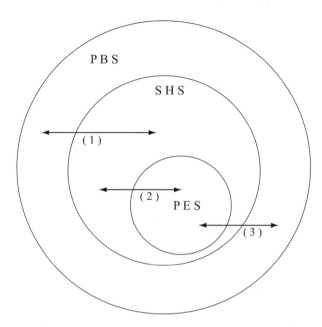

Figure 9.2   Systemic interactions

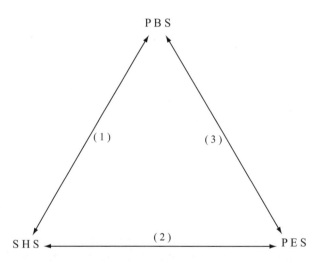

Figure 9.3   Systemic interactions (simplified)

and, on the other hand, the physical-biological reactions in the long duration of time, namely, an everlasting blessing to a peaceful and prudent use or a drastically limited accommodation of a bellicose and prodigal use.

When it comes to the extreme politico-economic abuses of the physical-biological environments, the super-system may impose a blanket penalty/catastrophe upon entire mankind through Interaction (1). Against this predicament of contemporary and future humankind, we need to contemplate a positive and viable solution. It is seen from the simplified diagrams that the nature of interactions within the system of human societies, as depicted in Interaction (2), may influence the characteristics of Interaction

(1) and Interaction (3). There are, however, many entrenched and vested interests in Interaction (2). This implies the obvious fact that the overall human behaviors may determine generally what we have to face over the long term. Thus, we must look for a positive and viable solution as regards the human-invited predicament in Interaction (1) rather than Interaction (2) or (3). Through Interaction (1), over many thousands of years, human societies have generated their respective Cultures that encompass value systems, knowledge, experiences, wisdom and mores, among other things. Thus, it is rather reasonable to incorporate the endeavors into the enrichment of diverse Cultures for the promotion of Sustainable Development.

Essentials of Developmental Interactions

The present general argument goes that we need a broad and integral long-term framework for Sustainable Development. As essentials for an integral approach, we must deal summarily with the interaction of highly dynamic factors conducive to Sustainable Development, such as improving human behavior, capacity, collaboration and material-spiritual balance, all of which are largely determined by the society-specific cultures (Cultures). In order to have these factors interact effectively with one another, we must introduce a *fifth element* as a sound driving force (on the basis of respective Sound Cultures)—"human motivation for a safe, sound, comfortable and enlightened life"—that corresponds to the *general personal ethos,* seeking a sound, active and fruitful longevity. For the present purpose, the motivational force is represented by the growing long-term orientation of the general public to the future (*society-general future orientation*). Such a general orientation may work for harmonizing socioeconomic development with our broadly defined global environment. It also works for regenerating, improving and accumulating the viable human heritage-diverse society-specific cultures (Cultures)— owed primarily to the nature of interactions between the respective societies and the broadly defined global environment (Environment).

All the integral five dynamic factors—behavior, capacity, collaboration, material-spiritual balance and sound motivation—interact with socioeconomic development and environment enhancement as well as with the strategic environments for Sustainable Development, which will be elaborated in the following section. Such interactions are simplified and summarily depicted in Figure 9.4 (Hiwaki 2001c). Areas A and B represent the spheres of activities for socioeconomic development and environment protection/ enhancement, respectively. The overlapping area between A and B is shown as Area C, containing the integral five dynamic factors of behavior, capacity, collaboration, material-spiritual balance and sound motivation, which represents the sphere exerting influence both on A and B. An expansion of the overlapping area both in absolute size and relative share in the combined areas A and B reflects a growing influence of the combined dynamic factors. These three spheres also interact mutually with the all encompassing Area D, which represents the sphere of strategic environments for Sustainable Development. This aspect of mutual influences is crucially important in the formulation of our simplified mathematical expression of Balanced Socioeconomic Development: $T/r = 1—(B/V)$, which is elaborated on in Theoretical Appendix 2 as "Value-Real Interactions" (or a spiral "virtuous circle" for socioeconomic development).

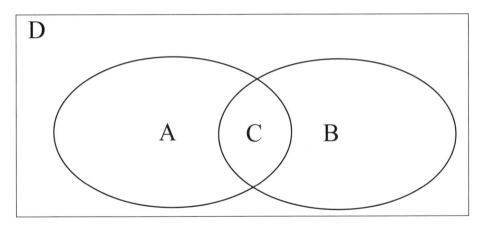

Figure 9.4   Essentials of developmental interactions

Essential Strategies for Sustainable Development

The above five dynamic factors—behavior, capacity, collaboration, material-spiritual balance and sound motivation—that interact with developmental and environmental enhancement, may represent the *heart* of the system relevant to Sustainable Development. This refers to the importance of "human capital" broadly defined. Human capital in this book encompasses the basic skills of reading, writing and calculating, vocational and professional skills, intelligence, wisdom, knowledge, ingenuity, creativity, imagination, insights, foresight, benevolence, courage, public spirit, self-control, long-term perspectives, good health, communicational skills, linguistic and other Culture-related abilities, to mention only major ingredients. Such broadly defined "human capital," being embraced by the society-specific culture (Culture), relates effectively to all the following five strategic environments of "fair learning," "fair role-sharing," "fair cost-sharing," "fair employment" and "fair international trade" (Hiwaki 2001c). These strategic environments may represent the *mind* of the system relevant to Sustainable Development. A continuous full cooperation between the system's *heart* and *mind* is expected as the working of the environment-humanity interacting system of Sustainable Development. Thus, the system as a whole may fulfill its functions as desired, so as to achieve and maintain Sustainable Development.

FAIR LEARNING ENVIRONMENT

As indicated in Figure 2.4, Area D represents the strategic environments which interact with Areas A, B and C for their mutual improvements for Sustainable Development. One crucial element here is the *fair learning environment* for a sound and comprehensive human development, which can be encouraged by the reorientation and redirection of educational endeavors worldwide. Appropriate educational innovations can change the prevailing orientation of memory-centered activities toward the orientation of thought-frame enhancement for comprehensive human development (see Chapter 18). For such innovations, we need to mobilize and coordinate all modes of education, including home, school, community and virtual varieties. This means that the educational innovations must address all the life processes of individual persons, cultivating capacities for the overall and holistic understanding of human processes and systems, and bringing out more positive and constructive long-term attitudes and behaviors of the general public.

Put differently, such educational innovations emphasize a broad-based, multifaceted and diverse learning opportunity, not only for skills but also for human values, sentiments, awareness, attitudes and capacities both in the developing and the industrialized nations, on the basis of respective Holistic Culture Enrichment. More specifically, the educational innovations must positively stimulate individual persons and the general public for greater awareness of human historical processes; better insights into the past, present and future; more appropriate and continuous endeavors for their cumulative and synergistic effects; more enlightened long-term perspectives; stronger long-term orientation to the future; more compassionate human relations; more serious concern about intrinsic human needs; and greater appreciation of diverse Cultures, among other things, for intellectual, aesthetic, spiritual, moral and overall human development—Comprehensive Human Development—to be elaborated on in Chapter 18.

FAIR ROLE-SHARING ENVIRONMENT

Another essential element is the *fair role-sharing environment* for public functions, in terms of an earnest and sincere commitment to the so-called "principle of subsidiarity" (the concept introduced into the Maastricht Treaty for establishing the European Union) by all levels of public entities, including local, national, regional, international and prospective global authorities, with a clear understanding that the supreme power resides in the human social constituents of respective societies. This principle has come to be generally understood as a "golden rule" applicable to the allocation of public functions and responsibilities among the various levels of government, on the criteria that public functions must be performed at the most efficient/effective level, closest possible to the citizens/social constituents. In essence, the principle is intended to encourage an intimate cooperation between all levels of government as well as a smooth coordination of public functions to augment government effectiveness and minimize the social costs of governance. This principle must be incorporated into all the public functions conducive to the above-mentioned educational innovations, socioeconomic development, enhancement of the global environment, enrichment of diverse Cultures, orientation toward compassionate human relations and improvement of other socioeconomic amenities. In short, the worldwide realization of such a principle is essential for Sustainable Development.

FAIR COST-SHARING ENVIRONMENT

A third essential element is the *fair cost-sharing environment* for Sustainable Development by means of the specific-purpose taxation. It is worth introducing a global value-added tax of one standard rate (for instance, 1 percent to begin with) on the value-added by all natural and legal persons in the world. There are numerous merits of this taxing method, including relatively large revenue from the broad tax base; stimulation of general cooperation and human solidarity; improvement in general awareness of both development and environment problems; no conceivable distortion to international trade; inducement to economizing resource use and elongating product-use duration; much fairer taxing methods from historical viewpoints contrasting to the emission-based taxes; and useful methods against the "transfer price" tax evasion, among other things, to be elaborated in Chapter 22.

As for the expenditure of the tax revenue (also see Chapter 22), we may think of financial support for reforesting, protecting ecosystems, spreading the educational innovations, researching for technical improvement of recycling resources, innovating preventative methods against environment deterioration, improving the natural, cultural, humanitarian and peaceful environments, and transferring mutually and worldwide the appropriate knowledge, technology, experience and wisdom for Cultural enrichment and Environment enhancement as well as for improvement of the overall strategic environments for Sustainable Development. Most importantly, the tax revenue can be used for a long-term reduction of the North-South friction and income disparity as well as for a long-term inducement to worldwide collaboration and solidarity for Sustainable Development.

FAIR EMPLOYMENT ENVIRONMENT

The fourth essential element in the strategic environments for Sustainable Development is the *fair employment environment* that perpetually enriches the diverse Cultures across the world (see Chapter 23). The all-encompassing holistic Culture, representing cumulative endeavors of individual persons and society in numerous generations to weave together a great variety of social fabrics in time and space, is the one having a desirable tendency to enrich itself over time and work for general peace, comfort and decency as well as for the common good—Sustainable Development. Then, a Culture-enriching employment encourages a harmonious and synergistic interaction of the Culture with the fair market function for augmentation of both the Culture and market activities over time.

Two basic principles must be embraced for such interaction between the specific Culture and the general market function. The first principle asserts that the market must account for both the market-specific and the Culture-embraced general knowledge/skills, for these knowledge/skills are generally incorporated into the socioeconomic activities within the society. In other words, the market must pay equitably and adequately for both of these mutually augmenting knowledge/skills. Payment only or mostly for the market-specific knowledge/skills may grossly distort the formation and allocation of the mutually augmenting knowledge/skills, simply encouraging the market-biased ones. The second principle asserts that all individual persons, all firms and all levels of government must strive synchronously for the continuity and advancement of both the Culture-embraced general and the market-specific knowledge/skills. Such endeavors may reinforce the Cultural base and augment the capacities of individual persons, peoples and prospective global community to pursue Sustainable Development.

FAIR INTERNATIONAL TRADE ENVIRONMENT

The last, but not the least, essential element in the strategic environments for Sustainable Development is the *fair international trade environment* that emphasizes the merit of Cultural diversity and Culture-respecting fair competition, downgrading the prevailing emphasis on the "level-ground" absolute competition across the world (see Chapter 24). International trade upholding such free competition across the world has fallen into a degenerate function of exploiting anything easily obtainable or surmountable and any humans lacking strong voice and/or power. This means that the prevailing international trade under the market fundamentalism (Market) favors the rich and strong among individual persons, firms and nations at the cost of all the rest. It goes without saying that this favoritism under the "law of the jungle" and the ideology of "might-makes-right" has trampled on Cultures everywhere and has devastated the broadly-defined global environment (Environment).

Such a fair trade environment, here, refers to a global attitude in favor of long-term *socioeconomic* balance in trading activities. Each society has its unique characteristics, comprising specific history, value system, climate, location, disposition, attitude, creativity, education, technology, factor endowment, polity, policy, institution, risk, orientation to the future, and so on. These characteristics have interacted with one another within a society over a long duration of time to form its unique Culture. Broadly speaking, any neighboring societies have tended to trade with each other on the basis of their somewhat different capacities in production and their different tastes in consumption, which have been largely nurtured and conditioned by the different Cultures. Then, the encouragement for Cultural enhancement and diversity, rather than standardization and uniformity, may guarantee the continuity and dynamism of international trade for the common good—Sustainable Development. A general rethinking as such may encourage the diverse enrichment of Cultures, while improving conditions for fair international transactions.

Concluding Remarks

The three different and yet coherent images/perspectives—the diagrammatically expressed relationship of the human world and the global environment—may provide a glimpse into our complex world that we have to keep in mind when dealing with the theoretical framework for Sustainable Development. Such complex images may also require us to deal with at least the five dynamic factors (the *heart* of the system) that systematically interact with the five strategic environments (the *mind* of the system) for the environment-humanity interacting system of Sustainable Development. The discussion in this chapter of the general images/perspectives of human-global interactions, dynamic factors and strategic environments will now relate to the discussion of politico-legal environment, major premises/assumptions and the core process of Balanced Socioeconomic Development envisioned in the theoretical framework in the following chapter.

10 *The Basic Theoretical Framework*

In Chapter 9 we examined the diagrammatical expressions of the general conditions relevant to Sustainable Development and the necessary strategic environments. In this Chapter I will first discuss a more general and overarching politico-legal environment necessary for lasting and amicable collaborations in our complex world (Hiwaki 2009b). Second, I will explain our major value premises for the present theoretical framework focusing generally on Sustainable Development that includes local, national, regional and global levels (Hiwaki 1995Jb, 1998a). Third, as a special feature of the present theoretical framework, I will introduce the normative and analogical development path—Optimal Development Path (ODP)—that emphasizes the importance of societal Value Aspect in the balanced socioeconomic development. Fourth, I will discuss briefly the people's own invisible hands ("Own Hands") as a complement to the classical concept of market ("invisible hand") for such socioeconomic development (Hiwaki 1996a).

Fifth, as an important feature of the present framework, I will explain the assumption of demand-supply consistency in the long term. Finally, I will briefly clarify the characteristic process of balanced socioeconomic development on the basis of perpetual interactions between the society's Value Aspect and Real Aspect for a "virtuous circle," reflecting the Cultural enrichment that improves the social value system and socioeconomic activities. To begin with, I will now take up the required shift in the "politico-legal" environment for necessary global collaborations for human sustainability (Hiwaki 2009b).

Politico-Legal Environment

The modern "liberal democracy" and "laissez-faire economics" might have assumed, to begin with, too much idealized and/or fictitious social constituents, namely, "autonomous and self-sufficient individuals." This implies that such assumption, by necessity, has contradicted the reality of general "fresh and blood," in view of the then emerging unspeakable modern disparity in the human conditions (the income/wealth/amenity disparity among individual persons and among societies at large), as well as in view of the grossly different treatment of fellow humans, both *intra*-national and *inter*-national. The modern "liberal democracy" and "laissez-faire economics" might have relied on a tacit "invisible guiding hand" for the evolution of general citizens as "individuals." Or, more realistically, such modern political and economic ideologies were tactically manipulated to set aside the particular and exclusive humans as "individuals" for reigning over the rest of humanity. Such absurd idealization of general human constituents as well as such a hideous plotting of the exclusive "individuals" may make sense, only if it was a villainous deception by the beneficiary of such political and economic ideologies for unification of the world.

"UNITY IN DIVERSITY" FOR THE MODERN LAW-GOVERNING STATE

It has come as no surprise that a wide range of contradictions and distortions in the real workings of the modern "liberal democracy" and "laissez-faire economics" have emerged. Such contradictions and distortions, as a matter of course, have contributed to enriching and empowering the beneficiary as the modern power structure (Big Market). Strongly supported by modern market fundamentalism (Market) comprising expansionism, utilitarianism, exclusionism (self-interest), free-market competition, sanctification of private property, "might-makes-right" ideology and "divide-and-rule" strategy, the principle of "Unity in Diversity" has helped dilapidate the "communal value systems" across the world and accelerate moral, cultural and environmental devastation in the meantime. Such politico-legal principle can be largely construed as the cause and result of the modern and contemporary human reality characterized by the disparate income/wealth/amenity among peoples and societies.

In our contemporary world, it is not only the financial and industrial circles, but also the government agencies (having collaborated as accomplices for alleged "liberal democracy" and "free market competition" as well as catering to the Big Market) that have promoted contemporary economic globalization and fellow exploitation on the basis of Market-driven capitalism. Accordingly, it is now aptly reckoned that all financial, industrial and governmental entities worldwide, upholding together the politico-legal principle of the modern "law-governing state"—Unity in Diversity—have devastated the diverse society-specific cultures (diverse Cultures) and the global environment (the Environment comprising natural, peaceful, humanitarian and other environments). The liberal politico-economic ideologies (incorporated into the Market), enshrined by the modern politico-legal principle, have been empowered to propel expansion and exploitation in the face of increasingly severe Environment and resource constraints, as well as in the face of the growing disparity of income/wealth/amenity worldwide. Consequentially, the principle of Unity in Diversity, together with the "might-makes-right" ideology, has not only devastated its own credibility but also seriously damaged the viability of human future.

NECESSARY SHIFT IN THE POLITICO-LEGAL PRINCIPLE

In view of the value foundation relevant to Unity in Diversity, I surmise that the modern value system has been extremely lopsided in favor of the Big Market, emphasizing *materialism* (absence of the spiritual concern), *individualism* (absence of the social concern), *progressivism* (absence of the traditional concern) and *egotism* (absence of the mutual concern). Moreover, all such materialism, individualism, progressivism and egotism have reinforced one another, while all these mutually reinforced values/ideologies have been constantly fueled by the modern *antagonism*—"free-market competition." Thus, the relevant value foundation for the modern politico-legal principle has become extremely divisive and disorderly—directly against *the order of nature*.

No wonder, the "sound communal value system" consisting of the general harmony, human integrity, social solidarity, societal continuity and relational mutuality, which is necessary for maintaining healthy human communities, have been severely damaged, endangering the future survival of humanity. In my opinion, we humans have now come to face the inevitability of embarking on Sustainable Development, after the reckless expansion of "money and material" in modern and contemporary times, causing a variety of unnecessary misery and devastation. If we want to avoid a *collective suicide*, we should strive to learn how to live more peacefully, behave more decently, share more equitably and collaborate more readily for the subsistence of all people on our Insular Planet. For such living, behaving, sharing and collaborating, we should adopt a much more flexible spiritual and intellectual attitude, respecting and understanding the diverse Cultures that have been nurtured through Neolithic and historical processes under different geographical, climatic and environmental conditions.

Likewise, we should open our eyes to the circulatory life and nature, the natural system of human-inclusive symbiosis and the development of polytheistic spirituality. Also, we should restrain ourselves from indulging in the "rat-race" of insatiable wants chasing the emancipation of lusts, which was escalated for the benefit of the Big Market on one pretext or another. Further we should learn to avoid confrontational/aggressive politico-economic behaviors. Furthermore, we should replace the *inhuman* concept of modern *rationality* by the generally approachable and more tolerant concept of *reasonableness*. Moreover, we should enrich our diverse Cultures to become reasonably sound. This cannot be overemphasized in our argument for a *paradigm shift*. Sustainable Development for human subsistence in perpetuity may naturally require the *paradigm shift* that entails the sound enrichment of diverse Cultures for regenerating and reinforcing the respective "sound communal value systems" which support a more appropriate politico-legal principle to replace the existing Unity in Diversity.

"INTEGRITY IN DIVERSITY" FOR SUSTAINABLE DEVELOPMENT

In pursuit of Sustainable Development, we need to grope for an *"open democracy"* on our Insular Planet, based on a more balanced and integral value system. Such *"open democracy"* may sharply contrast with the modern *"closed democracy"* that is *confined* within the respective national borders. A politico-legal framework coherent to Sustainable Development—"Integrity in Diversity"—is highly realistic and reasonable on our Insular Planet blessed with the diverse societies and Cultures. The term "Integrity" here indicates a *voluntary and collaborative* attitude essential to the age of Sustainable Development, in contrast to the *forcible* implication of the term "Unity" for unification.

Thus, Integrity in Diversity denotes the politico-legal principle appropriate to the prospective global community, where all peoples and societies collaborate *voluntarily* with one another to generate and uphold the *open democracy*. Such a democracy may recognize, respect and make the most of the different social conditions and Cultural heritages. Accordingly, the new politico-legal framework may base itself on the broad and common *communal value system* of reasonably sound society-specific cultures (Sound Cultures) across the world. Such harmonious value systems may be represented by the interactions of integral value balances between the spiritual and the material, between the collective and the individual, between the traditional and the progressive, and between the own and the other's social values (see Chapters 15 and 16). Such a *communal value system* of harmoniously integrated value balances may best provide a viable value foundation for the politico-legal principle—Integrity in Diversity.

Also, such a *communal value system* corresponds to the intrinsic "value system" of the Sound Culture that treasures the overall social harmony comprising the mutually reinforcing human integrity, social solidarity, societal continuity and relational mutuality.

Such a *communal value system* of overall harmony for the prospective global community may, no doubt, be conducive to Sustainable Development. This means that the politico-legal principle in its actual implementation need to be complemented by the sound judgments and voluntary collaborations of the respective peoples and societies based on their respective Sound Cultures within the prospective global community. For such a prospective human community comprising a vast variety of societies and Cultures, it is fundamentally important to nurture the "congenial spirit of collaboration" as well as to maintain and enhance the common and harmonious *communal value system* (integrity, solidarity, continuity and mutuality), together with the complementary value system (humanity, reliability, flexibility and viability).

NEW DEMOCRACY BASED ON A "COMMUNAL VALUE SYSTEM"

The on-going repeated financial crises and economic downfalls worldwide in the midst of rampant *intra*-national and *inter*-national competition, strife and warfare consequential to the modern "derogatory" self-interest inculcation, seem to toll the death of the principle of Unity in Diversity for the *"closed democracy,"* originated in the modern environment of self-centered and high-handed "law-governing state" as well as of self-seeking materialistic colonial expansion. Such principle, indeed, must leave the arena in favor of the collaboration-enhancing principle—Integrity in Diversity—for the *"open democracy"* of the prospective global community.

We humans can no longer afford the exorbitant cost of fighting each other to determine the winner/survivor according to the "law of the jungle," catering unknowingly to the unifying and standardizing principle of the "law-governing state" in favor of the Big Market that upholds and practices the "might-makes-right" ideology. Given the increasingly severe constraints on the environment and resources, we must seek human subsistence in a more reasonable and harmonious way, with the collaborative endeavors of all peoples and societies on the basis of the reasonably *sound communal value system* of the Sound Cultures. Such collaborative endeavors may, no doubt, uphold the politico-legal principle of Integrity in Diversity for the *"open democracy."* For harmonious human subsistence in the age of Sustainable Development, Integrity in Diversity may make much better sense than otherwise.

Value Premises/Assumptions for the Theoretical Framework

The present theoretical framework adopts a *new temporal definition* of "short term" and "long term" for a broad explanation of the balanced socioeconomic development that relates to the changing social value system firmly based on each dynamic holistic Culture. The present concept of "long term," therefore, means the long-enough duration of time for a change in the existing social value system, while the present concept of "short term" refers to the absence of such a change. The core value premise of the present theoretical framework for a balanced socioeconomic development consists of a perpetual trilateral "virtuous circle" of Cultural enhancement, human development and socioeconomic development. Such a core premise implies that the balanced socioeconomic development of each society can be accomplished as part of such "local virtuous circle" that may evolve eventually toward a "global virtuous circle" of Culture of Peace, Global Humanity and Sustainable Development (see Chapters 29 and 30). Our major assumptions, to be discussed briefly in the following, include the importance of dynamic diverse Cultures, constant human development, integral approach to development, the people's own invisible hands and the human mutual/communal interest.

DYNAMIC DIVERSE CULTURES

First, the present theoretical framework assumes the sound enrichment of the diverse society-specific cultures (Cultures) as the paradigm shift, to be encouraged worldwide with collaborative and perpetual endeavors. Such Cultural enrichment may take place through a complex interaction among the environmental, social, political, economic, psychological, educational, institutional and technological policies. This assumption of paradigm shift is pivotal, since it relates to the "local virtuous circle" of Holistic Culture Enrichment, Comprehensive Human Development and Balanced Socioeconomic Development. The dynamic Cultural function is facilitated by the "cultural-value proxy" that represents the long-term society-general time preference. In other words, the Cultural enrichment changes the social value system and, in turn, alters the society-general time preference ("cultural value proxy") to reveal the society's changing will and choice about the future socioeconomic development.

CONSTANT HUMAN DEVELOPMENT

Second, the present theoretical framework assumes a constant human development, for such human development represents the most important component essential for any viable socioeconomic development. The theoretical framework, therefore, stipulates the conditions for such socioeconomic development by means of the Necessary and Sufficient Conditions mathematically derived from the basic theoretical construct (see Theoretical Appendix 6). Such a viable development requires both a continuous rise in the material-spiritual living standard (Necessary Condition) and a continuous reinforcement in the long-term future orientation of the general public (Sufficient Condition). A constant satisfaction of both the Necessary and the Sufficient Conditions may, therefore, suggest the importance of accelerated increase in human-capital formation broadly defined and require the perpetual endeavor for personal-character building, spiritual development and human-capacity improvement on the basis of Cultural enrichment as well as on the basis of the growing long-term society-general future orientation.

INTEGRAL APPROACH TO DEVELOPMENT

Third, the present theoretical framework assumes the value premise of long-term integral approach to socioeconomic development that embraces the dynamic Culture and the changing material-spiritual, politico-economic and human-development environments as well as the changing global environment, in view of both the short-term and long-term needs of the respective people and societies. The theoretical framework for Balanced Socioeconomic Development refers analogically to each society's Value-Real interactions (see the "Descriptive Process of Development" in this chapter) and, for simplicity, the Optimal Development Path (ODP). Such an ODP, being "Culture-bound" and "changeable" over time, assumes the society's Value Aspect as strongly influencing the socioeconomic development. The ODP embodies the *lead-lag assumption*, meaning that the society-general future orientation leads that of the economy specific future orientation in the balanced socioeconomic development (see Chapter 11).

PEOPLE'S OWN INVISIBLE HANDS

Fourth, the present theoretical framework assumes the long-term socioeconomic development directed inherently by the people's own invisible hands (Own Hands), which represent the people's future orientation and long-term perspectives based on the constant enhancement of personal and societal thought-frames. Being constantly reinforced by the sound Cultural enrichment, the Own Hands are, in turn, assumed to guide and complement the "short-run" classical market function ("invisible hand") to accommodate both short-term and long-term human needs and to mitigate broadly defined "market failure" as well as the "short-run" oriented "policy failure," in order to bring about a balanced socioeconomic development. Also, the Own Hands are assumed to influence the long-term demand and supply through a simultaneous and equivalent effect on saving and investment over time. With this *third course of idea* (different both from the classical Say's law and the Keynesian anti-Say's law), the present framework asserts a simultaneous and equivalent influence of the Own Hands upon the growth of both saving and investment over time, without being prepossessed by the "short-run Keynesian paradox of thrift" that may imply inconsistent growth in saving and investment.

HUMAN MUTUAL/COMMUNAL INTEREST

Finally, our theoretical framework assumes the "mutuality-oriented" human nature. The new concept of human nature, not entirely denying the classical notion of "individual self-interest," emphasizes the importance of innate "mutual interest" or "communal interest." For the present theoretical framework, it is inevitable to modify the classical concept of human nature by a new definition: that is, *Human social constituents cannot entirely preclude self-interest but can restrain it for common and mutual interest.* The term "social constituents" here replaces the classical term "individual," for we cannot presume ordinary persons in our real world to live up to the definition of "individual," which harks back to the "self-sufficient and autonomous individual" as initially defined by Parmenides of Elea in ancient Greece about 2,500 years ago (Graham 2005). Such "individual" seems to imply "totally independent" of any Cultures, while ordinary "living persons" are largely the products of their Cultures and cannot thrive cut off totally from their respective Cultures.

Optimal Development Path and Balanced Development

It is assumed here that *society-general* future orientation has precedence over the less general, *economy-specific* future orientation. Put differently, the society-general will and interest has precedence over the economy-specific will and interest. The latter is revealed by the declining long-term real interest rate (Trend Interest Rate "r") in response to the declining long-term society-general time preference rate (Trend Time-Preference Rate "T"). The lead-lag assumption in the society's Value Aspect points to the other feature of the present theoretical construct, namely, the generalized two-way path of normative and analogical socioeconomic development—ODP.

Such a normative path is the analogy of a rather reasonable (*not* optimum in the strict mathematical sense) schedule derived from the continuous *lead-lag* interactions over time between T and r. In other words, such an ODP is derived theoretically from the assumed continuous changes of the Basic Ratio (T/r) in accordance with the changing social value system. The two-way development path (ODP) as shown in Figure 10.1 (Hiwaki 1993Ja, 1995a), suggests a general theory of socioeconomic development. It portrays, on the one hand, the positive processes of Growth (F-D) and Maturation (D-O) and, on the other, the negative processes of Retrogression (O-D) and Breakdown (D-F) (elaborated in Theoretical Appendix 4). The positive processes on the ODP indicate, perhaps, more relevant development. Such a development here refers to the Culture-bound development that integrates social and economic developments in harmony with the environment. It also integrates harmoniously the material and spiritual needs, the short-term and long-term needs, the personal and societal needs and the changing generational needs.

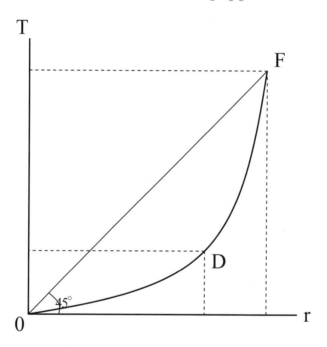

Figure 10.1 Optimal Development Path

Own Invisible Hands and Classical Invisible Hand

It is also aptly assumed that the balanced socioeconomic development depends on the strength of people's own invisible hands (Own Hands to be elaborated in Chapter 13). Own Hands represent the people's future orientation and long-term perspectives based on their "own" society-specific culture (Culture). Own Hands are assumed to be superior to the *visible* hands of the government—the "short-run" oriented governmental policies—and act as complementary (*not* a substitute) to the classical "invisible hand," which may mean the society-specific "short-run" fair market function. In our present assumption,

Own Hands guide and complement the "short-run-"oriented market function to mitigate the existing "market failure" broadly defined as well as the "short-run" oriented "policy failure," in order to bring about the Balanced Socioeconomic Development.

People's knowledge, wisdom and mores (as part of the relevant Culture), coinciding with the future orientation and long-term perspectives (Own Hands), no doubt, summon a sociopolitical will to overcome most of the prevailing "market failure" and "policy failure." "Market failure" usually refers mainly to the market limitation regarding spill-over effects, public goods, inter-generation resource allocation and distribution of income. In an even broader term, Daly and Cobb, Jr. classify "market failure" into three broad categories (see Chapter 5), namely, (1) the tendency for competition to be self-eliminating, (2) the corrosiveness of self-interest on the moral context of community that is presupposed by the market, and (3) the existence of public goods and externalities (Daly and Cobb 1994). Our present broadly defined "market failure" encompasses, in addition, the *inequitable* market transactions, both *intra*-national and *inter*-national, and also the consequential *long-term effects* of such transactions, as already discussed in Chapter 5.

The sound-and-fair "short-run" market function ("invisible hand"), despite such defects, is important and useful in the "short-run" economic transactions of monetary economies. Own Hands, well-embraced by the relevant Culture and constantly reinforced by the sound Cultural enrichment, can mitigate such market defects by complementing and guiding such "short-run" market function to provide a better coordination of short-term and long-term socioeconomic activities, a greater internalization and reduction of externalities, a better inter-generation resource allocation, a more effective protection and supply of common and public goods, a fairer and more equitable distribution of income, and so on. Thus, Own Hands and "invisible hand," together, can induce the Balanced Socioeconomic Development and may even usher in the Age of Sustainable Development.

Demand-Supply Consistency

Also, as indicated above, Own Hands are assumed to influence long-term demand and supply through a simultaneous and equivalent effect on saving and investment over a long duration of time. In other words, our long-term framework is impartial to demand and supply of investable funds. We also regard the long-term aggregate demand and supply as being *interdependent* and *balancing* each other in the long term, constantly guided by Own Hands. Such aggregate demand is simultaneously created with the corresponding aggregate supply and, vice versa, increasing the demand and supply together under the continuous enhancement of people's future orientation and long-term perspectives (Own Hands).

This suggests the *third course of idea* that is different from the classical Say's law and also from the Keynesian anti-Say's law. Together with this assumption of the third course of idea based on the simultaneous effects of Own Hands both on the long-term aggregate saving and investment, our long-term theoretical framework may largely eliminate the usual demand-supply mismatch. In other words, the Keynesian "paradox of thrift" in the "short-run" thinking of inconsistent growth of saving and investment can be eliminated in our *long-term* approach, for Own Hands (the force reflecting the future-orientation and long-term perspectives) bring about a simultaneous increase in the aggregate saving and investment over time.

As a final feature, the current theoretical framework may constitute a theory of Sustainable Development, as a logical consequence of balanced socioeconomic development at local and national levels. The growing future orientation of the general public, indicating a keener interest in the sound enrichment of the Culture, encourages the acceleration of comprehensive human development to broaden the personal and societal perspectives and enlighten the social constituents to become more future-oriented. Such perspectives and enlightenment, in turn, may encourage the balanced socioeconomic development and alter the social value system in favor of Sustainable Development.

This process of "virtuous circle" may accompany the synergistic interactions among personal-spiritual development, human-capital formation and thought-frame enhancement, all relevant both to the comprehensive human development and the sound Cultural enrichment, in the face of the increasingly limited resources and the devastated global environment (Environment). Such "virtuous circle" and synergistic interactions may work to alter the current lifestyles toward the less material and more mental, less quantitative and more qualitative, less short term and more long term, and less present and more future comfort and satisfaction.

Descriptive Process of Development

An explicit and harmonious integration of complex mental, temporal and physical phenomena is assumed essential for the present long-term theoretical framework that emphasizes the importance of a paradigm shift to the holistic enrichment of each society-specific culture (Holistic Culture Enrichment). This being mentioned, it is assumed that a long-term force arising from such overall phenomena changes the long-term *society-general* "present-time" preference rate (Trend Preference Rate) to reveal the society's open-ended will and harmonious choice regarding the future, based on the dynamic holistic Culture. In the positive process of Balanced Socioeconomic Development, the society-general future orientation is postulated to be enhanced as the Trend Preference Rate declines.

The *economic* will and interest regarding the future is summarily represented by the long-term *economy-specific* "present-time" preference rate (Trend Interest Rate). In the positive process of balanced socioeconomic development, the *economy-specific future orientation* is postulated to be strengthened as the Trend Interest Rate declines in some coherence with the Trend Preference Rate. This indicates our assumption of the particular *lead-lag* interaction between the Trend Preference Rate (*general* will and interest of the *system*) and the Trend Interest Rate (will and interest *specific* to the *sub-system*): that is, the former leads the latter for the "virtuous circle." The lead-lag assumption reflects the likely tendency that the social environment/atmosphere conducive to socioeconomic development must precede the economic risk-taking for such development, for the economic risk-taker may usually contemplate on the long-term matching profitable opportunities in the society.

Such a "virtuous circle" is initiated by Holistic Culture Enrichment. Since such Cultural enrichment is largely incorporated into intellectuality, general capacity, productivity, spirituality, personal character and thought-frames of the social constituents, it may naturally stimulate the simultaneous and synergistic processes of Comprehensive Human Development and Balanced Socioeconomic Development. Then, such Cultural enrichment, human development and socioeconomic development, by reinforcing the personal and societal capacities as well as the society-general future orientation, may provide the entire social constituents with the solid Cultural and social foundations for venturing into the unknown future. Thus, the paradigm shift for encouraging the sound enrichment of each Culture across the world is assumed to initiate each society's Balanced Socioeconomic Development for generating, in due course of time, the overarching Sustainable Development.

Holistic Culture Enrichment may trigger a perpetual *trilateral virtuous circle* of human development, socioeconomic development and Cultural enrichment. Such a trilateral virtuous circle (or, more precisely, a trilateral "spiral enhancement") reinforces the personal and societal capacities as well as the future orientation of the social constituents at large. The reinforced society-general future orientation (or the decline in the Trent Preference Rate), inducing a somewhat coherent future orientation in the economy-specific activities (or the decline in the Trend Interest Rate), most likely, induces an increase in savings and investments simultaneously and equivalently over time.

The increased investment in the overall human and material capital, as a matter of course, enlarges the society's total capital stock that further reinforces, in turn, the economy-specific and society-general future orientation. Also, the increased investment naturally results in the on-going expansion of the society's broadly defined aggregate output (or the long-term aggregate value-added) of tangible/material and intangible/spiritual nature. The expanded society's aggregate output, while increasing savings and investments further, entails the on-going *trilateral virtuous circle* of socioeconomic development, human development and Cultural enrichment.

Such a virtuous circle, in turn, reinforces the society-general future orientation to start a renewed and continuous interaction of the society's spiritual and material aspects (or the Value-Real Interaction elaborated in Theoretical Appendix 2). Over the long duration of time, the future orientation, both society-general and economy-specific, will be sufficiently strengthened to help the social constituents generate the "self-preserving," "self-organizing" and "self-evolving" qualities and capacities. Then, such a paradigm shift for the sound enrichment of diverse Cultures across the world, being upheld tenaciously and vigorously by the grass-root endeavors of each society as well as by the worldwide movement of New Enlightenment, humanity may eventually achieve an Integral Development of Global Community (see Chapter 28 for further details).

Concluding Remarks

In order to meet the challenge of Sustainable Development, the lead-lag assumption between the Trend Preference Rate and the Trend Interest Rate in the society's Value Aspect is crucial to understanding the well-balanced socioeconomic development on the Optimal Development Path (ODP) that relates to a *general theory of development*. The complementary assumption that refers to the people's own invisible hands (Own Hands) and the classical "invisible hand" is important to guarantee the Balanced Socioeconomic Development (see Chapter 14). The assumption of "market failure" broadly defined facilitates a vision relevant to long-term instability and insecurity of the real world (see Chapter 5). The assumption of the dynamic and long-term balance between saving and investment may illuminate the importance of personal and societal wills and spirits for the Balanced Socioeconomic Development which links consistently the microeconomic and macroeconomic phenomena through Comprehensive Human Development and Holistic Culture Enrichment.

The Necessary and Sufficient Conditions for the Balanced Socioeconomic Development may tighten our theoretical proposition (see Theoretical Appendix 6). The Necessary Condition represents the long-term improvement of spiritual and material "living standard" relevant to the general public, while the Sufficient Condition indicates the long-term enhancement of the society-general future orientation. More importantly, the Sufficient Condition prescribes the nature of the Necessary Condition, for instance, by shifting the consumption from the short-term focus to the short-and-long-term balance, from the quantity bias to the quality orientation, and from the material centeredness to the spiritual-intellectual-cultural emphasis in the process of Balanced Socioeconomic Development.

11 *The Basic Ratio and the Optimal Development Path*

In the theoretical framework discussed in Chapter 10, the Basic Ratio (T/r) is the left-hand term common to all the equations of the basic construct (see explanations in Theoretical Appendices 1–5). The given Basic Ratio represents the long-term interaction between the Trend Preference Rate (T) and the Trend Interest Rate (r). An extra-long-term schedule of the Basic Ratio, schematized and scheduled as the normative and analogical Optimal Development Path (ODP), portrays the changing interactions between the general societal trends in the people's orientation to the future (continuous changes in T) and the economy-specific trend in the future orientation (continuous changes in r). The economy-specific orientation to the future is deemed here as normally conservative, due to the deep-seated interest of economic actors in the existing factor endowments, socioeconomic environment, organizational culture, management, institutions and technology, among other things. It is assumed in the present long-term framework, therefore, that the reinforcement of *society-general future orientation* (decline in T) on the basis of Holistic Culture Enrichment leads the *economy-specific future orientation* (decline in r) in the process of Balanced Socioeconomic Development. We will now delve into the long-term *lead-lag assumption* that represents the nature of the normative ODP.

Lead-Lag Assumption

One of the pivotal assumptions in our long-term socioeconomic framework is the *lead-lag assumption* or the assumption of synergistic interactions on the basis of the *lead-lag* relationship between the Trend Preference Rate (T) and the Trend Interest Rate (r). A typical interaction between T and r is assumed to occur in the following simplified sequences. An initial decline in T causes, on the one hand, a coherent decline in r and provides, on the other hand, a simultaneous and synchronous influence on the aggregate long-term saving, investment and capital income. The simultaneous influence on the long-term saving and investment implies the third course of idea that is dissimilar either to the classical "Say's Law" or to the Keynesian "anti-Say's Law."

Martin Bronfenbrenner in his *Macroeconomic Alternatives* (1979) comments on "Say's Law," as follows. "With few exceptions, the classical economists accepted, in one or another form, a principle ascribed to Adam Smith's French disciple Jean Baptiste Say called Say's Law of Market. Say's Law maintains that, in the aggregate, supply creates its own demand, so that aggregate supply and demand functions are identical, and no aggregate demand function is required of a system containing an aggregate supply function (or 'production function')." Michio Morishima, being a neoclassical economist, declares in his *Modern Economics as an Idea* (1995) that demand does not adjust to supply in the real world. Instead, he goes on to say that saving (supply) adjusts to investment (demand). In my argument, however, the same and common force that embraces the long-term *society-general time preference* (Trend Preference Rate) induces simultaneous/ synchronous changes in demand (investment) and supply (saving) in the long term. In other words, the long-term aggregate saving and investment simultaneously influenced by the common factor—the decline in the Trend Preference Rate (reinforcement in the *society-general future orientation*)—may increase, respectively, the aggregate demand and supply to equilibrate in the long term.

Perhaps, the change in the Trend Preference Rate may affect different societies differently (at least in terms of the magnitude), due to their particularity in historical experiences, cultural and religious influences, politico-economic systems, socioeconomic structures, endowment of productive factors, demographic characteristics, levels and kinds of technological progress, particular risk factors, degrees of openness to the world and so on. This is one reason why one universal/global standard (regulation or idea) should *not* be imposed on all societies across the world. The Trend Preference Rate changes in accordance with the dynamics of the holistic society-specific culture (Culture), and, hence, the shape of the curve in Figure 10.1 (in Chapter 10) may *differ* subtly among societies and may *not be constant* over time for any societies. Still, their respective schedules of the Basic Ratio (T/r) can be depicted as a "bow-like" curve concave to the 45-degree ray, given the society's Balanced Socioeconomic Development.

The *lead-lag assumption* is incorporated into the "bow-like" curve, in which the Trend Preference Rate (T) initiates changes and induces the Trend Interest Rate (r) to follow in a coherent manner. This assumption may be considered reasonable and justifiable in view of the present long-term framework for the Balanced Socioeconomic Development.

Suppose, for example, that a dictator or a powerful bureaucratic machine, without a general consent or without a reasonable "democratic" procedure, initiated a substantive investment aiming at a rapid economic development. Suppose also that the investment was financed by borrowing from overseas, as well as by domestic fund-raising either by a forced saving or a more direct reallocation of resources and redistribution of income. This may seem to cause the *lead-lag* relation to be reversed. Such an autocratic method of development not firmly rooted in nor supported by the people's *appropriate* "future orientation," however, may not necessarily cause T and r to decline, nor their *lead-lag* relation to be reversed. At best, both T and r may remain unchanged. In the most likely scenario, the economy may fall into a "vicious circle," where the national debts as well as the people's misery and resentment may compound in the long term. Eventually, such a regime may end up with the loss of credibility (the Credibility Trap, as explained in Chapters 2–4: see also Chapter 12) as well as with much higher T and r at hand (or retardation of the society-general and economy-specific motivations for economic development).

Strictly from an economic viewpoint, the *lead-lag assumption* has a strong bearing on the general diminishing "productivity," as well as the changing "extra-profit rate" (to be elaborated in the following section) that is determined mainly by the Cultural undercurrent. Investors among all economic entities, both natural and legal persons alike, may generally perceive over time a declining average rate of return to investment in the continuous use of the prevailing production methods and the existing stock of capital. A new investment, however, may be undertaken only when they begin to perceive new socioeconomic needs coupled by an increase in the "extra-profit rate." This can be said especially when the required new investment is "lumpy." An increasing trend in the average "extra-profit rate," however, must await a further downward adjustment of the Trend Preference Rate (T) in the Growth Process. This argument will be more easily understood after the following discussion on the *long-term dynamic theory of interest*.

Optimal Development Path-Based Dynamic Theory of Interest

At this juncture, it is necessary to comment summarily on my idea relevant to the *theory of long-term interest* in a dynamic setting of Balanced Socioeconomic Development. Such a theoretical setting, therefore, differs somewhat from that of Irving Fisher's rather "short-run" theory of interest (Fisher 1930). Nevertheless, I fully agree with the *core essence* of his pioneering theory of interest and owe to him immensely in my theoretical development, not only of the dynamic theory of interest but also of the long-term socioeconomic framework. Fisher, in his meticulous and seminal theory of interest, attempted to synthesize the "impatience" (similar to the concept of "time preference") theory of interest and the "return over cost" (relevant to "productivity") theory of interest.

Fisher, elaborating on the year-to-year ("short-run") rate of interest, came to the conclusion that the "maximum total desirability is found when the rate of time preference is equal to the rate of interest," and that the maximum total "desirability" is to be found in the case of the income stream possessing the maximum present value satisfying the condition that "the rate of interest is equal to the rate of return over cost." This implies that the optimal rate of interest or the equilibrium rate of interest is found when it equals the rate of return over cost and the rate of time preference. Or, the equilibrium rate of interest reconciles the rate of time preference (representing the "impatience") with the rate of return over cost (representing the "productivity"), assuming *perfect competition* (Fisher 1930).

In other words, Fisher effectively "explained the rate of interest by (1) the supply of loans, brought forward by persuading people to forgo present consumption, and (2) the demand for loans, emanating from the prospect for productive investment" (Allen 1993). Since Fisher assumes *perfect competition* in his theory of interest, the market forces tend to bring about the saving-investment equilibrium, as well as the equilibrium market rate of interest equal to the average time-preference rate and the average productivity. Fisher's theoretical conclusion, briefly stated, may mean the following "short-run" *marginal* equilibrium: that is, assuming "the income stream possessing the maximum present value" (or "the maximum total desirability"), the rate of interest is equal to the time preference rate and the productivity growth, as far as the "short-run" economic activity is concerned.

One significant departure of the present concept of long-term interest rate (Trend Interest Rate) from Fisher's theory of "short-run" interest rate refers to the feature that the long-term time preference rate (Trend Preference Rate) is never equal to the long-term interest rate (Trend Interest Rate), except for the two extreme points on the Optimal Development Path, namely, Point F and Point O (see Figure 10.1 in Chapter 10). Another significant departure refers to the presently assumed property that the Trend Interest

Rate is "Culture-bound," following coherently the change in the "Culture-bound" Trend Preference Rate with a time lag. Such a concept of long-term real interest rate (Trend Interest Rate) can be explained by the *long-term dynamic theory of interest*, on the basis of a much broader, deeper and more general view of normative socioeconomic development.

The Trend Interest Rate (r) that is influenced by the "Culture-bound" Trend Preference Rate (T) over the Balanced Socioeconomic Development refers directly to the Optimal Development Path (ODP) or the "bow-like" curve embodying the *lead-lag assumption*. Thus, the present *long-term dynamic theory of interest* may imply a *long-term interest theory of development* incorporated into our normative and analogical ODP. The ODP has the function of equilibrating the long-term saving, investment and capital income (S = I = R: the long-term equilibrium condition for the Balanced Socioeconomic Development) as well as the function of facilitating the Trend Interest Rate—the Economic Rate of Interest (ERI)—to equilibrate with the Trend Preference Rate—the Social Rate of Interest (SRI)— *plus* Social Premium for Development (SPD or "extra-profit rate") in the *normative* process of socioeconomic development.

Thus, the present *long-term dynamic theory of interest*, being initially based, in principle, on Fisher's theory of interest, has evolved to explain a *dynamic* trend of the long-term real interest rate as depicted by the "bow-like" *interest-rate schedule* of ODP in Figure 11.1 (Hiwaki 2000b). The "bow-like" curve also represents the long-term dynamic change of the parity between the long-term time-preference rate *specific to the economic sector* (ERI) and the long-term time-preference rate of the *people in general* (SRI) *plus* the "extra-profit rate" (SPD) as appropriate inducement to economic risk-taking. The Trend Interest Rate (r), indicating the long-term economy-specific time-preference rate, corresponds to the Economic Rate of Interest (ERI), while the Trend Preference Rate (T), representing the long-term society-general time-preference rate, corresponds to the Social Rate of Interest (SRI).

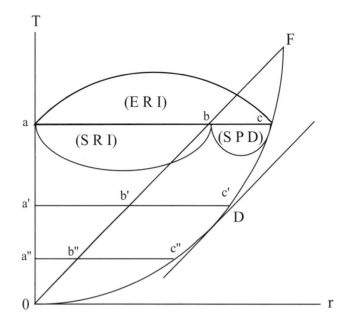

Figure 11.1 ODP with SRI, ERI and SPD

The *lead-lag assumption* specific to the relationship between the Trend Preference Rate (T) and the Trend Interest Rate (r), therefore, implies the "lead-lag" interactions between the SRI and the ERI, where the portion of "lag" refers to the SPD. Placed in this theoretical context, the ERI must be on par with the long-term "productivity" (*average* not *marginal* "productivity"), as well as with the Trend Interest Rate (the economy-specific time preference rate). With this understanding, I will now proceed to explain the *long-term interest theory of development* based on the ODP in Figure 11.1. In this diagram, for instance, the Trend Interest Rate (r) at the given point on the ODP (Point c) can be measured as the horizontal distance from Point a to Point c. This Trend Interest Rate (equivalent to the ERI), as indicated above, represents the long-term "productivity" of the given capital stock relevant to the development process at Point c.

Now, the corresponding Trend Preference Rate (T), equivalent to the SRI, can be measured as the horizontal distance from Point a to Point b. Also, the rate pertinent to the Social Premium for Development (SPD or equivalent to the long-term "extra-profit rate") is measured by the horizontal difference between the Trend Preference Rate and the Trend Interest Rate, namely, the distance from Point b to Point c. Generally speaking, then, the Economic Rate of Interest (ERI) at any given point on the ODP (for instance, ac, a'c' or a"c") corresponds to the respective Trend Interest Rate, and the Social Rate of Interest (SRI) at any given point on the ODP (ab, a'b' or a"b") to the Trend Preference Rate. This indicates that the ERI is always greater than the SRI (or, ab < ac), except for the unlikely two extreme points on the ODP (Point F and Point O). The difference between the ERI and the SRI always indicate the SPD (meaning the "extra-profit margin" or the long-run margin of the producer's excess profit matching the extra risk of development) at any given point on the ODP (representing the Balanced Socioeconomic Development).

A growing long-term "extra-profit rate" (over the range of the Growth Process F-D) implies that the economic entities, both natural and legal persons, may take their development actions in view of the increasing Social Premium for Development (SPD) as well as of the reinforced *society-general future orientation* (Trend Preference Rate). As a consequence, such economic entities may greatly contribute in the long term to the cause and purpose of the people in general for the Balanced Socioeconomic Development. Put differently, it is the *growing* "future orientation" of the people in general (the reinforced *society-general future orientation*) that provides the essential impetus and opportunity as well as the most fundamental vitality for the well-balanced socioeconomic development to take place on the basis of Holistic Culture Enrichment.

In short, I am arguing for the following identities to hold in the process of Balanced Socioeconomic Development for the Trend Preference Rate (T) and the Trend Interest Rate (r), respectively:

1. T = the long-term time-preference rate (the long-term "impatience") of the people in general = the long-term *social* discount rate = Social Rate of Interest (SRI); and
2. r = the long-term time-preference rate of the economic sector = the long-term "productivity" = the long-term *economic* discount rate = Economic Rate of Interest (ERI).

I am also arguing for the changing "extra-profit rate" of long-term nature (Social Premium for Development: SPD) to exist generally as the development inducement in the process of Balanced Socioeconomic Development, except for the two extreme points (Point F and Point O) on the ODP.

Special Features of the Optimal Development Path

The above *lead-lag assumption* simply indicates that any long-term reinforcement of the people's future orientation is accompanied by the decline in the Trend Preference Rate (T), which, in turn, causes the coherent decline in the Trend Interest Rate (r). In other words, the average economic actor, figuratively speaking, may up-grade his/her future orientation after confirming the reinforced *society-general future orientation*, in view of the long-term development risk properly covered by the Social Premium of Development (SPD). Such SPD may imply the on-going benefits from Holistic Culture Enrichment and Comprehensive Human Development. The *lead-lag assumption*, when it stipulates the long-term *normative* process of socioeconomic development, gives rise to the "bow-like" schedule (Optimal Development Path) specific to the relevant society.

The "bow-like" path refers figuratively to the most desirable long-term path specific to the society and reflects the society's dynamic Culture that holistically embraces the society's environmental, historical, political, social, economic, psychological, demographic, technological and institutional features and changes, among other things. Put differently, the Optimal Development Path (ODP) is the society-specific normative and analogical path representing the relevant *lead-lag* interaction between the *society-general future orientation* and the *economy-specific future orientation*. It is also important to note from the two-directional ODP that there is *no unique and universal point*—no stationary state—on or off the ODP to converge over time. Thus any given point on the ODP represents the "desirable" point of long-term *transitional* nature at the given process of normative development. In other words, any given point on the ODP is no more than a long-term passing point in the overall two-way dynamic processes of Balanced Socioeconomic Development.

Another feature of our normative/analogical development path refers to the two extreme theoretical points, Point O and Point F, where the Trend Preference Rate is equal to the Trend Interest Rate (or T = r). Point O occupies the lower extreme position—"utopia"—on the ODP, where both T and r have come to the respective "zeros" and equality. This point is the "utopian" theoretical position, because any real human beings and/or any real human societies cannot possibly arrive at such a position. Thus, this point is called here the "socioeconomic heaven." In this "heaven," each and every person, having an *infinite* future orientation, may be characterized as being immeasurably/infinitely enriched as well as completely satisfied, both mentally and physically. Strictly interpreted, the Basic Ratio (T/r) at Point O (where 0/0) is *indeterminate*, but it is assumed here to be an approximate unity of the respective rates (T and r) *infinitesimally* close to the origin. This implies that the society is so affluent as to go on consuming in perpetuity all its production without eroding its capital base forever.

The other extremity found at the upper end of the ODP (Point F) may indicate the worst possible theoretical position, where T and r are tending toward the parity at their highest possible levels. Such a position is called here as the "socioeconomic hell," where the people being completely "present-oriented" are consuming all what they produce and, thus, rapidly wearing off its capital base. Such society has no choice but to collapse eventually. At the "socioeconomic hell," the Basic Ratio (T/r), becoming unity at the highest possible rate of both T and r, implies that the society is too poor to save or to invest and also that the society eventually degenerates and collapses under the condition of T/r = C/V = 1.

Concluding Remarks

For people at large the "positive" Balanced Socioeconomic Development is more relevant and desired than a "negative" one. Peoples and societies, however, tend to be dynamic and interactive, as well as emotional and impulsive to some extent, often finding themselves in unexpected situations and conditions. Our two-directional ("positive" and "negative") Optimal Development Path can provide normative and analogical perspectives for such unexpected situations and conditions. For this purpose a detailed discussion on the four processes of Growth, Maturation, Retrogression and Breakdown is provided in Theoretical Appendix 4. Also, the two-directional ODP may serve for comparison and contrast with probable digression/derailment in reality of a variety of socioeconomic development away from the normative and analogical ODP. Such examples of derailment in modern times will be discussed in the following chapter.

12 *Optimal Development Path and Actual Development*

An Optimal Development Path (ODP), by definition, indicates a normative socioeconomic development, meaning that any actual corresponding development may differ from it to some extent. Although each ODP is theoretically considered society-specific, it cannot in reality be perfectly independent/intact of "might-makes-right" behaviors of neighboring countries and/or some lopsided value system of the modern capitalist civilization. Behaviors particular to the contemporary world, being highly *infective*, can become overwhelming and easily be justified by the-then "mainstream" philosophy and Economics. In retrospect, however, the resultant human disasters caused by such behaviors and the corresponding value system often seem absurd and unjustified at the least. I will now review analogically the modern tendencies in socioeconomic development in contrast to the probable society-specific normative ODPs.

Imperialist Paths versus Optimal Development Paths

It is important to note that there is no guarantee for any society in the actual world to start on or stay on the normative/analogical development path (ODP). No society, therefore, can claim that its development has been strictly following the ODP. In reality, a society may take a course to the right or to the left of the society-specific ODP or a course crisscrossing the ODP. The actual development paths of the modern colonial powers, such as Great Britain, the Netherlands and France, might have constituted the examples of socioeconomic development derailed widely to the right of their respective ODPs. With their respective Industrial Revolutions as turning points, they expanded their colonial empires and reinforced their control over and exploitation of their respective colonial resources, incomes and markets, and accomplished their own rapid socioeconomic development much faster than otherwise, meaning the socioeconomic development was based only on their own human and material resources at home.

These three modern powers, for example, avidly took advantage of both the human and material resources of Asia, Africa and other areas, as well as monopolizing the product markets of their respective colonies. It is highly probable, therefore, that these colonial powers, amassing inordinate profits and accumulating enormous wealth by the "colony-derived" *savings*, might have followed for some lengthy periods their respective developing paths much to the right of their "proper" ODPs (their normative ODPs in the *absence* of colonies). This implies that their own "Imperialist" schedules of the Trend

Interest Rates (that included the *extra monopoly profits* derived from their colonies) tended to be much higher than their "proper" Trend Interest Rates (in the absence of the colony-derived monopoly profits), respectively, for all the corresponding points on the ODP. Or, it implies that their "proper" Trend Preference Rates (Social Rates of Interests: SRI) did not have to decline as much or as fast to build up capital for their rapid and impressive accumulation of wealth and socioeconomic development.

In other words, their respective "Imperialist" ODPs (the ODPs including the colony-derived monopoly profits as the Imperialist's own development inducement)—their *actual* development paths—may have formed the portion of their particular curves more steeply sloped (or bulged rightward) than the cases of their "proper" and normative ODPs. Portions of their *actual* development paths lying far to the right of the respective "proper" ODPs imply that these modern colonial powers might have exaggerated their "extra-profit rates" (including the monopoly profits, to be sure) by exploiting colonies and, thus, growing much faster in both income and wealth than otherwise. Thus, such "Imperialist" development, perhaps, may have represented the *modern Imperialist* cases of "market failure" (contrasting with the cases of "market failure" relevant to the contemporary economic globalization discussed in Chapter 5).

Keynesian and Collectivist Policies versus Optimal Development Paths

Another example is the case of those countries which adopted the Keynesian fiscal and monetary policies of "demand management" in the face of the Great Depression and thereafter. Such countries have often resorted to *ad hoc*, intermittent and "trial-and-error" measures with an untiring bureaucratic zeal in managing the so-called "effective demand" in both recessionary and expansionary periods, on one pretext or another, based on the explicitly "short-run" Keynesian theory. In the meantime, they have practically ignored possible *long-term adverse consequences* of their "short-run" fiscal and monetary policies, which by and large amounted to "policy failure" (that may have also expanded the so-called "market failure") in the context of *long-term* socioeconomic development. Their application of the Keynesian monetary policy often changing artificially the official interest rates—drastically up and down—to dislocate market interest rates, as well as their artificial application of the Keynesian fiscal policy, "customarily" or "bureaucratically" manipulating government expenditures often too much, too often, too late, for example, may have distorted their long-term socioeconomic development, to say nothing of the wasted resources and the accumulated government debts over time.

Such monetary and fiscal policies may have forced the economic actors in the respective societies to make *incessant misjudgments* in the timing and size of investment, production and consumption, among other things. Many so-called "advanced nations" adopting such *ad hoc* tapping of interest rates, as well as of bureaucratically manipulating fiscal expenditures and/or tax revenues, for more than half a century, may have not only wasted world resources but also left their actual development paths to widely crisscross their respective ODPs. Such nations also distorted their socioeconomic development eventually at the cost mainly of developing and underdeveloped nations. Such abuses of the "short-run" Keynesian policy-oriented and/or "national-interest biased" economic growth/development, perhaps, represented over time the typical cases of accumulated "policy failure" and expanded "market failure" to the heavy cost of the underdeveloped societies as well as of the future generations of all peoples.

A third example involves the authoritarian societies in the former Soviet Union, Eastern Europe and other planned economies. The administrators in the respective nations, intentionally disregarding the appropriate market function ("sound-and-fair" market function as representing important human wisdom and heritage) and, perhaps, the will of their respective populations, often seemed to have concerned themselves with their strategies aiming at political, economic and military supremacy over their capitalist counterparts. Perhaps, Balanced Socioeconomic Development, even if it mattered, was only of secondary importance, as far as their leaders and policy makers were concerned. Accordingly, their economic planning, only reflecting their *hopeful* estimation of investment, production and consumption, most likely let their societies stray widely from their natural courses and, perhaps, much to the left of their respective ODPs, by suppressing *excessively* the profit incentive and utilitarian motive of their people. Thus, their economic planning may have resulted in gross "policy failure," distorting their socioeconomic development and wasting both natural and human resources. Such humanities-disregarding and market-ignoring development, perhaps, represented the case of combined "market failure" and "policy failure."

The Japanese Misguided Path versus the Optimal Development Path

A last example refers to the post-war society of Japan, whose development during the reconstruction period, following the devastation and defeat of the Second World War and the Allied Occupation, can be characterized by the administrators' strong initiative and leadership as well as by the employment system peculiar to post-war Japan. The basic tenet adopted for the nation's economic recovery and reconstruction was that *business recovery* had to come first and foremost. The policy stance was named as the Ishibashi Line after the journalist-turned politician and Japanese Keynesian—Tanzan Ishibashi—who emphasized the "business first" ideology; where business recovery had to be achieved before the consumption recovery. Martin Bronfenbrenner looks back in one of his article on Japan (1950): "In retrospect, this position became the top priority for the postwar economic policy," and such "ideology-embedded" policy has prevailed to the present as the powerful thought of leading Japanese "liberal" politicians.

Furthermore, the nation's economic reconstruction had to be accomplished by a rapid capital formation, which, in turn, had to be financed by domestically generated savings, whether voluntary or forced, taking full advantage of the thrift-oriented insular people. This ideology of "producer favoritism" coincided with the adoption of the *long-term stable employment system*—"life-time employment" system—initiated by large and well-established firms during and after the Korean War. The adoption of the employment system by these firms initially aimed at securing steady and reliable employees to prepare for the worldwide economic expansion after the European recovery from the damage caused by war. The employment system also appealed favorably to the existing workforce in general (who had suffered severely from the instability and lack in job opportunities during the immediate post-war period) as well as to the new and prospective workforce at large.

As a result, the expanding economic activities, along with the increased adoption of the employment system, may have induced optimism and enthusiasm about the future particularly in the households of industrial workers and have helped to reinforce the society-general orientation to the future. This reinforced future orientation, unexpected in the outset, may have set the pattern for the ensuing period of rapid economic growth accelerated by the society-general future orientation. Such future orientation contributed to rapid concerted increases in the aggregate saving and investment, especially from the middle part of the 1950s to the early 1970s. Consequentially, the "producer favoritism" encouraged the corporate sector to establish strong vested interests in its fastest possible growth, often at the cost of the household sector (including workers, consumers, savers, depositors and taxpayers). Indeed, the producer's access to handsome profits and retained earnings became a top priority of the leading business club (*Keidanren*) who often underhandedly persuaded the liberal politicians and bureaucratic leaders for the sake of an ever-escalating capital formation and the consequential boost in economic activities.

An early post-war policy package of the "producer favoritism," for example, consisted of the practical ban on the import of consumer durables in favor of the domestic substitutes; the high domestic prices to appropriate the producer's "export subsidies" for cultivation of markets overseas; the public investment biased to business and industrial infrastructure; and the tax reduction on plant-and-equipment investment. Also, the policy package included the stepped-up depreciation of capital and the government-guaranteed "over loaning" (providing loans in excess of the respective bank capacities by the guarantee of the Bank of Japan and the Ministry of Finance) specific to large and established firms, just to mention a few examples. Such a policy package undoubtedly gave an extra push for the capital formation in the corporate sector, almost always at the cost of workers and consumers. Thus, it was intended for the benefit of the producer with important resources allocated *en masse* to the stock of industrial capital, which was often manipulated to become obsolescent "prematurely" or *depreciated* at an "extraordinary" pace for the sake of "underhanded" corporate income tax reduction.

Such "producer favoritism," coupled with the private sector's adoption of a *stable long-term employment system* ("lifetime employment" system) during the Korean-war procurement boom and thereafter by almost all the established and growing firms, boosted the profits and growth prospects. The employment system, in particular, is inclined to tame the workforce to become more amicable and cooperative to the management and to nurture in the same workforce a much more moderate long-term "impatience" (reinforcement of *society-general* long-term future orientation), which together indirectly suppressed the market interest rate and the average wage hike in the economy at large for a lengthy period of time. High consumer prices consequential to the domestic substitution of durable consumer goods, together with a declining societal time-preference rate consequential to the employment system, were no doubt conducive to the rising aggregate saving and investment ratios for nearly 20 years until the early 1970s. The fast-rising saving ratio, especially of the household sector, helped meet the ever-expanding investment needs of the corporate sector at a low market interest cost, which was also manipulated by the government and financial system (at the pressure of *Keidanren* and other business leaders associations) with the "business first" ideology.

Thus, the post-war "producer favoritism" and the employment system of the established firms were tantamount to the rapid income redistribution away from the household sector to the corporate sector. The latter sector, as a consequence, has become the society's "blackhole" that gobbled up the rapidly growing income and wealth to build up and vastly strengthen its power over the people as well as over the government. In addition, it can be easily deduced that the actual long-term interest rates applied particularly to the capital formation of large and/or well-established corporations may have tended to be much lower than the ones implied by the relevant Trend Interest Rate—the Economic Discount Rate—and much lower than the rate of productivity gain. In other words, actual market interest rates applied particularly to the investment loans for the large and established firms tended to be very low, often at the cost of household sector—a constant low interest rate manipulated against the household savings (taking advantage of the thrift-oriented insular people). This may imply "hidden extra-profit rates" or "underhanded income transfer" from the household sector to the business sector to boost corporate "extra-profits" and to accelerate corporate power as well as its stock of capital. This may have indicated the long-term accumulation of social inconsistencies (against social harmony and mutual trust) to lead the society to the Credibility Trap (see Chapter 3).

The Japanese case may have represented a typical "double standard," favoring the large firms at the cost of households (particularly, workers, consumers, depositors and taxpayers) at large, perhaps, due to the extraordinary conditions after the Second World War, the ideology of "Catch-up with the West," the "business first" ideology and the naive liquidation of the diverse and coherent Japanese society-specific cultures (Cultures). Thus, some observational statements describing Japan, as "the producer sovereign nation," "the corporate state," "Japan incorporated" and "the rich country with the poor people," may speak more aptly and eloquently of Japan's grossly lopsided socioeconomic development than the Western condescending appraisal—"the oriental miracle." Such Culture-ignoring "business-first" development, perhaps, may have represented the combined case of "market failure," "policy failure" and "Culture failure," which has made the Japanese path destined to the Credibility Trap.

Concluding Remarks

All the examples of development schemes explained above are now coming to a blind alley with the severe constraint on the environment, resources and humanities. Although it is very difficult to depict and explain persuasively the theoretical ODP, I have described the normative path as an *analogy* relevant to the present theoretical framework. It is important to examine a variety of past and present development examples on the basis of such normative and analogical ODPs that represent the dynamic incarnation of the "Culture-bound" Basic Ratio (T/r). Simple as it is, the analogical ODP, symbolizing a general theory of development as well as an interest theory of development, is *a powerful tool* to examine different characteristics of long-term socioeconomic development in terms of diverse Cultures and societies. The normative ODP reminds us of the importance of Balanced Socioeconomic Development that is basically different from the lopsided and short-lived development models by various economists based on modern civilization. As an important guiding force for the Balanced Socioeconomic Development, in the following chapter I will deal with the "Culture-embraced" people's own invisible hands (Own Hands) that direct the "short-run" capricious market force in the long term and elaborate on one dynamic component of the Own Hands—personal and societal thought-frame enhancement—which is conducive to society's long-term perspectives and appropriate value renewal.

13 *People's Own Invisible Hands and Value Renewal*

The normative Optimal Development Path (ODP) may suggest the necessity of improving socioeconomic values for the Balanced Socioeconomic Development. In this chapter, I will deal with the people's own invisible hands (Own Hands) as the most important factor that upgrades personal and societal values for long-term collaborative endeavors. The present concept of "Own Hands" (the people's long-term orientation and perspective as well as their personal and societal thought-frames, based on the Holistic Culture Enrichment) presumes the possibility of *conscious* collaborative endeavors of the social constituents *for* their satisfaction of short-and-long-term diverse needs as well as *against* the impending Environment devastation and the Market force accelerating the income-and-wealth disparity (Hiwaki 1995d, 1996a). Such *conscious* collaborative endeavors may very well expand the people's time-frame relevant to the *future* and also enhance the awareness of the crucial connections of human well-being with the sound-and-diverse Cultures and the healthy Environment. The expanding human time-frame and the growing human awareness, then, may encourage further collaborative endeavors for the satisfaction of more diverse and longer-term human needs. Such human collaborative endeavors that interact with the expansion of the human time-frame may enhance the Own Hands.

Thought-Frame Enhancement for Value Renewal

The enhancement of personal and societal thought-frames pertaining to the overall time and space ("thought-frame enhancement" for short) may indicate the continuous process of synergistic interactions between the investment in broadly defined human capital and the expansion of the people's *future* time horizon. The "thought-frame enhancement," requiring acceleration of investment in such human capital, is necessary for a value renewal in favor of Sustainable Development. The present definition of "*effective*" human capital covers a wide variety of human capacity, which is over and above the minimum knowledge/skills and the minimum endowment of the Cultural heritage embodied in the "simple labor." The open-ended "*effective*" human capital encompasses, among other things, vocational and professional knowledge/skills, intelligence, wisdom, ingenuity, creativity, imagination, insights, foresight, public spirit, long-term perspectives and so on (see Chapter 10).

Thus, the "*effective*" human capital is postulated here as indispensable not only in production-related activities but also in all other positive human activities, encompassing consumption, waste management, environmental conservation and enhancement, personal health, self-learning, self-enlightenment/actualization, inter-personal relations and political participation, to mention only the major elements. These attributes of the "*effective*" human capital, when constantly enriched and incorporated harmoniously into the social constituents at large, may improve effectiveness, wisdom, ingenuity and thoughtfulness in all human socioeconomic activities and also enhance continuously the personal and societal thought-frames as a component of the Own Hands.

I will argue in this chapter that the acceleration in human-capital formation interacts synergistically with "thought-frame enhancement." A built-in mechanism for such synergistic interactions is one of the important features of the present long-term socioeconomic framework. The framework may provide a comprehensive *linkage* between the economic activities and all the other human activities via changes in the Trend Preference Rate that is also closely related to the Own Hands. Such Own Hands may broadly represent the people's orientation to the future and long-term perspectives on the basis of sound Cultural enrichment. Such a general socioeconomic force—Own Hands—may, most likely, guide and complement the market function of "short-run" orientation (the classical "invisible hand") for the Balanced Socioeconomic Development harmonious with the Environment. Then, the enhancement of the Own Hands by the reinforced society-general future orientation may accompany the thought-frame enhancement that improves the socioeconomic values and interests appropriate for Sustainable Development. The curve implying the "thought-frame enhancement" is now depicted as Curve H in Figure 13.1 (Hiwaki 1995a, 1996a), the derivation of which is discussed in Theoretical Appendix 7.

The horizontal axis in Figure 13.1 shows the people's *conscious* horizon for the *future* time (Ft) and the vertical axis shows their investment in human capital broadly defined (Ih). The origin relevant to the horizontal axis indicates a total absence of the *future* in the people's thought-frame (an extreme theoretical point). Thus, Curve H sloping upward and convex to the horizontal axis represents the synergistic interactions between the expansion of the people's conscious *future* time and the acceleration of the broadly defined human-capital formation. Curve H also implies the schedule of the "thought-

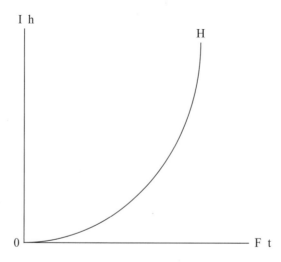

Figure 13.1 Thought-frame enhancement

frame enhancement." These features of the curve suggest our reasoning that the personal and societal thought-frames can be cultivated and enhanced by their Culture-*conscious* and *forward-looking* endeavors for rapid investment in human capital broadly defined.

Though simple in its appearance, Curve H provides a variety of implications, besides expressing the schedule of synergistic interactions. Curve H extending to the right implies, first, that the people's *future* time can expand or that the Own Hands can be continuously improved. This also implies the probable continuous decline in the long-term *society-general* "present-time" preference. Second, the increasing slope of Curve H implies an acceleration of human-capital formation, suggesting that the accelerated cultivation of human capacities is essential for the enhancement of the personal and societal thought-frames ("thought-frame enhancement"). Third, the same increasing slope implies the personal and societal inability of expanding *infinitely* the "conscious time horizon" relevant to the future (or probable limitation for expanding the people's *conscious future*).

All these features may emphasize the importance of synergistic interactions between the human-capital formation and the people's orientation to the future and long-term perspective (Own Hands). Such synergistic interactions not only encourage the "thought-frame enhancement" but also contribute toward the fair and equitable distribution of income that may include "psychic/emotional" income. The acceleration of human-capital formation and the expansion of the people's *future* time horizon, together, may enhance quantity, quality and diversity of human capital and its importance to the society so much so that the broadly defined "*effective*" human capital grows in the long term as the most important factor relevant to production, consumption and all other human socioeconomic and mental activities.

This facet of synergistic interactions, then, provides a new ground and rationale for the fair and equitable distribution of income based on the growing quantity and quality of diverse human capital as well as based on the increasing opportunities for cultivation and employment of human resources. A corollary of such income distribution is an enhancement of personal self-respect, self-reliance and self-command as well as mutual respect, mutual reliance and mutual collaboration, all of which, in turn, may induce a more desirable and comfortable sociopolitical environment respective to each society. The rationale for this sort of fairness in income distribution, together with the corollary of enhanced self and mutual capacities for the human self-preservation, self-organization and self-evolution, suggests a new phase of capitalism (or, perhaps, more appropriately called "*collaborative humanism*") that centers on the improvement of human capacities and collaborations. In this new phase, the Own Hands guide and complement the market function to promote the Balanced Socioeconomic Development in harmony with the Environment—an appropriate step toward Sustainable Development.

Own Invisible Hands and Sustainable Development

As seen above, the Own Hands that guide and complement the classical "invisible hand" are deemed favorable for each society's Balanced Socioeconomic Development, as well as for harmonization of the socioeconomic development with the Environment. This implies that knowledge, wisdom, intelligence and long-term perspectives, coinciding with the reinforcement of future orientation among the social constituents at large, are expected to summon the sociopolitical will to overcome the broadly defined "market failure" and "policy failure," albeit partially in the beginning. Then, the Own Hands may induce a change in the social value system in favor of *conscious* collaborations for the common good—Sustainable Development. For, the Own Hands strengthened continuously over time may inevitably shift the sociopsychological weights steadily from the "present orientation" to the "future orientation" and expand the *conscious future* in the thought-frame of the people at large. The longer the *conscious future* becomes, the greater the chance of promoting Sustainable Development. The importance of the wholesome Environment for human life, especially for healthy living, mental enrichment and aesthetic enjoyment, can be comprehended more easily and readily by the people with a longer-term and future-oriented thought-frame that is firmly based on the long-accumulated Culture.

The "physical" time, after all, is common and impartial to all life and matter on the earth and represents broadly the on-going process of natural evolution in the open-ended circulatory system. Accordingly, the "physical" time can be regarded as an essential factor in governing the dynamic interactions in the global system consisting of the "biosphere," the "sociosphere" and the "psychosphere" (Koizumi 1994). It is inevitable, therefore, that the people's "sociopsychological" awareness of the past, present and future on the basis of the Culture tends to be largely constrained by the universal "physical" time as well as by the "physiological" time of human beings. People's "sociopsychological" time, however, tends to be much more flexible than either the "physical" time or the "physiological" time, and can be expanded far into the future by education and, especially, by means of personal and societal endeavors for the broadly defined human-capital formation, which are conducive to the Comprehensive Human Development.

The time stream of past, present and future, consisting of the people's "sociopsychological" time-frame, is in fact continuous and indivisible. If people's "conscious future" is expanded long enough, they may grow wiser to be able to treat themselves, others, the diverse Cultures and the Environment more carefully for the sake of a more comfortable and viable human life in the future. The past-respecting, present-concerned and, simultaneously, future-looking characteristics of people, all of which are summarily represented by the changing Trend Preference Rate (implying the changing long-term *society-general future orientation*), can offer a meaningful implication both for the socioeconomic development and the Environment protection. Thus, a continuous *society-general* weight shift from the "present orientation" to the "future orientation" can be regarded as meaningful and favorable for Sustainable Development. Put differently, such general weight shift, if wisely promoted over time, can serve the cause and purpose of Sustainable Development.

The classical "invisible hand" combined with the "individual self-interest" in our contemporary world may encourage a rapid economic growth or a rapid expansion of materially-biased production, but such rapid expansion may work to the detriment of the wholesome nature and the "psycho-physical" well-being of people at large. The "invisible hand," indeed, is supposed to offer useful price signals for "current" production and consumption. Such market function, when guided and complemented by the Own Hands (the people's growing future orientation and long-term perspectives based on the enhancement of thought-frames), may respond more effectively to both the short-term and long-term needs for human well-being over the long duration of time. For, human well-being may require harmoniously integrated material, physical, personal, spiritual, aesthetic, intellectual and psychological needs of both the short and long terms. Such comprehensive and complex needs are inevitably based on the people's close and wholesome relationship with the Culture and the Environment.

The Own Hands, which represent the most fundamental vitality and motivation in socioeconomic development as well as the best available human capacity for possible human reconciliation with the natural process of the Environment, may have a good reason to occupy the pivotal position in the present long-term socioeconomic framework. A decline in the Trend Preference Rate (implying the reinforced *society-general future orientation*), reflecting to a great extent the improvement of the Own Hands, may enhance human awareness in such a way as to change the socioeconomic value system, most probably, toward favoring Sustainable Development. In other words, the people's awareness of their ultimate reliance on the Environment for satisfaction of both their short-term and long-term needs may be enhanced through the acceleration of investment in the broadly defined human capital, which simultaneously contributes to the Own Hands and the Culture.

Thought-Frame Enhancement and Maturation Process

The present long-term socioeconomic framework, as seen from the diagrammatic exercise (see the derivation of Curve H in Appendix 7), may facilitate such a *value renewal* by means of the *built-in* dynamics for "thought-frame enhancement." Thus, the present argument addresses squarely the question of *value renewal* appropriate for Sustainable Development. Such a *value renewal* may require an acceleration of broadly defined human-capital formation, which interacts with the expansion of people's *future time horizon* in the long-term framework. In other words, it is assumed that the acceleration in human-capital formation tends to expand the people's *conscious future time horizon* (most relevant to the "*sociopsychological time*," in particular), and this expansion within the people's thought-frame, in turn, may accelerate the investment in human capital to continue the "virtuous circle."

In this very process of "virtuous circle" or a repeated synergistic interaction between the expanding conscious future time horizon and the accelerated human-capital formation, societal will and personal motivation may grow in search of more satisfying and reasonable long-term lifestyles. In such a process, the Own Hands strengthened over time may guide the "market function" for an appropriate *inter-generational* allocation of resources for a greater satisfaction of the people in work and leisure as well as for a fuller life based on Cultural and Environmental soundness. Put differently, people's growing orientation to the future and their improving long-term future perspectives may help accelerate the human-capital formation for "thought-frame enhancement" that may naturally facilitate over time the well-balanced socioeconomic development harmonious with the Environment.

For this sort of "virtuous circle" to take root, processes on the ODP should provide the best possible condition and the normative criteria. In the Maturation Process, the people with growing human-capital formation as well as with growing interest in the diverse and extra-long-term human accomplishments—diverse Cultures—may comprehend the synergistic interactions of various phenomena, socioeconomic activities and major sectors in their societies. In this very process, people may acquire a deeper awareness of human well-being inextricably connected to both Cultural and Environmental soundness. Also, people may acquire a greater capacity for the mediation of conflicting interests, which is implied by the closing gap between the Social Rate of Interest (SRI) and the Economic Rate of Interest (ERI) in the Maturation Process.

Concluding Remarks

It is in the Maturation Process that an increasing number of both natural and legal persons (all social constituents) may acquire a greater self-respect, self-reliance and self-command, which are harmonious with mutual respect, mutual reliance and mutual collaboration. Such growing sound human qualities amount to the human-capital enrichment that promotes the Comprehensive Human Development. Now, on the basis of the promoted human development, people may be adopting their lifestyles for more mental satisfaction and becoming more future oriented, sound-Culture pursuing and globally concerned. Such alteration of lifestyles may also involve the process where the Own Hands get reinforced for guiding the classical "invisible hand" effectively and wisely as well as for promoting the process of "thought-frame enhancement." Then, the Maturation Process on the ODP, along with the "thought-frame enhancement," may offer the best possible chance for Sustainable Development—a balanced global socioeconomic development harmonious with the Environment.

14 *Paradigm Shift and Balanced Development*

In this final chapter of Part 2, I will discuss first our *universal proposition* that encompasses the four processes of the Balanced Socioeconomic Development (Growth, Maturation, Retrogression and Breakdown on the Optimal Development Path (ODP)). The universal proposition goes: Positive or negative socioeconomic development depends primarily on the strength of the society-general future orientation and long-term perspective relevant to the Own Hands. This universal proposition consists of two closely related propositions. One is the "sunny-side" proposition asserting that a steady rise in the society-general future orientation induces the Balanced Socioeconomic Development (as implied in the Sufficient Condition in Theoretical Appendix 6). The other is the "reverse-side" proposition to the effect that a continuous decline in the society-general future orientation induces degeneration in the socioeconomic development. I will discuss here only the positive aspect, concentrating on the "sunny-side" proposition. Also, I will deal briefly with the necessary paradigm shift for the Balanced Socioeconomic Development.

The Sunny-Side Proposition and Extra-Profit Rate

The "sunny-side" proposition—the positive aspect of the universal proposition for the Balanced Socioeconomic Development—refers first to the Growth Process that is characterized by the growing horizontal gap between the Social Rate of Interest (SRI) and the Economic Rate of Interest (ERI) up to Point D on the ODP, where the gap becomes the largest as seen in Figure 14.1 (same as Figure 11.1). In this process, as the SRI declines rapidly, the ERI tends to adjust to the SRI only "passively", hence, lagging more behind the SRI. In other words, such an adjustment takes place only when the economic entities sense the growing future orientation of the people in general and/or only when the Social Premium for Development (SPD) expands. The term "passively" refers to a rather slow and "reluctant" decline of the ERI in adjustment to the decline of the SRI. The proposition in this phase on the ODP bases itself mainly on the rapid reinforcement of the society-general future orientation.

Put differently, the "sunny-side" proposition asserts that the fundamental source of socioeconomic vitality arises from the people's general enthusiasm and optimism for the future as well as from their growing motivation for the long-term betterment of socioeconomic conditions based on the on-going Holistic Culture Enrichment. Such general tendency in the Growth Process is accompanied by the "virtuous circle" of accelerated personal and societal endeavors for the Comprehensive Human Development and the resultant improvement in the overall socioeconomic conditions. Such a

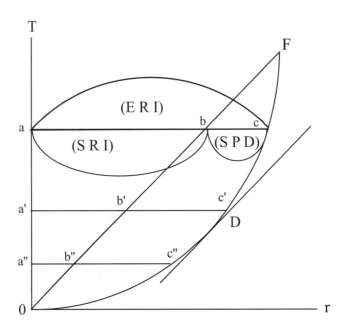

Figure 14.1 ERI adjusting to SRI

"virtuous circle" may even allow the real socioeconomic activities to overtake the general expectation, in such a way as the growth momentum gains in strength and allows the realized growth rate to exceed the expected one.

Next, the "sunny-side" proposition refers to the Maturation Process that is characterized by the closing gap between the Social Rate of Interest (SRI) and the Economic Rate of Interest (ERI), indicating the declining "extra-profit rate" (SPD). This process reflects the steady and "positive" adjustment of the ERI to the SRI. The term "positive" here refers to the willing/matured/constructive attitude of the economic entities toward the *society-economy harmonization* for further socioeconomic development. The *"sunny-side" proposition* for this phase on the ODP bases itself on the strengthened people's own invisible hands (Own Hands). The Own Hands now indicates a rapid enhancement of the people's long-term future orientation and perspective as well as the enhancement of personal and societal thought-frames based on the on-going Holistic Culture Enrichment. Such reinforcement of the Own Hands also reflects the on-going Comprehensive Human Development. In other words, the proposition may indicate a rapid *society-economy harmonization* on the basis of society-wide awareness and willingness of the imperative personal and societal self-command for reasonable well-being in the future.

The proposition also reflects the accelerated personal and societal endeavors for the all-embracing and broadly defined human-capital formation based on the on-going Holistic Culture Enrichment. In short, the "sunny-side" proposition relevant to the Maturation Process suggests that the *fundamental vitality* in socioeconomic development generally consists of the "virtuous circle" between the constantly reinforced society-general future orientation and the *"effective"* human-capital formation for self-fulfillment, self-enlightenment and, perhaps, self-actualization and self-transcendence. Such a "virtuous circle" may nurture the people's "sound dreams and desires" for the future as well as their mutual credibility, reliability, understanding and collaboration. Thus, the "sunny-side" proposition suggests that the people, with their constantly strengthened Own Hands, may supply over time all the necessary human resources to satisfy their pursuit of the Balanced Socioeconomic Development harmonious with the Environment, simultaneously promoting the Holistic Culture Enrichment and Comprehensive Human Development.

The Paradigm Shift and Sustainable Development

The brief discussion above of the "sunny-side" proposition indicates that the Own Hands, being strengthened steadily by the on-going Holistic Culture Enrichment, may propel society toward the Balanced Socioeconomic Development which is harmonious with the Environment. This proposition implies that the fundamental vitality for socioeconomic development generally consists of the "virtuous circle" between the people's growing orientation to the future and their farsighted long-term endeavors for cultivation and enhancement of personal and societal capacities on the basis of the on-going Holistic Culture Enrichment. Thus, the "sunny-side" proposition itself may encourage the paradigm shift (Holistic Culture Enrichment in each and every society) for Sustainable Development. That is; the steadily strengthened Own Hands by such Cultural enrichment, through the processes of Growth and Maturation, will guide the people toward the appropriate and viable socioeconomic development in each and every society as a long-term perpetual approach toward Sustainable Development.

In these Growth and Maturation processes, the weight in the capital formation may *shift* gradually at first and rapidly thereafter from the *material capital* to the diverse-and-integral *human capital* broadly defined. Along with the weight shift, the accelerated human-capital formation may induce a greater and more widespread personal ownership of human capital at large. An integrated diverse variety of broadly defined human capital that is embodied in each person may develop personal and societal capacities to command the appropriate and reasonable cycle of production, consumption and waste disposal over time, while taking care of the Environment conservation. The advancing personal and societal capacities, as well as the evolving far-sighted long-term approaches to cultural, social, economic, political, psychological, aesthetic, intellectual and environmental activities based on the sound Cultural enrichment, may nurture, among the social constituents, a healthy and critical outlook toward the issues of public and common interest. This nurtured critical outlook, in turn, may lead the respective peoples and societies to go beyond their short-term vested interests and develop a keener awareness as to the necessity of long-term collaboration for public purposes and the common good—Sustainable Development.

Accordingly, ideas pertinent to global sustainability (Sustainable Development) and wholesome human enrichment (Global Humanity) may gain strength steadily and induce a gradual shift away from the strictly "market-centered" competitive behaviors inculcated by the market fundamentalism (Market). Also, the ideas of global sustainability and wholesome human development may encourage more profound personal and societal capacities relevant to knowledge, awareness, wisdom, credibility, prudence, public spirit, harmony and self-command on the basis of the respective Cultural enrichment. In other words, the development of personal and societal capacities may respond positively and collaboratively to rectify the contemporary predicaments of diverse Cultures and the

Environment. Such predicaments may demand personal and societal endeavors as well as international collaboration for the respective Balanced Socioeconomic Development which is harmonious with the enrichment of diverse Cultures and the Environment. The generation and propagation of such ideas, endeavors and concerns worldwide as well as the collaborations among people and societies are subsumed in our Maturation Process which is deemed the most appropriate process toward Sustainable Development.

Paradoxical though it may seem, the existing diversity among nations and societies in the degrees of economic development is a blessing and a good starting point in the *perpetual* pursuit for Sustainable Development. The people of industrially advanced nations and the affluent minority of developing nations, who comprise only a fraction of the world population, currently produce and consume a great majority of the world's resources and products. This reality may offer a key question on the issue of Sustainable Development. Sustainability of the prospective global human community can be realized only by means of the personal and societal value renewal (the paradigm shift for sound Cultural enrichment). Naturally, it involves "big IFs."

"IF" the people of industrially advanced nations, feeling reasonably satisfied (or saturated) with the existing material wealth, would shift their socioeconomic values steadily toward the *less material-oriented* production and consumption, and much more toward the respective Culture-oriented esthetic-spiritual-intellectual production and consumption for a greater mental and spiritual satisfaction, the exploitation of already scarce natural resources could be moderated to avoid a further rapid depletion of non-renewable resources as well as a further rapid deterioration of the Environment. "IF," again, such a shift in values and interests could be successfully coordinated among the industrially advanced nations and "IF" such new collaborative endeavors for the common good (Sustainable Development) would become known to the many developing nations, the latter nations could find the room and scope for their socioeconomic development to satisfy their basic human needs, perhaps, without imposing much extra burden on the present state of the Environment. "IF," also, such developing nations could be persuaded sooner or later by the *good example* of the industrially advanced nations, the world could advance toward Sustainable Development.

The above conditional argument may sound optimistic but, perhaps, it is not far-fetched or impossible. Such a collaborative initiative—presumably taken by the advanced nations to create greater harmony between their socioeconomic development and the Environment, as well as the greater concern of harmonizing human interests in a more viable future—can offer a good example of the socioeconomic development for all nations. As a consequence, the developing nations may learn how to restrain the material use for their respective socioeconomic development and become highly encouraged to respect and enrich their own Cultures for Comprehensive Human Development. Such an initiative and good example coupled with the New Enlightenment that earnestly pursues Sustainable Development, encouraging a greater international cooperation and collaboration for the sound enrichment of the diverse Cultures across the world as well as freeing people and societies from the pervasive shackles of market fundamentalism (Market), may eventually promote a worldwide collaboration for Sustainable Development, providing at the same time a brighter prospect for the currently stagnating, discouraged and disillusioned nations and societies.

In order for such "big IFs" to become rather plausible "ifs," however, the people of the industrially advanced nations must start striving urgently for a breakthrough in the paradigm shift. Perhaps, one potent channel for such a breakthrough is an appropriate long-term educational policy that enhances over time the thought-frames of their respective peoples, enriches their respective Cultures and discourages the Market-centered values and mindset. For such long-term educational strategy, full-fledged and whole-hearted collaborative endeavors by both governments and non-government organizations are required in order to provide a socioeconomic environment that encourages, to begin with, a fairer and more equitable *intra*-national distribution of income, wealth and amenity. Such a socioeconomic environment may be based on much more integrated personal and societal capacities than the ones determined by the short-term Market orientation. Also, the socioeconomic environment must encourage much more respect for the poor and weak than hitherto. In this respect, we must remind ourselves constantly that any of us and our descendants may come to belong to the poor and weak as a result of a variety of drastic sociopolitico-economic changes in the long duration of time.

Once the benefit of socioeconomic gains begins to be distributed more equitably among the respective social constituents at large with a greater fairness to the "broadly defined" human capital, as well as among fellow citizens across the world, humankind may take a step forward toward a position where each society may come to entertain a more appropriate mental frame for the fairer income distribution within the prospective global community. In the present long-term theoretical framework, the income distribution based increasingly on the broadly defined human capital (that incorporates into the on-going Comprehensive Human Development and Holistic Culture Enrichment) may become desirable for and conducive to reasonable "personal equity" in respective societies. Such a dynamic concept of equitable income distribution may provide a more reasonable starting line for all people, as far as personal motivation is concerned, for the *integral* (rather than specialized) human capital formation in the respective societies.

The Paradigm Shift and Income Distribution

The above-mentioned concept of fair and dynamic income distribution, as a matter of course, requires the difficult task of evaluating the *"effective"* human capital embodied in the socioeconomic activities of the social constituents individually and generally. An appropriate facilitation of this task in each society may evolve gradually in the long term by means of the reinforced Own Hands (the people's long-term future orientation and perspectives based on the enhancement of personal and societal thought-frames) that guide and complement the "short-run invisible hand."

Such fair and equitable income distribution, then, may induce an accelerated investment in the broadly defined human capital that is largely incorporated into the respective Cultures in the long term. Such an accelerated human-capital formation may, in turn, become conducive to the personal and societal integration of physical, intellectual and spiritual development with the thought-frame enhancement. Also, such human-capital formation may contribute to the synergistic integration of the growing satisfaction (arising from the fair and equitable income distribution) with self-fulfillment and self-actualization of the social constituents at large. All such on-going integrations, simultaneously enriching the respective Cultures, may, in turn, reinforce the Own Hands in the respective societies to guide and complement the classical "invisible hand" for an appropriate evaluation of *"effective"* human capital in socioeconomic activities.

Furthermore, a much fairer distribution of income, based primarily on the rapidly growing stock of diverse and integrated human capital in the Maturation Process, may induce the development of personal and societal capacities to enhance mutual respect, credibility, reliability and self-command among the social constituents. Still further, such income distribution may be conducive to an enhanced understanding of the inevitable "mutuality" among the social constituents in the long term. Put more positively, such income distribution may give rise to the growing endeavors of the social constituents to coordinate themselves, domestically and internationally, for mutual survival and a thriving society. Moreover, such income distribution may help the social constituents become increasingly aware of the necessary harmony between their personal and public purposes, between their diversified freedom and social responsibility, and between their competition and cooperation. All these endeavors may, most likely, be conducive to harmonizing the socioeconomic development with the Environment for Sustainable Development.

As many societies and nations eventually move into the Maturation Process with the paradigm shift for the sound enrichment of diverse Cultures across the world, their respective constituents (with more comprehensive, complex and yet harmoniously integrated human capital, and no doubt keenly aware of the common good) may consciously seek much fairer income distribution domestically and internationally. Eventually, such human capital embraced by the respective Sound Cultures, superseding the physical and financial capitals in both absolute and relative importance, may encourage a much fairer income distribution worldwide that contributes to Culture of Peace, Global Humanity and Sustainable Development. In other words, such human capital would inevitably assume the pivotal role as the most important factor in the maturation phase of socioeconomic development worldwide.

Concluding Remarks

The paradigm shift for the sound Cultural enrichment worldwide, indeed, indicates one fundamentally different idea from that of the classicist paradigm. The paradigm shift in the present context specifies the shift from the classical paradigm comprising "self-interest" and "invisible hand" to the totally new paradigm, upholding the sound and perpetual enrichment of the holistic Culture in each society for Comprehensive Human Development and Balanced Socioeconomic Development. Such Cultural enrichment may naturally encourage a constant "thought-frame enhancement" as well as a growing "common and mutual interest" of the social constituents. Also, such Cultural enrichment may constantly reinforce the Own Hands in each society for complementing and guiding the classical "invisible hand" over the long term for the accomplishment of more appropriate and deserving socioeconomic development—Sustainable Development.

3 *Cultures and Comprehensive Human Development*

After a lengthy discussion in Part 2 on the theoretical framework and its ramifications, in Part 3 I will first discuss the concept of sound society-specific culture ("Sound Culture"). After defining the term Sound Culture, I will refer to the concept of "sound creativity" directly relevant to Sound Culture (Chapter 15). Next, I will explain the characteristics of Sound Culture in terms of multi-faceted integral ideas and thoughts in ancient Japan. Then, I will reconfirm the importance of diverse Sound Cultures across the world for Sustainable Development, drawing on the "Seventeen Article Constitution" of Prince Shotoku in early-seventh century Japan, which embodies an illuminating wisdom complex that alludes to the Sound Culture relevant to our Insular Planet (Chapter 16). The concept of Sound Culture will, then, be related to Comprehensive Human Development (Chapter 17). With such human development in mind, I will then discuss a variety of potential innovations in education for counter-balancing the prevailing Market (Chapter 18). Finally, I will argue that the perpetual sound enrichment of diverse Cultures is essential for personal and spiritual maturation relevant to Sustainable Development (Chapter 19).

15 *Sound Culture and Sound Creativity*

In this chapter, I will discuss a definition of "Sound Culture" and a theoretical foundation for the development of "Sound Creativity" in relation to the Culture-based Comprehensive Human Development that roughly consists of long-term personal and spiritual development, human-capacity improvement and thought-frame enhancement. To begin with, I will offer an argument against the contemporary distortion of the so-called "creativity" that does not satisfy our tentative definition of Sound Creativity, due mainly to the modern and contemporary emphases on the lopsided value system. In other words, the failure in general of the contemporary "creativity" qualifying the term "Sound Creativity" is considered to be mainly due to the dominance of the market fundamentalism (Market) that contradicts its own viable future as well as peaceful human coexistence and survival. Then, Sound Culture will be explained as the necessary and sufficient conditions for developing Sound Creativity. Finally, I will argue for the importance of emphasizing Sound Creativity for Sustainable Development.

Distorted Creativity in the Contemporary World

Modern and contemporary societies of the industrially advanced world, perhaps, have been strongly influenced and conditioned by "drastic and explosive" Western reactions to the tight, repressive and oppressive medieval binds of Catholicism and absolute monarchy on human freedom in general. Such "explosive" reactions may have taken place in the sequence of Renaissance, Reformation, Enlightenment, Industrial Revolution, Imperialistic Expansion and Economic Globalization. This process can also be viewed from the consequential "wide swing of the pendulum"—from the extremely "constrained freedom" toward the opposite extreme with its dogmatic pursuit of materialism, progressivism, individualism and egotism, along with excessive emphasis on liberal democracy and the market fundamentalism (Market).

Such extreme transformations of thought, polity, economy, attitude, behavior and lifestyle, no doubt, have weakened the modesty and restraint of the Western world. Accordingly, it has grossly distorted and/or devastated the diverse Cultures of the remaining world, in particular, by means of modern and contemporary colonialism, rationalism, reductionist scientism, progressivism, laissez-faire economics, expansionist industrialism, "money-breeds-money" global economy and the Market-driven IT revolution. Today's emphases on the dogma of "free market competition" and the ideology of "might-makes-right," therefore, may very well imply the excuse for the world power structure—the Big

Market—for their predatory accumulation of wealth and power as well as being an excuse for their perpetual domination of the world (see Chapter 6).

Such modern and contemporary transformations and disfigurations of the world, together with the "masked" excuses incorporated into modern economic theories that strongly favor the capital-rich individuals and the industrially advanced societies, have toppled the internal harmony of diverse Cultures across the world. Thus, the modern, "modernized" and "modernizing" societies today are taken to be extremely lopsided in their emphases on values and interests. They favor excessively the *competitive, material, individual, progressive* and *own-societal* values and interests at the sacrifice of the *congenial, spiritual, collective, traditional* and *foreign-societal* values and interests. With such biased values and interests, all these societies may trifle, if not entirely deny, the importance of societal and human *harmony, integrity, solidarity, continuity* and *mutuality,* which are all crucial to maintaining the soundness of the respective Cultures as well as to sustaining the respective societies into the future (Hiwaki 2006b).

Then, the so-called "creativity" encouraged and nurtured by the Market in the modern and contemporary world is largely *disqualified* to be Sound Creativity, as far as our definition is concerned. The term Sound Creativity is meant here as one that *contributes* to the perpetual human subsistence, well-being and maturity for peaceful co-existence and symbiosis with the Environment. This definition suggests that the Market can largely be construed as the *negative force* against the development of the Sound Creativity. No wonder, we have been facing increasingly instable and insecure living conditions as well as an extremely uncertain and cloudy human future, despite the abundance of on-going human "creativity." The increasing poverty and miseries in a growing proportion of the human population, as a result of the Market-biased "creativity"; the increasing threat to life in a growing sphere of the world as a result of the Market-incarnated exclusion; and the accelerated concentration of wealth and power in a decreasing number of individuals as a result of the Market-intrinsic absolute and predatory competition, all together, have led us to the unwanted choices of global tyranny by either the Big Market (power structure of the contemporary world) or the Big Brother (dictator in the Orwellian World), as already discussed in Chapter 6.

Harmonious Integration of Opposite Values

For a Culture to be sound in our contemporary world, it must be able to maintain the integral harmony relevant to the "*sound communal value system,*" as depicted in Figure 15.1 (Hiwaki 2008b). The diagram, to begin with, shows the human *integrity (humanity)* based on the integral balance of *spiritual* and *material* values. Second, it refers to the social *solidarity (reliability)* based on the integral balance of *collective* and *individual* values. Third, it indicates the societal *continuity (flexibility)* based on the integral balance of *traditional* and *progressive* values. Finally, the diagram shows the relational *mutuality (viability)* based on the integral balance of *own-societal* and *foreign-societal* values. All the harmoniously integrated value balances in the diagram are *inter-related* and *inter-active* as indicated by the respective *three directional* feed-forward and feed-back arrows.

This implies that any development of drastic imbalance in one or another of the four integral value balances, unless it is remedied readily and constantly by the personal and societal endeavors as well as by the *integral-harmonious force* depicted in the center, negatively affects all the remaining value balances to the detriment of Sound Culture. In other words,

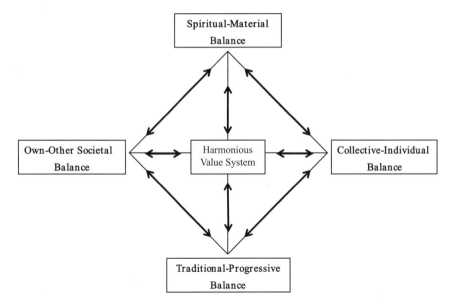

Figure 15.1 Harmonious value system

the personal and societal endeavors must constantly enrich the Culture to maintain the internal consistency among the four respective balances of social and human values by the strong harmonizing power. The sound enrichment of the Culture for its internal consistency requires the constant Comprehensive Human Development of the social constituents, which interacts closely with the Balanced Socioeconomic Development.

For such a purpose, a Culture-oriented continuous investment in human capacity, by both personal and societal endeavors, has to be accompanied by coherent "soft-and-hard" investment in the social infrastructure that interacts synergistically with human-capacity enhancement. Such coordinated investment in human capacity and the social infrastructure may enhance the joint personal and societal capacities, simultaneously enriching the relevant Culture, being conducive to developing the Sound Creativity and contributing to Comprehensive Human Development and the Balanced Socioeconomic Development. These multi-faceted coherent processes of synergistic interactions, particularly the *trilateral virtuous circle* of the on-going Cultural enrichment, human development and socioeconomic development, refer broadly to our theoretical framework for developing Sound Creativity.

Sound Creativity and Human Development

Sound Creativity, defined as one that contributes to perpetual human subsistence, well-being and maturity for peaceful co-existence and symbiosis with the Environment, excludes most of the modern and contemporary varieties of so-called "creativity." Such excluded "creativity" here may refer to the new ideas coming out of the *transient sharpness*, particularly in terms of self-seeking and lopsided motivation. Put differently, such "creativity," a seemingly brilliant idea, may refer to short-term commercial and acquisitive purpose, make-shift government policy, violence-related innovation and temporary and local solutions, of one kind or another, which do not take into consideration the broad and complex human aspects and the short-and-long-term prospects of the whole society, not to speak of the prospective global community.

More importantly, Sound Creativity must base itself on Sound Culture. The term "Sound Culture," as already indicated, denotes the one that can maintain the dynamic and consistent harmony of social and human values in perpetuity. In a sense, such a Sound Culture serves as the "time-space carrier" for the continuity of people and society, the "societal immune system" for the mental health and amenity of people and society, and the "social glue and lubricant" for harmonious personal and societal relations. Thus, Sound Culture indicates the normative and theoretical foundation for developing Sound Creativity that is closely related to Comprehensive Human Development that roughly consists of personal-and-spiritual development, human-capacity improvement and thought-frame enhancement.

It is quite reasonable, therefore, to define Sound Creativity on the basis of the Sound Culture that embraces the broad and intrinsic *sound communal value system* consisting of social *harmony*, human *integrity*, social *solidarity*, societal *continuity* and relational *mutuality*. Such inclination of the Sound Culture, generating harmonious and integral balances in all the spiritual-material, collective-individual, traditional-progressive and own-other values as shown in the above diagram (Figure 15.1), may naturally contribute to the development of Sound Creativity. The development of Sound Creativity, in turn, is naturally conducive to the enrichment of the Sound Culture. Thus, we may consider the depicted diagram of integral social harmony to serve as our "simplified" *indicator and criteria* of Sound Culture, which, in turn, satisfies the foundational requirement for developing Sound Creativity. In other words, we may consider the constantly enriched Sound Culture as the *necessary* and *sufficient* condition for developing Sound Creativity.

Concluding Remarks

What we must aim at, by all means, is the development of Sound Creativity for the sake of reasonably stable, decent, harmonious and secure life-and-living of all humanity. As a first step, therefore, we must start restoring and enriching our diverse Cultures across the world for the purpose of generating the respective Sound Cultures. Thus, it is highly important to emphasize the *congenial, spiritual, collective, traditional* and *other-societal* values in our very attitude, behavior and lifestyle, de-emphasizing the presently emphasized *competitive, material, individual, progressive* and *own-societal* values. By such emphasis and de-emphasis, we may be able to gradually generate the sound Cultural function that may enhance the broad and intrinsic *sound communal value system* (harmony, integrity, solidarity, continuity and mutuality).

Such sound function, in turn, is conducive to developing and sorting out Sound Creativity among all kinds of so-called "creativity." By this Cultural function, we may eventually be able to develop and utilize only Sound Creativity that contributes perpetually to human subsistence, well-being and maturity for peaceful co-existence and symbiosis with the Environment. Only by developing Sound Creativity on the basis of Sound Culture, perhaps, we humans may be able to realize a viable and peaceful world. In other words, by focusing on the sound enrichment of the diverse Cultures (the *paradigm shift*) as well as on the development of the Sound Creativity, we may be able to mark a first step toward Sustainable Development.

16 *Sound Culture and Wisdom Complex*

It is my opinion and conviction that Sustainable Development depends on the long-enduring human heritage of reasonably sound and diverse society-specific cultures (Sound Cultures). Such Sound Cultures may provide the respective tangible-intangible Cultural foundations for present and future socioeconomic and other human activities, adjusting to the respective environments and the available resources. The Sound Culture defined in the previous chapter is to be reconfirmed in this chapter by means of a circular "wisdom complex" derived from the "Seventeen Article Constitution," promulgated by Prince Shotoku of Japan some fourteen centuries ago (Hiwaki 2008b). In view of our Insular Planet with its increasingly severe constraints on the environment, resources and humanities, the normative definition of the Sound Culture with its value system may become an appropriate basis for enriching the diverse Cultures across the world for the common good—Sustainable Development.

Culturally Distorted Contemporary World

Most of our contemporary societies and respective Cultures may have been largely diluted or corrupted by mutually reinforcing, lopsided, pervasive thoughts and ideologies, such as the modern *antagonism, materialism, individualism, progressivism* and *egotism*. Such lopsided thoughts and ideologies, having been asserted proudly, vigorously and recklessly by the contemporary power structure (the Big Market) as the glories of the modern civilization, may be constantly reinforced by intrinsic antagonism (predacious competition), particularly with the overarching crude "might-makes-right" ideology. Moreover, the mutual reinforcement among such lopsided thoughts and ideologies may have led our contemporary world to an incontinent direction, to the detriment of our future.

Thus, our contemporary societies, all together, may continuously hurtle toward a chaotic and helpless state, involving all people and other ecological beings. Such a contemporary state, with its lopsided value system, is symbolically depicted in Figure 16.1 (Hiwaki 2008b). In the diagram the modern antagonism, materialism, progressivism, individualism and egotism interact with one another on the basis of laissez-fare economics with competition and ambiguous "liberal democracy," to ferment and accelerate into perpetuity the general "disparity-animosity spiral," which no natural and sound communities can accommodate for long.

Accordingly, our contemporary global sociocultural tendency, reflecting the schizophrenic or divisive characteristics (long-term "destructive" characteristics) of

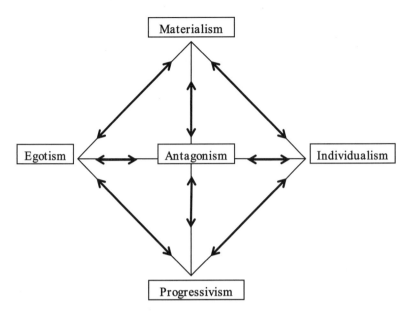

Figure 16.1 Untenable value system

modern civilization with the relevant two *alter egos* ("reductionist scientism" and "market fundamentalism"), may assert superficially the utopian values, such as, freedom, equality, fraternity, charity and human rights, on the one hand, and encourage in reality the inconsistent crude behaviors based on the "law of the jungle," aggressiveness, acquisitiveness, extravagance, exclusion and cruelty. All the crude behaviors may converge on the "might-makes-right" ideology, to the fatal detriment of the diverse Cultures that have been the respective natural foundations for the present and future socioeconomic and other human activities across the world. The incompatibility of these contemporary values and behaviors may have reinforced the explosive and chaotic tendency toward an imminent man-made catastrophe, of one kind or another.

More than 60 years ago, Indian Mahatma Gandhi (1869–1948) confronted the modern contradictions with his illuminative "Seven Social Sins"; (1) Politics without Principles, (2) Wealth without Work, (3) Pleasure without Conscience, (4) Knowledge without Character, (5) Commerce without Morality, (6) Science without Humanity, and (7) Worship without Sacrifice. Even earlier than this, a sage in Japan was intuitively aware of the uncivilized and acquisitive West, and was very wary of the modern civilization. Saigo Nanshu (Tamamori Saigo 1827–1877), who never left Japan, insightfully saw through the Western civilization as nothing but "barbarian in nature," commenting to his students (Inamori 2007):

> *Civilization is the term that rightly glorifies the broadly prevailing conduct of reason pertinent to the just way. It doesn't mean large and solemn palaces, gorgeous robes or showy appearances … If the West is truly civilized, it must have guided the "uncivilized" societies on the basis of loving hearts. It is undoubtedly "barbarian" to have treated in particular the "uncivilized", "unknowing" and "unreasonable" societies cruelly and mercilessly only for the sake of its own profits …* (this passage was translated into English by the present author).

Diagrammatical Definition of Sound Culture

In order to avoid an imminent man-made catastrophe, it is never too late for us humans to rectify our thoughts, values, lifestyles and behaviors, by emphasizing the *harmoniously integrated value balances* of the diverse Sound Cultures, such as spiritual-material balance, traditional-progressive balance, collective-individual balance, and own-other societal balances, as depicted in our diagrammatic definition of the Sound Culture in Figure 16.2 (same as Figure 15.1 in the previous chapter). In order to maintain such a Sound Culture, therefore, each "paired opposite values" must be respectively *integrated harmoniously* as well as *balanced equitably* in the process of dynamic Cultural enrichment. For this purpose we need to cultivate ourselves constantly for collaborative endeavors as well as for complementary integration of such "paired opposite values." In other words, we humans must work very hard to enrich our respective Cultures on the basis of the "*cosmic universe*" (Roessler, Lasker and Hiwaki 2007) rather than the prevalently and, perhaps, wrongly asserted "*chaotic universe*" of the "Big Bang."

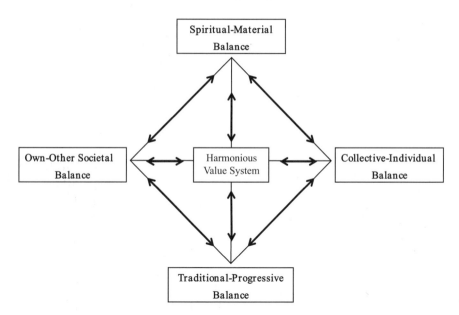

Figure 16.2 Sound value system

The Sound Culture, no doubt, encourages the mutual reinforcement of human *integrity* (*humanity*), societal *continuity* (*flexibility*), social *solidarity* (*reliability*) and human *mutuality* (*viability*), as shown in Figure 16.3 (Hiwaki 2008b). The complementary and integral spiritual-material, traditional-progressive, individual-collective and own-other value balances may, respectively, contribute to the *Integrity*, *Continuity*, *Solidarity* and *Mutuality* for the overall social *Harmony*. Thus, the mutual interaction and harmonious integration of such Cultural values, put all together, may refer to an integral complex of human wisdom for peace, harmony and comfort. Such a "wisdom complex" may exert synergy effects for the long-term *intra*-social and *inter*-social harmony to bring about reasonable peace, comfort and satisfaction for all people in perpetuity.

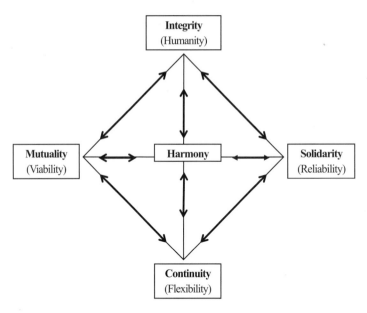

Figure 16.3 Sound and viable value system

The Seventeen Article Constitution

A model Sound Culture that encompasses an integral complex of human wisdom for peace, comfort and satisfaction ("wisdom complex") is revealed by the in-depth inquiries of Kenichi Tanaka (2002) into the "Seventeen Article Constitution" promulgated by Prince Shotoku of Japan in 604 AD. The Constitution was recorded in an eighth-century compilation of Japanese history entitled *Nihon Shoki*. Different from our contemporary meaning of "national legal canon," the "Seventeen Article Constitution," when *normally* interpreted, is no more than a moral code or a collection of maxims aimed at the then bureaucrats, aristocrats and chieftains (Tiedemann 1974). It is, however, a rich fountain of "wisdom complex," when interpreted *deeply* as done by Tanaka. The Constitution was promulgated when Prince Shotoku (the Crown Prince) was regent to Empress Suiko, during the great transformation of Japan with the mutually conflicting philosophies and religions of indigenous (Shintoism) and foreign origins (Confucianism and Buddhism), as well as the vested interests of militant chieftains and political factions.

Tanaka examined the Constitution for half a century, and discovered several coherent versions of "wisdom complexes" relevant to the troubled period of Prince Shotoku's leadership. The spirit and thought of such "wisdom complexes," no doubt, have been conveyed to the present day as important undercurrents of the Japanese Culture, as seen clearly in *Royal Road to Life: Learning from the Teachings of Saigo Nanshu* (Inamori 2007). The coherent messages of the "wisdom complexes" are highly relevant to our time of great turmoil and, perhaps, indispensable in our world that has come to a blind alley in terms of the environment, resources and humanities with its haphazard expansionism compounded by the egoistic and antagonistic "competition."

The Overarching Wisdom Complex

In the Constitution, Prince Shotoku asserts in the outset (Article 1) the most important Cultural value—"Harmony" (*Yawaragi*). This concept indicates "the meaning before all meanings" or "the word most intrinsic to the Japanese nationhood," according to Kenichi Tanaka. The concept of "Harmony" may very well correspond to the intrinsic nature of the Japanese Culture, largely encompassing the essential implications of modern semantics, ontology and epistemology, according to Tanaka's philosophical interpretation. This interpretation is based on his multi-faceted inquiries into the Constitution, which encompass studies of (among others) Buddhism, Confucianism and other Chinese thoughts, Shintoism and other ancient Japanese beliefs, and the Western postmodernism including the ideas of Carl Gustav Jung.

Following the concept of "Harmony," Prince Shotoku points to the Buddhist tenet of "Three Treasures" (*Sanbo*) in Article 2, implying the segmented whole (holism) of "meaning" (Buddha's Teaching), "existence" (the Law of Nature) and "consciousness" (Buddhist Devotion), which all together may correspond and contribute to the intrinsic and holistic Japanese "Harmony." He then refers to the Shintoist concept of "Emperor's Words" (*Mikotonori*: the decreed ruler's words) in Article 3, which literally indicates the "divine will" (or "metaphysical national mind") conveyed through the Emperor. This Japanese tenet primarily represents the concept of "existence" according to Tanaka. This may also imply the national and societal "continuity" or "continuous existence" through the Imperial lineage. Next, Prince Shotoku focalizes on the Confucian concept of ritualistic "Morality" (*Iya*) in Article 4, which primarily indicates the "consciousness," according to Tanaka. This may refer to the national and societal "solidarity consciousness."

After this, Prince Shotoku explains the four steps to the "way of wisdom" in Articles 5 to 8. These four articles, according to Tanaka, imply first "encountering with the intrinsic meaning" (Article 5), second "being cordial and moral" (Article 6), third "being awakened" (Article 7), and finally "dismissing one's self" (Article 8). Following these steps, Prince Shotoku brings us to the concept of "Mutuality" (*Makoto*) in Article 9. According to Tanaka, this concept indicates the "divine trust" in the conscience that resides in the people. Then, it may refer to the "viability" in the mutual relationship of individual persons and societies or "mutual trustworthiness" (*mutuality*) for peaceful coexistence.

This is to conclude the metaphysical "wisdom complex" contained in the first half of the Constitution (Articles 1 to 9). This "wisdom complex" is relevant to the *metaphysical nationhood*, according to Tanaka. It, in turn, relates to the one pertinent to the *physical nationhood* described in the latter half of the Constitution (Articles 10 to 17). The first half of the Constitution, therefore, indicates the metaphysical theme of "nationhood" and refers to the "supreme wisdom" from the standpoint of the *nationhood* (*not* from any *personal* standpoint). Then, the latter half of the Constitution is the pragmatic "wisdom complex" that indicates how such metaphysical "national wisdom" or the most essential "meaning of nationhood" realizes on the social constituents. This awareness of nationhood, in turn, reinforces the most intrinsic and holistic "Harmony" of the nationhood.

The Sound Communal Value System

The overarching expression of the "wisdom complex" in terms of the metaphysical nationhood—*Shotoku Mandala* (for simplicity)—shown in Figure 16.4 (Hiwaki 2008b), may suffice for our present purpose. As seen in the diagram, the concept of "Harmony" is located in the center of *Shotoku Mandala*. This concept of "Harmony," meaning the most intrinsic and holistic nationhood of Japan, may imply "soundness of the nationhood." It may also imply coordination, integration and harmonization of all different domestic and alien divisive elements within the nation. To the north of "Harmony" is located the concept of "Three Treasures" that combine the Buddha's Teaching, the Law of Nature and the Buddhist Devotion. The concept of "Three Treasures", being central to the Buddhist tenet, may imply the importance of the national/social/human *"integrity"* (or "soundness of the national/social/human character").

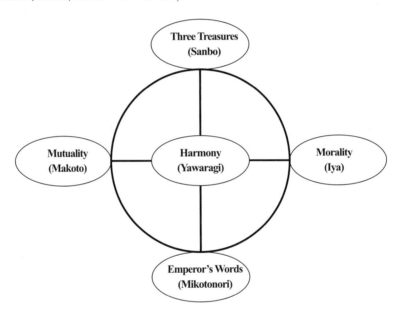

Figure 16.4 *Shotoku Mandala*: Sound value system

The concept of "Emperor's Words"—the important Shintoist tenet—is placed to the south of "Harmony" to indicate the "divine will for the just way" as being conveyed through the words of the Emperor. This concept may also imply the importance of national *"continuity"* (or "soundness in the national succession"), for it may refer to the continuity of the Imperial lineage, implying Prince Shotoku's hearty wishes for the wholesome nationhood to continue into eternity. In fact, the Japanese Imperial lineage has been continuous for, perhaps, some 1,800 years (or some 2,600 years in term of the "mythological" interpretation)—the longest existing dynasty in the world. To the east of "Harmony" is located the Confucian tenet of ritualized "Morality." This concept may imply the importance of national *"solidarity"* (or "soundness of the national cohesion") on the basis of the Confucian ritualistic moral/manner code that might have largely corresponded to the intrinsic Japanese mores and traditions. Now, the circular system of "wisdom complex" comes to completion with the concept of "Mutuality" to the west of "Harmony." This concept of "Mutuality" (*Makoto:* trustworthiness), implying the "divine trust in the people," emphasizes the importance of "viable human relationship" or the "*mutuality*" in the international/national/social relationship (or "sound mutual relationship"), may imply the most important value for any national/social relations. Such "Mutuality" is, in turn, considered corresponding and conducive to the most intrinsic and holistic Japanese nationhood—"Harmony."

Shotoku Mandala may correspond broadly to the normative "Sound Culture" depicted by the present author in Figure 16.2 and Figure 16.3. "Harmony" (*Yawaragi*) in *Shotoku Mandala*, implying the "soundness of the most intrinsic nationhood," can be interpreted to correspond to the "harmonious value system" in the Sound Culture. "Three Treasures" (*Sanbo*), implying the "soundness of the national/social/human character," can be interpreted to correspond to the harmoniously integrated "spiritual-material" value balance or the human "*integrity*" in the Sound Culture. "Emperor's Words" (*Mikotonori*), implying "soundness of the national/societal succession," can be interpreted to correspond to the harmoniously integrated "traditional-progressive" value balance or the national/societal "*continuity*" in the Sound Culture. "Morality" (*Iya*), implying "soundness of the national/social cohesion," may correspond to the harmoniously integrated "collective-individual" value balance or the national/social "*solidarity*" in the Sound Culture. Finally, "Mutuality" (*Makoto*) in *Shotoku Mandala*, implying "soundness of the international/societal relationship," can be interpreted to correspond to the harmoniously integrated "own-other" value balance or the national/societal "*viability*" in the Sound Culture.

Concluding Remarks

Treasure harmony and avoid discords by all means. (Prince Shotoku)

Gain new insights through reviewing old materials. (Confucius)

In view of our contemporary strife, confusion and turmoil (due mainly to our contemporary lopsided value system and lifestyles and the consequential egotist "competition-induced" disparities and animosities), on the one hand, and our contemporary yearning for Sustainable Development, Culture of Peace and Global Humanity, on the other, it is about the time to see our modern and contemporary thoughts, behaviors and lifestyles in a new light. Living on our Insular Planet, with the increasingly severe constraints on the environment, resources and humanities, we need to pursue an alternative avenue for a viable future. Perhaps, we need to encourage a steady shift in the legal paradigm from the standardizing premise of Unity in Diversity to the harmonizing premise of Integrity in Diversity for the age of Sustainable Development on the Insular Planet (see Chapter 10), as well as the socioeconomic paradigm shift for the sound enrichment of diverse Cultures (see Chapters 14, 29 and 30). We should at least rely more on the long-enduring wisdom of our diverse Cultures across the world rather than searching for immediate and transient solutions elsewhere, which almost always worsen the problems in the long term. Moreover, we should strive for Sustainable Development by enriching the diverse Cultures through our determined collaborative endeavors to meet the challenges of our age.

17 New Enlightenment for Comprehensive Human Development

Having discussed in the previous two chapters the concept of "Sound Culture," I will first discuss in this chapter the importance of comprehensive and integral human cultivation (Comprehensive Human Development) on the basis of "Sound Culture," and with reference to the on-going economic globalization propelled by the market fundamentalism (Market). In examining this connection, I will take up the undercurrent evolution of modern civilization together with its particular aggressiveness as well as the consequential fate of non-Western societies and their diverse society-specific cultures (Cultures). Second, modern civilization and its contemporary incarnation (*alter ego*)—Market—will be explained in terms of the adverse effects on Cultural diversity and soundness. Finally, I will argue that Comprehensive Human Development requires restoration and enrichment of diverse Cultures across the world, not only by the personal and societal endeavors in each society but also by the particular worldwide movement—the New Enlightenment.

Human Development and Modern Rationality

To seriously tackle the root causes of the worldwide human predicaments compounded by Market-propelled globalization, we must have an explicit and appropriate aim for wholesome and integral human development—Comprehensive Human Development. Here, the term "Comprehensive Human Development" indicates personal and spiritual development as well as human-capital formation and personal-societal thought-frame enhancement on the basis of sound Cultural enrichment. Such human development worldwide may require restoration and enrichment of diverse society-specific cultures (Cultures) across the world. Through collaborative endeavors worldwide for Comprehensive Human Development, a keen awareness needs to be generated with regards to the prevailing economic dogma and ideology, which assert the trinity of "free competition," "free market" and "free trade" for alleged human well-being and progress as well as the strictly Market-oriented values and the "might-makes-right" ideology.

Such dogmas, values and ideology have provided the material abundance to excess for the very small minority of rich and strong at the cost of the great majority of poor and weak, both *intra*-nationally and *inter*-nationally, and have led almost all people to distort their personal development as well as to degrade their humanitarian values. Many conscientious people in the world have long begun to doubt, apprehend and criticize the on-going economic globalization propelled by the market fundamentalism (Market). It is, however, important now to relate such doubt, apprehension and criticism to a worldwide movement of the New Enlightenment for the constructive causes toward Sustainable Development as well as toward Culture of Peace and Global Humanity. The New Enlightenment as such, no doubt, encourages a worldwide restoration and enrichment of diverse Cultures.

The on-going economic globalization, propelled by the Market as well as supported by the Market-driven IT revolution, has its own claim of rationality. For our purposes here, the Market is assumed to have its own ethos that is individuality interested, short-term engaged, competition propelled, outward/centrifugal directed, expansionist product-flow oriented and private-property centered, as defined in Chapter 8 and discussed elsewhere. The Market, asserting the "trinity of freedom," often pretends to have the theoretical rationality for efficient allocation of resources. The Market presumes that non-Western societies adapt themselves to the Western value system, instead of maintaining the complex and different values of their diverse Cultures. Accordingly, the perpetual and absolute competition entirely under the "standardized" rules of the game is assumed to bring forth the best possible results for the "haves" and the powerful among all global market participants. Such results may include an income distribution which is much more favorable to the "haves" at the cost of the "have-nots" and the constant "bullish" massage for investment and innovative activities that lead to a continuous invigoration of global market activities with a further depletion of global resources and devastation of the Environment.

Given such a "Market-sovereign" worldview, the world power structure (Big Market) and all the "haves" and the strong are often tempted to propagandize that the Market is meant for "the greatest happiness of the greatest number," given that economic globalization has increased the aggregate global output. The propaganda may never convince all people, since the majority is not egalitarian or rational. It is well known now that humans cannot be strictly egalitarian and rational as envisioned by the enthusiasts of the Enlightenment in the seventeenth and eighteenth centuries (see Chapter 8). The modern capitalism (or the modern civilization) that evolved in close relationship with the "Intellectual Revolution" (the Enlightenment) and the Industrial Revolution has never treated all humans rationally or equally to the letter. Instead, the protagonists and supporters of modern capitalism have severely divided fellow humans for irrational and selfish treatment. Some important divisive treatment includes those between Christians and pagans, between the "haves" and the "have-nots," between the populations of the suzerains and those at the mercy of such suzerains, and between the workers of the industrially advanced nations and those of the developing nations, not to speak of racial and sexual discrimination.

These examples of overt discriminations and irrational treatments under modern civilization may invalidate the triumphant claim of the Enlightenment that provided a strong influence on the thoughts and theories of Modern Economics. If humans are neither rational nor homogeneous, the most important theoretical claim of Modern Economics, that the "free-market competition" brings forth the efficient allocation of resources, may lose its validity, as already examined (see Chapter 5). Alternatively, some may argue either that those industrialists and multinational corporations have behaved irrationally or that such rampant discrimination among humans has indeed been rational. Or, it can be suspected that the very economic argument was devised as theoretical support for the power structure (Big Market) in modern civilization or, more broadly, for the Western supremacy over the rest to continue forever.

A glance at a United Nations Development Programme (UNDP) statistics (UNDP 1994) clearly reveals that the global distribution of income, even in the latter half of the twentieth century, intensely and increasingly favored the rich at the cost of the poor, despite a humanistic allusion by the Western leaders. As already discussed in Part 1 (Chapter 7: Overview of the Contemporary World), the global income share of the rich (the top 20 percent of the world population) increased from 70 percent to 85 percent in the 30-year period between 1960 and 1991, reducing the income share of the rest from 30 percent to 15 percent. When it comes to the very poor (the bottom 20 percent of the world population), their already meager income share of 2.3 percent in 1960 was further reduced to 1.4 percent in 1991. Put differently, the income share of the top 20 percent of the world population in proportion to that of the bottom 20 percent increased from the 30 times in 1960 to the 60 times in 1991. Such a trend of severe income disparity worldwide has been continuous even today. Then, we must ask ourselves: Is it *rational* to increase a cleavage in the world between rich and poor?

Modern Civilization and Cultural Diversity

It is easily apprehended that a great majority of the world population is today placed in a highly handicapped position in comparison to the people of the Western world. The Western people and societies, through the last five centuries of mutual rivalries as well as intellectual contacts and socioeconomic exchanges, have come to share broadly the sentiments, spirits, experiences, knowledge, wisdom and mores, among other things, implicitly or explicitly relevant to modern civilization. Put differently, such people and societies, with somewhat common Christian and/or Greek-Latin heritages, may have gradually come to share rather similar sentiments, thoughts, ideas, values, technologies, polities, institutions, organizations and legal instruments relevant to modern civilizations, while largely retaining their respective Cultural integrity. Such modern civilization-oriented Cultures, though highly diverse in their own right, are naturally much more confined than the diversity pertinent to all Cultures in the world.

The concept of "Culture" is generally assumed here to have its own ethos that is community interested, long-term engaged, cooperation propelled, inward/centripetal directed, continuity-accumulation-oriented and common-property centered (as characterized in Chapter 8). The pervasiveness of the West-European civilization, having been variously influenced and shaped by diverse Western Cultures, may imply a particular "aggressiveness" that has fully mobilized the Market together with armament. For example, it is quite reasonable to argue that many of those stagnated and/or underdeveloped societies today were once victims of the Colonialist-Imperialist powers that had intentionally destroyed the diverse native Cultures and thereby robbed their vitality, as explained in terms of the Credibility Trap (see Chapters 2 to 4). Given such power-backed "aggressiveness" that characterized modern capitalism, many non-Western societies have had no other choice than to imitate, blindly or reluctantly, the modern ideas, thoughts, values, lifestyles, customs, institutions, organizations, technologies, polities and rules, among other things.

It is, however, impossible to have emulated or replicated internally the most essential spirits, motives and experiences contemporary to the evolution of modern civilization. Despite the strenuous endeavors of adapting themselves to modern civilization, most of the non-Western societies and people have been doing no better than narrowly surviving without much hope for the future. They may have been totally or badly deprived of their respective Cultural foundations for their present and future socioeconomic and other human activities, as well as their important human and material resources and the respective Cultural integrity. The modern civilization is quite alien to many Cultures of the non-Western world. Thus, they have been much handicapped *culturally*, to begin with, in their endeavors to cope with the relevant Western languages as well as with the Market and the Market-driven globalization, which demand the "absolute" competition under the Market rule.

Moreover, the non-Western societies have been pressed or forced to give up their respective Cultures as obstacles for partaking in the compelling and compulsive economic globalization. In other words, they have had no choice but to pay the exorbitant prices to adapt themselves to the modern civilization, facing the world controlled by the Big Market (the power structure of the world). Such prices may have implied the respective sacrifices of long-cherished knowledge, wisdom, technologies, skills, mores, values, means of communication and so on, embedded firmly in their respective Cultures. More specifically, such horrendous prices and sacrifices may have included their hard-won human capital, confidence, credibility, identity and mutual trust under the respective Cultures.

As a consequence, the non-Western people may have been compelled to pay a further price in terms of the loss of stability, security and vitality of the respective societies. Much worse, they might have foregone their social centripetal forces as well as their mental-spiritual continuities of past, present and future. Even with such sacrifices, their endeavors to adapt themselves to the modern civilization might not have guaranteed the prosperity of their social constituents at large and respective posterities, for the non-Western societies have been incessantly exposed to the civilization-originated and profit-motivated rapid changes as well as compelled to face the unfair and unreasonable "free-market competition" under the Western "law of the jungle"—the "level-ground" absolute competition. Most likely, such adaptation might have only subjugated their present and future generations to Western societies as well as to the faceless and merciless power structure of the world (Big Market).

Human Development and New Enlightenment

The Sound Culture (reasonably sound Culture) may be assumed to have provided humans with the Cultural catalysis and synthesis in their inter-personal relations as well as in their relations with the relevant natural and man-made environments. Such a Culture may generate a centripetal force on the basis of the Culture-bound mutual trust and credibility, and relate both horizontally and vertically to the social constituents that consist of all individuals, families, firms, civil organizations and governmental entities. Such a Sound Culture may also facilitate societal interactions for *intra*-generation coordination, *inter*-generation solidarity, *inter*-national amity and person-society-environment synergy in the process of socioeconomic development. After all, such a Sound Culture may accommodate and encourage the general human ethos that favors a sound, active and fruitful longevity within the constraints of the relevant environments and resources.

Such qualifications of the Sound Culture may indicate a rich potential as the foundation of the Comprehensive Human Development, which primarily consists of personal and spiritual development and human-capital formation as well as of personal thought-frame enhancement. In other words, we assume that a worldwide endeavor for the restoration and enrichment of diverse Cultures is conducive to such human development, which simultaneously provides a strong impetus to the Balanced Socioeconomic Development across the world. Such human development and socioeconomic development, indeed, may work for the harmonious "triple balances" between matter and mind, progress and tradition, and individual and community. As qualified in the previous chapters (Chapters 15 and 16), if the people are mindful of an additional balance between their own societal values and those of other societies, they may generate the dynamic Sound Culture in the prospective global community for symbiosis with other societies, Cultures and the Environment.

Such harmonious and integral Cultural enrichment here emphasizes the Cultural integrity, credibility, respectability, flexibility, openness and dynamism over time. Such Cultural characteristics may *require* and, at the same time, *induce* the strong and continuous *society-general* orientation to the future as well as the earnest and untiring personal and societal endeavors for Comprehensive Human Development. To take the greatest advantage of such Cultural characteristics, the relevant social constituents must strive *consciously* to build up the strong *centripetal force* of the society, by deepening and broadening the Culture-bound *mutual trust*. For this purpose, the Culture has to be restored and enriched to offer the holistic and common foundation for Comprehensive Human Development. Such personal and societal endeavors, however earnest and vigorous, have to be reinforced by additional and tireless attempts to communicate and harmonize with the surrounding diverse societies, as well as with the worldwide development of a constructive human environment, based particularly on peaceful and humanitarian endeavors.

Further still, such endeavors of the respective people and societies must be sanctioned, encouraged and supported by a growing and long-lasting worldwide movement of the New Enlightenment (as defined in Chapter 8). Such global movement, on the one hand, must aim at the freeing of all peoples and societies from the shackles of the politico-economic dogma comprising "free market," "free competition" and "free trade" and the ideology of "might-makes-right," both of which fanatically embrace the Market in favor of the Big Market. On the other hand, such a global movement must work for the sound enrichment of diverse Cultures as well as for personal, spiritual and intellectual development across the world, and bring into play the *common and constructive cultural traits* of all peoples and societies. The eventual purpose of the New Enlightenment is to encourage worldwide human motivation and capacity for collaborative long-term perpetual endeavors for Sustainable Development, Culture of Peace and Global Humanity, which all together may represent the world's important contemporary issues.

Concluding Remarks

The Market-propelled and IT-supported economic globalization has degraded personality and spirituality at large through the devastation of diverse Cultures across the world. It may also seem to seduce all of us into becoming infantile and mechanical entities, by rapidly altering us to behave like the incarnations of producing and consuming machines simply guided by the market signals. Such contemporary tendency can never constitute a viable proposition for the future of the humanity. Then, what alternative do we have for the future? The only viable alternative in the face of the pervasive Market, perhaps, lies in the daring challenge of consorted local and global endeavors (along with the New Enlightenment) for the restoration and enrichment of diverse Cultures, as well as for the pertinent human development (Comprehensive Human Development) across the world to counteract and tame the abrasive and reckless Market, so as to cater to the respective and diverse Cultures.

18 *Innovative Education for Diverse Sound Cultures*

In this chapter a broad scope of innovative education will be presented and examined in relation to Comprehensive Human Development (as discussed in Chapter 17). This scope will refer to the enhancement of personal and societal thought-frames conducive to the relevant human values, attitudes and behaviors favorable for dealing with the important issues of the twenty-first century. To begin with, these important issues will be identified in relation to the concepts of the Culture, the Environment and the Market. Second, a relevant theoretical framework for developing personal and societal capacities will be elaborated upon. Third, I will introduce a schematized chart of synergistic influence, which shows a conjectural scope of the mutual relationship among education, thought-frame, behavior and other relevant factors. Fourth, an appropriate direction of educational endeavors will be suggested in view of the awesome force of the Market. Fifth, I will introduce and discuss several innovative possibilities of education, which, when used together, may help solve the important global issues. Finally, I will conclude the chapter, referring to our frameworks for human development.

Globalization and Important Issues

The importance of thought-frame enhancement can be discussed in terms of the social-value enhancement for combating the general mental desolation and lifestyle devastation in the age of "digitized globalization." The term "digitized globalization" refers to the combined forces of the market fundamentalism (Market) and the Market-driven revolution in communication ("digital revolution") for economic globalization. Both the Market and the "digital revolution" can be implicated to have trampled on the existing diverse society-specific cultures (Cultures) across the world and the broadly defined global environment (Environment) that includes natural, cultural, humanitarian, peaceful and other relevant human environments.

The term "Culture," as defined in Chapter 8 and elsewhere, means the all-encompassing holistic society-specific culture that refers generally to the long-term accumulated whole of personal and societal experiences, knowledge, wisdom, mores, norms, linguistic and non-linguistic communicational skills, to mention only the major elements. The "accumulated whole" implies the synergistic interactions of the natural and legal persons within their own society and their interactions with other people, societies and Cultures, in addition to the Environment. Such a Culture must be positive and constructive, at least, to the particular people and society. The dynamic Culture, therefore, must have the positive purpose of securing subsistence, well-being and peace for the relevant people and society. In contrast, the term "Market" means the prevailing market fundamentalism that upholds only the market-related values and favors only the winners in the market. The Market goes largely against non-Western values and lifestyles, as well as against their diverse Cultures. Thus, the Market has trampled on them across the world, viewing them as obstacles to its expansion and prevalence all over the world. Also, the Market has devastated the Environment, exploiting it mercilessly and endlessly as "free goods."

Such devastation of our diverse Cultures and the Environment by the Market has been undermining security, stability, identity, interdependence and long-term orientation of households, firms, governments and societies without any exceptions. In addition, the Market, by introducing highly convenient "short-run" efficiency-oriented digital devices, has drastically altered and reshuffled our accustomed lifestyles, value systems, human development, employment practices, human relations and social order almost entirely. When the Market ushered in the global computer age, we humans may have been driven to face the reality of irreversible changes in all aspects of our lives. This may have happened too fast, too much and too soon for the general public to catch up with, become accustomed to and to live with. The Market, by means of the "digital revolution," has been exaggerating the instability of socioeconomic activities, the uncertainty in future prospects and the insecurity of employment, income and living.

Hidden behind the Market and the "digital revolution" is the *world-standardizing/ unifying* faceless power structure of the modern civilization (Big Market). The civilization may have demonstrated the zeal resembling that of religion for the "Market sovereignty," which differs vastly from either the "consumer sovereignty" or the "producer sovereignty." The modern civilization naturally embodies the ideas of the Enlightenment in the seventeenth and eighteenth centuries, such as rationalism, egalitarianism, self-interest, free-market competition, individualism, liberal democracy and human evolution/progress. Such ideas may have fanned and misguided the people at large to support and sanction the modern "acquisitiveness"—the "naked" profit motive—and the modern diplomatic excuse—"national interest"—in terms of global economic and political activities, resulting in the Market having its "own way" against all reasons to have the future world reigned perpetually by the Big Market.

Given the awesome force of the Market, that has no compass bearing on any guiding light for the future of humanity, we humans may have very limited struggling space, if any, for an alternative way of life with reasonable security, stability and decency. If we can generate an active worldwide consensus on such an alternative lifestyle, we can expect to leave a healthy Environment to future generations. In securing such an active consensus, we need to cultivate the general will for enhancing our thought-frames (that is, personal and societal scopes of thought in time and space) as well as for enriching our diverse Cultures. This is the challenge to deal squarely with the formidable Market— the unifying, standardizing, controlling instrument/force and the ideology of "might-makes-right."

By enhancing our personal and societal thought-frames and enriching our diverse Cultures, we may effectively approach the major global issues, such as Sustainable Development, Culture of Peace and Global Humanity. All these issues that contradict the pervasive Market may point to the respective alternative ways of life, which encourage cooperation, solidarity, harmony, security, stability and viability for all the generations to come. Also, in attempting to enhance our thought-frames, we can comprehend more easily the importance of restoring and enriching our diverse Cultures for ready collaborations worldwide. Such endeavors may call for the recourse to *educational innovation* for Comprehensive Human Development. For this reason, I consider it highly important to delve further into the relationship between education, thought-frame and behavior in the present discussion.

Framework for Multilateral Value Enhancement

In order to take up the issue of the Comprehensive Human Development, I would like first to discuss the idea relevant to the enhancement of personal and societal thought-frames. Our premise for such thought-frame enhancement indicates that, in order to overcome the devastating forces of the Market and the "digitized globalization," we must enrich and strengthen the counteracting forces of diverse Cultures all over the world. For this purpose, we need to commit ourselves to cultivating and enhancing our personal and societal thought-frames for Comprehensive Human Development. A continuous enhancement of such thought-frames may expand the time frame of our market activities and all the other activities. In other words, a general elongation of our time frame alone may help change our market behaviors in favor of Balanced Socioeconomic Development and, hence, Sustainable Development.

The theoretical process of thought-frame enhancement is shown in the first quadrant in Figure 18.1 (Hiwaki 1996a). The horizontal axis (Ft) represents the average future orientation of the social constituents (implying the planning range of the society), and the vertical axis (Ih) the personal and societal investment in the human capital broadly defined. The origin of the diagram (O) implies a theoretical point referring to the absence of both future orientation and human-capital formation. The upward sloping curve (Curve H) suggests the theoretical time-space process of *thought-frame enhancement*, which may represent a continuous mutual and synergistic interaction between the human-capital formation (space) and the future orientation (time). In

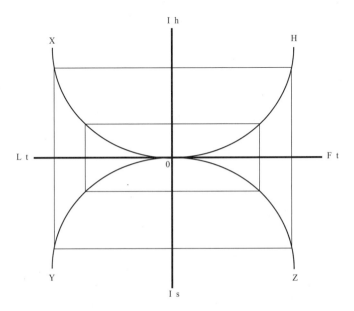

Figure 18.1 Complex value enhancement

essence, Curve H indicates that, as the investment in the broadly defined human capital expands, the average social constituents become further oriented to the future to have an enhanced scope of thought in time and space (see Theoretical Appendix 7). The thought-frame enhancement may feed synergistically back to stimulating the human-capital formation. This implies the intrinsic and perpetual process of thought-frame enhancement envisioned in this chapter.

In addition, this diagram as a whole represents a broader perspective to explain the synergistic enrichment of overall personal and societal capacities relevant to Comprehensive Human Development. The upper and the lower vertical axes in Figure 18.1, representing the variables amenable to government long-term policy, may indicate the various levels of investment in human capital (Ih)—enrichment of personal capacity—and the various levels of investment in the soft-and-hard social infrastructure (Is)—enrichment of the societal capacity. These policy-amenable variables also indicate the people's endeavors for personal and societal capacity enrichment as well as for enrichment of the relevant Culture.

The horizontal axes may imply the much less policy amenable variables that rely on the constant and complex personal and societal endeavors as well as on the roundabout and indirect effects of the capacity-enriching activities represented by the upper and the lower vertical axes. The horizontal axes on the right and the left, respectively, indicate the average orientation to the future (Ft) and the average life expectation (Lt) of the social constituents. In other words, the right-hand axis implies a variety of planning ranges of the society, and the left-hand axis a variety of the people's expected life spans.

The mutual and synergistic interactions of the four axes may lead to Comprehensive Human Development. Also, these axes, respectively, stand for the "personal-capacity enrichment" (Ih), the "societal-capacity enrichment" (Is), the "future-plan elongation" (Ft) and the "life-prospect elongation" (Lt). Their respective "intra-quadrant" interactions represent the process of *thought-frame enhancement* (Curve H) based on the interactions between the "personal-capacity enrichment" (Ih) and the "future-plan elongation" (Ft); the process of *human-value enhancement* (Curve X) based on the "personal-capacity enrichment" (Ih) and the "life-prospect elongation" (Lt); the process of *lifestyle enhancement* (Curve Y) based on the "societal-capacity enrichment" (Is) and the "life-prospect elongation" (Lt); and the process of *common-goal enhancement* (Curve Z) based on the "societal-capacity enrichment" (Is) and the "future-plan elongation" (Ft). All the four *enhancement* processes (Curves H, X, Y and Z) interact with one another continuously to depict a well-coordinated outward expansion of the *rectangular plane*. Regarding the theoretical framework depicted in Figure 18.1, a more detailed discussion will be presented later in Chapter 28.

The Schematized Flow in Human Development

The theoretical framework for multilateral value enhancement, representing Comprehensive Human Development, may naturally effect direct and indirect influence on both Holistic Culture Enrichment and Balanced Socioeconomic Development. I will now relate the above theoretical framework to the flow-chart framework that is assumed to illustrate a Culture-enriching educational innovation, influencing the personal-and-societal thought-frame enhancement as well as the improvement of personal-and-societal behaviors. Suppose the introduction of innovative education for the Cultural enrichment, through the policy-amenable axes of both the personal-capacity enrichment (Ih) and the societal-capacity enrichment (Is) in Figure 18.1. The innovative education can interact synergistically with the personal and societal experiences, information and thinking process. Such education may influence the personal and societal thought-frames as well as their awareness, values, attitudes and eventually behaviors, as shown in the flow-chart schematized in Figure 18.2 (Hiwaki 2003a, 2005c) with the assumed feed-forward and feed-back effects.

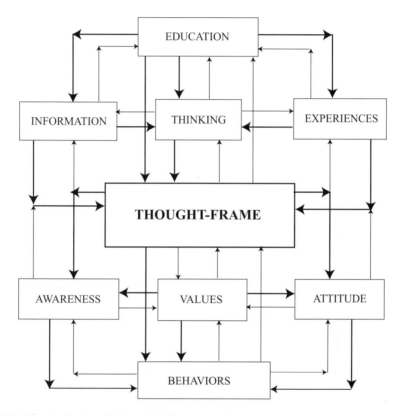

Figure 18.2 Flow chart of thought-frame enhancement

The above flow-chart is designed primarily to relate a significant Culture-enriching educational innovation to the consequential enhancement in the personal and societal thought-frames and behaviors (indicated by the bold-line arrows), accommodating also the important feedback effects (indicated by the thin-line arrows). In this flow-chart, such innovative education is assumed to interact synergistically with personal and societal experiences, thinking and information for the enhancement of their thought-frames. Thus enhanced thought-frames are now assumed to influence their awareness, values, attitudes and eventually behaviors. Such improvements in awareness, values, attitudes and behaviors may now feedback to enhance the personal and societal thought-frames. Such compounded enhancement of the thought-frames through the *feed-forward* and *feed-back* processes may now advance Comprehensive Human Development, Holistic Culture Enrichment and Balanced Socioeconomic Development.

New Educational Direction

As hinted at in the beginning of this chapter, the onslaught of global standardization by the inhuman force of the Market has been devastating our lives, the diverse Cultures and the Environment, with the popular support and sanction of the lopsided modern value premise that represents competition-biased modern capitalism, liberty-emphasizing modern democracy and lust-emancipating Modern Economics (as discussed in Chapter 5). The value premise of modern civilization may have regarded any other civilizations and Cultures as "barbarous" and/or "threatening," and aimed, accordingly, at the global standardization of the values and rules under "Market sovereignty." At the same time, the ideology ("might-makes-right") and the instrument/tool (Market) of modern civilization accelerate the "disparity-animosity spiral" all over the world to the demise of the humanity and humanities. Such prejudice and ideology in the modern capitalist civilization take us nowhere but to mental desolation in a schizophrenic desert, dehumanized chaos in the real-and-virtual world and the eventual man-made catastrophe of the devastated Environment and depleted natural resources.

An appropriate innovation of Culture-enriching education, therefore, is called for in order to overcome such awesome predicaments accelerated by the pervasive Market. Such an educational innovation must effectively enrich the human capacity to induce reasonable human stability, security, health, comfort, integrity and harmony. Also, such educational development is necessary for the simultaneous/synchronous processes of enhancing our personal and societal thought-frames and enriching our diverse Cultures. The enhanced thought-frames and enriched diverse Cultures, in turn, may contribute to the active consensus that is conducive to the simultaneous and synchronous processes of Sustainable Development, Culture of Peace and Global Humanity. These important global issues seem to favor amicable and harmonious mutual relations on the basis of their intrinsic common purposes and to encourage the long-term, Culture-bound, humanities-enhancing, harmony-treasuring and longevity-favoring lifestyles.

Such relevant educational innovation, to begin with, may require a redirection of the existing educational methods practiced particularly in the modern and advanced nations. For, the people of such nations may have been made blind and numb to the long-term lethal effects of the Market and the Market-driven "digitization." Such innovational redirection must change the prevailing cramming-oriented reductionist system of modern education toward a more integral, meaningful and, perhaps, more rewarding and enjoyable education for thought-frame enhancement as well as for Cultural enrichment and diversity. In such innovational redirection we need to involve, mobilize and coordinate all modes of education, including home, school, community and virtual varieties. Also, such new direction must address the life-long education of human social constituents to induce their appreciation and enjoyment of the sound diverse Cultures and their Culture-embraced personal-spiritual-intellectual development. Such innovative endeavors in education may redirect the social constituents at large toward the much stronger future orientation by investing constantly in their broadly defined human capital which is favorable and available for the common purpose—the integral development of the prospective global community, encompassing Sustainable Development, Culture of Peace and Global Humanity.

Further, all the educational innovations must aim at having individual social constituents cultivate essential abilities for overall and holistic understanding of the human historical relations to the Environment as well as of the circulatory view of life and nature. Still further, such innovations must bring out more positive and constructive long-term attitudes and behaviors in natural and legal persons and the general public. Moreover, such educational innovations must emphasize broad-based, multifaceted and diverse learning opportunities, not only for knowledge and skills, but also for values, aesthetic sentiments, awareness, attitudes and long-term perspectives for personal and spiritual development under the respective Cultural enrichment. This implies that educational innovations are meant not only for the effectiveness of bread-winning but also for the enhancement of human values and qualities in the respective people and societies through the sound enrichment of the respective Cultures.

Concrete Educational Innovations

FOR BROADER COMPREHENSION AND AWARENESS

We need educational innovation to stimulate all of us, individually and collectively, in order to achieve a greater awareness of the extra-long-term accumulative human endeavors that have taken place worldwide, prehistorically and historically. This has the purpose of encouraging all natural and legal persons to understand that geographical locations, climates, terrestrial and celestial occurrences, historical incidents and so on, have been, respectively, important causes of the different social, political, economic, linguistic, technological and even educational developments. Such an educational innovation must be intended to encourage the understanding of human endeavors in the very struggle for survival, subsistence, well-being, stability, integrity, comfort, harmony and human development. Such an innovation must, at the same time, discourage a simplistic conclusion based only on the end results or the existing prevalent tendencies.

FOR KEEN INSIGHTS INTO HUMAN NATURE AND HISTORY

Second, closely related to the afore-mentioned innovation, we must work for educational innovation to bring out better insights into the past, present and future. This is to discourage the sterile method of studying history by memorizing often-distorted accounts by different historians and rulers, describing dynasties and events, such as conquests, wars, territorial expansion and economic development mostly from the viewpoint of the winners. Indeed, educational innovation should encourage a broader perspective for short-term, long-term, diverse and synergistic effects of the various historical occurrences of different societies in the past, the present and possibly into the future. Further, this type of educational innovation must be intended to encourage individual persons to challenge the established interpretations by resorting to new approaches with different angles, standpoints and perspectives. Moreover, such an innovation should encourage individual persons to develop keen insights into human nature and history and derive many useful lessons for a balanced human cultivation in the future.

FOR INTER-RELATED KNOWLEDGE ACCUMULATION

Third, we need an educational innovation to encourage a more comprehensive and integral approach to the learning process as well as to the learning environment, in order to bring about more cumulative and synergistic effects of what is learned. This is to encourage individual persons to relate one phenomenon with another more effectively and profoundly, and to synthesize and integrate within their respective minds the learned concepts, thoughts, ideas and theories in different subjects as well as in different experiences and occasions. This type of educational innovation must be intended to discourage study just for the sake of memory and to encourage study for the sake of enriching the knowledge foundation of learners. At the same time, it must be aimed at encouraging the continuous accumulation of knowledge for the sake of broadening and deepening the scope of understanding and viewing the intricate, complex and synergistic interactions of various types and fields of knowledge. Eventually, it must be aimed at having continuous inter-related knowledge accumulation of different subjects and objects, relating closely to the earnest quest for the common good—Sustainable Development.

FOR LONG-TERM FUTURE PERSPECTIVES

Fourth, we need educational innovation to nurture a more enlightened long-term perspective and a stronger orientation to the future. This is to encourage the construction of a broad and rich foundation of knowledge and experience, not only for paving the way toward future studies but also for viewing the various phenomena locally and globally as well as for understanding them from the long-range, historical and humanitarian perspectives. It should also encourage serious concern for the well-being of our future generations as well as for the health of the Environment. This type of educational innovation must be intended to avoid the narrow, shallow, simplistic and reductionist views of the world from the self-centered and short-term perspectives. It must also be aimed at developing the ability to look into not only the immediate but also the long-term consequences of our individual behaviors, business practices and government policies.

FOR UNDERSTANDING HUMAN ETHOS AND RELATIONSHIPS

Fifth, we need educational innovation to encourage more compassionate, generous, tolerant and symbiotic human relations as well as more serious concerns about the intrinsic and basic human needs. This should encourage asking various questions about the health of our respective Cultures in view of the prevailing lifestyles, which are largely and increasingly detached from the natural environment, societies, local communities and even families. Also, it should review broadly the relationship between human nature and intrinsic human needs in the short and long terms, as well as in different sexes, ages and stages of personal life. This type of educational innovation must be intended to avoid thinking in terms of insatiable wants and desires. Such an innovation must develop the ability to compare and contrast material and spiritual needs, and aim at the human ethos of sound, active and fruitful longevity as well as at close, tolerant, generous and compassionate human relations and social interactions.

FOR INTER-CULTURAL UNDERSTANDING AND MUTUAL RESPECT

On top of all the above, we need educational innovation to encourage affinity to our own respective Cultures and, at the same time, understanding of the other peoples and Cultures. This should encourage finding the important meaning of the long-accumulated holistic Cultures to the respective peoples. Also, it should encourage thinking about the importance of Cultural identity for one's mental health, comfort and integrity, as well as for one's fitting private and public lifestyles. Further, it should examine and treasure the Culture-bound environment for human relations, manners, language, festivities, ceremonies, sentiments, hospitality and so on, for a comfortable and worthy personal and social life. This type of educational innovation must be intended to cultivate a greater appreciation of and respect for, the diverse Cultures in the world and to encourage our mutual endeavors for the enrichment of the respective Cultures.

FOR WELL-BALANCED HUMAN DEVELOPMENT

The above-mentioned *interactive-integrative* educational innovations are by no means exhaustive, but the examples are of paramount importance. All these educational endeavors must aim at well-balanced human development in the intellectual, aesthetic, spiritual and moral spheres, as well as aim at the enhancement of personal and societal thought-frames in time and space. Introducing such educational innovations into our frameworks of human development in the above Figure 18.1 and 18.2, we may now expect the meaningful interactions of education, knowledge, experiences and active thinking to enhance the personal and societal thought-frames, as well as to bring about appropriate behaviors, for the sound enrichment of our respective Cultures. Such continuous processes of thought-frame enhancement and Cultural enrichment may provide for intra-society collaborations and viable cooperation worldwide in order to deal effectively with our important global issues for the integral development of the prospective global community.

Concluding Remarks

It is, indeed, difficult just to think about dealing effectively with the important global issues, such as Sustainable Development, Culture of Peace and Global Humanity. It is, however, almost impossible to start dealing with them without containing, neutralizing and Culture-orienting the *world-standardizing* pervasive force of the market fundamentalism (Market). The Market has not only trampled on the society-specific public goods (diverse Cultures) but also devastated the global public goods (Environment). The Market with its *antagonistic competition* and ruling ideology of "might-makes-right" also has initiated and accelerated the deadly "disparity-animosity spiral" in our contemporary world. In containing the Market in our mindset and dealing with the important global issues, therefore, we humans must urgently start collaborating, both locally and globally, for retrieving, restoring and enriching our diverse Cultures all over the world. We must also pay much keener attention to the close and intrinsic relationship, in particular, between the diverse Cultures and the Environment, so that they are fully respected by all persons and societies.

Then, our collaborative endeavors to enrich the diverse Cultures must proceed with the *enhancement of our thought-frames* in order to avoid a possible pitfall of the *exclusive and nationalistic* approach to our respective Cultures. Thus, we must innovate and develop our education particularly for both thought-frame enhancement and Cultural enrichment so that we will be able to deal effectively with the impending global issues based on our wholehearted collaborations and earnest endeavors. Through the development of such innovative education, especially in the industrially advanced nations, we may gradually modify and remedy our *"modernized"* mentality and attitude to rid of our "simple-minded" and "self-righteous" pursuit of freedom, convenience, individuality and private property. Thus, we will be able to cope with the impending regression/degradation of humanities, as well as with the distorted and wasteful exploitation of human capacities and natural resources. The Culture-enriching educational endeavor for enhancing our thought-frames may prove to be the most important starter for the process of human-value enhancement and human development (Figure 18.1), as well as for the synergistic process of changing our socioeconomic behaviors (Figure 18.2).

19 *Cultural Enrichment and Personality*

In this chapter I will consider the important role of education in a contemporary world characterized by inundation of information and fast-changing living environment. I will examine again the importance of innovative education and its role in thought-frame enhancement and the consequential change in behavior which favors possible solutions for the important global issues of Sustainable Development, Culture of Peace and Global Humanity. Then I will argue for the potential effects of such innovative education on Cultural enrichment and personal maturation, attempting to explain the complexity of such a relationship. Furthermore, the policy implication for personal maturation is offered in terms of the educational endeavor to rectify the transient-happiness-centered ideology of modern and contemporary times.

Innovative Education and Holistic Cultures

The innovative education discussed in the previous chapter consisted of a great variety of potential innovations aiming at worldwide Comprehensive Human Development and the enrichment of the diverse Cultures, *not* at the narrow nationalistic endeavor for Cultural superiority or exclusiveness. In the previous chapter, such innovations were directed particularly toward the people of industrially advanced nations, with the implication that the general social constituents in such nations were needed to mature to comprehend, in particular, the great variety of distortions existing in the modern and "modernized" world. Thus, such innovations were meant to encourage: greater awareness of the numerous and different historical processes; better insight into the past, present and future; more comprehensive cumulative and synergistic learning; more enlightened long-term perspectives and stronger future orientation; more compassionate, generous and tolerant understanding with regards to human relationships; and the more serious concerns about intrinsic "spiritual-and-material" human needs; greater affinity to one's own Culture and more profound understanding of other Cultures as being essential to the well-being of the respective societies.

All these broad aspects of educational innovations may relate largely to the enhancement of personal and societal thought-frames that may be conducive to intellectual-and-spiritual development, personal maturation, broad human-capital formation and development of long-term perspectives. All these together may roughly comprise Comprehensive Human Development. Such human development, when widespread in the world, may naturally encourage the worldwide enrichment of existing diverse Cultures. A particular emphasis in the present discussion, however, focuses on a "virtuous circle" as well as a synergistic interaction among innovative educations, thought-frame enhancement, personal maturation and Cultural enrichment. Each of these has a variety of facets and dimensions and, hence, their relations may be neither direct nor linear.

Modern Education and Personality

Formal education, if it is appropriately constituted and instituted, may, over time, be conducive to personal maturation as well as to personal and societal thought-frame enhancement. So-called "modern education," however, mainly emphasizes the *memorization* of the "standardized" or "established" Western knowledge, as far as the *imitation* of the Western educational system by many non-Western societies is concerned. In other words, such "modern education" may emphasize a fast and accurate memorization of Western knowledge and technical methods, without due regards to the history, thought, spirit, experience and Cultural background which gave rise to modern civilization as well as to the modern inquiry and education. Education as such, however, can add little to thought-frame enhancement and personal maturation, particularly when ignoring the indigenous heritages of own Cultural foundations. Typical students, being forced to cram and/or skim only what is emphasized in the classroom, may very often experience the degeneration of their thought-frames, which are firmly based on the respective Cultures, and they may start leaning toward the misguided *ego-centric* variety of existence, being practically detached from their own Cultures.

Through such "modern education," many people of non-Western societies may have been conditioned or forced to think that anything "Western" is advanced and suitable for imitation for their own survival as well as for their own political and socioeconomic development. Thus, such education is recognized and encouraged for their very survival in a world under the control of Western societies. By means of such "modern education," people in non-Western societies may have been accustomed to expect that all humans are naturally bent toward *self-centered* development, growth, expansion or progress as emphasized by both Western and non-Western leaders, often with their hidden motivations and vested interests.

Even the modern development of technology, hinging generally on finding, inventing and collecting knowledge, however, has been mostly the product of historically and mutually antagonistic conditions experienced in Europe during modern times. Thus, such technological development cannot vouch for "human progress/development," contrary to certain self-righteous dogmatic belief. For, the conditioning through "modern education," very often, has implied that non-Western Cultures could be slighted, despised and destroyed, as a matter of course. Under the circumstances, the indigenous peoples themselves have been made party to the Cultural degradation so that it could proceed *irreversibly* or *irrevocably* to the detriment, at least, of their own personal maturation.

"Personality," being both Culture-based and person-specific, may mature, perhaps, only under favorable Cultural and socioeconomic environments, for "personality" *per se* may not be construed as "progressive" or "advancing" *a priori*. In that case, the general degrees of personal maturation cannot be compared inter-culturally or historically. It may not be far-fetched to say that Abraham Maslow (Gobble 1970) did not hypothesize on the progress of "personality" and/or "human nature" in his five-stage pyramid. If we happen to consider his hypothesis as referring to "personality," we must limit our interpretation of the hypothesis to the extent that it applies strictly to the chronological comparison of a specific person in a specific stable Culture with his/her material and spiritual needs as variables. Even this constrained interpretation cannot persuade all, since a normal person, as being much more complex than a linear chronological existence, may exhibit simultaneously two or more characteristics of Maslow's five stages. Professor Ayten Aydin rightly described the hypothesis as "Maslow's human behavior pyramid" in her elaboration and extension of Maslow's hypothesis (Aydin 2003).

Market Fundamentalism and Personal Maturation

If the above implied grasp of "personal development" is reasonable, the imitation of modern education by non-Western societies may only contribute over time to an expansion of new information and, perhaps, new knowledge *at the sacrifice of* the respective long-accumulated, indispensable Cultures. In the meantime, such an imitation may contribute little, either directly or indirectly, to personal maturation of the people. This may create serious problems to such societies over a long duration of time, as can be surmised from the conditions of the former colonies all over the world, where the indigenous people were neither completely wiped out nor almost totally replaced by new settlers as in USA, Canada and Australia. (Incidentally, I am not recommending or praising this type of colonization at all.) All the other former colonies seem to have serious *hangover* from their devastated or dilapidated Cultures. For, they lost their solid Cultural foundations, upon which their personal maturation, spiritual development, intellectual enhancement and human-capital formation had to be *firmly based*, for the effective interaction of such improvements as well as for mutual reinforcement and synergy effects.

To a great degree, however, almost all people and societies in the world are on board the "same boat" nowadays, since the market fundamentalism (Market), with its emancipation of lusts, selfishness and "now-orientation," has been trampling on almost all Cultures across the world. This implies that almost all children in the world may have been much less motivated to engage themselves in the *long-term endeavor* for knowledge accumulation, spiritual development, intellectual enhancement, and much less inclined for personal maturation. As a consequence, the so-called "infantization"or "robotization" of persons may have been encroaching on the human world, much faster and more intensively than normally expected from the thought of modern capitalism. The effects of materialism, individualism, egotism, antagonism, progress-oriented expansionism instigated by the pervasive Market, together with its sweeping attack on the diverse Cultures across the world, may have already "infantized" or "robotized" the people at large to lead only the *"short-run-oriented"* lifestyles. Worse still, without hope of personal maturity in the absence of firm Cultural foundations, they may have already been led only to accelerated instability, uncertainty and insecurity worldwide on the way to human-made *irreversible and unavoidable* disasters.

Own Culture and Personal Maturation

Our discussion may now require a brief review of the diagram on "thought-frame enhancement" shown in Figure 18.2 in the previous chapter. The diagram depicts that the flow from "innovative education" all the way to "behavior" and the feedback from "behavior" to "education" are both conducive to the enhancement of th personal and societal thought-frames. It, however, does not refer to the effect on personal maturation at all, for the implied relationship is naturally much more complex. One possible thread of connection to personal maturation, though non-linear, can be construed in terms of the changes in awareness, values, attitudes and behaviors via thought-frame enhancement and the feed-back effect of reinforced "personal" thought-frame. One's "personality" may mature through appropriate and holistic enhancement of personal awareness, values, attitudes, behaviors and thought-frame.

Such a channel of "personality" improvements alone, however plausible, may not guarantee their direct inducement to personal maturation, since any individual "personality" needs to be solidly based on the "own" Culture. Then, the aim of the Cultural restoration, reproduction and enrichment has to be intensively incorporated in educational innovations, so that the personal thought-frame enhancement incorporates the "own" Cultural enrichment, possibly to effect personal maturation. In other words, the process of strongly determined personal and societal endeavors for the sound enrichment of "own" Culture through educational innovations may become necessary for personal maturation.

The modern view, greatly biased toward the *"alleged"* universal phenomenon of "strictly rational and equal humanity," has often been asserted through modern thought and education, whereas most humans have been neither universalized nor standardized to show the "strictly rational and equal" tendency. Such a modern view can be taken generally as *fallacious* and even *disastrous* when it comes to personal maturation that must be both person-specific and "own" Culture-based. What we can do possibly for effecting the personal maturation of the social constituents, then, is to encourage and facilitate their collaborative endeavors for Comprehensive Human Development, by means of educational innovations that assert strongly the "own" Holistic Culture Enrichment.

Concluding Remarks

According to J. H. Randall, Jr, author of *The Making of the Modern Mind* (1976), human nature refers to a highly complex one of impulse, passion and emotional preference, not only of rationality. "Human nature, as plastic as it is, cannot be distorted too far or changed too suddenly without danger." Humans are social constituents, who live and develop in groups, and "what they are is largely a product of traditions and customs of the group" (or, a product of the "own Culture" in the present context). If his interpretation of human nature is still valid and reasonable, educational innovations which are conducive to enhancement of personal and societal thought-frames as well as to the restoration, reproduction and enrichment of the "own" respective Cultures may induce human development inclusive of personal maturation over time. In other words, only such educational innovations solidly based on the "own" Cultures may facilitate personal maturation.

Thus, it is time, and still not too late, that the governments of all nations, all international organizations and others concerned with the state of the world, heeding the policy implication hinted in the above, begin to collaborate and encourage global and local endeavors for the "own" Culture-based educational innovations that aim at the respective Comprehensive Human Development, as well as at the enrichment of the respective Cultures. For, the "on-going" deprivation and dilapidation of our "own" diverse Cultures may amount to *a total denial* of our own respective "personality" and our possible personal maturation. To be realistic, we cannot move into the "Maturation Process" in our socioeconomic development without the personal maturation of our social constituents at large. This is the reason why such Culture-embraced personal maturation is important for Comprehensive Human Development, Balanced Socioeconomic Development and Holistic Culture Enrichment and, hence, for the global issues of Sustainable Development, Culture of Peace and Global Humanity.

4 *Methodology for Sustainability*

In Part 4, I will discuss the institutional and methodological implications for Sustainable Development. First, I will deal with a functional guideline for the integral approach to Sustainable Development (Chapter 20). Next, the Optimal Development Path will be discussed in view of the stabilization of "worldwide social cost" (Chapter 21). Then, the worldwide "unitary rate" value-added environment tax will be examined as supplement to the main engine—general human spirit and will—for working Sustainable Development. In view of this connection, I will also discuss a prototype of a global governance system for Sustainable Development (Chapter 22). Further, I will argue for a viable Culture-enhancing employment system (Chapter 23). Next, I will elaborate on a viable long-term theory of international trade that harmoniously integrates and enriches diverse Cultures and the prospective global community (Chapter 24). Lastly, I will propose the synchronous "local-and-global campaigns" for Sustainable Development on the basis of the dynamic enrichment of diverse Cultures (Chapter 25).

20 *Functional Approaches to Sustainability*

In view of the integral approach to theory, strategy and global governance system, I will now discuss a functional guideline for the multi-dimensional proposal that combines Cultural, educational, legal and systemic approaches to Sustainable Development. For these multiple approaches to be most effective, they must all fit into one another to constitute one coherent integral process and methodology. This indicates an assumption relevant to various synergistic interactions of the respective approaches. Such a methodology may, indeed, give rise to many favorable synergy effects, as well as greater functional effectiveness at a much lower cost over time. For this purpose, I will introduce in this chapter an appropriate guideline for the integral methodology.

Strategic Environment and Cultures

IMPORTANT FACTORS RELEVANT TO THE INTEGRAL METHODOLOGY

The purpose of this chapter is to discuss a functional guideline for the multi-dimensional approach to Sustainable Development, emphasizing the integral methodology. To begin with, a comprehensive long-term theory of Sustainable Development is a *must* as the normative basis for creating a coherent strategic environment and global governance system. Second, the necessity of such a strategic environment for Sustainable Development is assumed to be of humanities-enhancing nature compatible with the sound enrichment of diverse Cultures across the world. In other words, the strategic environment must encompass policies for fair learning, fair role sharing, fair cost sharing, fair employment and fair international trade, based on the constant enrichment of diverse Cultures (as discussed in Chapter 9).

A third point is to indicate the necessity of an integral, flexible and transparent system of global governance that is devoted specific to Sustainable Development and the closely related issues, such as Culture of Peace and Global Humanity. Such a governance system must cater to a wide spectrum of both the short-term and long-term needs/interests in the prospective global community. A final point refers to the requirement of coherence among such a theory, strategic environment and governance system conducive simultaneously to Sustainable Development, Culture of Peace and Global Humanity for their integral development.

Accordingly, the present chapter emphasizes the necessity of the sound and diverse Cultural enrichment for Sustainable Development. In this respect, it is important to deal with the question of neglected or devastated diverse Cultures. Such diverse

Cultures have suffered from severe degradation by the awesome force of the Market, which, being antagonistic to the diametrically opposite nature of diverse Cultures, has aggressively exploited and trampled on them. Thus, the present discussion stresses the necessity for counter-balancing the ferocious force of the Market, by means of restoration and enrichment of the diverse Cultures across the world. Based on this premise, I will deal with the combination of Cultural, educational, legal and systemic approaches to Sustainable Development. These four functional approaches may naturally have their favorable effects, respectively, and, when put together, the most desirable *synergy effects* on the promotion of Sustainable Development.

Four Functional Approaches

CULTURAL APPROACH

The present functional approaches to Sustainable Development consist of Cultural Approach, Educational Approach, Legal Approach and Systemic Approach. The definition and characterization of the society-specific cultures (Cultures) have direct relevance when discussing the Cultural Approach. For the sake of *conscious and earnest* worldwide endeavors for the sound enrichment of diverse Cultures, this approach aims at working for the *sound Cultural common grounds* (or "sound communal value systems" of the respective Sound Cultures)—the long-term harmonious and integral value systems—in favor of Sustainable Development. Put differently, the promotion of Sustainable Development is sought on the basis of each and every society's balanced socioeconomic development, assuming that such development is inevitably linked with Cultural enrichment.

Also, the Cultural Approach seeks a roundabout effect of Cultural enrichment through market activities, assuming that the "sound-and-fair market function" be gradually incorporated into diverse Cultures. Such an integral effect may naturally be conducive to the worldwide *socioeconomic transformation* in favor of Sustainable Development. Sustainable Development, promoted through the worldwide enrichment of diverse Cultures that *ameliorate* the acrimonious Market, perhaps, is the last resort left for the re-humanization of human societies. Such re-humanization is particularly important, in view of the on-going Market-driven globalization pushing the explosive *disparity-animosity spiral* to the detriment of a viable human future.

Moreover, Market-driven globalization has been accompanied by the vicious circle of the Market mindset, comprising the degradation of humanities, the devastation of diverse Cultures and the destruction of the Environment, thus working entirely and increasingly against Sustainable Development. Then, the *conscious and earnest* enrichment of diverse Cultures is not only indispensable for Sustainable Development but also most effective to end the Market-invited explosive vicious circle. Such Cultural enrichment may also promote appropriate human-capital formation, human-character building and human thought-frame enhancement in the respective societies. All such aspects of human development, indeed, are conducive to the worldwide *socioeconomic transformation* in favor of Sustainable Development. They have a strong relevance to the Balanced Socioeconomic Development of each and every society as well as to the protection and improvement of the Environment.

EDUCATIONAL APPROACH

Our Educational Approach has a particular relevance to such Cultural enrichment, for the most essential and intrinsic function of education in any long-endured society is the *reproduction* of the own Cultures and the *sound communal value system*. Such a reproduction process of Culture also plays an important role in Comprehensive Human Development. The function of education, therefore, is indispensable for Cultural reproduction and sound human development, as well as for nurturing the long-term future orientation of the social constituents. Each Culture may consistently connect the past, present and future of the relevant society through the sound process of Cultural enrichment. Thus, the Educational Approach must promote the sound enrichment of diverse Cultures across the world, mobilizing formal education, community education, family education and a "virtual" variety of education to produce versatile and effective educational activities for Cultural reproduction as well as for the worldwide *socioeconomic transformation* toward Sustainable Development. Then, the Educational Approach must seek not only a steady reform in school systems and curricula but also many innovations in the various forms of education.

The Educational Approach, indeed, requires an innovative education for integrating and harmonizing the general lifestyles with the respective Cultures. It also requires an innovative education to harmoniously integrate the human "spiritual and material" needs, based on the reinforced long-term future orientation and perspectives. Further, this approach requires an innovative education to promote appropriate spiritual, intellectual and aesthetic environments and rectify the "prevailing rational, efficient and reductionist" environments. Furthermore, it requires the worldwide educational encouragement for food, clothing and shelter to be harmonious with the respective peoples, Cultures and the Environment.

Still further, it requires innovative education to discourage excessive material and pecuniary wants and encourage more heart-warming, compassionate and relational needs. Moreover, our Educational Approach requires an appropriate education that promotes the long-term perspectives, principles and policies for the worldwide *socioeconomic transformation*. Broadly speaking, the purpose of this approach is for the freeing of people from the shackles of the materially biased and convenience-seeking lifestyles of "egotist and short-run" nature: that is, a *general emancipation* from the Market.

LEGAL APPROACH

A third agenda item relates to our Legal Approach, which is intended to create the legal framework for the promotion of Sustainable Development on the basis of the politico-legal principle—*Integrity* in Diversity—of *open democracy* (discussed in Chapter 10). Such a legal framework, by the very nature of Sustainable Development, must be of the "supranational" kind firmly based on the *sound common grounds* (or sound communal value systems) of diverse Cultures. Such a "supranational" framework must encompass a wide spectrum of levels, for example, from the grassroots of the individual-volunteer level to the collective national level and to the broad globalized level. The term "supranational" framework here refers to the legal framework superseding the respective national constitutions and other legal canons for the sake of the worldwide *socioeconomic transformation* based on the *sound common grounds* of diverse Cultures. Thus, the term "supranational" framework refers to the legal framework that directly guides the authorities of nations, states, prefectures and municipalities, as well as the leaders of firms, civic groups and the general public of the respective societies, for the process toward Sustainable Development.

Such a "supranational" legal framework requires the delegation of substantial national power to the "supranational organization" and also to the states, prefectures and municipalities of the respective nations for the global-and-local promotion of Sustainable Development. Thus, the legal framework must provide broad and general content of a highly persuasive nature capable of withstanding the scrutiny of national ratification procedures. Moreover, such content must be most appropriate and effective for the worldwide *socioeconomic transformation* toward Sustainable Development, including the broad measures for enriching the diverse Cultures as well as for educational reforms and innovations. Also, the legal framework must be broadly binding upon all the public and private entities across the world, as well as providing an effective means against violation. Further, the legal framework must provide for the functions and authorities to pursue Sustainable Development, as well as to provide the ways and means to the "supranational organization" appropriate for the functions and authorities.

SYSTEMIC APPROACH

Lastly, but not least important, our Systemic Approach deals with the "supranational organization" and its systemic network for the global-and-local promotion of Sustainable Development. It is quite obvious that the "supranational organization" alone can have only limited effects, without the general support of the diverse peoples who are well aware and convinced of the *sound Cultural common grounds* (namely, the long-term harmonious and integral communal value systems) of diverse Cultures. Such organization necessitates the Culture-connected general support of and commitment from national governments, state-and-local authorities, firms and civic organizations as well as the general public of the respective societies/nations. Such diverse parties of the support network, consisting of all public and private entities, are normally connected by the respective dynamic Cultures.

This implies that the Systemic Approach must address the question of how to create worldwide coherent awareness and consciousness of *sound Cultural common grounds* (or sound communal value systems) among the parties concerned of the support network for the systemic collaboration with the "supranational organization." In order to be effective to and responsible for the promotion of Sustainable Development, the "supranational organization" must also have within itself the credible legislative, administrative and judiciary functions and authorities, *unbiased* as much as practicable, to diverse Cultures, societies/nations, politico-economic backgrounds, racial-ethnic-sex-age groups and religious creeds (see "Global Governance Systems for Sustainability" in Chapter 22).

For such functions and authorities, the "supranational organization" must have its versatile structure and capacity, which primarily cater to the existing diverse Cultures and their sound enrichment for Sustainable Development. Thus, the "supranational organization," through its versatile structure and capacity, must encourage the respective societal/national initiatives for sound Cultural enrichment and the Balanced Socioeconomic Development. Such "supranational organizations," in their policy guidance to the national-prefectural-municipal authorities, must take into consideration the levels and characteristics relevant to the socioeconomic development of the respective societies, their histories and customs, their sizes and ethnic composition of populations and their geographic, climatic and environmental conditions.

In order to have the "supranational organization" checked regularly for its appropriateness and effectiveness, it must also have the credible external entities to inspect and audit regularly. Further, it must interact directly and indirectly with the above-mentioned public and private entities for the constant, mutual and viable feed-forward and feed-back effects. Furthermore, the "supranational organization" must have an appropriate role-sharing structure with the international organizations, national governments, local authorities, non-government organizations and private corporations for the most effective *socioeconomic transformation* in favor of Sustainable Development.

Concluding Remarks: Concerted Approach

As explained above, the Cultural Approach to Sustainable Development emphasizes the sound enrichment of diverse Cultures across the world. Such Cultural enrichment by itself implies a concerted endeavor for the Comprehensive Human Development and Balanced Socioeconomic Development, which stimulates a long-term future orientation of the social constituents relevant to each and every society. Such a Culture-enriching approach can be linked closely with the Educational Approach, which recognizes the intrinsic educational function as the dynamic "cultural reproduction," aiming at sound Cultural enrichment in each society. Such a Cultural reproduction process must also aim at providing a solid foundation for Comprehensive Human Development and reinforce the *long-term society-general future orientation* in favor of Sustainable Development. These approaches, when supported by the Legal Approach with a binding "supranational" legal framework (that is based on the *sound common grounds* of the diverse Cultures), may no doubt multiply the total effectiveness.

Such a legal framework must provide for the creation of the "supranational organization" and its ways and means. This is where the Systemic Approach comes in. The versatile "supranational organization" and its network of collaboration with the existing public and private sectors across the world may have to strive for forming and harmonizing broad and worldwide policies for Sustainable Development on the basis of a broad theoretical framework. Thus, all the four approaches may definitely require one another for many a favorable synergy effect and become most effective when they constitute one integral multi-dimensional approach. It is now important to combine all such theoretical framework, strategic environment and global governance system with the functional guideline relevant to the coherent Cultural, educational, legal and systemic approaches. Simplistic as it is, the present functional guideline is meant to aim at the coherence of the components to acquire general understanding, conscious collaborations and earnest support for the sustainability of the prospective global community.

21 *Social-Cost Stability for Sustainability*

Sustainable Development will be discussed here in terms the logical and global consequences of Balanced Socioeconomic Development in each society. This theoretical discussion will make the assumption that such development interacts constantly in a "virtuous circle" with Holistic Culture Enrichment and Comprehensive Human Development. Based on this assumption, I will suggest that such virtuous and integral development in each society, and all over the world, may provide a stabilizing tendency in the overall deterioration of the global environment (Environment). This tendency can provide a consistent influence on the "worldwide social cost." In other words, a great variety of balanced development, based on the sound enrichment of the respective Cultures, can gradually contain and stabilize the current explosive "worldwide social cost."

Balanced Socioeconomic Development

Given the divergent conditions of contemporary societies all over the world, it is impossible to imagine a situation where all societies move automatically in unison in favor of Sustainable Development. Thus, I will suggest here an alternative way to Sustainable Development, where each society seeks Balanced Socioeconomic Development at its own speed and style. Such balanced development here indicates development on the basis of balanced short-and-long-term needs, consisting of balanced material-and-spiritual, personal-and-societal, and traditional-and-progressive needs. All these balanced needs of each society are closely related to reasonably sound Culture. In order to justify this alternative avenue, we must show, at least theoretically, that Sustainable Development is a global process consequential to Balanced Socioeconomic Development in each and every society, despite the different processes in speed and style of the diverse societies.

This theoretical discussion assumes the condition that each society's Balanced Socioeconomic Development interacts in a "virtuous circle" with the sound enrichment of society-specific culture (Holistic Culture Enrichment) and the comprehensive development of its human constituents (Comprehensive Human Development). The term Holistic Culture Enrichment here indicates sound Cultural enrichment. The term Comprehensive Human Development reflects a general improvement in the thought-frame, personality, spirituality and capacity of the human constituents in the relevant society.

With such compounded development in each and every society, the global world may find a stabilizing tendency in the overall deterioration of the broadly defined global environment (Environment). Such stabilizing tendency in the Environment may provide a consistent influence on the "worldwide social cost" relevant to the balanced global socioeconomic development. In other words, a great variety of Balanced Socioeconomic Development respective to diverse societies, interacting in a "virtuous circle" with the holistic enrichment of the respective Cultures and the comprehensive development of the respective human constituents, may be able to stabilize over time the rate of increase in the "worldwide social cost," both apparent and hidden. In short, I will argue that such a balanced worldwide socioeconomic development can usher in the age of Sustainable Development.

Theoretical Explanation of Balanced Development

BOW-SHAPED OPTIMAL DEVELOPMENT PATH

In a nutshell, the theoretical construct of a society's Value Aspect being constantly equated with the Real Aspects offers the basis for the simplified diagram of the Optimal Development Path (ODP). Figure 21.1 depicts the generalized "bow-shaped" ODP in the two-dimensional setting with the Trend Preference Rate (T) on the vertical axis (Axis T) and the Trend Interest Rate (r) on the horizontal axis (Axis r), with the intermediary 45-degree ray (Ray). The Ray, indicating the parity between T and r in its entire range, may represent the fiction that the *economy-specific* future orientation always converges on the *society-general* future orientation. The bow-like ODP dismisses the fiction that implies the "economic *risk-free* development" with no extra "social cost." A gradual conversion,

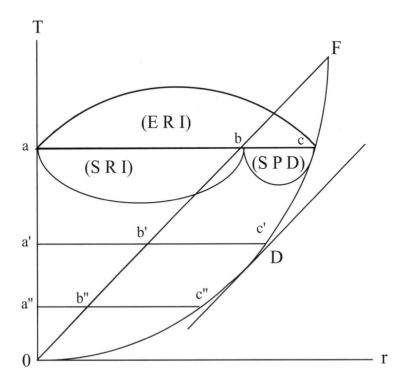

Figure 21.1 Optimal Development Path and social cost

however, may take place in the Maturation Process (D-O on ODP), implying that the maturation of the social constituents invites the gradual stabilization of the overall "social cost." Such overall "social cost" may include both paid and unpaid costs, which arise from the so-called "economic development."

The slope of the ODP at Point D refers to the slope of the Ray, indicating that the change in T equals the change in r only at that particular point on ODP. The process of Balanced Socioeconomic Development—downward movement on the ODP—can be interpreted into two positive development phases of the Growth Process (F-D) and the Maturation Process (D-O). For the present purpose, the two phases of positive development are considered relevant in view of Sustainable Development. The Growth Process starts from Point F and ends at Point D (the Growth-Maturation turning point), while the Maturation Process starts from Point D and ends somewhere in the vicinity of Point O.

Optimal Development Path and Worldwide Social Cost

ECONOMIC RISK-TAKING AS AN EXTRA SOCIAL COST

A particular horizontal distance between the specific point on Axis T (or specific value of T, such as a, a', a") and the corresponding point on the ODP (or the specific value of r, such as c, c', c") is assumed to show the "analogical" rate of increase in the *overall cost* of development. The particular horizontal gap between the Ray and the ODP (or the rate of the Social Premium of Development (SPD) at that particular point on the ODP, such as bc, b'c', b"c") is assumed here to represent the marginal rate of increase in the "social cost" of development at the particular point on the ODP. The particular gap can be interpreted here simply to show an *extra burden* on the Environment over time, due to the new development activities that necessarily require an extra cost of the *economic risk-taking*. Such risk-taking, in turn, is assumed here to impose the risk-equivalent "social cost" (in terms of resources) on the relevant society that pursues Balanced Socioeconomic Development. Then, such an extra "social cost," as an analogy, may impose an extra load on the Environment and the prospective global community.

The extra rate of increase in the "social cost" is assumed incurred when an appropriate amount of extra profits (in terms of resources) is extracted (eventually) from the finite Environment as the relevant incentive for *economic risk-taking* (for further socioeconomic development). Depending upon the history, political condition, geographical location, climate, security and natural resources, all different societies may encounter their respective costs of *economic risk-taking* at their respective points of development processes and, hence, their different depths (or different concavities) of the bow-shaped diverse ODPs. For the moment, such differences are *ignored* for our rough global generalization as well as for simplicity of our present diagrammatic exposition. I am interested here only in the *tendency of overall increase* in the "worldwide social cost:" that is, whether it implies *stabilizing* or *exploding*.

OVERALL SOCIAL COST AND EXTRA SOCIAL COST

As seen from the diagram, the overall analogical "social cost" (measured horizontally by r, for the present purpose) may increase at a decreasing rate throughout the positive development on the ODP. The growth of the analogical *extra* "social-cost" relevant to *economic risk-taking* for a further development, shown by the horizontal gap (between the Ray and the ODP at each relevant point on the ODP), expands rapidly from Point F (no gap) in the Growth Process and becomes maximal at Point D. Such a gap, however, starts shrinking rapidly in the Maturation Process (D-O) that is the most relevant process for Sustainable Development. This implies that, if all or most societies in the world move into the Maturation Process, the extra "worldwide social cost" may increase at a decreasing rate.

STABILIZATION OF WORLDWIDE SOCIAL COST

Such a worldwide movement into the Maturation Process is the *necessary* condition for the eventual stabilization of the "worldwide social cost" but not the *sufficient* condition. In order to achieve the *sufficient* condition, humankind must change and mature personally and spiritually through constant Comprehensive Human Development, for such human development alone can accomplish the sound and balanced socioeconomic development. The constant human development in each society, as a matter of course, requires a sound Cultural foundation. This is the very reason why the paradigm shift for the perpetual sound enrichment of diverse Cultures across the world is a *must* (sufficient condition) for accomplishing Sustainable Development.

Constant Comprehensive Human Development can help draw the bow-like ODP closer to the Ray, which implies the *changing concavity* of the ODP. This also implies two things: one reflecting a diminished importance of the SPD as a development incentive, and the other reflecting a likely quickened movement into the Maturation Process. Both of these effects of such Comprehensive Human Development on development processes may imply the stabilizing tendency of the overall "social cost." These effects and consequences on worldwide socioeconomic development may imply an enhanced Culture of Peace and Global Humanity. Such Comprehensive Human Development based on the sound enrichment of diverse Cultures across the world may bring forth worldwide peace, compassion, tolerance, future orientation, mutual understanding and collaborative consciousness, to constantly reduce the *risk factors*.

The Global Optimal Development Path and the Analogical World

Using the above diagram, Figure 21.1, I will now depict the three groups of societies on the same ODP (ignoring the different concavities of the respective groups, for simplicity) as representing our "analogical world," namely, Groups C, C' and C" located at the respective Points (c), (c') and (c") on the analogical "global ODP," assuming all the societies are pursuing their respective Balanced Socioeconomic Development. In the present analogical scheme, Group C" at Point (c") has already moved beyond Point D into the Maturation Process, while Group C' has just reached Point (c') and Group C at Point

(c) has been much behind but moving rapidly away from Point F. The horizontal gap between the Ray and the ODP for Group C' is the largest among the three groups and is still expanding, and the gap for Group C is much smaller than the case of Group C' but gradually expanding. The gap for Group C" is greater than the case of Group C but it is now steadily shrinking.

We may interpret from this analogical exposition that the extra "worldwide social cost" can be made to stabilize over time, so long as all societies are pursuing Balanced Socioeconomic Development and Comprehensive Human Development on the basis of on-going Holistic Culture Enrichment. Under such conditions, we may expect a variety of appropriate changes in the components of the Environment (natural, cultural, institutional, technological, humanitarian and peaceful environments) over such development on the ODP to work mutually for stabilizing the overall deterioration of the Environment. If all or most societies in the world follow their ODPs strictly in the same positive direction, the stabilizing tendency may prove to be continuous. If the global ODP is drawing closer to the Ray over time through constant worldwide Comprehensive Human Development, the prospects may be brighter.

Concluding Remarks

The above theoretical discussion of stabilizing tendency as regards the "worldwide social cost" is based on a rough and loose analogical interpretation of the *extra* "social cost" (for further development) increasing at a decreasing rate in the Maturation Process, supported by constant worldwide Comprehensive Human Development. Such worldwide human development, also conducive to the worldwide population stabilization and decrease, can reduce the extra burden relevant to the "worldwide social cost" attributed to further socioeconomic development. Although such a discussion captures neither the complex totality of "worldwide social cost" nor the specific reality of the world surrounding us, the theoretical exposition, as rough and loose as it is, may at least indicate the *appropriate direction* as regards our necessary endeavors for Sustainable Development. It can never be overstressed here that the sound and perpetual enrichment of diverse Cultures, being incorporated into the respective peoples, can induce their *sound communal value systems* for Balanced Socioeconomic Development. A *corollary* of the present argument is that any international development-and-environment assistance must shift its aim and tenet to supporting the "trilateral virtuous circle" of Holistic Culture Enrichment, Comprehensive Human Development and Balanced Socioeconomic Development in each recipient society.

22 *The Main and Supplementary Wheels for Sustainability*

The New Enlightenment places a strong emphasis on the freeing of all peoples and societies from the shackles of both the market fundamentalism (Market) and the scientific fundamentalism (Scientism). It also emphasizes the long-term worldwide campaign and collaborative endeavor for personal, spiritual and intellectual development across the world in order to bring the common and constructive traits of diverse Cultures into play. Therefore, the most important function of the New Enlightenment is to encourage the restoration and sound enrichment of diverse Cultures across the world. The effect of such a worldwide endeavor to gather fruit, however, may influence too slowly to alleviate the suffering of many of our fellow humans and avoid the irreversible devastation of the broadly defined global environment (Environment).

The "market approach," together with the "scientific approach," is reinforcing an output-and-consumption growth that is too rapid, in the face of severe constraints on the environment and resources. This is the reason why the main wheel of *human will and spirit*—the "voluntary" wheel of conscious initiative—needs to be reinforced by a supplementary wheel of "compulsory" policy endeavors for Sustainable Development. In this chapter I will elaborate on such policy endeavors, paying particular attention to the desirability of a unitary "global value-added environment tax" with the relevant expenditure policy.

The Main Wheel: Human Will and Spirit

MODERN TWIN ALTER EGOS: MARKET AND SCIENTISM

Modern capitalism with its twin "alter egos"—the market fundamentalism (Market) and the science fundamentalism (Scientism)—has emphasized, among other things, material above mind, human above nature, greed above life, liberty above security, individual above society, short term above long term, quantity above quality, change above continuity, flow above stock, revolution above evolution, progress above tradition, competition above cooperation, and exploitation above conservation. Thus, our challenge for Sustainable Development is certainly an awesome task against the powerful Market of "modern greed-propelled material monoculture" based on the "might-makes-right" ideology.

The other of the twin "alter egos"—the Scientism—or the so-called "scientific approach" has ignored, consciously or unconsciously, the symbiotic and holistic existence of nature and humanity. Viewed retrospectively, in its innate attempt, the Scientism has endeavored to subjugate nature to mankind, often, with its arrogant, shallow, partial, short-sighted, unbalanced, improvident, radical, sloppy or marginal knowledge. This "scientific approach," together with the "market approach," has not only devastated the natural environment but also led, over time, the great majority of humans to misery, instability, uncertainty and insecurity, leaving them impoverished, dehumanized, apathetic, disappointed, discontented, embittered and/or despairing. Such an incontinent development has been pursued under the explosive "emancipation of lusts" by both the "market approach" and the "scientific approach" for the sake of the contemporary power structure—the Big Market.

HUMAN WILL AND SPIRIT FOR SUSTAINABILITY

Of late, however, we sense a steady surge of *human will and spirit* for Sustainable Development. This favorable surge has been accompanied by the reflection on the consequence of such "lust emancipation" as well as by the repentance on the imprudent adoption of "market approach" and "scientific approach." Such *human will and spirit* must no doubt constitute the main wheel for Sustainable Development, which still needs to be encouraged and nurtured by tenacious and untiring endeavors across the world. Such *will and spirit* may need to be accompanied by an earnest wish to replace the imprudent modern lifestyle with a viable alternative. Such an alternative may have to be compatible with the decent livelihood of all people as well as with the severe global constraints on the environment and resources. Also, such *will and spirit* needs to be supported by the keen awareness that the egotist "free-market competition" for the endless pursuit of material abundance and convenience cannot pave the way for a harmonious, comfortable and decent life for all humankind.

There is also a steady surge of awareness that modern capitalism, however pervasive it might be, cannot persuade all people into following the values, rules and methods prescribed only by the one-sided historical and cultural momentum of modern societies. Such an emerging awareness, together with the New Enlightenment, may point to the importance of integrating the *common and constructive cultural traits* widely shared by diverse Cultures. Here, the term "New Enlightenment" may mean the evolving quest for a viable human future, freeing all people and societies from the shackles of the modern "alter egos" (Market and Scientism) and encouraging sound Cultural enrichment and human development for Sustainable Development.

Global Value-Added Tax

Our theoretical framework of Sustainable Development is formulated mainly to emphasize the importance of *human will and spirit* based on the strong orientation to the future for accomplishing Balanced Socioeconomic Development in each society as well as in the prospective global community. Such *will and spirit* need to be encouraged and nurtured in the process of the paradigm shift which emphasizes the perpetual and sound enrichment of diverse Cultures across the world. In order to assist the properly directed *human will and spirit*, we may need a well-coordinated supplementary wheel that can accelerate the global process toward Sustainable Development. Such a supplementary wheel—a unitary rate environment tax on all the value-added across the world—may have an important role to play in conveying the message of just and equitable collaboration, by avoiding the insinuation of "bullying" or "witch hunting."

SUPPLEMENTARY WHEEL: GLOBAL FISCAL POLICY

The supplementary wheel may become an extra driving force when the message is substantiated by an earnest and trustworthy "global fiscal policy." The term "global fiscal policy" here indicates the policy of one-rate global value-added tax, together with the relevant policy of expenditure. The global fiscal policy must contribute simultaneously to global environment conservation and Balanced Socioeconomic Development, particularly in favor of under-privileged people and societies. Such a policy scheme will be discussed here to illustrate the long-term favorable effects upon both human livelihood and the global environment. As the term taxation implies, it is the *one-rate tax* to be collected from both natural and legal persons across the world at each stage of value-added for market transactions.

One serious drawback of the tax scheme to be pointed out at the outset is that so-called "value-added tax" is currently practiced only by a minority of nations, such as the ones in the European Union. This implies a nomenclatural unfamiliarity. Another drawback is the difficulty in calculating an appropriate *unitary* tax rate. To a great extent, such a tax rate depends on the initial scope of policy endeavors that are aimed at accomplishing Sustainable Development. Also, once determined, the rate of global unitary tax may have to be changed over time, according to the changing conditions of the global environment as well as changing human needs. Further, there are so many unknowns surrounding the global issue (Sustainable Development) that the process of "trial and error" adjustment may be both inevitable and advisable. Thus, it is appropriate to begin with a rounded figure such as *one percent* of all the value-added all over the world. With such a tax rate, we can expect the revenue to be no less than US$600 billion, given the rounded world GDP of US$60 trillion a year. Such a huge amount per year may allow for a variety of meaningful global-policy endeavors for Sustainable Development.

MERITS OF ONE-RATE GLOBAL ENVIRONMENTAL TAX

In comparison to the few drawbacks outlined above, there are numerous merits to adopting the "one-rate global value-added tax." First, the tax system can collect a great amount of revenue with a relatively *light burden* (thinly spread burden) to each natural and legal person, by asking all producers (and eventually all consumers), irrespective of the "advanced" and the "developing" nations, to contribute according to their output. Second, the proposed *one-rate tax* on value-added for market transactions, implying roughly the same rate of increase in the *production cost* everywhere, does not seem to distort international trade much. Third, by asking all producers of natural and legal persons directly or indirectly for such a reasonable contribution, the environment tax may theoretically cultivate in almost all persons a sense of mutual responsibility, collaborative consciousness and solidarity for the common good—Sustainable Development.

Fourth, such a value-added tax may theoretically encourage all producers to *avoid waste* in resource use and improve productivity, as well as all consumers to favor quality more than quantity for a *longer and tender product use* ("a better product for a longer use") when it comes to both capital goods and consumer durables. Fifth, in view of current mainstream products that combine hardware, software and service under the on-going "new international division of labor," which encourages the firms and workers of the advanced and the developing nations to collaborate for joint production, the one-rate value-added tax induces, theoretically, all these nations to assume *joint responsibility* both for production and the environment.

Sixth, the on-going shift in the comparative advantage of the advanced nations *to* the so-called "service" industries (including financial, insurance, patent and franchise services) can be deemed a result of the progression from their heavy and/or chemical industrialization, a period which polluted and devasted the Enviroment, exploiting worldwide resources for too long. Then, the same tax rate on the high value-added "services" of the advanced nations can be considered *reasonable* from a "historical" viewpoint, despite the production of "services" generally polluting the natural environment less than the production of "goods."

Seventh, the one-rate tax across the world can theoretically be collected from all *multinational corporations*, even if some of them have a habit of practicing the so-called "transfer price" for the evasion of profit-and-income taxes. Finally, with the end of the "cold war" as well as with the acceleration of the so-called "economic globalization," the newly formed structure of *international interdependence* has theoretically reduced the obstacles of non-cooperation, indifference and a free ride. As a result, the taxable area now encompasses almost all the countries in the world.

Appropriate Use of the Tax Revenue

The system of *one-rate value-added tax* can be considered *fair and reasonable* as explained above and also *appropriate* for the sustainability of global community, as it can collect a large amount of revenue from high value-added producers (individuals, firms and nations) and a smaller amount of revenue from low value-added ones. The tax system can become even more appropriate for the promotion of Sustainable Development if the tax revenue is used to help encourage a constructive human collaboration, solidarity and coordination for the common good, continuous reduction of the North-South gap in income and wealth, two-way initiative and understanding between Western and non-Western societies, and an enhanced environment of peace and harmony within and among all societies.

Some concrete examples of potential expenditure may, to begin with, include the one on ecosystem conservation. Second, another important expenditure could be on the educational project to reorient and redirect the general public, particularly of the industrially advanced nations, to seek alternative thoughts, attitudes and lifestyles compatible with the severe global constraints. Third, the tax revenue could be fruitfully spent on the restoration and sound enrichment of diverse society-specific cultures (Cultures) to stop the "vicious circle" between the poverty and the population explosion of the "Culture-devastated" societies (largely the victims of the past colonialism/imperialism and the contemporary subjugation by the economic globalization). Fourth, the tax revenue could be best spent on encouraging the *trilateral virtuous circle* of Holistic Culture Enrichment, Comprehensive Human Development and Balanced Socioeconomic Development in each and every society. Fifth, the tax spending could aim at encouraging the harmonious integration of common positive and constructive traits of diverse Cultures (comprising *sound communal value systems*) for the promotion of Sustainable Development.

Sixth, the "global fiscal policy" could subsidize the *long-term, non-profit* endeavors for viable technological innovation ("sound creativity") that economize on non-renewable resources and/or improve productivity in all resource use, creating a steady reduction of the environmental load in production. Seventh, the tax revenue could be effectively spent on encouraging the research endeavors that address the preventive policy of Environment deterioration as well as the sweeping reform for the protection of the natural environment, in particular. Finally, long-term continuous support can be provided by expenditure on *non-profit, non-government* endeavors for improving peaceful, humanitarian and cultural environments for all people. These examples of tax uses refer only to the obvious and broad categories among many other policy potentials. Most importantly, all such expenditures need to be effectively coordinated and prioritized over time for the promotion of Sustainable Development.

Diagrammatic Explanation of Global Fiscal Policy

Based on the assumed introduction of the "value-added environment tax" and the relevant expenditures, I will now attempt to explain their broad theoretical implications on global demand and supply, as well as on global economic development and Environment protection, as shown in Figure 22.1. The upper section of the diagram (above the origin) shows the standard explanation that compares the changes of the global aggregate demand and supply in terms of the global Gross Domestic Product (GDP) (G), shown on the horizontal axis, as well as in terms of the relevant price levels (P), shown on the vertical axis. The diagram in the lower section (below the origin) indicates the curve of environment cost (E), which relates directly the sum of the environment tax revenue (T), shown on the vertical axis, to the respective global GDP (G) on the horizontal axis.

The initial demand and supply curves are indicated by Do and So, respectively, in the upper section of the diagram (above the origin), and the environment-cost curve Eo on the lower section (below the origin). At the intersection (X) between Do and So, we find the most simplistic global GDP (Go) and the related price level (Po), on the assumption that all markets in the world are functioning appropriately. Now, the introduction of the curve for the environment cost (Eo) that is not usually accounted for in the most simplistic analysis shifts the supply curve to SEo. Such an introduction of environmental cost points to a new intersection (A), which indicates the resultant lower GDP (Go') and higher price level (Po'). Based on this result, the simplistic "*development*" protagonist may take a negative stance to the environment protection, while the simplistic "*conservation*" protagonist may argue that such an economic drawback should be tolerated for the sake of conserving the global environment.

Our theoretical argument, however, *does not* cater to *either* of the above two simplistic arguments, for we think that the economic development does not have to suffer at all even in the "short run" as the result of accounting for the environment cost. Along with the supply shift to SEo, the demand also shifts to Do* with the additional expenditure

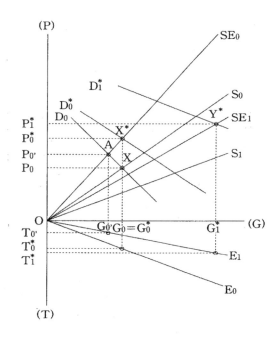

Figure 22.1 Global value-added tax and development

equivalent to the tax revenue (To*). Thus, the GDP now indicates the one (Go*), which is equivalent to the initial GDP (Go). In other words, the "short-run" equilibrium is achieved at the new intersection (Xo*) between the demand curve (Do*) and the supply curve (SEo), indicating the GDP (Go = Go*). The global price level, however, rises to Po* (including 1 percent value-added tax) in the "short run," reflecting the *new value system* pertinent to Sustainable Development, which properly recognizes and internalizes the environmental cost of the economic development.

Over the long duration of time, the environment-cost curve may shift from Eo to E1, reflecting a reduction of the environment load and cost as well as the downward adjustment of the "unitary tax rate." Such a change can be realized by the enhanced *will and spirit* for Sustainable Development as well as with the policy effects both of the environment tax and the equivalent expenditure. In the meantime, the global GDP expands to the new level (G1*) at the new intersection (Y*). This long-term "global fiscal policy" may imply a further shift (reducing the unitary tax rate) of the environment-cost curve along with the GDP growth that is based on Comprehensive Human Development, reflecting the restoration and sound enrichment of diverse Cultures across the world. This, indeed, indicates a potential process toward Sustainable Development.

Global Governance Systems for Sustainability

The above supplementary wheel (the "global fiscal policy") may imply the necessity of a "supranational organization" empowered with the taxation and expenditure. Whether we like it or not, we will need an appropriate global governance system for such a "global fiscal policy" that implies the presence of a highly integrated, flexible and transparent system of global governance for Sustainable Development. Such a "supranational" global governance system in a simplified example, in essence, consists of four closely interacting components, namely, Deliberative Body of law-making and budgetary competence (D), Generality-oriented Commission (G), Particularity-oriented Commission (P), and Court of Arbitration and Justice (J). The mutual relationship of the four components can be depicted as in Figure 22.2 (Hiwaki 2001c).

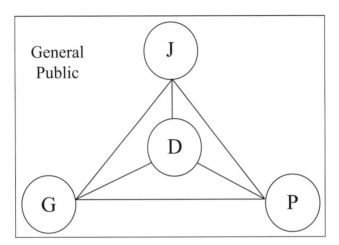

Figure 22.2 Global governance system

Conceptually speaking, such a governance system must be a dynamic and flexible one as well as an organic whole. In other words, its components must interact constantly in all directions to develop their total effectiveness by sharing leadership, knowledge, experience, expertise and wisdom, without having any sectarian biases. The Deliberative Body (D) consists of three forums, namely, Summit Forum, Political Forum and Civil Forum.

DELIBERATIVE BODY (1): SUMMIT FORUM

The Summit Forum must be represented by all the incumbent heads of State in the world. These heads of State meet at least once a year to decide, by a two-third majority, on the matters most fundamental to the purpose of Sustainable Development. Such important matters may include the "fundamental legal framework" and the "global unitary rate of value-added tax" that provide the exclusive financial resource for the governance system. To be effective, such decisions in the Summit Forum must be approved by the two-third majority both in the Political Forum and the Civil Forum, and must also be ratified by the simple majority in the respective national congresses that represent at least 90 percent of the world population. All the other regulations and budgetary matters based on the "fundamental legal framework" can be decided to make them effective by the simple majority both at the Political Forum and the Civil Forum.

DELIBERATIVE BODY (2): POLITICAL FORUM

Representatives to the Political Forum must be selected from politicians by the national election in each nation for a 6-year term with the possible second-term re-election. Their total number should not exceed a manageable limit (within the range of 300–400) and each member nation is allocated their number of representatives on the basis of at least one per nation, and thereafter according to the economic size of the nation. The elected representatives should have proficiency in *one* or more of the *four core issues*, namely, socioeconomic development, Cultural enrichment, human development and environment conservation/development. Also, the nations allotted more than one representative must see to it that such specialties are represented, as much as is feasible, without duplication.

DELIBERATIVE BODY (3): CIVIL FORUM

Similarly, representatives to the Civil Forum must be selected by national election in each member nation from active members of various civil groups, professional and academic institutions and non-profit organizations. The representatives of the Civil Forum may have a four-year term of office with a possible second-term re-election, and there should be a range of 300–400 seats. Each member nation is allocated their number of representatives on the basis of at least one per nation, and thereafter according to the population size of the nation. Such elected representatives also should have proficiency in *two* or more of the *four core issues*, namely, socioeconomic development, Cultural enrichment, human development and environment conservation/development. Also, the nations with more than one representative must see to it that such specialties are represented, as much as is feasible, without duplication. Further, it is advisable that each representative to the Civil Forum is assisted by a "consultative body" composed of active experts from civil groups, professional and academic institutions and non-profit organizations in his/her nation.

The representatives to all three Forums can introduce bills to their respective Forums. Such a bill introduction within the Political Forum and the Civil Forum must fulfill the one condition of saving time and avoiding fruitless debates. At least two of the four "Working Groups" jointly and equally represented by both the Political and the Civil Forums, specializing in the respective *core issues*, must endorse the bill introduction by a simple majority. Any such bill also has to be passed by a simple majority both at the Political Forum and the Civil Forum.

COURT OF ARBITRATION AND JUSTICE

Now, we turn to three other components of the proposed global governance system. The Court of Arbitration and Justice (J) may not only interpret appropriateness of the relevant laws and activities of all the nations but also mediate in conflicts between the member nations, all essentially based on the "fundamental legal framework" and the related regulations conducive to Sustainable Development. It may also mediate between the Generality-oriented Commission (G) and the Particularity-oriented Commission (P) in case of conflicts over jurisdictional and administrative questions. In addition, the Court can introduce an arbitration bill to the Summit Forum, the Political Forum and the Civil Forum when a debate and deliberation in any of the three forums is deadlocked.

GENERALITY-ORIENTED COMMISSION

The Generality-oriented Commission (G) has administrative competence where one standard ruling across the world is called for, such as an emission standard for hazardous wastes, a global standard for open-sea fishing and explorations and fair-trade policy, as well as for broad and general environment protection. This Commission can introduce bills for standard regulation to any of the three deliberative forums with one important condition. In order to save time and avoid fruitless debates, such bills have to be endorsed by at least two of the four "Working Groups" jointly and equally represented by the Political and Civil Forums of the Deliberative Body (D).

PARTICULARITY-ORIENTED COMMISSION

The Particularity-oriented Commission (P) has administrative competence where a special ruling is called for, such as local protection of species and ecosystems, reforestation of specific areas, purification of a contaminated river or lake, encouragement of a specific nation's socioeconomic development, Cultural enrichment, human development and environment protection. This Commission also can introduce bills for special regulation to any of the three deliberative forums. Again, in order to save time and avoid fruitless debates, such bills have to be endorsed by at least two of the four "Working Groups" in the Deliberative Body (D).

OTHER IMPORTANT ASPECTS OF THE GOVERNANCE SYSTEM

The respective heads ("Presidents") of (J), (G) and (P), being approved by the respective two-third majorities of all three Forums, jointly represent the global governance system for a four-year term. Each and all (J), (G) and (P) must undergo, respectively, a thorough review every three to five years conducted by both the Political Forum and Civil Forum, as regards the appropriateness and transparency in the handling of various cases, issues and regulations. All four components of the global governance system cater to the wide spectrum of short-term and long-term needs and interests of the global community, as well as to the process toward Sustainable Development. In essence, they are responsible to all natural persons of the prospective global community. In order to maintain their competence, flexibility and transparency in a dynamic world, all these components must constantly look for the best and most appropriate personnel and must also be able to tap into the expertise of private firms, non-profit organizations, academic institutions, professional associations, civil groups and all levels of government entities and international public organizations.

Concluding Remarks

The most important wheel for Sustainable Development, no doubt, is the appropriately cultured *human will and spirit*. Such *will and spirit* may very well be encouraged by the keen awareness and knowledge of the imminent human predicaments as well as by the sound enrichment of diverse Cultures. The enhancement of human thought-frames on the basis of such sound Cultural enrichment may be conducive to the long-term broad perspectives that an appropriate improvement of thoughts, attitudes, behaviors, lifestyles and value systems, based on the reasonably sound respective Cultures (diverse Sound Cultures), can eventually work for Sustainable Development. It may, however, be necessary to supplement such potential *will and spirit* by means of the policy wheel, such as the above "global fiscal policy," given the contemporary time frame limited by both the Market value system and the severe constraints on the Environment, resources and humanities. For persuasion and effectiveness, such policy endeavors must be *"fair and equitable"* to all societies, particularly avoiding the negative insinuation of "bullying" or "witch hunting."

The so-called "Kyoto Protocol" has been struggling with the limitation of active participation and expected results. One important defect of the Protocol is the idea that it is solely based on the *unchanged* modern mentality and the lopsided value system of materialism, individualism, progressivism, egotism and antagonism, as well as on the *modern emancipation* of all variety of lusts. Other important defects refer to its "witch-hunt" characteristics, "might-makes-right" ideology and reliance on the speculative market transaction of "emission rights." For the worldwide endeavor for human sustainability in the face of the *modern triple failures* ("market failure," "policy failure" and "Culture failure"), it is imperative to take a new direction other than the extension of the modern twin "alter egos" (Market and Scientism).

It goes without saying that the long-term worldwide campaign, collaborative consciousness and global governance system for Sustainable Development calls for the New Enlightenment, in order to help encourage and support the main wheel of *human will and spirit* for Sustainable Development. The importance of the paradigm shift for the sound enrichment of diverse Cultures cannot be overstressed here. In other words, the paradigm shift has now become *inevitable* in view of the contemporary human demise reflecting the explosive "disparity-animosity spiral" and "want-and-lust emancipation" under the on-going population explosion. Moreover, it is crucially important to be aware that *no extension* of the "modern" endeavors based on the lopsided value system can promote Sustainable Development.

23 *Culture-Enhancing Employment*

This chapter focuses on the theoretical difference between the *Market practice* of human-resource employment with negligible (perhaps negative) payment for the Culture-oriented contents of labor services and a newly proposed alternative practice of the *Culture-enhancing employment* with adequate payment. In the theoretical examination, the *Market practice* of human employment may, in a few generations, eradicate the important Culture-oriented contents in general so that people face a *non-viable* future without the necessary Cultural foundation. In contrast, the *Culture-enhancing practice* may expand and reinforce the Cultural foundation and, as a result, the Culture-rich human resources can carry out a perpetual socioeconomic development into the future. These two opposite cases will be examined in a diagrammatic comparison/contrast, to show as clearly as possible that *a full payment* for human resources—inclusive of adequate payment for the Culture-oriented contents—based on the *Culture-enhancing practice* is much more advantageous over time than the *Market practice* of little payment for the Culture-oriented contents.

Employment, Cultures and Market

The issue of human employment, by necessity, must address the Cultural foundation, since the broadly defined Culture is largely incorporated into the workforce that is, perhaps, the most important and indispensable component of the relevant society. It is the very Culture-oriented contents that are intimately incorporated into the underlying *general* capacity of the social constituents in all socioeconomic activities. Such a *general* capacity offers human-based market activities, for it is a truism that the market functions itself largely based on the holistic Culture that embraces important values such as honesty, reliability and mutual concerns of the social constituents. Theoretically speaking, the so-called "market" by nature treats any things abundant as "free goods," including the abundant Culture-oriented contents in the workforce. It is no wonder, therefore, that the market fundamentalism (Market) exploits the abundant Culture-oriented contents of human resources thoroughly to the point of practical exhaustion.

Such exploitation implies that the very abundance of the Culture-oriented *general* capacity works against itself in the market system. This gives rise to a serious paradox that the "market approach" degrades the Cultural values and functions over time, eventually obliterating the long-endured Cultural foundation that is essential for market activities to continue and expand. Perhaps, this paradox suggests a *fatal flaw* of the short-sighted "market approach" and, for that matter, it is the *basic flaw* of modern Economics that relies heavily upon the dogma of "free-market competition." The Market that adheres dogmatically to the "market approach" has naturally been the very cause of the on-going Cultural and Environmental devastation.

Put differently, the very short-sighted and expansionist product-flow-oriented ethos of the Market leads diverse Cultures and the Environment to their eventual exhaustion, despite the fact that their existence is most essential to human life, socioeconomic development and continuation of market activities. In order to rectify the on-going tendency of an undesirable hurtling toward Cultural exhaustion as well as toward the eventual dead-end to market activities, the "Culture-enhancing and Culture-integrated" employment system may become inevitable, among other things. Such an employment system may lead to a harmonious and synergistic interaction between Culture and the "sound-and-fair market function" for enriching the Culture and augmenting the market activities. Also, such interaction may indirectly contribute to the conservation and development of the Environment. Thus, such Culture-and-market interaction is the focal point in our present discussion of the "Culture-enhancing and Culture-integrated" approach to the employment of human resources.

Employment: Culture versus Market

The theoretical approach to a "free and competitive market" goes back to the publication of *The Wealth of Nations* by Adam Smith in 1776. Western societies, regardless of understanding Adam Smith correctly or not, have largely adapted themselves over time to the way of thinking based on the politico-economic concepts of the "invisible hand" (often interpreted as "free and competitive market") and the "self-interest" (often a derogatory representation of human nature). Also, modern economists, inculcated by such classical Economics, have spread the thought and concepts throughout the world. Concepts such as "invisible hand" and "self-interest," when exported to non-Western societies by force or persuasion, have drastically degraded their Cultural foundations by rewarding mainly the market values of scarce resources as well as by upholding the competitive market model of employment.

Such a shortsighted "market approach" has drastically underestimated the abundant Culture-oriented contents of human resources and mostly rewarded the scarce *market-demanded skills*. The shortsightedness has paid little attention to the long-endured Cultural foundation that is indispensable over time for the continuation and expansion of market activities. This denigration of the Cultural worth over time may have resulted in the impoverished Cultural foundation, upon which newly *market-demanded skills* of often lopsided/unbalanced sophistication have been formed by the increasingly smaller proportion of such sophisticated workers. Thus, the Cultural denigration, accompanied by the growing disparity in income, wealth and amenity among the social constituents, may have induced contemporary socioeconomic polarization and politico-economic animosity across the world.

The term "Culture," representing the cumulative endeavors of people in numerous generations to weave together a great variety of personal, social and environmental fabrics in time and space, is assumed here as the one having a desirable tendency to enrich itself over time and, simultaneously, work toward general peace and comfort of the people. This interpretation emphasizes the *keynote* of Culture, namely, the Cultural inclination toward mutual peace and amenity. This rather simplistic statement of Cultural inclination is useful for contrasting the Culture with the Market in their respective effects on employment. In my opinion, a harmonious interaction between the Culture and the "sound-and-fair" market, dealing appropriately with the highly important Cultural contents of human resources, is conducive to the synergy of the peaceful invigoration of market activities and well-balanced socioeconomic development. For such synergy effects, the presently proposed long-term model of employment may offer useful analogical and analytical frameworks as well as meaningful policy implications.

Any employment practices need to consider the Cultural foundation of the respective societies to function reasonably well. The arrival of modern industrial societies, however, has induced a gradual abstraction of labor from the underlying diverse Cultures to reinforce the force of the Market. According to the Market, economic activities are deemed totally dependent upon "demand and supply" under the assumption of "free-market competition." "The broad argument is that, given free and informed competition among workers and employers, each worker must be paid the value of his contribution to production" (Reynolds et al. 1978). Such employment assumes, among other things, many small-scale employers competing for labor, with no collusion among employers or among workers and adequate channels of information. This "short-run" *competitive employment*, however, is a far cry from the actual employment practices of many large, powerful and, often, monopsonistic/oligopsonistic employers. In view of the market neglect of both diverse Cultures and the natural environment, among other things, we have reasons to doubt that the wages determined by market can account for the full costs in the long term, namely, the cost of acquiring *market-effective* special skills and *culture-effective* general skills, as well as the cost of sustaining the Cultural foundation and the Culture-embracing environment.

Economic Globalization and Employment

An "idealized competitive model" of employment is usually credited to the neoclassical school of Economics and can be traced back again to *The Wealth of Nations* by Adam Smith (1776). The book revolutionized the idea of economic development with the above-mentioned concepts of "invisible hand" and "self-interest." The later application of these concepts in the course of the Industrial Revolution and the Imperialistic pursuit of power not only ignored the value of diverse Cultures but also set conditions convenient to the abstraction of "labor" from the underlying Culture for the sake of the short-run competitive model of employment. Moreover, the "invisible hand" has come to treat the long-living and spiritually inclined workers similar to material goods or machines. Such *inhuman* treatment has seldom taken heed of the known "peculiarities" of labor markets, particularly, the inseparability of worker from his/her labor services (Marshall 1959).

The concept of "self-interest," on the other hand, has helped reduce human motivation to a "short-run" self-centeredness and encouraged a self-seeking and aggressive character among workers. The two concepts—"invisible hand" and "self-interest"—regardless of the meanings initially intended, have made the employment "cut-and-dry" and the values of humanities and human motivations grossly distorted over the long duration of time. As an extension of individual "self-interest," the national self-interest ("national interest") has somehow excused the modern powers to indulge in Imperialism and neo-Imperialism (economic globalization), to deprive other people and societies of their essential resources and, in the process, spread the thoughts and lifestyles pertaining to such politico-economic concepts.

It is no wonder why we often come across the well-worn argument favoring the competitive model of employment. Such an argument is allegedly based upon the features common among the modern, "modernized" and "modernizing" industrial nations, despite the existing differences, such as "size, climate, geographic characteristics, language, cultural traditions, and form of government" (Reynolds 1978). The competitive model has been supported by almost all business organizations in the Western world and presumed by many adherents to the neoclassical school as an "authentic" model applicable across the world. Now that the economic globalization has become the *leitmotif* (reigning ideology), the logic of global capitalism asserts itself under the wing of global corporations and financiers (as agents of the Big Market), reviving the crude "law of the jungle" to the detriment of diverse Cultures and humanities everywhere.

Accustomed to their own convenient definitions of "self-interest," almost all the global/multinational corporations and financiers, with their economic, financial and political influences beyond their national boundaries (and usually backed by their mother-country governments), have attempted to lord it over or to impose their own rules on almost all societies across the world, ignoring the cultural and natural environments. Speaking of the far-reaching nature of the on-going economic globalization, William Greider in his *One World Ready or Not* (1997) puts it: "The past is up-ended and new social values are created alongside the fabulous new wealth ... Yet, masses of people are also tangibly deprived of their claims to self-sufficiency, the independent means of sustaining hearth and home. People and communities, even nations, find themselves losing control over their own destinies, ensnared by the revolutionary demands of consumers." Even George Soros, an enigmatic person, in *The Crisis of Global Capitalism* (1998) declares, too: "It is market fundamentalism that has rendered the global capitalism unsound and unsustainable."

The revived "law of the jungle" under the guise of authentic and ideal "free-market competition" has exerted the drastically negative effects on diverse Cultures, regardless of rich and poor countries, shattering their already slighted values. This predicament of diverse Cultures, in turn, has affected the lives of workers everywhere, as many global corporations and financiers together try to change working conditions and even reshuffle workers throughout the world on one pretext or another. They have been replacing the highly paid workers in the industrially advanced nations by means of the worldwide network of sophisticated computers, as well as by the exploitation of cheap labor in the developing nations (see Chapter 5).

Market-Centered Employment

The diverse Cultures and the Market, respectively, are blessed with inherent dynamism of different kinds. To speak simplistically, the diverse Cultures tend to deepen and enrich themselves over time, while the Market tends to expand and strengthen itself. In other words, the "Culture" tends to reproduce and accumulate itself, while the "Market" tends to expand its controlled territory. Such dynamic characteristics of the diverse Cultures and the Market, respectively, coincide with the above-mentioned *ethos* of the Culture and the *ethos* of the Market. If we can find the way in our contemporary world to have the "sound-and-fair" market function serve the diverse Sound Cultures properly, respecting and enriching them, all people and all societies throughout the world may benefit incalculably. However, if we let the Market stifle the diverse Cultures, all of us may lose drastically and irreversibly. It is important to recognize that both the diverse Cultures and the "sound-and-fair" market function constitute the indispensable human heritages.

DIAGRAMMATIC EXPLANATION OF COMPETITIVE EMPLOYMENT

We have, however, been witnessing the Market-driven economic globalization stifling diverse Cultures across the world. If we simply look on as passive observers, all Cultures will most likely be trampled upon in all regions of the world, soon to a point beyond the hope of recovery. This, however, may not be the end of the story, for such doom on the Cultures will certainly visit the Market, too, leading it to an unforeseen dead end. To explain this simplified surmise, I will take a diagrammatic approach to the well-known competitive model of employment first. Now, let us begin with a reasonably rich Cultural foundation (O1) as shown in Figure 23.1, prior to the introduction of the market system into the picture (Hiwaki 1999b, 2001b). In the initial long-term period, the market demand for labor services (*market-effective special skills*) leads to forming an echelon of human capital (H1). For simplicity, the market is assumed to pay the workforce only for the *market-effective special skills*.

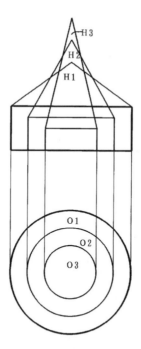

Figure 23.1 Culture-impoverishing employment

This means that the market ignores the indispensable support of the *culture-effective general skills* that are provided simultaneously by the same workforce. In other words, the market treats the Culture and the *culture-effective general skills* strictly as "free goods." Such a lopsided/unbalanced rewarding scheme, of course, entails a serious consequence in the contemporary world where "money speaks." The following generation of workers, sensing the paltry contribution of the *culture-effective general skills* to their prospective income (neither in terms of "monetary" reward nor "psychic/emotional" reward of recognition), may naturally become discouraged and shy of acquiring the *culture-effective general skills*, thus diminishing the Cultural foundation over generations.

Now, in response to the market demand for new *market-effective special skills*, a second echelon of human capital (H2) is to be formed on the diminished Cultural foundation (O2). Such capital formation may, at best, relate only partially to the existing stock of human capital. Those workers responding to the market demand are now amply rewarded, despite their reduced orientation to the Culture. Ignoring again the Culture-oriented contents in the labor services, the market discourages the next generation of workers from acquiring the *culture-effective general skills* to impoverish their Cultural foundation still further. Upon this much-diminished foundation (O3), a third echelon of human capital (H3) needs to be formed in response to the change of market demand, and so it goes on, toward the eventual obliteration of the Culture as insinuated in Figure 23.1. Such drastic Cultural degeneration may, sooner or later, lead the very market to the dead end.

IMPLICATIONS OF COMPETITIVE EMPLOYMENT

In the above analysis we intentionally ignored, for the sake of simplicity, the actual practices of *competitive employment* rewarding the workforce in one way or another for the Culture-oriented contents. Being pressed for a greater profit, corporate managers in our contemporary world, however, may usually take a short view of things and consider the immediate market conditions first and foremost. Thus, even in the actual situation we can safely assume that the sequences such as H1 to H2 and to H3 tend to be quite uneven and largely disconnected from one another. In our simplified illustration, each different generation of workforce responds in its own way to the shift of market demand. Also, the average workers may become increasingly detached from the Culture over the sequences. This may, in turn, imply that the market faces a growing difficulty and uncertainty in its own expansion.

Under the above setting, newly demanded *market-effective special skills* of increasing sophistication may most likely be acquired by a decreasing proportion of the workforce, thus accelerating both the socioeconomic polarization and the politico-economic animosity. Also, the people in general may tend to lose over time their sophisticated command of language (part of the Cultural foundation), when the growing specialization of skills may require more intricate and effective communication among the specialized and also between the specialized and the non-specialized. Further, the social constituents may tend to lose the Cultural catalysis in their inter-personal relations amid the growing reality of "cut-throat" competition and "cut-and-dry" lifestyle.

Moreover, people tend to lose their Culture-bound sense of responsibility and public spirit in the midst of an explosive "freedom" generated by "free market competition," "emancipated lusts," "liberal democracy" and the rapid income growth of the "market-specialized minority." A point may be reached, at which more and more businesses have to operate on more shaky Cultural ground, facing increasingly uneasy, self-seeking, capricious, infantile workers and consumers. Mutual reliability and trust among the social constitutents may tend to dissipate rapidly, resulting in the practical collapse of market and social order (see the "Credibility Trap" in Chapters 2 and 3).

Culture-Enhancing Employment

Alternatively, we can at least choose in theory a more appropriate employment system, namely, the "Culture-enhancing and Culture-integrated employment" that reinforces both the Cultural foundation and the "sound-and-fair" market function, simultaneously. Our theoretical model encourages a harmonious and synergistic interaction between the Culture and the "sound-and-fair" market function with two basic principles. The first principle asserts that the "sound-and-fair" market function must account reasonably for both the *market-effective special skills* and the *culture-effective general skills*, paying for both the skills equitably and adequately. The second principle asserts that all firms and all levels of government must encourage and strive for the continuity and enhancement of both the *culture-effective general skills* and the *market-effective special skills* to have both the skills accumulate steadily and reinforce mutually over time. Such endeavors naturally enrich the Culture and reinforce the Cultural foundation for socioeconomic activities and augment synergistically the abilities of individual persons and societies in the changing world.

DIAGRAMMATIC EXPLANATION OF CULTURE-ENHANCING EMPLOYMENT

I will now contrast the "Culture-enhancing and Culture-integrated" model of employment with the above *competitive employment* model, beginning again with a reasonably rich Cultural foundation (O1), as seen in Figure 23.2 (Hiwaki 1999b). Following the introduction of "sound-and-fair" market function into society, an echelon of human capital (H1) is to be formed according to market demand. Equitable and adequate

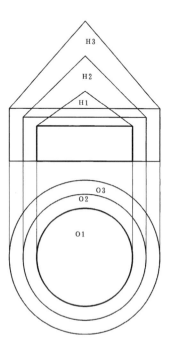

Figure 23.2 Culture-enhancing employment

payments for both the *culture-effective general skills* and the *market-effective special skills* facilitate Comprehensive Human Development and the sound enrichment of Culture, augmenting the market activities at the same time. The payment scheme encourages the synergistic "complementing" interaction between both skills to increase their productivity and reinforce the Cultural foundation over time. Such treatment of both skills may contribute to the well-balanced and Culture-embracing sophistication of the people in general.

Upon such reinforced Cultural foundation (O2) a second echelon of human capital (H2) is to be formed in response to the change in market demand. The equitable and adequate payments for both the *culture-effective general skills* and the *market-effective special skills*, again, may enhance the compatibility of both skills to produce their synergy effects to the quantity and quality of production. Accordingly, such a payment scheme increases the joint productivity of such skills, along with the processes of balanced-comprehensive human development and the reinforced Cultural foundation. Likewise, a third echelon of human capital (H3) is to be formed on an even richer foundation (O3) to meet a further shift in market demand, and thus goes on to enrich the Culture and augment the market activities, simultaneously, as depicted in the above diagram.

IMPLICATIONS OF CULTURE-ENHANCING EMPLOYMENT

In this manner, Culture-enhancing employment facilitates the harmonious and synergistic interactions between the Culture and the "sound-and-fair" market function to enhance the thought-frames (namely, personal and societal scopes of thought in time and space) and the lifestyles in general. Correspondingly, such an employment system may improve future prospects and the "virtuous circle" of Holistic Culture Enrichment, Comprehensive Human Development and Balanced Socioeconomic Development. In a world of Cultural diversity, therefore, both the *culture-effective general skills* and the *market-effective special skills*, which are accounted and paid equitably and adequately, may become crucially important for pursuing sound Cultural enrichment, appropriate human development and well-balanced socioeconomic development in each society.

Exposing the core idea of the "Culture-enriching and Culture-integrated" approach to employment in the above, I am fully aware of the formidable nature of challenge. Given the on-going thrust of the market fundamentalism (Market) as well as the accumulated momentum of economic globalization, the Market emphasis on the short-sighted *competitive employment* may prevail throughout the world into the foreseeable future. Thus, I am quite apprehensive of such a future consequence, particularly because the self-seeking global corporations and financiers have been practically turned loose to spread *grossly profit-motivated messages* in the world economy. The crudest imaginable Market may be well on the way to digging its own grave by trampling on the diverse Cultures across the world and thereby forever depriving all humans the opportunity to enhance their thought-frames and lifestyles as appropriate to Sustainable Development. This may, indeed, amount to the detriment of our contemporary world and our future generations. It may also imply that we forever lose our opportunities to work for Sustainable Development, Culture of Peace and Global Humanity for the integral development of the prospective global community.

Concluding Remarks

The present argument is straightforward. As a step to rectify the prevailing bias toward the crudest Market orientation of "short-run" nature, the "Culture-enhancing and Culture-integrated" employment may become indispensable for Sustainable Development. Such employment can offer a much greater scope than otherwise for human development, enjoyment, achievement, fulfillment, identity and lifestyle as well as for health, comfort and amenity. The "Culture-enhancing and Culture-integrated" employment may also provide us with a far greater chance for the equitable distribution of income, wealth and amenity as well as for Holistic Culture Enrichment, Comprehensive Human Development and Balanced Socioeconomic Development.

I am of the opinion that the market function can be *cultured* to have both the short-term and long-term orientation as well as the Culture-enhancing emphases. Put differently, our short-sighted Market mindset reflects nothing but our contemporary short-sighted thinking, attitude and behavior *inculcated* in modern times. This modern and contemporary tendency can be rectified, if we so will, by our resolute endeavors to enrich our respective Cultures and to cultivate an ever-greater dimension in our thought-frames. Such endeavors will, no doubt, change our value systems, lifestyles and socioeconomic activities. Then, the idea of adopting the "Culture-enhancing and Culture-integrated" employment may not be far-fetched after all. Such employment may integrate the specific Culture with the "sound-and-fair" market function for reinforcing each society's Cultural enrichment, human development and socioeconomic development, which are all important *local* prerequisites for Sustainable Development.

24 Culture-Enhancing International Trade

In this chapter, I will introduce a *long-term theory* of international trade that is conducive to viable and thriving trade as well as to Sustainable Development. International trade under the "free-market competition" of "short-run nature" tends inevitably to exploit any seemingly abundant, easily obtainable or surmountable resources and any humans lacking strong voice and power. This implies that international trade may devastate diverse Cultures and the Environment and impoverish people and societies at large to the detriment of itself. An alternative approach to international trade may be the viable long-term approach based on the sound enrichment of existing diverse Cultures across the world to quicken the development process toward the socioeconomic maturation of all the trading societies.

Backgrounds and Assumptions

It goes without saying that Sustainable Development of the prospective global community requires a drastically new approach to international trade. Here, we may adopt a shorthand definition of Sustainable Development as a long-term global process of the Balanced Socioeconomic Development compatible with protection and enhancement of the Environment. So far, modern economists at different times have asserted various factors and aspects of trading societies as the important causes of international trade. They have separately chosen absolute advantage, comparative costs, different factor endowments, scale advantage, technological difference, government industrial policy and so on. Whether static or dynamic, these *partial* approaches that explain only limited aspects of international trade have assumed the necessity of "free-market competition" and "full employment" within trading societies. To be sure, international trade under the prevailing "short-run free competition" (without "full employment" in reality) tends inevitably to exploit any resources easily obtainable or surmountable and any humans lacking strong voice or power.

This implies that international trade under the pervasive Market has favored the rich and strong among natural persons, firms and societies at the cost of the rest. It also implies that such international trade has devastated holistic diverse Cultures and the Environment as well as the innate human well-being that rests with peace and order. Such international trade does not contribute to overall human progress or happiness. Peace and order as an innate blessing of Sound Culture is also an innate requirement of a viable international trade. Moreover, it is almost a truism that a Culture of Peace serves as an essential global foundation for Sustainable Development.

One important assumption here refers to the sound enrichment of diverse Cultures and the Environment, respectively referring to the "societal public goods" and the "global public goods." Another important assumption here asserts that a continuous growth of *society-general orientation to the future* all over the world is essential both to Sustainable Development and international trade. Such future orientation is indispensable to Holistic Culture Enrichment, Comprehensive Human Development and Balanced Socioeconomic Development in each society. Making such general assumptions, I will argue for a *long-term integral approach* to international trade—"Culture-enhancing and Culture-integrated" theory of international trade. In essence, the present approach, by favoring the long-term and general human benefits, emphasizes the process of *mutually maturing interaction* of all trading societies, which provides a favorable impetus to the Balanced Socioeconomic Development in each society and Sustainable Development of the prospective global community.

Economic Discipline and Sustainable Development

INTERNATIONAL TRADE AND ECONOMIC GLOBALIZATION

Under the on-going process of Market-driven globalization, governments look for growing economy and power, firms for growing sales and profits, consumers for growing abundance and convenience, and economists for growing competition and efficiency. In these circumstances, international trade may have played a highly important role. A worldwide expansion of international trade has increased the world's total production, sales, profits, abundance and convenience, while expanding the income disparity, the skewed allocation of resources and the instability of the human and the ecological world.

The Market-driven globalization, which is almost totally *flow-biased* and very much in favor of the rich and strong, has given top priority to the "short-run" benefits at the cost of the long-term needs of people and societies in general. The "short-run" benefits are no doubt important for all humans, since we wish to be fed, clothed and sheltered comfortably in our daily lives. Achieving a good balance between the short-term and long-term needs is, however, much more important to humans (who have a relatively large brain and a long expected life among mammals) needing to satisfy spiritual, intellectual and aesthetic desires, along with material needs, not to mention hope for the future.

International trade as an important economic activity today must cater to such compounded and complex human needs and desires both in the short and long terms. With severe constraints on the global environment and resources, however, international trade must also play a role in enhancing the progress of Sustainable Development. In other words, international trade must contribute to Comprehensive Human Development and the human welfare of all present and future generations. Various vested interests, however, may prevent governments, firms, consumers and even economic thinkers from changing the prevailing *short-run-biased* thoughts and practices of international trade. As far as the large majority of present-day economists are concerned, their vested interests constitute the modern and neoclassical economic thoughts and the resultant body of theories and tools. Such economic thoughts, theories and tools apparently entertain the peculiar dogmas regarding human nature ("self-interest"), market function ("invisible hand") and "free-market competition" (natural liberty).

LOPSIDED ECONOMIC THEORIES AND APPROACHES

Typical economists these days usually resort to the *marginal*, *partial* and *"short-run"* approaches on the convenient assumption of "other things being constant," not only applying these approaches to the theoretical exercises of complex economic issues but also to the more practical exercises of policy formulations. Naturally, other things are always changing in various ways, but such economists tend to dismiss the contradiction, often, with the deceptive and expedient argument that the assumption of "other things being constant" can approximate the reality in a "very short run." They also make it a custom to assert the *golden rule* of "free-market competition," without condemning (often, closing eyes to) the prevailing unfair competition—the "level-ground" absolute competition—between and among the grossly disparate trading parties. In asserting such a *golden rule*, they argue particularly for the "efficient allocation" of resources and the expansion of economic activities, often closing their eyes to the ill effects on "equitable income distribution" and viable human subsistence. Such economists always carry the banner for "competition" and "efficiency," despite the intrinsic theoretical deficiency.

General human needs and orientation may usually require a long-term perspective, as well as an integral approach. In other words, such a perspective and approach may relate closely to the necessity of protecting and enriching diverse Cultures and the Environment. For the lasting accommodation of complex human needs, therefore, a drastic new approach to international trade has to be based on the societal and global "public goods"—diverse Cultures and the Environment. Such a new approach is indispensable, in view of the biased and dogmatic development of the prevailing economic theories that pay little attention to the lasting needs of people and societies.

Indeed, the prevailing trade theories have encouraged growing biases and economic disparities among different societies and social constituents, and contributed to the rapid deterioration of diverse Cultures and the Environment. A fundamental flaw of such theories is exemplified by the following serious paradox. The Market tends to degrade the Cultural foundation that is essential for market activities to continue and expand. Such mainstream theories, catering to the Big Market, must have promoted the "short-run" oriented uniformity over diversity and created deceptive/illusionary values for both the exploiter and the exploited. Likewise, such theories must have forced humans to largely ignore the non-material potential for pursuing higher human goals and viable future. Our present discussion, therefore, serves as an attempt to to rectify such defects and biases of our economic discipline.

An Alternative Theory of International Trade

Now I will deal briefly with the essentials relevant to the "Culture-enhancing and Culture-integrated" approach to international trade, based mainly on my "interest theory of development" as part of the present long-term theoretical framework. This theoretical exposition emphasizes the dynamic role of international trade for worldwide Culture-to-Culture communication, which amount to *mutually maturing interactions* based on the Optimal Development Paths (ODPs). Such dynamic interactions, in turn, may call for positive, long-term and future-oriented interactions of consumers, producers and governments in international trade. These sorts of trade interactions can be facilitated by the function of international trade as multi-media communication between the demand and the supply of traded goods and services. I will also briefly discuss the major implications of the "Culture-enhancing and Culture-integrated" theory of international trade to Sustainable Development.

DIAGRAMMATIC EXPLANATION OF ALTERNATIVE THEORY

In order to facilitate the discussion of the present long-term integral approach to international trade, I will now assume three sample societies for simplicity, namely, Societies X, Y and Z with their respectively characterized ODPs, as shown in Figure 24.1. Society X is assumed to be already at the Growth-Maturation turning point (x), Society Y at a high point of the Growth Process (y), and Society Z near the beginning of the Growth Process (z). To begin with, these sample societies distinguish themselves with their ODPs of different "bow-like" shapes as well as with their positions on their ODPs. Such distinctions may roughly reflect their respective histories, value systems, dispositions, attitudes, creativity, education, technology, factor endowments, scale advantages, locations, climates, polities, policies, institutions, risk factors, orientations to the future, and so on. Such diverse features of the societies, by interacting with one another through trade, may deepen the uniqueness and attractiveness of Culture-embraced goods and services in international trade.

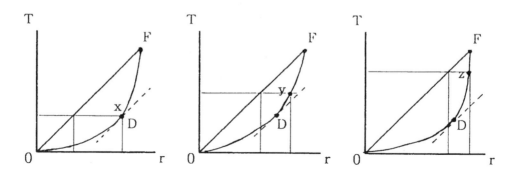

Figure 24.1 Three different Optimal Development Paths

Based on the interpretation of the ODPs in Figure 24.1 (Hiwaki 2000b), the respective sample societies face their different realities relevant to the long-term social discount rate (Social Rate of Interest (SRI)), the long-term economic discount rate (Economic Rate of Interest (ERI)) and the "extra-profit margin" (Social Premium for Development (SPD)). Generally speaking, the ERI tends to vary among societies, reflecting the different characteristics as mentioned above. Accordingly, the "extra-profit margin" that amounts to the difference between the ERI and the SRI may vary widely among these societies, largely reflecting their socioeconomic priorities in time and space at the given positions on their respective ODPs.

The different characteristics and priorities of the respective societies may constitute both causes and results of the difference between the ERI and the SRI. With such difference, these societies interact through the *mutuality-oriented* (*not* self-seeking),

Culture-respecting (*not* Market-centered) and *Culture-integrated* international trade, to the consequence of more pronounced *absolute, comparative, scarce and unique advantages* of each society. Such interactions, in turn, enrich their respective Cultural foundations to induce more expanded and upgraded activities of international trade on the basis of their *changing* ODPs.

GENERALIZED CULTURE-ENHANCING INTERNATIONAL TRADE

In view of the numerous societies with their respective ODPs and at their respective positions on the ODPs, the present "Culture-enhancing and Culture-integrated" theory of international trade asserts generally that all societies can trade with one another on the basis of their Cultural enrichment constantly incorporated into the respective ODPs. Also, it generally asserts that such enriched Cultural characteristics can lend continuity and dynamics to international trade on the basis of more pronounced respective *absolute, comparative, scarce and unique advantages*. Such respective advantages may encompass more enticing practical features, integral harmony and aesthetic sophistication, among other things, as far as the traded goods and services are concerned. Moreover, the "Culture-enhancing and Culture-integrated" dynamic theory, in essence, relates trading activities generally to the diverse Value Aspects of all societies, which closely relate to the *absolute, comparative, scarce and unique advantages* based on the respective Cultural enrichment.

Each differentiated Culture can generally relate to the specific history, geographical location, climate, value system, polity and other characteristics of each society in the present "long-term-and-dynamic" theory of international trade. Put differently, the respective characteristics of each society may largely correspond to the relative uniqueness of the Culture—the unique "societal public goods." The "Culture-enhancing and Culture-integrated" theory, therefore, requires *Culture-respecting* fair competition (*not* the "level-ground" absolute competition) and *mutuality-inclined* cooperation and interdependence. Also, it requires continuous enhancement of the Environment—the "global public goods"—in order to expand and upgrade international trade continuously. It goes without saying that Culture of Peace, an important element of the Environment, must prevail for the stability and continuity of international trade.

Trade as an Interaction for Mutual Maturation

The above discussion of the "Culture-enhancing theory" emphasizes that international trade may originate in and thrive on the diverse and dynamic Cultures worldwide. Viewed in this manner, we may come to a better understanding of the human reality that almost all societies in the world are better off by trading in one way or another, on the basis of the Culture-integrated personal and societal capacities for production and the Culture-oriented needs and tastes for consumption. Indeed, numerous societies traded with one another largely on the basis of Cultural differences before the modern age, and for that matter, long before modern trade theories were postulated on the basis of the modern lopsided value system.

The modern explanations of trade may sound *rational* in the "modern" light of enshrined private property, misguided individualism, flow-oriented expansionism, supremacy-seeking industrialism and inhuman efficiency emphasis. Emphasizing the importance of "free-market competition" for the "short-run" efficiency of allocation and/ or the other hidden purposes, the modern explanations, however, largely slighted and/ or intentionally neglected the intrinsic importance of the historically, geographically and climatically differentiated Cultures that serve as the most fundamental basis for international trade. As a result, the modern trade theories may have purposefully distorted the human attitudes toward the most important societal and global "public goods"—diverse Cultures and the Environment.

To rectify the traditionally biased theories, the present *integral approach* argues for the following: the "short-run," competitive, aggressive and expansionist market function and the long-term, cooperative, ameliorating and continuity-oriented diverse Cultures have to be harmonized and mobilized for human comfort, health and welfare as well as for fair and integral interdependence. Now that the importance of the differentiated diverse Cultures and their mutual interactions through international trade has been asserted, we can speak more positively the prospect of Sustainable Development. Given the differentiated diverse Cultures leading to international trade, the trade-induced interactions among the diverse Cultures can now be regarded as an important vehicle to nurture proper respect to all Cultures. The continuous and sound enrichment of the respective Cultures on the basis of long-term orientation to the future may offer the expanded and upgraded opportunities not only for international trade, but also for human development, socioeconomic development and enhancement of the Environment.

In other words, the Culture-to-Culture interactions through international trade may stimulate one another among the different societies to promote their respective and mutual processes of Holistic Culture Enrichment and Comprehensive Human Development. Such interactions also amount to the *mutually maturing interactions* for Balanced Socioeconomic Development on their respective ODPs. Through such positive interactions, all societies can influence one another to quicken their respective processes of socioeconomic development, so that they can move far more quickly toward and into their respective Maturation Processes. This is the process of *mutually maturing interactions* of all trading societies, which may accelerate the global process of socioeconomic activities toward Sustainable Development on the basis of the constantly reinforced *absolute, comparative, scarce and unique advantages*.

Trade as Multimedia Communication

Such "Culture-enhancing and Culture-integrated" international trade can also function as multimedia communication in the prospective global community. The more enlightened consumers of Society X, for example, can start demonstrating their demands for the goods and services in the international market, which enrich the diverse Cultures and enhance the Environment. All consumers and all workers in the trading societies are the eventual beneficiaries of the expanded and upgraded international trade on the basis of the Culture-embraced *absolute, comparative, scarce and unique advantages* that are reinforced constantly by diverse Cultural enrichment. They can also directly interact with their counterparts in Societies Y and Z via the Internet to exchange important information about internationally traded materials, goods and services, and to collaborate for the cause of Sustainable Development.

Through such "grassroots" demonstrations and interactions for the sake of more appropriate consumer-and-worker behaviors, such enlightened consumers and workers all over the world can also positively influence, both internally and externally, the thoughts and behaviors of the less enlightened ones for the sound enrichment of their respective Cultures as well as for the enhancement of the Environment. Particularly, the enlightened consumers, as they grow in number, can guide the behavior of producers in different countries by their enlightened demands for goods and services. Such demand may encourage domestic and foreign producers to pay proper respect to diverse Cultures and the Environment, and also to cooperate for the cause of Sustainable Development.

Then, the consumer-to-consumer, consumer-to-producer and producer-to-producer interactions in domestic and international markets may encourage or discourage the supply and demand of goods and services, depending on their favorable or unfavorable impacts on diverse Cultures, the Environment and the process toward Sustainable Development. Put differently, international trade in the computer age can work as a complex worldwide network of multimedia communication for appropriate information, ideas, attitudes, behaviors and lifestyles favorable to Sustainable Development that depends on the continuous enrichment of diverse Cultures across the world as well as on the continuous enhancement of the Environment. Further, such international trade under the New Enlightenment, that embraces consumers, workers, scholars, business leaders and government authorities in general, can increase the strong impetus to a *virtuous circle* of Holistic Culture Enrichment, Comprehensive Human Development and Balanced Socioeconomic Development, to induce a favorable condition for Sustainable Development.

Such multimedia communication as a function of international trade can take a long stride when supported by the favorable endeavors of local, national, international and transnational governments, as well as by the cooperation of enlightened stakeholders of multinational and global corporations. One possible consequence of the "Culture-enhancing and Culture-integrated" international trade, given such a favorable turn of events, may enhance the recognition that the perpetual enrichment of diverse Cultures, as well as the perpetual enhancement of the Environment, is indispensable to the present and future needs of all people and societies. A further consequence may mean a worldwide and wholehearted endeavor for the cultivation of enhanced thought-frames in all people. This, for example, may lead to a general understanding that the sound enrichment of each and every Culture provides a growing opportunity not only for international trade, but also for Comprehensive Human Development and Balanced Socioeconomic Development favorable to the process of Sustainable Development.

A third possibility may refer to the consequence of a closer intergovernmental cooperation and stronger transnational leadership to enhance the harmonious balance between the short-term and long-term socioeconomic activities, according to the needs of all diverse people and societies. Also, this possibility may provide the relevant stimulation for multinational and global corporations to adjust to the *Culture-respecting* fair competition and the *Culture-enhancing* employment and international trade. The closer the intergovernmental cooperation and the stronger the transnational leadership for sound enrichment of diverse Cultures, the greater the overall motivation and impetus will be for creating an appropriate global governance system for the better coordination of the worldwide endeavors that enrich diverse Cultures and enhance the Environment. All these likely consequences, together, can be conducive to speeding up the process toward Sustainable Development.

Implications of Culture-Enhancing Trade Theory

The long-term Culture-enhancing approach to international trade offers some far-reaching implications, by contributing to the development of new thought and attitude for international trade as well as to the development of a new transnational politico-economic environment for well-balanced socioeconomic development. The present approach, emphasizing the process of *mutually maturing interactions,* differs clearly from the classical and neoclassical emphases on the "free and competitive market" for "short-run efficiency" and economic expansion without proper consideration of consequential social costs and maladies across the world. Such classical and neoclassical emphases, given the severe constraints on the natural environment and resources, may most probably favor only the rich and powerful among people, firms and societies for the perpetuation of their control over the world.

The present proposition stresses global human development and collaboration in pursuit of Sustainable Development as well as in perpetuation of the general welfare of present and future generations. Going much beyond the classical and neoclassical assertions of the "short-run" mutual benefits and the interdependence of economies, without paying heed to the contagion of "win-or-lose" competition and "life-or-death" income disparity, the present proposal of the Culture-and-Environment embracing approach to international trade may work for common and lasting benefits to all people and societies across the world. These benefits, no doubt, arise from the sound enrichment of diverse Cultures and the appropriate enhancement of the Environment, as well as from the thriving international trade and the enhanced aggregate value-added (including enhanced mental/emotional rewards, improved product quality, broadened variety of exchanges and augmented international harmony) relevant to each trading society.

Further, the present integral approach to international trade emphasizes the expanding trade activities based on the Culture-induced *absolute, comparative, scarce and unique advantages.* This approach also emphasizes long-term dynamic interactions among the ever-flourishing diverse Cultures, strengthening the very foundations of the upgraded and appropriate trade expansion for the benefit of all consumers and workers of the prospective global community. Such an approach may have further unexpected implications in favor of human development and enlightenment of all societies. Moreover, the "Culture-enhancing and Culture-integrated" theory of international trade warns against the unwise choice of adhering to the inhuman dogmas of market fundamentalism (Market). Such dogmas may, most likely, ignore the earnest human wishes for global peace and divide all people into the "haves" and the "have-nots," with the inevitable consequences of accelerated human misery and security costs, the compounded social maladies and the inevitable Cultural and Environmental devastation.

Concluding Remarks

The "Culture-enhancing and Culture-integrated" approach to international trade can promote the sound and continuous enrichment of diverse Cultures and lifestyles through the long-term stable process of *mutually maturing interactions* and *multimedia communication.* Such interactions and multimedia communication may nurture a Culture of Peace among all people across the world, as well as a growing orientation to the future and long-term perspective. Also, the "Culture-enhancing and Culture-integrated" approach may induce the *trilateral virtuous circle* of Cultural enrichment, human development and socioeconomic development, and be conducive to a collaborative and amicable nature for the prospective global community.

Further, such a theory of international trade on the basis of the "Culture-enhancing and Culture-integrated" *absolute, comparative, scarce and unique advantages* of the respective societies may, most likely, overcome the inadequacies and excesses of our contemporary lifestyles based on the mainstream trade theories. Furthermore, the present "Culture-enhancing and Culture-integrated" approach may be conducive to paving the way toward Sustainable Development, by generating the collaborative endeavors among all peoples for the respective *trilateral virtuous circles*. Moreover, the present approach may contribute to the peace-promoting Culture-to-Culture *multimedia communication* and *mutually maturing interactions* among all trading societies through their sound enrichment of diverse Cultures.

25 Culture-Hinged Campaigns for Sustainability

The market fundamentalism (Market) seems to have worked against the humanities and the human aspiration for Sustainable Development, by devastating both the Environment and the diverse Cultures. This understanding is *crucial* to counteract and rectify the Market-driven lifestyles and to have recourse to the sound enrichment of the existing diverse society-specific cultures (Cultures). In this Chapter I will argue for the importance of both the society-specific and the worldwide campaigns for Sustainable Development on the basis of the perpetual enrichment of diverse Cultures. Simultaneous and synchronous campaigns as such hinge on the *common ethos* of the Sound Cultures, that is, a community-interested, continuity-aimed, accumulation-oriented, cooperation-propelled, long-term-engaged, full-life-favoring, inward-ameliorating, peace-seeking and common-value-centered ethos. The main purpose in this discussion is to illustrate the Culture-hinged social interactions both in the society-specific and the worldwide settings for Sustainable Development.

The Transient Over-Riding the Permanent

Today we face a world that is extremely biased toward material expansion. This world allows and encourages the self-righteous pervasion of the Market which has forced incessant changes in taste, fashion, thought, method, behavior and lifestyle, as well as a worldwide escalation of competition, antagonism and cruelty. The Market, devastating diverse Cultures and the Environment, has negated and destroyed both personal integrity and accumulated knowledge/wisdom relevant to those diverse Cultures, which have grown with the strong will, endeavor and perseverance of the respective people and societies over the long duration of time. All such ill and drastic effects of the Market has entailed an accelerated instability in employment, income and living, as well as a bottomless degradation in personality, spirituality, humanity and humanistic capacities at large, without providing any light for a better future. These unfortunate consequences have biased human nature toward transient pleasure and convenience against life-long mutual and public concerns.

In view of the on-going degradation of diverse Cultures and the Environment in our contemporary world, it is nearly impossible to imagine that the dominant and pervasive Market is capable of working for the human ethos of sound, active and fruitful longevity and the human desire for Sustainable Development. Instead, the Market, upholding naked materialism, egotism and expansionism, has imposed its exclusive "short-run" values all over the world. The Market has demanded free competition, free market and free trade with its ideology of "might-makes-right" for the aggrandizement of the contemporary power structure (the Big Market). The main aim in the present discussion, therefore, is to argue for the importance of the Culture-hinged society-specific and worldwide campaigns against the Market-distorted mindset, life and lifestyle, as well as to illustrate how such Culture-hinged campaigns need to tame the Market and pave the way to Sustainable Development.

The Overall Relationship Illustrated

With the pervasive Market working against the human ethos, as well as against the human desire for a viable future, there remains no potent way other than the recourse to enriching existing diverse Cultures for a viable life and peace. Such Cultures have been much weakened by *human faults and negligence*, particularly by the modern human indulgence in materialism and egotism, which all together have reinforced the Market, sacrificing the potential and desirable effects of diverse Sound Cultures. Thus, by the process of elimination, the sound enrichment of the existing diverse Cultures that embody the characteristics almost opposite to the Market, perhaps, is the only available means left today to counteract and restore the Market to the initially envisioned function of a "sound-and-fair" market.

This is the reason why we need to contemplate the Culture-hinged campaigns for Sustainable Development. To begin with, such campaigns have to be based primarily on the *common ethos* of diverse Sound Cultures: that is, the community-interested, continuity-aimed, accumulation-oriented, cooperation-propelled, long-term-engaged, full-life-favoring, inward/ameliorating, peace-seeking and common-value-centered ethos. Any holistic Culture that has been formed over an innumerable number of years may provide people and society with a common foundation for values, beliefs, mores, tastes, customs, mutual relations, organizations, institutions, education, technology, communication, expressions, aesthetics and lifestyles, among other things.

DIAGRAMMATIC EXPLANATION OF CAMPAIGNS FOR SUSTAINABILITY

The Culture-hinged campaigns, here, literally mean that both society-specific and worldwide campaigns encourage the sound enrichment of diverse Cultures on a reasonable and steady path toward Sustainable Development. As shown in Figure 25.1 (Hiwaki 2005d), Sustainable Development can be promoted by both the society-specific and the worldwide campaigns. Such campaigns may also promote their coordinated mutual interactions for greater synergy effects. Any advancement in the process toward Sustainable Development may feedback favorably to these campaigns through a continuous "virtuous circle." In the worldwide campaign (the left-hand box), the New Enlightenment must play a central role for the general enrichment of the diverse Cultures, while a strong societal will for Cultural enrichment is the motivating factor in the society-specific campaign (the right-hand box). In their coordinated mutual interactions, the worldwide campaign may consistently and continuously support the respective society-specific endeavors by creating a favorable worldwide atmosphere for the sound enrichment of diverse Cultures. At the same time, the respective society-specific campaigns may contribute steadily to the worldwide campaign by directly enriching their respective Cultures.

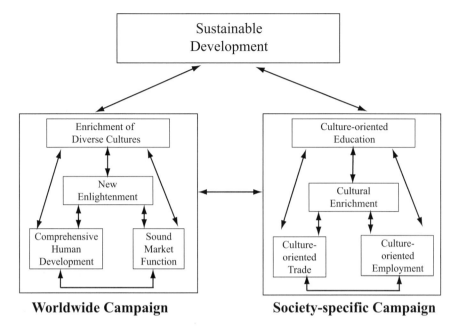

Figure 25.1 Campaigns for Sustainable Development

Worldwide Campaign for Sustainability

As seen from the left-hand box, the worldwide campaign includes the *mutually reinforcing* multiple interactions. The New Enlightenment coordinates the sound enrichment of diverse Cultures all over the world. Such Cultural enrichment, in turn, supports and propagates the New Enlightenment in the respective societies. Also, the New Enlightenment favors both Comprehensive Human Development and the "sound-and-fair" market function. Such human development and market function, in turn, feedback to propagate the New Enlightenment. The worldwide endeavor for sound enrichment of diverse Cultures encourages both Comprehensive Human Development and the "sound-and-fair" market function, while such human development and market function work for the sound enrichment of diverse Cultures. Comprehensive Human Development all over the world encourages the "sound-and-fair" market function and augments the sound enrichment of diverse Cultures, while such market function and diverse Cultures augment Comprehensive Human Development. Finally, the "sound-and-fair" market function is conducive both to Comprehensive Human Development and the sound enrichment of diverse Cultures, while such human development and enriched diverse Cultures encourage the "sound-and-fair" market function.

BRIEFING ON THREE CONCEPTS

The three concepts—"New Enlightenment," "Comprehensive Human Development" and "sound-and-fair" market function—may require a brief review. The New Enlightenment is the prospective worldwide movement for Cultural enrichment and diversity as well as for Sustainable Development. It may counteract the Market-driven lifestyles and enhance the human thought-frames that represent individual/personal and collective/

societal scopes of thought in time and space. Comprehensive Human Development is aimed at enhancing the personal integrity, humanities, human values and human capacities, which may prove to be most important to counteract the Market-driven digital revolution and economic globalization. Such human development consists of thought-frame enhancement, intellectual-and-spiritual development, personal-character building and human-capacity improvement. The "sound-and-fair" market function, referring to the facilitation of both domestic and international market transactions, indicates the fair and equitable accommodation of Culture-integrated human labor, goods and services throughout the world. The mutual and supportive interactions of the New Enlightenment, Comprehensive Human Development and the "sound-and-fair" market function may coordinate the continuous enrichment of the existing diverse Cultures across the world for the process of Sustainable Development.

Society-Specific Campaign for Sustainability

The society-specific campaign is depicted in the right-hand box (Figure 25.1) to encompass the *mutually reinforcing* multiple interactions in each society. An earnest societal endeavor emphatic on Cultural enrichment promotes and coordinates Culture-oriented education, employment and international trade, while such education, employment and trade feed back their support to the Cultural enrichment. The Culture-oriented education that promotes community-interested, continuity-aimed, accumulation-oriented, cooperation-propelled, long-term-engaged, full-life-favoring, inward-ameliorating and common-property-centered inquiries and learning encourages the reorganization of production and employment in terms of the Cultural emphases. Such an education also encourages the realignment of international trade on the basis of Culture-oriented values and skills, as well as on the basis of personal and societal characteristics of the relevant societies. Such employment and trade, at the same time, may augment a Culture-enhancing curriculum in formal education and revitalize the interest of families and communities in the sound enrichment of their own Culture.

The steady and strong orientation of employment toward the own Culture promotes Comprehensive Human Development in the broadly defined Culture-enhancing education and reorients international trade toward the exchanges of products that embody the Culture-intensive features of knowledge, skills, experiences and wisdom—the Culture-embraced *absolute, comparative, scarce and unique advantages*. Such redirection of education and international trade, in turn, induces a further Cultural orientation of employment that rewards the personal accumulation of Culture-based experience, knowledge, wisdom, attitudes, behaviors, skills and long-term perspectives. The "Culture-enhancing and Culture-integrated" international trade promotes Culture-embraced *advantages* through a more intensive cultivation of Cultural characteristics. Such international trade necessitates the realignment of Culture-oriented education and Culture-enhancing employment as well as the constantly enriched characteristics of the Culture. Such education and employment, in turn, reinforce the Culture-embraced *absolute, comparative, scarce and unique advantages* in international trade.

Concluding Remarks

As usual, the discussion regarding such a desirable redirection of our lifestyles for Sustainable Development as well as such an illustration of the perspective relevant to the Culture-oriented education, employment and international trade, may constitute an easier part of the issue, in comparison to their translations into *real and effective* actions, both worldwide and society-specific. The motion and momentum of modern capitalism, however, having been reinforced over the last three centuries on the basis of materialism, liberalism, progressivism, individual egotism and expansionism, seem to be unstoppable or impossible to redirect.

Most people, perhaps, may feel either powerless against the gigantic wheel of history or feel easier to follow the on-going trend more than any other alternatives. Also, most people may be, in one way or another, too busy to think beyond their own daily businesses. Much worse, many cynical condescending intellectuals may be in the pretension of resigning themselves to their fate, boasting their insights and foresight to the effect that even the best possible alternative can easily degenerate into an unexpected and undesirable consequence or a disaster in the given reality of the human world. Despite such hurdles, however, it is important for us who aim at the socioeconomic transformation for Sustainable Development to carry the torch high and profess our best possible alternatives on all possible occasions.

5 *Harmonious and Integral Development*

In order to sum up my exploration into Sustainable Development, I will deal first with appropriate global governance for the important global issues, particularly related to the nature of democracy in the prospective global community (Chapter 26). Second, in relation to such global governance, I will propose for our viable future a positive/constructive socioeconomic policy relevant to the Society of Longevity which is closely related to Sustainable Development (Chapter 27). Third, the complex nature of the Balanced Socioeconomic Development (local Sustainable Development) will be explained through the Multilateral-Value Interaction—the Culture-enriching socioeconomic and human development (Chapter 28). Fourth, I will argue for a simultaneous resolution of the impending global issues—Sustainable Development, Culture of Peace and Global Humanity (Chapter 29). Finally, the proposed paradigm shift for the simultaneous resolutions of the major global issues will be summed up succinctly and analogically by a diagram of "local-global linkage" for the integral development of the prospective global community (Chapter 30).

26 *Democracy for Our Insular Planet*

In this chapter I will delve into a serious and important question: whether the freedom-emphasizing modern democracy based on rational, self-sufficient and autonomous individuals is appropriate to our insular planet (Hiwaki 2009b). The term "insular planet" here refers to Planet Earth with its growing severity of constraints on the environment and resources. To begin with, I will discuss the arduous and unsuccessful experience of Japan in adapting itself to the modern democracy. Japan, as an "insular country," has long been characterized by its diverse society-specific cultures (Cultures) and its severe constraint on resources. Next, I will examine the reality of our insular planet and argue against the modern democracy for the governance of the planet's complex population and societies. Finally, I will summarize a variety of elements and conditions important for the particular "democracy" that is appropriate to the people of the insular planet in the Age of Sustainable Development.

Modern Democracy and Insular Japan

The freedom-emphasizing modern democracy that, on the basis of rational, self-sufficient and autonomous individuals, evolved out of the lengthy period of fermenting under the particular heritage that includes historical, geographical, cultural, political, spiritual and philosophical backgrounds in the Subcontinent of Europe. Such a particular political institution, indeed, could not have been easily emulated, adopted or copied by a society with a totally different heritage. In our contemporary world, however, non-Western societies have copied, followed or pretended at least to understand modern liberal democracy, in order to associate and trade with the industrially advanced Western countries. Modern democracy in our contemporary world is often presumed in our international treaties/agreements, along with the associated tenets of "private property" and "free-market competition." To adapt oneself to modern democracy is, by nature, an extremely difficult challenge to most non-Western societies, including a seemingly "modernized" and "democratized" society like Japan (Hiwaki 2005a).

It is known well that Japan does not share the West's historical, geographical, cultural, political, spiritual and philosophical heritage. The only seeming similarity with the West European region is that Japan also underwent its own feudalism and absolutism at the same times (Umesao 1997), perhaps, by a historical coincidence. Japan adapting itself to the modern democracy was, figuratively speaking, a kind of perverted experience; the result of having to fit oneself into ready-made alien clothing with total disregard to one's own physical characteristics and cultural aesthetics. There is no doubt, however, that Japan failed in its attempt to achieve this, after many audacious, painful and embarrassing endeavors. Japan has attempted "democratization" of itself in two steps: the first based on its own motivation (or the fear of being colonized by the Western nations) and the second on the American initiative. First, emerging from the gun smoke of the Meiji Restoration—the Social Revolution in 1868—Japanese leaders, under their own initiative, started forcing "modernization" of the nation by setting up a quasi-constitutional monarchy, as well as imitating the Western models of educational, legal, industrial and military systems.

In its zeal and haste to show Westerners it was an "enlightened" nation, the leaders of Japan overdid themselves, rapidly changing the very material of Japanese lifestyles, whilst slighting their long-standing traditions, practices and mores. The superficiality of these lifestyles did not convince either the Westerners or the Japanese, while the neglect of traditions, practices and mores gradually undermined the Japanese identity as well as the overall integrity of Japan's diverse and largely coherent society-specific cultures (Cultures). In the meantime, the general public, receiving rather vague and often misleading information on the West, had to struggle with new rules, institutions, organizations and lifestyles as well as with new ideas and concepts rooted in Western values, such as individuality, rationality, equality, freedom, privacy, competition and efficiency. When it came to such value-laden ideas and concepts, most people only could pretend to understand them superficially through translations and formal education, while missing the meanings that were intrinsic to the experiential, behavioral, spiritual and philosophical peculiarities of the Western world.

Moreover, Japan followed and imitated Western Imperialism, against the teaching and warning of Yokoi Shonan, the influential thinker assassinated in 1869 (Tokunaga 2005). He urged that Japan should enrich the nation and strengthen its force, *not for supremacy* but for good and peaceful governance of itself based on *people's good conscience*. The overall integrity of Japan's diverse Cultures, which nurtured the people's *good conscience*, however, was soon treated as an obstacle both to "modernization" and the ambition for "Imperialistic" pursuit. The powerful bureaucracy after the Social Revolution, built on top of the 260-year-old experience of the full-dress bureaucracy in the Edo period, began to impose its own will on the course of the nation and forced the people of Japan into repeated warfare—the Shino-Japanese War, the Russo-Japanese War, the First World War and the Second World War. As a result of its unconditional surrender and defeat in the Second World War, Japan totally lost the trust of neighboring nations, as well as its self-confidence as a nation, not to speak of the territories it lost as a result. The second attempt at the "democratization" of the Japanese began in the spiritual, moral and cultural vacuum that occurred after this unconditional surrender. This time the initiative came from the occupying US army led by the American Commander-in-Chief, Marshall Douglas MacArthur. The occupation's hasty efforts to democratize Japan was ambitious and extensive, encompassing the Constitution, value system, education, business, agriculture, labor and so on. The attempt to implement "American-style liberal democracy" and "free market economy" as quickly as possible was the highest priority. Thus, the occupation dismissed or banned anything connected to Japanese traditions, practices and mores, encouraging or forcing, at the same time, Anglo-American values, rules, thoughts and lifestyles. The occupation also worked hard for the post-occupational control apparatus—the US-Japan Security Treaty that allowed many US bases in Japan— to keep the nation under the close scrutiny and control of the US as well as to make Japan serve the Pacific bastion against communism.

The subsequent US patronization of Japan into the "free world," on the basis of the US-Japan Security Treaty and support from Japan's pro-American political party, helped Japan to throw all its energy and talents into post-war industrial recovery and the ensuing economic development. With the rapid economic development, however, the Japanese people generally became self-complacent and gradually lost their interest in political participation, leaving their fate in the hands of the unchanging one-party rule for half a century. Such unchanging politics, almost totally obedient to the strategic interest of the US, which was guided or directed underhandedly by the powerful post-war bureaucracy, also discouraged the Japanese people to engage in public spirit or of political participation. Moreover, post-war education, with its basis in memorization of concepts, rules and facts, as well mass-media reports of opportunistically pre-interpreted or prefabricated political opinions in favor of "Americanization" of the nation, has not encouraged public concern or independent thinking.

After all, the long-standing and deep-running "insular climate" for collaboration, harmony and order directly and emotionally contradicted the newly propagated ideas of individual rationality, self-sufficiency and autonomy with the accompanying value-laden "free-market competition," aggressiveness and profit-seeking egoist mentality. The individualistic, assertive and confrontational attitudes and behaviors inculcated by the "liberal democracy" and "free-market competition" had been deemed "self-righteous," "uncooperative," "uncompromising" or "disharmonious" in view of the accustomed *insular climate*. As a result, the people in general were deeply confused, with little awareness of the native background, spirit, attitude and behavior intrinsic to the modern democracy. Thus, most Japanese people began to interpret derogatively or opportunistically the concepts of self-interest, competition, equality, freedom, human rights, aggressiveness, acquisitiveness, individualism and so on, based on the visible behaviors of the "liberal democratic" market fundamentalism (Market). Thus, Japan has not only failed to assimilate itself into the modern democracy but also gradually lost its identity and direction as the *insular* country, after repeated attack from within and without, on the traditions, customs and mores embedded in its diverse Cultures.

"Insularized" Planet Earth

As if it had totally forgetting the painful and unsuccessful experience of blindly imitating the West, Japan, with little freedom of choice post-war, jumped on the bandwagon of being led by the US, along with many European countries. That is, Japan pursued the course of new economic colonialism ("new Imperialism") at the cost of poor societies, as well as of hasty economic expansion at the cost of the Environment and resources and even at the cost of its own people who had by now been inculcated in favor of the "producers-sovereignty." In a sense, Japan was all only following the well-trodden path of modern "liberal democracy" and its twin brother, market fundamentalism (Market). Together, these provided the on-going impetus for the worldwide emancipation of "insatiable lusts" for private property, goods and services.

Accordingly, most of the societies on Planet Earth, influenced by the industrially advanced "democratic" countries, have become enthused with economic expansion, capital accumulation, resource exploitation, acquisitiveness, extravagance and even fraudulent behaviors, as if the natural environment, resources and human endurance were unlimited. Thus, our contemporary world, as a result of economic globalization, is now faced with the growing severity of global resource constraints, which, together with the grossly lopsided modern value system, has produced the extremely skewed distribution of income, wealth and amenity, both *intra*-nationally and *inter*-nationally. The increasing proportion of the poor in the growing global population eloquently speaks for the growing inequity, poverty, instability, exclusion and, often, cruelty. Figuratively speaking, Planet Earth has turned into an insular planet, as far as the increasing severity of constraints on the natural environment and resources and their immediate effects on all humanity are concerned.

Natural and human resources have been excessively and brutally exploited under economic globalization. The global environment (Environment) also has suffered devastation, due to the resultant heavy pollution, global warming and destruction of ecosystems. The diverse Cultures worldwide have been liquidated by the Market to leave the mutual trust and the societal solidarity collapsing everywhere. In addition, the IT Revolution and technological innovations relevant to communication and transportation have accelerated global accessibility as well as the concentration of power, giving the impression of a much shrunken Planet Earth. These and other related drastic changes have made the confrontational behaviors of peoples and societies alarmingly hazardous and detrimental to human survival in the future. In other words, both growing global production and individual acquisitiveness through "free-market competition" and "emancipation of individual lusts" have been made untenable on the insular planet.

Likewise, the on-going rapid shift of income, wealth, resources and amenity from poor to rich across the world on the basis of the rampant "economic colonialism" has accelerated the physical difficulty and the political fatality. Under the severe constraints of the insular planet, therefore, it has become extremely difficult to continue our politico-economic activities which are based on acquisitive confrontation of assumed rational, self-sufficient and autonomous individuals; to continue our output growth based on the "insatiability" of human wants as well as on the Market mindset; and to continue the deficient and lopsided "market approach" to resource allocation and income distribution. Now, it seems inevitable for us to argue against the modern "liberal democracy" that allows the free and massive individual-and-collective deviations from the common good—Sustainable Development.

New Democracy on the Insular Planet

At its very inception, modern "liberal democracy" seems to have assumed more idealized social constituents than "flesh and blood" can stand. As a result, gross misconceptions and distortions in the real workings of democracy have emerged, even in Western societies where democracy first arose. "Democracy," as such, must have reasonable expectations with regards to the social constituents and ought to be adjusted to the people based on their own Cultural heritage, in order for it to be effective and produce viable results.

In these Western societies, however, modern "liberal democracy," that has justified and encouraged utilitarianism, private property, a laissez-faire economy, well-being, peace and order, has widened the gap between the rich and poor, as well as accelerated moral, Cultural and Environmental degradation. Moreover, it is extremely costly;

worldwide military expense (security costs) alone now amounts to the total value-added of the poorer half of the human population. This implies also the incalculable waste of human efforts and material resources, not to speak of the damage to the Environment. Under the condition of the insular planet, therefore, modern "liberal democracy" should be drastically reoriented, redesigned or discarded, rather than enshrined as a universal principle.

Dwelling on the insular planet now, we must strive to learn how to live more amicably, share more equitably and collaborate more readily for the survival of all people and societies, as well as for the decent life of all humans. For these purposes, we should generate "open democracy" on the principle of "Integrity in Diversity," by forfeiting the existing "closed democracy" based on the standardizing principle of "Unity in Diversity," as elaborated upon in Chapter 10. Also, we should replace the steep and humanly unreachable *rationality* in the strict modern interpretation, by gentle and humanly approachable *reasonableness* of a more tolerant and equitable world. Further, we should restrain ourselves from indulging in either our *insatiable* wants or our *confrontational* politico-economic behaviors.

Further still, we should open up ourselves to a flexible mental and intellectual aspiration that respects and understands the *circulatory view* of life and nature, the system of *symbiosis* for the mankind-inclusive whole natural world, and a world that cherishes a sound variety of subjective-objective spirituality without the strict binds of monotheism. Particularly, in view of the "democratic" adaptation of ourselves to the idea and lifestyle encompassing Sustainable Development, we should cherish the congenial spirits of collaboration, sharing and solidarity based on the diverse and Sound Cultures, eliminating at the same time the "might-makes-right" ideology that encourages excessive competition, exclusion and cruelty. For a more comprehensive and systemic approach, we should pursue the long-term policy that encourages the *trilateral virtuous circle* among Holistic Culture Enrichment, Comprehensive Human Development and Balanced Socioeconomic Development in each and all societies.

Concluding Remarks

As quoted above, the teaching and warning of Yokoi Shonan, urging that Japan should enrich the nation and strengthen its force, "*not for supremacy* but for good and peaceful governance of itself based on the *people's good conscience*," is worth repeating here. Such an idea can be very well emulated by the world at large and wisely incorporated into the above-described "open democracy" based on the diverse-Culture-treasuring "Integrity in Diversity". It may enrich the "tolerant and broad-minded" attitude appropriate to the practice of "open democracy" on our insular planet. Such a democracy can contribute to Global Humanity (humane ways of sharing income, wealth and amenity on the basis of Comprehensive Human Development) and Culture of Peace (global climate for the peaceful cooperation through dialogue and reconciliation on the basis of fundamental "*sound common communal values*" of the diverse and reasonably sound Cultures). Given such an "open democracy" for Sustainable Development, it may not be far-fetched to believe that all countries on our insular planet evolve gradually to be motivated to disarm themselves.

According to William Graham, Professor of the University of Toronto, "Whereas, in the self-sufficient consciousness the autonomous individual has dominion of other animals and the world of nature in general (including women, children and laborers), the Collaborative Consciousness of Relational Individuals recognizes and affirms differences and diversity" (Graham 2005). Indeed, it is indispensable to rethink and redefine our fellow humans as "relational individuals," for most of us/them, worldwide, may naturally exhibit such characteristics. Also, we would do well to count on the collaborative consciousness of *Culture-respecting* relational individuals for the promotion of Sustainable Development, Culture of Peace and Global Humanity. Moreover, "open democracy" on the basis of the "diverse-Culture-treasuring" principle of Integrity in Diversity, as well as on the basis of collaborative-conscious relational individuals, may suit our insular planet best.

27 A Society of Longevity and a Positive Perspective

Now, I will take up another important issue—Society of Longevity—which is compatible with Sustainable Development, Culture of Peace and Global Humanity in our prospective global community, as well as related closely to the aforementioned Balanced Socioeconomic Development, Holistic Culture Enrichment and Comprehensive Human Development in each society. Society of Longevity refers to our future perspective of a wholesome society embodying a "positive and integral" socioeconomic policy for the accomplishment of full life, good health and meaningful career (Hiwaki 1997, 1998c). Its comprehensive socioeconomic policy may contrast very well with the "passive" and "patchwork" social policy prevailing in our advanced industrial nations. The present vision of a wholesome society may not just be a dream or a fantasy. It is the vision of a viable society to be shared by many "newly enlightened" people on the way to Sustainable Development. Maybe we are already heading for such a society, by the force of historical imperative.

For the Society of Longevity to fully blossom, however, untiring personal and societal endeavors for "positive and integral" reforms may be required in the prevailing systems of social values, education, medicine and employment, to mention only the major ones. In creating such a future state of society, the cultured awareness of growing life spans may expand our conscious time horizon and planning scope, encouraging a longer-term perspective and future orientation. This could trigger a "virtuous circle" of Comprehensive Human Development, Holistic Culture Enrichment and Balanced Socioeconomic Development in each and all societies. Such a *trilateral virtuous circle* may facilitate the necessary reforms for a longer, healthier, more active, more meaningful and comfortable life, as well as a greater scope and experience for finding our potential talents, worthy careers and fitting lifestyles. Then, the Society of Longevity may serve the integral goals of Sustainable Development, Culture of Peace and Global Humanity.

Full Life, Good Health and a Meaningful Career

Today, we sense a negative air surrounding the discussion of once coveted "longevity" when it is within the reach of almost all people. Indeed, the widely known "welfare state" is presently posing a serious problem among the forerunner societies, due mainly to the ever increasing financial burden that erodes other social priorities. In a sense we are staggered at a technical question regarding the *inter*-generational transfer of resources for the care of the increasing elderly and, perhaps, we are wasting much time on it.

I think it is about the time to ask ourselves a crucial question: Do we have the *will* to pursue a "positive and integral" socioeconomic policy aiming at a longer, healthier, more active, more meaningful and comfortable life for all? Such a socioeconomic policy represents an alternative to the prevailing "passive" social policy relevant to the "welfare state." The "positive and integral" policy is, in my opinion, not only compatible with, but also conducive to Sustainable Development, Culture of Peace and Global Humanity in the prospective global community. Further, it is highly conducive to Balanced Socioeconomic Development, Comprehensive Human Development and Holistic Culture Enrichment in each society.

The reason why the prevailing social policy is considered "passive" can be found in its "remedial" characteristics. The "welfare state" offers a remedy for the Market-driven disparity in income distribution. In other words, the moral hazard of self-seeking modern individuals and the short-sighted forces of the Market have exaggerated the income disparity among people to require a transfer of resources from the beneficiary of the Market to the ill-favored in a broad sense. If this is the case, the implied income transfer must take place largely "*intra*-generationally" rather than "*inter*-generationally." In practice, however, the "welfare state" has placed a strong emphasis on the transfer of income from the young to the elderly—*inter*-generational redistribution—especially when it comes to the public pension and medical expenses. This practice, in the face of a demographic shift, has made the current social policy doubly "passive"—remedial and demographic passivity. Put differently, the rising proportion of the elderly in the social constituents has made a sufficient income transfer increasingly difficult over time.

In view of short-sighted market forces and pervasive egoistic self-interest, both of which erode human welfare and the natural environment, I now propose a "positive and integral" socioeconomic policy that may be conducive to the Society of Longevity with a *happiness triangle* comprising the mutually reinforced *full life, good health* and *meaningful career*, as depicted in Figure 27.1 (Hiwaki 1997). Such a wholesome society, that bases itself on the synergistic interactions among the important human conditions of the *happiness triangle,* is also conducive to Sustainable Development by the implied requirements of long-term social, economic and ecological perspectives of our physical and mental health, as well as of our continuous socioeconomic development. A full blossoming of the Society of Longevity, therefore, hinges on the "positive and integral" reforms in the prevailing social value system as well as the systems of medicine, employment and education.

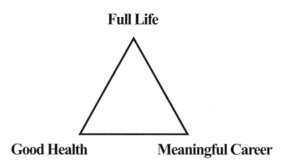

Figure 27.1 A happiness triangle

The Society of Longevity implies the necessity of manifold changes in our social priorities. To begin with, social priorities must change from the prevailing justification of overarching and egoistic individual "self-interest" to a greater reliance on individual and collective "mutual interest" in the collaborative endeavor to accomplish such a *happiness triangle* for people generally. Priorities must also change from the prevailing emphasis on the material-biased satisfaction to the reinforced cultivation of greater satisfaction on the bases of mental, spiritual, aesthetic, intellectual and emotional sources. Further, priorities must change from the prevailing "remedial" social policy to a long-term "preventive" socioeconomic policy encompassing medicine, career development and other welfare requirements.

Further still, priorities must change from the prevailing job opportunities largely based on the market-centered "division of labor" to the ones encouraging the Culture-embracing "harmonious integration" of personal capacities for worthy and lifelong careers. Moreover, priorities must change from the prevailing market-oriented and intellectuality-slanted education in the formal setting of schools to a flexible "lifetime continuing education" for the Culture-based and intellectuality-aesthetics-spirituality-balanced investment in personal capacities, with much better coordination and integration of the educational roles appropriate to home, school and community.

Toward Positive Socioeconomic Policy

According to Michio Morishima, Professor Emeritus of the London School of Economics, nobody would tolerate a group of greedy individuals for long, unless the wealth accumulated by their monetary greed is restored, in one way or another, to people at large. Hence, there exist two kinds of actions in the upper structure of society to protect the individuals thriving by their monetary greed. One is the action for law and order to protect them directly. Another kind refers to indirect means of protection or actions to pacify the rest of the people through promotion of social welfare. Thus, modern capitalism consists of the narrowly-defined "capitalist" sector as the lower structure of the capitalist system and the welfare-education sector as the upper structure. The former cannot survive without the latter in the long duration of time, and vice versa (Morishima 1995).

In tacit agreement with Morishima's view regarding the complementary structures in the capitalist system, sociologist Totaro Okada, after his laborious study on the writings of William Beveridge, T.H. Marshall, Richard Titumuss, Paul Halmos and Robert Pinker, notes that social services of the "welfare state" have been typically developed since the beginning of the twentieth century in Great Britain to cope with the social problems of the capitalist industrial society (Okada 1995). These notions imply that the current system of social welfare has not developed for itself as proof of human progress or kind-hearted compassion, but largely to protect the interest of the society's acquisitive and wealthy sector. So-called "social welfare," then, has developed as a reaction to Market-generated miseries, especially as a measure to justify human market behaviors based on the grossly distorted value system, the overarching emphasis on *egoistic self-interest*, in particular. In this sense, I consider the prevailing welfare system "passive."

Surveying the fiscal difficulty of social policy, which many advanced industrial nations encounter on the basis of the prevailing "*inter*-generational" income transfer under the on-going demographic trend, Lester C. Thurow in *The Future of Capitalism* (1996) questions the viability of the present "welfare state" from a different angle. He views negatively the compatibility of "*inter*-generational" transfer with the democratic process, where the growing number of elderly look after their own "self-interest" and vote for themselves an ever greater income at the cost of the young, consequently exacerbating the fiscal difficulty and leading to a new class struggle. "In the years ahead, class struggle is apt to be redefined to mean not the poor against the rich but the young against the old." This passage by Thurow, though politically "twisted," eloquently speaks against the prevailing social policy at the mercy of "demographic shift."

Such negative implications can also be seen in the naming of the on-going demographic trend, using terms such as the "aging society" and "graying population." They usually insinuate the increasing societal costs of medicine and pension paid for the rising proportion of the retired elderly, the growing negative effects on socioeconomic vitality under the declining proportion of young-and-working people and the accelerating organizational and institutional stiffening concurrent with the demographic shift. Indeed, the costs of medicine and public pensions are increasing rapidly today and, perhaps, other problems are also on the rise. We cannot, however, attribute all these problems to the demographic shift alone. All or, at least, part of these growing social maladies may have roots in our modern value system leaning heavily on the egoistic self-interest and the short-sighted Market, as well as on the "passivity" of the prevailing social policy.

In the 1970s, when the "welfare state" was not so negatively viewed, Gunner Myrdal, a Swedish Nobel laureate, made a much more "positive" statement (Myrdal 1972). That is, social reforms of the "preventive" kind, aiming at families and children, concerning housing, nourishment, health-keeping and education, especially when offered in kind, may reduce the future cost of individuals and society or improve future productivity. This indicates the core idea of the Scandinavian social policy: that is, *prevention is superior to remedy*. It is this type of "positive and future-oriented" idea that is a step in the right direction toward a "positive" socioeconomic policy.

Our present argument may push the idea further, by explicitly aiming at the "positive and integral" socioeconomic policy and welfare system for the Society of Longevity, compatible with Sustainable Development. Such policies and systems may serve as the cause of improving lifestyles, health care and career development of all people for the possible accomplishment of *full life*, *good health* and *meaningful career*. The mutually-reinforcing trilateral relations shown in the *happiness triangle* above imply not only the interactive possibility for such comprehensive accomplishment but also the respectively related areas in need of "positive" reforms, namely, the systems of education, welfare and employment. Put differently, the human conditions such as *full life*, *good health* and *meaningful career* depend on one another. That is: *full life* requires good health and a worthy career, *good health* requires an enjoyable *full life* coupled with a *meaningful career*, and a *meaningful career* requires *good health* and an enjoyable *full life*.

Policy for the Society of Longevity

A POSITIVE AND INTEGRAL EDUCATIONAL SYSTEM

The Society of Longevity requires a "comprehensive" socioeconomic policy for "positive and integrative" remodeling of the existing systems relevant to education, welfare and employment. To begin with, the "positive and integral" educational system coordinates and integrates the diverse educational functions of home, school, community and "virtual" variety on the basis of the Culture-embraced long-term perspectives and future orientation.

Such a system must aim at cultivating a full potential of individual persons as well as expanding their thought-frames to the fullest extent based on the following guidelines.

The "positive and integral" educational system must avoid a bureaucratic manual-based operation primarily based on precedents and formalism. Second, such an educational system must place the utmost emphasis on the holistic grasp of human past, present and future, rather than justifying only the modern trend and existent conditions. Third, the educational system must always remain flexible, receptive, insightful, critical and respectful toward the existing diverse Cultures as well as toward the changing ideas and values. Fourth, such an educational system must have a leading function to enrich the society's own Culture, by emphasizing respect for the other diverse Cultures across the world (see Chapter 18).

Last but not least, the educational system must have the purpose of serving all people, by contributing to their well-balanced and comprehensive human development, worthy careers and enjoyable lifestyles. It must not aim at promoting any special interests, including ones of industry, finance and State authority. Such a "positive and integral" educational system is conducive to expanding personal and societal thought-frames in time and space and, hence, enhancing personal and societal values and concerns for the "common and mutual interests" as well as downgrading the pervasive "*individual* self-interest" and "collective *national* interest."

A POSITIVE AND INTEGRAL WELFARE SYSTEM

A "positive and integral" welfare system is also called for. Such a welfare system must provide a solid socioeconomic foundation for empowerment of all people far beyond the maintenance of human dignity. It is for the purpose of encouraging the "positive and integral" lifestyles for all, which is Culture-embraced and Culture-enhancing. Such a welfare system must have the greatest emphasis on *preventive* welfare and medicine to enhance health, career, longevity and comfort. Also, it must provide for *continuing* education to enhance career development and self-actualization, and encourage the *mutual* responsibility for enriching the financial base for health maintenance, career development and income security. Here, I emphatically use the terms "preventive," "continuing" and "mutual" for the "positive and integral" socioeconomic policy.

The "mutual finance," namely, a well-balanced "*inter*-generational" and "*intra*-generational" finance, must not exclude reasonable "self-help" that is always encouraged as a top priority in personal welfare, but the "mutual help" must be available for all as the basic measure for furthering health, career, longevity and comfort as well as for securing human dignity. The well-balanced "*inter*-generational" and "*intra*-generational" nature of "mutual finance" based on the sound Cultural enrichment can deal with the demographic shift and the economic change and, at the same time, encourage the intrinsic nature of *relational mutuality*—"reciprocal help" and "interdependence."

A POSITIVE AND INTEGRAL EMPLOYMENT SYSTEM

Furthermore, the Society of Longevity requires a "positive and integral" employment system (or the "Culture-enhancing and Culture-integrated" employment system discussed in Chapter 23), which facilitates smooth mobility of workers to put the right person in the right place over time. Also, it is crucial for such an employment system to encourage, as much as practicable, "integration" of the Culture-embraced personal characteristics in intellectuality, personality, aesthetics, creativity, public concern, morality, spirituality, long-term perspective, future orientation, and so on. This is for the sake of career development and self-actualization as well as of fulfilling personal responsibilities for the common and mutual purposes.

By the "positive and integral" employment system, I mean not only the smooth mobility of workers but also their flexible career choices and redevelopment, positively and integrally supported by societal facilities and opportunities of "continuing" education and enlightenment. Moreover, by such a system, I mean not only the equitable employment opportunities free of discrimination by sex, race, ethnicity, creed, age and so on, but also the equitable "long-term rewards" without much slant by the short-sighted market forces (see Chapter 23). Besides, such an employment system must include the function to ameliorate mental and physical stresses in the work environment by means of the Cultural "glue and lubricant" for human relations.

A POSITIVE AND INTEGRAL VALUE SYSTEM

On top of everything else, the Society of Longevity requires a "positive and integral" value system with a modified "positive" personal self-image and general image of human nature ("mutuality-oriented" human nature), coupled with the Culture-based long-term perspective that integrates harmoniously mutual interest and self-interest. Such a value system, also harmoniously integrating "material-spiritual" values, "individual-societal" values and "traditional-progressive" values, may encourage the "positive" personal preference of the Culture-based future orientation and long-term perspectives rather than the present-intensive "short-run" orientation. In addition, such a "positive and integral" value system places a strong emphasis on the "positive and future-oriented thinking" that a challenge (or a preventive action) is superior to acquiescence (or a remedial action). On the basis of such "positive" human image, personal preference and thinking, the value system may interact synergistically with the systems of "positive and integral" education, welfare and employment to enhance opportunities for all to enjoy a longer, healthier, more active, fruitful and comfortable life and lifestyle. This vision of "positive and integral" enjoyment of long life constitutes the goal pertinent to the Society of Longevity.

Society of Longevity and Sustainable Development

The Society of Longevity that embodies such a comprehensive socioeconomic policy for the above systems of "positive and integral" values, education, welfare and employment is, no doubt, conducive to the Culture-based long-term perspectives, future orientation, human capital formation, career development, common-and-mutual interest, stress-ameliorated work environment and equitable-and-fair distribution of income. Also, the Society of Longevity favors preventive welfare and medicine, harmonious interpersonal relationships, "open democracy" for the prospective global community, stability in population growth, balanced socioeconomic development and conservation of the global environment. All these happen to be important conditions for Sustainable Development, to say nothing of Culture of Peace and Global Humanity. In other words, the Society of Longevity may "positively and integrally" promote general interest in Sustainable Development.

To begin with, the Society of Longevity generally encourages a longer, healthier, more active, fruitful and comfortable life. An expanding average life span, especially the "positively" cultured awareness of growing general life span, is conducive to the personal and societal expansion of *conscious* time horizon and planning scope. Put differently, our awareness of expanding life span may encourage our long-term thinking and future planning, and motivate us to increase investment in our personal and societal capacities. This process serves to expand our personal and societal thought-frames in time and space, enhancing our long-term perspectives and future orientation. Stated more straightforwardly, a general expansion of life span can trigger off a "virtuous circle" between the long-term future orientation and the comprehensive human development, to nurture higher goals and mutual concerns.

This "virtuous circle" facilitates the required reforms for the Society of Longevity that provides us greater scope and more varied experiences for finding our potential talents, worthy careers and fitting lifestyles, in order to pave the way, for all people, to a longer, healthier, more active, fruitful and comfortable life in the future. Such a life requires, in addition to the reasonably Sound Cultures across the world, both the wholesome global environment and the well-balanced socioeconomic development in the prospective global community (or Sustainable Development). In a sense, the Society of Longevity interacts mutually and perpetually with Sustainable Development. Such an interaction may, most probably, take place in the Maturation Process on our normative Optimal Development Path (ODP) as discussed in Theoretical Appendix 4.

Concluding Remarks

I have discussed my "positive and integral" perspective concerning the broader welfare system aiming at the synergistic interactions of full life, good health and meaningful career. Indeed, the human life span almost everywhere in the world is growing as improvements in medicine, nourishment, sanitation, welfare and education are made. At the same time, many advanced industrial nations, on the one hand, are struggling with the increasing cost of the "welfare state," given the growing number of the retired elderly and often the dwindling number of the young and incumbent workers. On the other hand, the world community, with an on-going polarization in income, wealth, education, technology and social welfare, is facing an increasing number of people at the bottom of the global income strata, suffering from starvation, malnutrition, and imminent death, not to mention lack of human dignity.

Given the growing human life span with the ominous population explosion, it is, perhaps, imperative to look for a "positive and integral" way to enhance human well-being in the future. Society of Longevity is a vision that requires a global "positive and integral" socioeconomic policy with the emphatically balanced *inter*-generational and *intra*-generational "mutual financing" scheme. This scheme can be supported by a willing elongation of the general work life concurrent with longer, healthier, more active, fruitful and comfortable life for all people, which constitutes the goal pertinent to the Society of Longevity. Earnest pursuance of such a wholesome world community of the future, in my opinion, is not only relevant but also conducive to the simultaneous resolution of the important global issues—Sustainable Development, Culture of Peace and Global Humanity.

28 *Multilateral-Value Interactions*

In this chapter I will introduce summarily a theoretical/analogical illumination as part of the present long-term theoretical framework for Sustainable Development. The diagrammatical explanation of *integral value development* will be related closely to Cultural enrichment, human development and socioeconomic development. In other words, I will introduce here Culture-enriching human development in terms of a theoretical diagram that refers to the dynamic interactions of multilateral personal and societal values. Such a diagrammatic presentation, emphasizing an important approach to Cultural enrichment and human development, will bring out the complex value interactions for socioeconomic development eventually helping to induce the global process of Sustainable Development.

Integral Value Development

Balanced Socioeconomic Development and Holistic Culture Enrichment tend to require a growing long-term future orientation in the personal and societal thought-frames that represent their scopes of thought in time and space. A continuous improvement of the general thought-frame is imperative for the maintenance and augmentation of societal vitality. Such thought-frame enhancement can interact over time with the enhancement of common goals, general lifestyles and basic humanities within each society. A favorable simultaneous process of the Cultural enrichment and the social-vitality augmentation will be shown by the multilateral value interactions in Figure 28.1, which involves the four inter-related axes as discussed briefly in Chapter 18.

Among these axes are the horizontal axis on the right-hand side for "future-plan elongation" (Ft); the horizontal axis on the left-hand side for "life-prospect elongation" (Lt); the vertical axis above the origin for "personal-capacity enrichment" (Ih); and vertical axis below the origin for "societal-capacity enrichment" (Is). The horizontal axes on the right and the left, respectively, suggest the scope of future orientation (Ft) and the range of life expectation (Lt). More specifically, the right-hand axis (Ft) implies the planning range of the society, and the left-hand axis (Lt) the expected range of average life span.

The upper and the lower vertical axes show respectively the range of human-capital formation (Ih) and the range of investment in soft-and-hard socioeconomic infrastructure (Is). Such investment in human capital and social infrastructure are considered amenable to the *long-term* government policies for the sound enrichment of the Culture. These policy-amenable axes also indicate the likelihood of effective government initiatives of a long-term nature, which stimulate personal and societal endeavors for improving the respective capacities. In other words, Cultural enrichment and personal-societal vitality

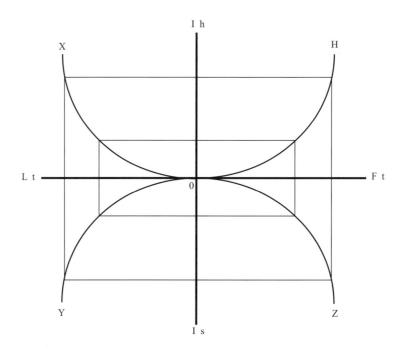

Figure 28.1 Multilateral-value enhancement

can be stimulated simultaneously over time by the *long-term* government policies. Also, such stimulation, perhaps, can reinforce indirectly the personal and societal orientation to the future and also influence indirectly the elongation of average life span that is blessed with health and vitality

A first theoretical process in Figure 28.1 refers to *thought-frame enhancement*—the augmentation of "intellectual and planning values." This process is shown by the curve sloping upward in the first quadrant—*Curve H*. The curve of *thought-frame enhancement* suggests a long-term continuous interaction between the growing future orientation (Ih) and the growing human-capital formation (Ih). Thus, moving upward on *Curve H* implies the process of human development in terms of "intellectuality and long-term perspective." A second theoretical process refers to the curve of *human-value enhancement*— the augmentation of "human and spiritual values." This process is shown by the curve sloping upward in the second quadrant—*Curve X*. The curve of *human-value enhancement* suggests a long-term continuous interaction between the growing human-capital formation (Ih) and the growing life expectation (Lt). Thus, moving upward on *Curve X* implies the process of human development in terms of "character and spirituality."

A third theoretical process refers to the curve of *lifestyle enhancement*—the augmentation of "health and living values." This process is shown by the curve sloping downward in the third quadrant—*Curve Y*. The curve of *lifestyle enhancement* suggests a long-term continuous interaction between the growing life expectation (Lt) and the growing investment in soft-and-hard socioeconomic infrastructure (Is). Thus, moving downward on *Curve Y* implies human development in terms of "soundness and aesthetics." A fourth theoretical process refers to the curve of *common-goal enhancement*—the augmentation of "long-term social and mutual values." This process is shown by the curve sloping downward in the fourth quadrant—*Curve Z*. The curve of *common-goal enhancement* suggests a long-term continuous interaction between the growing investment in soft-and-hard socioeconomic infrastructure (Is) and the growing future orientation (Ft). Thus, moving downward on *Curve Z* implies human development in terms of "long-term common and mutual concern."

A final theoretical process refers to the overall harmonious development that refers to Holistic Culture Enrichment, Comprehensive Human Development and Balanced Socioeconomic Development. This is the *Grand Process* expressed by the expansion of the rectangle that connects all the four axes and the four curves. In other words, the initial rectangle, connecting Ft, *Curve H*, Ih, *Curve X*, Lt, *Curve Y*, Is, and *Curve Z*, moves to expand itself harmoniously and integrally in the eight directions to form a larger rectangle. Thus, the *Grand Process* indicates the "mutually reinforcing harmonious interactions" among the eight respective processes to direct simultaneous and synchronous human development, socioeconomic development and Cultural enrichment.

Social Value System and Societal Viability

The Culture, with its broad and comprehensive definition as well as its multilateral value system, in particular, may become enriched along with the simultaneous movement away from the origin on the four axes and the four curves in Figure 28.1. More specifically, the future plan, the life prospect, the personal capacity and the societal capacity are all improving together with the *value enhancement* relevant to intellectuality and long-term perspective (*Curve H*), humanity and spirituality (*Curve X*), soundness and aesthetics (*Curve Y*) and long-term common and mutual concern (*Curve Z*). All these improving values, as mentioned above, are conducive to the simultaneous promotion of Holistic Culture Enrichment, Comprehensive Human Development and Balanced Socioeconomic Development. These multidimensional processes of value improvement, all together, may lead to the reinforcement of personal and societal vitality as well as the sound enrichment of the Culture. Such multi-faceted enrichment of the Culture and augmentation of the personal and societal vitality may, in turn, reinforce the society's *centripetal force* as well as the *mutual trust* among the social constituents for the viability of the society.

Thus, it is important to note that the *centripetal force* and *mutual trust* cannot be separated from either the dynamic Sound Culture or the Culture-based personal and societal vitality. When the Culture suffers devastation by the Market, the general public may defy the society as well as its leadership and become apathetic, defensive, self-seeking, present-oriented, nihilistic and/or disorderly. Then, the personal and societal vitality undergoes a continuous degeneration. This implies a perpetual degradation of human spirit, attitude and behavior. Such degeneration may, most likely, lead to the evaporation of *centripetal force* and *mutual trust*. With such degeneration of vitality, socioeconomic activities may certainly deteriorate to start reversing the movements on the four axes and the four curves in Figure 28.1.

More specifically, the elongation processes of future plan and life span, as well as the enrichment processes of personal and societal capacities may, most likely, turn backward and toward their respective and simultaneous deterioration. At the same time, the enhancement processes of thought-frames, human values, lifestyles and common goals may face the very similar fates. In other words, all the "positive-and-constructive" inclinations of the social constituents toward the society and the Culture may fall into "negative and destructive" inclinations or into a "vicious circle" reversing the *Grand Process*—the eight-fold processes of deterioration. Such societal and Cultural predicaments, indeed, may induce the Cultural degeneration as well as the personal and societal lethargy. Then, the society concerned cannot avoid a prolonged economic deterioration and social disorder, coupled with the Market-accelerated instability, uncertainty and insecurity. Such multitudes of prolonged social and Cultural maladies refer to the Credibility Trap—an extra long-term societal lethargy—resulted from the Cultural devastation.

Theory-Pertinent Policy Implications

From the above discussion, we can easily draw our theory-pertinent policy implications for the prevention of the Credibility Trap which is an *antithesis* to both "local" balanced socioeconomic development and "global" Sustainable Development. The Necessary Condition for Balanced Socioeconomic Development requires a long-term policy for encouraging "the on-going improvement of standard of living" (reflecting both mental and material enrichment) relevant to all people. Much more difficult, the Sufficient Condition for Balanced Socioeconomic Development requires an appropriate long-term policy for encouraging the enhancement of long-term *society-general* future orientation, coupled with the general *thought-frame enhancement*. The Sufficient Condition also prescribes the nature of improvement in living standard. Put differently, the aggregate consumption must grow over time, shifting it gradually from "quantity-oriented" to "quality-oriented," as well as from "material-centered" to "personality/spirituality/intellectuality-centered." Likewise, the aggregate labor income must grow in the long term, reflecting the improvement of human character, productivity and general capacity of the workers.

In accordance with the above policy implications, our theoretical framework for the interaction of society's Value and Real Aspects (see Theoretical Appendix 2) emphasizes the importance of long-term policies for encouraging the sound enrichment of the Culture in relation to human development and socioeconomic development. The continuous enrichment of the Culture is the most important precondition for the personal and societal vitality, mutual trust, reliability, integrity and interdependence as well as for the social centripetal force and the societal continuity.

Again, in accordance with all the long-term policies mentioned above, the framework of the multilateral value interactions (Figure 28.1) also suggests the importance of long-term policies to encourage the growth of Culture-enhancing human-capital investment as well as the coherent growth of investment in soft-and-hard socioeconomic infrastructure. Such a well-coordinated investment policy may stimulate the constant and concerted enhancement of personal and societal thought-frames toward a longer-term future orientation, which may have favorable consequences in Cultural enrichment, human development and socioeconomic development. Such a long-term policy may encourage "directly" the enrichment of personal-and-societal capacities and "indirectly" the elongation of future plan and life span, as well as the consequential enhancement of intellectual-and-planning values, human-and-spiritual values, health-and-living values and common-and-mutual values. Such improvement of Culture-enhancing personal and societal characteristics may, in due course of time, counterbalance and modify the Market-induced crude and inhuman values prevalent in our contemporary world.

Concluding Remarks

All in all, the above long-term policies that aim at Holistic Culture Enrichment may exert a strong influence on Comprehensive Human Development and Balanced Socioeconomic Development of the given society. At the same time, such long-term policies for Cultural enrichment, when adopted by a great majority of societies in the world, may become capable eventually to persuade the Market into generating a *"sound-and-fair"* market function for the benefit of all persons and societies in both the present and future generations as an important step toward Sustainable Development. Thus, our long-term concerted endeavors for the enrichment of diverse Cultures across the world may serve generally for the prevention and remedy of the Credibility Trap as well as for the invigoration of the respective societies and the prospective global community.

29 *Systemic Resolutions of Important Issues*

The global issues, such as Sustainable Development, Culture of Peace and Global Humanity, respectively, are highly complex ones, since they have grown over the long duration of time, interacting with many other issues, ideologies, policy failure, market failure, Culture failure and human failure, among other things. These three issues, however, have a mutual and intimate relationship with one another, and we need to grasp their intrinsic common nature/property in order to produce an *integral policy* for systemic solutions. In this chapter, I will discuss such integral policy.

Mutual Relationship of Global Issues

CULTURE OF PEACE

In order to facilitate a solid and meaningful discussion of the mutual relations between the global issues of Sustainable Development, Culture of Peace and Global Humanity, we need to briefly review them. To begin with, the term Culture of Peace refers to a worldwide cultural foundation for the pursuit of peace in national and international communities. According to Dr Federico Mayor, the-then Director-General of UNESCO (Mayor 1997),

> *A culture of peace consists of values, attitudes and behaviors that reflect and inspire social interaction and sharing, based on the principles of freedom, justice and democracy, all human rights, tolerance and solidarity, that reject violence, endeavor to prevent conflicts by tackling their root causes to solve problems through dialogue and negotiation and that guarantee the full exercise of all rights and the means to participate fully in the development process of their society.*

Peace has always been threatened by the ideology of "might-makes-right" that caters to the Big Market. Such ideology tends to encourage the freedom of inequitable competition in the individuality interested and private-property centered activities, producing always the insolence of the winner and the resentment of the loser. Peace can never be achieved under such conditions. I am of the opinion that peace must be cultivated with unflagging endeavor, enthusiasm and fair spirit through dynamic and harmonious relationships among all peoples at both individual and collective levels. War and peace (or enmity and amity) may arise from relative mental conditions of the same humans individually and collectively.

No lasting peace can be achieved without the totally committed endeavor to enhance our own thought-frames, as well as to make our own minds reasonably balanced and harmonious. Our thought-frames can be enhanced and our minds reasonably balanced only if they are solidly based on the relevant Sound Cultures with the respective *sound communal value systems*. This being mentioned, our tentative definition of Culture of Peace refers to a worldwide cultural environment and function to encourage and support all personal, national and international peace-making and peace-keeping endeavors for a harmonious and collaborative co-existence based on the diverse Sound Cultures.

SUSTAINABLE DEVELOPMENT

Next, the term Sustainable Development is defined by *Our Common Future* as "development that meets the needs of the present without compromising the ability of future generations to meet their own needs" (WCED 1987). The definition is based on the World Commission's conviction that "it is impossible to separate economic development issues from environment issues; many forms of development erode the environmental resources upon which they must be based, and environmental degradation can undermine economic development."

In the same spirit, we may paraphrase the definition of Sustainable Development as a viable worldwide process of Balanced Socioeconomic Development in harmony with the conservation and enhancement of the global environment. Here, the term Balanced Socioeconomic Development refers to the balance between social and economic development that integrates and harmonizes short-term and long-term needs, material and spiritual needs and personal and societal needs. The term "global environment" represents the broad definition that encompasses the natural, cultural, humanitarian and peaceful environments. Our paraphrased definition of Sustainable Development emphasizes the importance of Balanced Socioeconomic Development to all humans, present and future, as well as the importance of thoughtful use and treatment of the global environment. Thus, Sustainable Development hinges on the enhancement of human thought-frames and enrichment of diverse Cultures.

GLOBAL HUMANITY

Finally, the term Global Humanity here indicates an appropriate future-oriented socioeconomic attitude and policy to prevent future human miseries, frustration and mental desolation as well as social disruption and warfare across the world. In a sense, Global Humanity is a future-oriented wholesome globalism that asserts a general *preventive* idea (that is, prevention is better than cure). In his *Beyond the Welfare State* (1960), Gunnar Myrdal argues that every person who is born on the earth has a right to enjoy a minimum level of guaranteed subsistence.

The acceleration of the Market-driven globalization in the last 30 years has destabilized almost all lives on the earth and dehumanized living and working conditions. Such economic globalization has also caused unprecedented miseries worldwide and the impending bankruptcy of humanity. In view of all such abuses by the Market, I feel it important to strive for a future-oriented integral policy of prevention. Thus, our present definition of Global Humanity emphasizes the *preventive trinity* of human needs that include subsistence, health and education, and also favors positive and viable human prospects. Global Humanity, therefore, means here a future-oriented global socioeconomic policy on the basis of worldwide collaborative and preventive endeavors for our common future, involving all natural and legal persons and all levels of government for a guaranteed accommodation of minimum human needs for subsistence, health and education.

MUTUAL AND TRILATERAL RELATIONSHIP

To accomplish Global Humanity, where every person on the earth can enjoy the *preventive trinity* of human needs may necessitate a worldwide collaborative endeavor for peace (Culture of Peace), as well as a global process of Balanced Socioeconomic Development (Sustainable Development). To accomplish Sustainable Development, or the worldwide process of socioeconomic development in harmony with the Environment, may necessitate a worldwide endeavor for accommodating everyone with the preventive trinity of minimum human needs (Global Humanity) and also the Sound Culture-oriented peace-making endeavor (Culture of Peace). To build a Culture of Peace, which refers to the worldwide sound Cultural function and foundation for the process of peach-making and peace-keeping endeavors, may necessitate the viable process of global socioeconomic development (Sustainable Development) and a worldwide endeavor for accommodating the *preventive trinity* of minimum human needs for all people (Global Humanity). These mutually supportive and interactive relations are depicted symbolically in Figure 29.1 (Hiwaki 2005J), where Circles C, S and G represent, respectively, Culture of Peace, Sustainable Development and Global Humanity.

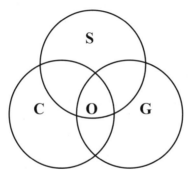

Figure 29.1 Supportive and interactive relations

Relations between Cultures and Global Issues

In addition to the above mutual relations, all these global issues assert, by necessity, a common mental attitude that upholds the global endeavors for human values, human development and humanities-directed solidarity as well as the general human ethos favoring sound, active and fruitful longevity. Such a common attitude is depicted by O in Figure 29.1 above. Also, the global issues commonly require both a conceptual space encompassing the entire world and a conceptual time encompassing the past, present and future of human history. Accordingly, the major global issues including Culture of Peace, Sustainable Development and Global Humanity are closely related to our diverse Cultures, for the existing Cultures, having endured the twists and turns of their long-term accumulation and enrichment processes, are inclined to grope and look for the long-term future. Further, such long-endured Cultures may naturally accommodate both the humanities-oriented endeavors and the longevity-favoring human ethos, which are more or less intrinsic to all the global issues in the above.

CULTURAL DIVERSITY AND DIFFERENT PRIORITIES

Facing their diverse socioeconomic and political realities, however, the respective Cultures and societies may differ somewhat from one another in their priorities regarding the common property that encourages such humanities-oriented endeavors and longevity-favoring ethos. Largely agreeing to the desirability of global and long-term perspectives, the respective Cultures and societies may reveal some ambivalence in such desirability. These likely differences among our Cultures and societies may eloquently speak for Cultural diversity, which must be taken as an undeniable reality of our world. Such Cultural diversity is, in a sense, an inevitable feature of the Cultures, since any Culture is largely a product of long-term human interactions with their respective neighbors, surroundings and climates, which may differ vastly depending on the locations on the earth (Diamond 1997). This awareness is crucial for any attempt to solve the global issues.

An equally important awareness concerns the necessity of amelioration relevant to modern and contemporary discriminations against non-Western Cultures. The awareness as such is particularly important in our contemporary times. The Market-driven pervasive *standardizing force*, sanctioned and reinforced by modern civilization on the basis of a particular faith and value system, has been devastating and liquidating the non-Western Cultures with an accelerated velocity and magnitude. Such world controlling and standardizing forces, when left alone, can accelerate human predicaments in terms of both localized and globalized conflicts of people and also in terms of the on-going devastation of the Environment. Such growing predicaments will be explained in the following section.

DESIRED SIMULTANEOUS APPROACH TO GLOBAL ISSUES

Presently, we are concerned with finding a way to deal effectively with the global issues. What I am aiming at, of course, is the worldwide realization of a *reasonably* secure, healthy and worthwhile life for all in the present and future generations. We humans may not be looking for a *paradise* of a unified faith, a scientifically envisioned *never* land, or a politico-economically concocted *utopia*. However difficult and remote it may seem, what we humans may need for ourselves is an active consensus worldwide on the desirability of a *secure, healthy and worthwhile life for all*. Such desirability may speak for both the humanities-oriented global endeavor and the longevity-favoring human ethos, however diverse the existing Cultures may be.

An active consensus on such desirability, therefore, may help lead to the simultaneous resolution of Culture of Peace, Sustainable Development and Global Humanity based on the sound enrichment of diverse Cultures. Such a process of Cultural enrichment and diversity may work for the enriched integral human capacities that reflect the dynamic and comprehensive human development. In contrast, it is quite certain that a mere expansion of economic activities in the world by Market-driven globalization, instead of improving the lives of all humans, leads only to widespread human misery through devastation of our diverse Cultures as well as of the Environment. A positive and favorable recognition and enrichment of diverse Cultures, therefore, is a first step to an end.

COMMON PROPERTY OF GLOBAL ISSUES AND DIVERSE CULTURES

Assuming broadly that the reasonably Sound Cultures tend to accommodate both the humanities-oriented endeavors and the longevity-favoring human ethos, we may relate the diverse Cultures to the major global issues in Figure 29.2 (Hiwaki 2005J). In the diagram, the area D denotes the diverse Cultures in the world. My contention here is that all the major issues of global importance contain the same common property (O) that upholds the humanities-oriented endeavors and the longevity-favoring human ethos, among other things. Now, such endeavors and ethos, both of which link the global issues with one another, are also closely related to the diverse Cultures across the world. Such complex, resonant and synergistic relations naturally lead to my argument for the sound enrichment of the diverse Cultures as the necessary condition for dealing effectively with global issues for the simultaneous and synchronous resolution of Culture of Peace, Sustainable Development and Global Humanity.

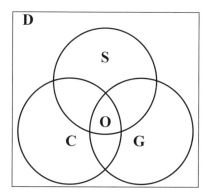

Figure 29.2 Cultures as related to global issues

Strategies for the Paradigm Shift

EDUCATION-DEVELOPING STRATEGY

One important factor for both the humanities-oriented endeavors and the longevity-favoring human ethos concerns the strategy of developing the Culture-enriching education worldwide. Such a redirected and innovative endeavor for educational development can change the prevailing cramming system of education (a "take-order" education for the Big Market) toward a more meaningful and, perhaps, more enjoyable education for the thought-frame enhancement as well as for the appreciation of Cultural enrichment and diversity (as discussed in Chapters 18 and 19). For this purpose, we need to mobilize and coordinate all modes of education, including home, school, community and "virtual" varieties. Such educational development must address the human life-long process to cultivate the capacity for overall and holistic understanding of human development processes and to bring out more congenial and constructive long-term attitude and behaviors in individual persons and the general public.

Such educational development must emphasize broad-based, multifaceted and diverse learning opportunities not only for knowledge and skills but also for values, sentiments, awareness, attitude, perspectives and integrative capacities. More concretely, it must positively stimulate individual persons and the general public for greater awareness of human development and historical processes. Also, it must bring out better insights into the past, present and future. Further, the educational development must encourage more appropriate and continuous endeavors for their *cumulative and synergistic effects*. Further still, it must nurture more enlightened long-term perspectives and stronger orientation to the future. Furthermore, it must lead to more compassionate and generous human relationships and more serious concern about *intrinsic human needs*. Moreover, the educational development must cultivate a greater appreciation of diverse Cultures and guide toward greater endeavors for Holistic Culture Enrichment (pursuing the paradigm shift). All these educational endeavors must aim at intellectual, aesthetic, spiritual, moral and overall human development.

EMPLOYMENT-DEVELOPING STRATEGY

Another important element concerns the strategy for developing the employment that favors the "Culture-enhancing and Culture-integrated" practice of employment (as discussed in Chapter 23). Such employment strategy must provide diverse employment opportunities not only for knowledge and skills but also for values, sentiments, awareness, attitude, perspectives and other Culture-oriented capacities. More concretely, such strategy must encourage the Cultural catalysis and synthesis for all the interpersonal relations within the respective organizations to avoid wasteful cut-throat competition and inhuman cut-and-dry work life. Also, the strategy must initiate to improve the Culture-embraced sense of responsibility, public spirit, reliability and mutual trust as well as the sound creativity based on the respective Sound Cultures. Further, such a positive development of employment must encourage a *harmonious and synergistic* interaction between the Culture and the "sound-and-fair" market function with two basic principles.

The first principle demands a well-balanced payment scheme, which accounts for both the "market-effective special skills" and the "Culture-effective general skills." These skills, containing respectively market values and broad Cultural values, are usually utilized together in economic activities for production and distribution of marketable goods and services. The second principle demands all individuals, all firms and all levels of government to strive, as much as practicable, for the continuity and enhancement of both the Culture-effective and the market-effective skills, so that almost all the skills can accumulate steadily over time for enrichment of the Cultural foundation. Such all-out endeavors can also augment the capacities of individual persons, peoples and societies to cope quite well with the dynamic world.

Such strategic development of employment practice with the two principles, in a sense, necessitates a gradual shift of economic activities toward Culture-oriented human development, which is much more relevant to the human needs of each society than the Market-oriented "want-and-desire" development solely for the profit motive of the acquisitively-slanted individuals. This employment strategy is intended to induce growing occupational opportunities for usually non-marketable but socially constructive human services. Such opportunities are desirable for the reinforcement or revitalization of local Cultures and communities, particularly for comprehensive youth development and social activities. Also, a variety of new occupations are required for the conservation and revitalization of the natural environment to offer natural, wholesome and aesthetic enjoyment to all people. These occupational opportunities with appropriate remuneration must be created by society as a whole for the sound enrichment of the Culture, as well as for the enhancement of the living conditions appropriate for Sustainable Development, Culture of Peace and Global Humanity. Such endeavors for the development of occupations may not only be able to create new employment opportunities but also transfer the human resources from the heavily Market-slanted economic activities to more humanly important Culture-oriented socioeconomic activities for mutual comfort and satisfaction.

INTERNATIONAL TRADE-DEVELOPING STRATEGY

Such endeavors may point to a third important strategy for the humanities-oriented endeavors and the longevity-favoring human ethos. This concerns the strategy for developing the "Culture-enhancing and Culture-integrated" international trade (as discussed in Chapter 24). Such a strategy may augment the merit of Holistic Culture Enrichment as well as the merit of Culture-respecting fair competition and cooperation against the prevailing Market-slanted "level-ground" absolute and antagonistic competition. Such strategy for the augmentation of international trade may prepare for more equitable and satisfactory lifestyles across the world, which is conducive to Sustainable Development, Culture of Peace and Global Humanity for the integral development of the prospective global community.

Any society has its unique characteristics comprising the history, value system, climate, location, disposition, attitude, creativity, education, technology, factor endowment, scale advantage, polity, policy, institution, risk factor, orientation to the future, and so on. These characteristics, interacting with one another over a long duration of time under the varying degrees of external influences, may have resulted in a unique holistic Culture. Therefore, any equitable international exchanges, broadly speaking, need to take place on the broad foundations of such diverse Cultures, which have largely conditioned their respective capacities in production as well as their diverse tastes and styles in consumption and social life. This suggests that each society, by means of the dynamic enrichment of its own Sound Culture, may naturally and constantly generate the "Culture-enhancing and Culture-integrated" *absolute, comparative, scarce and unique advantages* for international trade.

This is the reason why I argue for the encouragement of the specific Holistic Culture Enrichment (the paradigm shift), rather than standardization and uniformity concocted by the Market under the modern civilization. Put differently, an all-out endeavor for sound enrichment of our diverse Cultures may guarantee the continuity and dynamism of international trade. Culture-oriented cultivation and human development in all societies may lead to a growing demand and supply within and between societies on the basis of the constant refinement of the Culture-oriented consumption and social life of the respectively unique value-added output.

Also, the trade development on the basis of Culture-respecting sound competition may, no doubt, provide for the intrinsic short-term and long-term needs of individual persons, peoples and societies across the world as well as for the Culture-induced absolute, comparative, scarce and unique advantages in international trade. Thus, a general rethinking of international trade in line with the *Culture-respecting sound-and-fair competition and cooperation* may encourage the constant and sound enrichment of diverse Cultures, while improving the conditions for comfortable society-specific lifestyles and amicable human relations. Also, such rethinking may provide for the "mutually-maturing process" of *harmonious and synergistic* interactions between trading partners across the world.

Concluding Remarks

As I have argued repeatedly, it is important to revive and enrich our respective Cultures for the age of Sustainable Development. The sound enrichment of the existing diverse Cultures is a necessary condition for dealing effectively and simultaneously with Sustainable Development, Culture of Peace and Global Humanity. Such endeavor for enriching our diverse Cultures may also require the New Enlightenment that aims at the sound enrichment of the diverse Cultures, counter-balancing the pervasive Market supported by the global businesses and the governments of the advanced nations, as well as by the international organizations, such as the International Monetary Fund (IMF), World Trade Organization (WTO) and the World Bank. Also, such New Enlightenment must aim at facilitating the mutually enriching interaction between the diverse Cultures as well as generating the "sound-and-fair" market function. As indicated above, the process of Holistic Culture Enrichment leads to the enhancement in human-capital formation and the enrichment of general and diverse human capacities for Comprehensive Human Development. Also, the enrichment process of our diverse Cultures, in fact, works for Balanced Socioeconomic Development that naturally reflects the global enhancement of human values and humanities-oriented endeavors, as well as the worldwide reinforcement of the general human ethos favoring sound, active and fruitful longevity.

In other words, the dynamic process of Holistic Culture Enrichment in each society may naturally reinforce the community-interested, long-term-engaged, cooperation-propelled, accumulation-oriented and common-property-centered Cultural ethos and also accommodate the common values and attitudes intrinsic to the systemic resolution of the three important global issues (Sustainable Development, Culture of Peace and Global Humanity). Also, such values and attitudes, being reinforced by the New Enlightenment that encourages diverse Cultural enrichment for the growth of human motivation, capacity, solidarity and socioeconomic value balances for countervailing the market fundamentalism (Market), may encourage the Cultural effects for safer, healthier, more comfortable and more enlightened-and-enlightening lifestyles.

30 *Trilateral Virtuous Circles and Local-Global Linkage*

Sustainable Development requires a variety of local-global coordination and collaboration, which is, however, extremely difficult under the on-going economic globalization. The globalization has divided the world, by favoring the rich and strong whilst sacrificing the poor and weak. Given such worldwide politico-economic environment, any advancement toward Sustainable Development may become near impossible, unless humankind, sensing the imminent "human-invited" globe-scale catastrophe, makes an indomitable determination to pursue the paradigm shift. Indeed, the required global paradigm shift may amount to an all-out collaboration of human beings for the sound enrichment of the diverse Cultures (as discussed in Chapters 14, 15 and 16). Such Cultural enrichment in each society, interacting with both Comprehensive Human Development and Balanced Socioeconomic Development, may induce their perpetual "local" *trilateral virtuous circle*. Such a virtuous circle may, in turn, give rise eventually to a "global" *trilateral virtuous circle* among Culture of Peace, Global Humanity and Sustainable Development. There exists a close global and local correspondence between Culture of Peace and Cultural soundness, between Global Humanity and human development, and between Sustainable Development and socioeconomic development.

The Paradigm Shift for Sustainable Development

Sustainable Development is an open-ended perpetual process that requires conscious, earnest, tenacious and perpetual collaborations of all humanity for worldwide *socioeconomic transformation* by the paradigm shift. Sustainable Development, as a matter of course, cannot be achieved by a mere slogan and/or lip-service, nor can it be promoted by an extension of the on-going economic globalization with its lopsided value system. Such a value system of the Market-driven expansionism has been deeply inculcated by means of the modern *materialism*, *individualism*, *progressivism*, *egotism* and *antagonism*, as well as deceptively and vigorously encouraged by the self-seeking power structure of our contemporary world (Big Market). This indicates that Sustainable Development of the prospective global community may require the appropriate paradigm shift both locally and globally in order to counter-balance the existing pervasive Market value system. In a word, the new paradigm proposed in this book amounts to the sound and perpetual enrichment of diverse Cultures (the most intrinsic *common property* of the respective societies) by the collaborative endeavors of the respective social constituents.

Such endeavors must be pursued with an indomitable personal and societal determination as well as with an unyielding will to nurture the Sound Culture in each society. Such a Sound Culture is defined here as one capable of integrating and harmonizing the "seemingly" conflicting important values, so that the society can function harmoniously with the integral balances of such mutually opposing values (as elaborated in Chapters 15 and 16). Such important integral balances may include spiritual-and-material, traditional-and-progressive, personal-and-societal and own-and-other societal value balances. These value balances may refer, respectively, to the *human integrity, societal continuity, social solidarity* and *relational mutuality,* conducing to the most intrinsic communal value—*human and social harmony*—all of which must be maintained synchronously by the harmonizing dynamism of the Sound Culture.

Such a Sound Culture is presumed here to be nurtured by the constant and perpetual enrichment of the Culture that encompasses the continuous accumulation and contextualization of personal and societal experiences, knowledge, skills, wisdom, values, mores, customs, traditions, expressions and means of communication, among other things. The proposed paradigm shift for nurturing the respective Sound Cultures of diverse societies through their constant Cultural enrichment is also conducive to the perpetual *trilateral virtuous circle* among the on-going Holistic Culture Enrichment, Comprehensive Human Development and Balanced Socioeconomic Development in each society. This local *virtuous circle* may very well stimulate the global *virtuous circle* for the simultaneous and synchronous interactions of mutually supportive Culture of Peace, Global Humanity and Sustainable Development, to be explained in the following section.

The term Comprehensive Human Development here indicates a continuous cultivation of overall human capacities and community-interested sentiments/values on the basis of the dynamic Cultural enrichment (as elaborated in Chapter 17). Such human development may also encourage the *long-term personal common ethos* of "sound, active and fruitful longevity" and the *long-term common societal ethos* of "harmony, integrity, continuity, solidarity and mutuality." Further, such human development may represent the general improvement in the thought-frames, personality, spirituality and capacities of the individual and collective social constituents. Another term, "Balanced Socioeconomic Development," refers to the Culture-enhancing socioeconomic development with the conscious and integral concerns of reasonable balances in the short-term and long-term societal needs, encompassing the respective balances between social and economic needs, material and spiritual needs, personal and societal needs, and own and other's needs (as discussed in Chapters 12, 14 and 21). Further, such a Culture-enhancing socioeconomic development indicates the development in harmony with the Environment, on the basis of the on-going sound enrichment of the Culture.

Mutually Supportive Global Issues

As indicated above, the *trilateral virtuous circle* among Holistic Culture Enrichment, Comprehensive Human Development and Balanced Socioeconomic Development may encourage a synchronous and integral global promotion of Culture of Peace, Global Humanity and Sustainable Development. Such synchronous and integral interactions of the important global issues may suggest their relationship as mutually supportive prerequisites. Sustainable Development that requires the conscious and collaborative human endeavors for the respective socioeconomic development harmonious with the global environment is an essential prerequisite for both Culture of Peace and Global

Humanity. Culture of Peace that indicates both the domestic harmony and the international amity of all societies is an essential prerequisite for both Sustainable Development and Global Humanity. Global Humanity that is conducive to the accommodation of all humans with the minimum human needs for subsistence, health and education is an essential prerequisite for both Culture of Peace and Sustainable Development. Thus, all these global challenges relate to one another, conducing to their mutual reinforcement.

It goes without saying that Culture of Peace cannot be created globally out of nothing. It has to be solidly based on the intrinsic nature of local/societal Cultures that refer to the diverse and respectively holistic society-specific cultures across the world. Delving into the intrinsic nature of any long-enduring holistic Cultures, we may come to the most intrinsic value—*human and social harmony*—that encourages personal and societal integrity, mutuality, solidarity and continuity. Such intrinsic and common nature of diverse Cultures (*human and social harmony*) must be cherished by all human societies in order to nurture Culture of Peace in the prospective global community. In this manner, the constant enrichment of the diverse Cultures can be related to Culture of Peace. Likewise, Global Humanity should be based on the Comprehensive Human Development of each society. Such human development emphasizes the *comprehensive* nature of human development, which encompasses mental-and-physical health improvement, personal-and-spiritual development, knowledge-and-capacity advancement and personal-and-societal thought-frame enhancement. Thus, the Comprehensive Human Development asserts, at the least, the minimum requirement of subsistence, health and education for all the social constituents, which is also the basic tenet of Global Humanity.

It is almost self-explanatory that Sustainable Development requires Balanced Socioeconomic Development in each society. Such balanced development indicates the socioeconomic development harmonious with the Environment on the basis of the balanced short-and-long-term needs relevant to material-and-spiritual, individual-and-collective, traditional-and-progressive, and own-and-other-societal needs. Thus, Sustainable Development may be a logical and global consequence of Balanced Socioeconomic Development in each and every society. It is now apparent that there exists a close global and local correspondence between Culture of Peace and Holistic Culture Enrichment, between Global Humanity and Comprehensive Human Development, and between Sustainable Development and Balanced Socioeconomic Development.

Diagrammatic Explanation of Virtuous Circles

Central to all the *local* and *global* relations mentioned above, we may recognize the prominence of the diverse Sound Cultures. All human perpetual collaboration for the *paradigm shift* is necessary, indeed, for generating the reasonably sound diverse Cultures across the world. However difficult it may be, we humans must pursue the *paradigm shift* if we want to survive. This is the reason why I am emphasizing the sound enrichment of the diverse Cultures as the *paradigm shift* for a simultaneous and integral resolution of Sustainable Development, Culture of Peace and Global Humanity. For this purpose, the New Enlightenment (see Chapter 8) is crucial for encouraging and supporting *continuously* the local and global endeavors for the sound Cultural enrichment, as well as marginalizing the Market across the world. As seen in the following diagrammatic expression of "Local-Global Linkage," all such global issues have to be pursued *simultaneously* in view of methodological, strategic and cost effectiveness. They are the prerequisites to one another and the supportive stimulants to one another, as indicated by the two-way arrows in Figure 30.1 (Hiwaki 2008a).

Equally important, such global challenges must be firmly based in the local/societal challenges for Holistic Culture Enrichment (C), Comprehensive Human Development (H), and Balanced Socioeconomic Development (S), as shown to be the *inner* triangular interactions. These *local* challenges imply the mutually supportive interactions among (C), (H) and (S), as well as their *trilateral "two-way" virtuous circles* in perpetuity. Furthermore, the diagram indicates the mutual interactions and correspondences between the *local* and *global* challenges by the "two-way" arrows, as depicted between Balanced Socioeconomic Development (S) and Sustainable Development, between Holistic Culture Enrichment (C) and Culture of Peace, and between Comprehensive Human Development (H) and Global Humanity.

All together, the following diagram indicates the simultaneous and synchronous *local-global* interactions that provide the *linkage* between the perpetual "two-way" *local virtuous circle* (among the on-going Holistic Culture Enrichment, Comprehensive Human Development and Balanced Socioeconomic Development) and the *global "two-way" trilateral virtuous circle* in perpetuity (among Culture of Peace, Global Humanity and Sustainable Development). This point is most important here, for the diagram asserts the *local* foundations for the *global* challenges as well as the synchronous nature between the *local* and *global* endeavors for the sound and harmonious solutions of the *human-originated* complex problems.

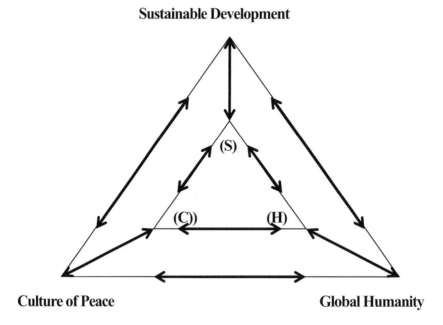

Figure 30.1 Local-global linkage

Concluding Remarks

The *trilateral virtuous circle* of the on-going Holistic Culture Enrichment, Comprehensive Human Development and Balanced Socioeconomic Development at national level may become the cause and result of acquiring "self-preserving," "self-organizing" and "self-evolving" human qualities and capacities for the sustainability of humanity and human community. When such a *trilateral virtuous circle* is encouraged and enhanced by the worldwide New Enlightenment for Sustainable Development, which strengthens the motivation to enrich the diverse Cultures across the world, discouraging the human mindset of market fundamentalism (Market) at the same time, such worldwide movement may help perpetuate the *paradigm shift* to accelerate the sound enrichment of diverse Cultures.

This implies that the *paradigm shift* may acquire over time a force and drive of its own for the *trilateral virtuous circle* of Sustainable Development, Culture of Peace and Global Humanity, supported by the enhancement of human qualities and capacities, as well as by the worldwide New Enlightenment. The *paradigm shift*, once it acquires its own force and drive, may accelerate the speed and magnitude of global collaborations for our common viable future—the sustainable and integral development of the prospective global community. In such a sustainable global community, the poetical analogy—"a choir of cultures"—where "each is able to sound its own note but able also to include the tones of all the others" in Christopher Budd's *Finance at the Threshold* (to be published by Gower Publishing Limited in 2011) may reflect our "sound communal value system."

Epilogue

Dr Aurelio Peccei, the President of the Club of Rome, stated the following some 30 years ago: "The most and pragmatic step society can take to become sustainable, I surmise, is to reduce and avoid waste. For, as Mahatma Gandhi said, our planet produces enough for our need, but not for our greed" (van Dam 1982). Also, in his message to the Tokyo Meeting in 1982 under the theme "Approaching The 21st Century: Global Problems and Human Choices," he predicted: "It will reveal that the human community, for all its splendid achievements and formidable assets, does not possess the self-organizing, self-preserving and self-evolving qualities" (Peccei 1982). Echoing Dr Peccei at the same meeting, Professor Howard Perlmutter of the Wharton School paraphrased the biologist Lewis Thomas: "Survival of the fittest doesn't mean that nature is red in tooth and claw, as the 19th century read the message of evolution, or that only the strongest, most dominating, and shrewdest will win. The fittest who survive are those who cooperate best with other living things" (Perlmutter 1982).

Professor George E. Lasker, President of the International Institute for Advanced Studies in Systems Research and Cybernetics (IIAS) in his paper on "Developing Collaborative Consciousness: Methodological Issues," argues for the importance of collaborative consciousness: "The collaborative consciousness is characterized by a propensity of an individual to relate to other humans and to cooperate with them in order to survive, to meet his needs and to build a better future for himself, for his family and for society" (Lasker 1998). In this context, he discusses his proposal of "Olympics of Good Deeds and Kindness, that would measure not the strength of muscles or the power of intellect, but the strength of goodness and greatness of spirit in a human heart and soul, and that would celebrate the acts of kindness and caring." By means of such Olympics, Professor Lasker would like to help reorder human priorities and values on the agenda of human concerns, to help promote the development of collaborative consciousness globally, and to help facilitate the transition from the Culture of War and violence to the Culture of Peace, freedom, harmony and cooperation for the whole of mankind.

New Enlightenment and Market Fundamentalism

Indeed, we humans need to be most serious about developing "collaborative consciousness," cooperating with "other living things," and developing our personal and societal "self-organizing, self-preserving and self-evolving qualities." For this purpose, we must collaborate consciously to bring about the New Enlightenment (perhaps, Olympics of the Good Deeds and Kindness is an appropriate starter), for enhancing sound human values, appropriate human development and humanities-oriented global solidarity as well as for enriching diverse Cultures. Also, we must consciously promote the New Enlightenment to support the *general human ethos* of sound, active and fruitful longevity as well as the *sociocultural ethos* of harmony, integrity, continuity, solidarity and mutuality (or *sound communal value system*). Further, we must consciously collaborate for the New Enlightenment to free all humans from the shackles of market fundamentalism (Market).

Such collaborative endeavors may lead us inevitably to the importance of Cultural diversity and soundness, which is conducive to a simultaneous and synchronous accomplishment of Sustainable Development, Culture of Peace and Global Humanity for the integral development of the prospective global community, by eliminating the crudity, cruelty, exclusion and inhumanity inherent in the Market and its ideology of "might-makes-right." Since the collapse of the Soviet Union, especially, the Market has gained momentum to emerge ever more dominant and has drastically increased the number of the starved and the starving by the billion in the world, taking crucial resources away from poor people and societies. Also, the Market has intensified the gap of living standards between those near the top and those near the bottom. Those who have a vested interest in the Market have now become bold enough to impose on the diverse human communities the so-called "global standards," showing openly their ambition and power to control the whole human community. Figuratively stated, the contemporary power structure—Big Market—is "red in tooth and claw," with its crudity, cruelty, exclusion and inhumanity.

The Paradigm Shift and Human Legacies

Moreover, the Market is escalating its forces, as a matter of course, to obliterate our most intrinsic public goods—diverse Cultures, for this very diversity, apparently, has been in the way of the Market. Likewise, the Market has revealed its extreme "short-run" orientation and limited perspective by devastating the most important public goods for human survival—Environment. It is not far-fetched to argue, therefore, that the Market has amplified the "market failure" and "policy failure" across the world (as discussed in Chapter 5 and elsewhere) by devastating the diverse Cultures that normally immunize the respective societies, countervailing against the contagion of crudity, instability and exclusion grossly exaggerated by the Market mindset.

In order to counteract the awesome forces of the Market, I believe, it is crucially important to nurture the *paradigm shift* for restoring and enriching appropriately the existing diverse Cultures across the world. The purpose here, however, is not only to counteract the Market, but also to encourage the "fair and viable market function" in diverse human societies. Furthermore, the perpetual sound enrichment of diverse Cultures—the *paradigm shift*—can encourage the Market to winnow away crudity, cruelty, instability and exclusion as well as to interact properly and constructively with the diverse Cultures and the Environment. Thus, the *paradigm shift* for perpetual and sound enrichment of diverse Cultures, by containing the pervasive Market mindset across the world, may enable individual persons and societies to become much more respectful to one another for the benefit of all humans and societies, particularly for the benefit of the future generations.

As indicated elsewhere (Chapter 8, in particular), both the intrinsic "sound-and-fair" market function (*not* the Market) and the diverse Sound Cultures represent important human legacies as well as indispensable "public goods." Both of them constitute human mindsets as well as the unique and strong features of the human world, though many of our contemporaries have been sold to the abrasive Market, disregarding both the intrinsic market function and the respective Cultures. Also, many of our contemporaries have become much more concerned with the short term than the long term, as well as much more heavily oriented toward the material than the spiritual. Furthermore, many of us have become aggressive, power hungry and keenly egoistic as well as self-centered, self-serving, self-seeking and intolerant of the other.

Our contemporaries have been inculcated through "modern" formal education, mass-media and liberal political thoughts to behave according to what the dominant power structure (the Big Market) advocates. All such education, media and politics in our contemporary world have been catering to the Big Market, not to mankind at large. This implies that we cannot expect any *alternative* politico-economic environment forever, unless we humans decide now to steadily pursue the alternative value systems and ways of life through the *paradigm shift*, perpetually enriching the diverse Cultures across the world and giving rise to the strong countervailing power against the lopsided Market that caters mostly to the Big Market.

Integrity in Diversity for Open Democracy

Given all the different and lopsided inclinations among our contemporaries, it is more than apparent that the simplistic "law-governing state" under the politico-legal principle of Unity in Diversity has an extremely limited capacity and perspective for ruling the diverse people and societies in the world. The rich can easily rise above and the poor can fall below the standardized laws and rules, particularly under the existing liberal politico-economic environment. Given the pervasive Market and its ideology of "might-makes-right" favoring the Big Market, such a unitary and simplistic "law-governing state" has exerted grossly "distorted" *undemocratic* effects to mankind at large. Thus, any *standardizing laws* on the premise of Unity in Diversity (such as a national constitution and the market rule), may have created a situation where some become much superior to others by the *nature* of the very "standard," unless all humans and societies are quite similar in all aspects.

In other words, any such laws and rules do not mean the same to all people. Besides, it is extremely difficult to assume all humanity is either good-natured or evil-natured. Perhaps, one can be good in one moment/situation and evil in another. One can also be good or evil, depending upon the view points and interpretations by the different Cultures. Then, the standardizing tenet of Unity in Diversity for the "law-governing state," referring possibly to the very state *only within* national borders at best, is much too narrow and too constraining to deal with highly complex humans, human societies and human Cultures. Also, the particular tenet, from the beginning, might have been developed in modern times to work for the benefit of the rich and powerful, who regarded themselves either as rulers or ones much superior to the "average" social constituents. Then, such a tenet, by necessity, goes directly against the so-called "democracy" of our common understanding. Thus, there is a good reason for the politico-legal principle of Integrity in Diversity to replace the principle of Unity in Diversity, particularly on our Insular Planet with its diverse Cultures and limited resources. In the prospective global community, an "open general democracy" may require the support of the principle of Integrity in Diversity (as discussed in Chapter 10), which necessitates the harmonious *sound communal value system* (comprising *human and social harmony, human integrity, social solidarity, societal continuity and relational mutuality*) relevant to the respective Sound Cultures (as discussed in Chapter 16).

In spite of the severe environment and resource constraints, the modern and contemporary emancipation of human "insatiable wants" under the lopsided and pervasive campaign for "liberal democracy" and "free market competition" has grossly complicated and destabilized the human conditions, lifestyles and behaviors. The explosion of individual insatiable wants does not seem to know any limits. Such an explosive growth of insatiable wants has naturally created enormous profit opportunities for those who are most acquisitively inclined.

The more acquisitive one is, the more profits one can obtain under the frantic market expansion led by the emancipation of lusts and greed. Also, the greater the obtained profits, the more powerful and more above the standardized laws such acquisitive individuals can become in our contemporary world. Moreover, the on-going liberal emancipation of human lusts and greed, as a matter of course, has produced an enormous human disparity in income, wealth, power and amenity. Such human disparity, in turn, can either induce legislation of new laws or twist the existing laws in favor of the rich and powerful. Owing to the complexity of human nature as well as the complexity of personal and societal settings, therefore, any standard laws and rules can create gross disparity in human conditions.

If the above argument is reasonable to people generally, it is much fairer to leave them more to rely on the humanities-inducing and harmony-enhancing diverse Sound Cultures (implying the respectively accumulated personal and societal experiences, skills, knowledge, wisdom, mores, communication and human relations, among other things) for collaboratively ruling the respective people and societies. It will no doubt require untiring endeavors to appropriately restore and enrich their respective Cultures toward reasonably sound ones in the face of changing world conditions. Such dynamic and perpetual endeavors for Cultural restoration and enrichment may naturally be entwined closely with human development and socioeconomic development to encourage the "local" *trilateral virtuous circle* of on-going Holistic Culture Enrichment, Comprehensive Human Development and Balanced Socioeconomic Development.

Sound Cultures and Respective Communal Value Systems

Moreover, all people in the world will have much better chance of survival and well-being by relying more on their respective Sound Cultures than on the Market that dictates the "law-governing state" and, at the same time, destroys the future of mankind by devastating both the diverse Cultures and the Environment. The process of restoring and enriching the diverse Cultures, however, inevitably requires the *paradigm shift* that necessitates untiring, perpetual and collaborative endeavors among all people and societies. Such a paradigm shift may trigger off the "local" *trilateral virtuous circle* pertinent to the diverse societies and kindle a greater hope for an enlightened and viable human future.

Under the reasonably sound Culture (as discussed in Chapter 16), the integral harmony of spiritual and material values (spiritual-material balance), implying an integral evaluation of human spiritual-and-material inclinations, refers to the intrinsic and potential *human integrity* that may go beyond the materialistic "human nature" of the transient society. The integral harmony of social and individual values (collective-individual balance), implying an integral evaluation of human personal-and-social inclinations, refers to the intrinsic and potential *social integrity* that may go beyond the unitary and individualistic "law-governing state" of the transient society. The integral harmony of traditional and progressive values (traditional-progressive balance), implying an integral evaluation of human past-present-future inclinations, refers to the intrinsic and potential *historical integrity* that may go beyond the unstable and uncertain life span of the transient society.

The integral harmony of one's own societal values and other's societal values (own-other societal balance), implying an integral evaluation of self-and-other inclinations in the human world, refers to the intrinsic and potential *mutual integrity* that may go beyond the insatiable and self-centered egotism of the transient society. All these spiritual-material, social-individual, traditional-progressive and self-other value balances, put together, constitute the harmony-embracing *sound communal value system* that can help maintain the health of local, national, regional and global communities. Thus, the reasonably sound Culture with such a *sound communal value system* may reveal an important hint for future human survival, well-being and peace. Also, such a Sound Culture may discourage excessive arrogance, acquisitiveness, aggressiveness and self-righteousness. Put differently, the Sound Culture definitely discourages the ideology of "might-makes-right," which justifies the egotism reinforced by greediness, extravagance and exclusion.

The Lopsided Value System and Human Miseries

Such a harmonious *sound communal value system* (comprising human and social harmony, human integrity, social solidarity, societal continuity and own-other mutuality), as the most important core of the respective Sound Cultures, may contrast clearly with the modern lopsided value system comprising *antagonism, materialism, individualism, progressivism* and *egotism*, which emphasizes the ideology of "might-makes-right." Such an emphasis may have deprived humanity of the self-preserving, self-organizing and self-evolving qualities that are conducive to a peaceful and viable future. Perhaps, due mainly to the lopsided value system, we humans have shown personal and societal arrogance and/or disrespect to the other peoples, societies and Cultures. In our modern and contemporary world, such arrogance and disrespect have often been exhibited against our predecessors' experiences, knowledge, wisdom and mores, which were accumulated in their respective Cultures through tenacious endeavors to live harmoniously, and also among diverse societies with their respective climates, resources and environments.

Having learnt little from our predecessors and long-accumulated diverse Cultures, and dealing only with transient ideas, humankind has suffered from undue and repetitive conditions caused by arbitrary, uncertain, unstable and insecure "trial-and-error" experiments imposed on us by the tyranny of the power structures of modern times." In other words, as a result of the insolence and arrogance of people generally, perhaps, the self-righteous and power-hungry Big Market, often ignorant of human and social complexities, has imposed convenient "trial-and-error" experiments on mankind and inflicted misery and agony on their contemporaries. Moreover, such arrogance and disrespect to their predecessors' endeavors and the respective diverse Cultures might have, indeed, deprived mankind of the chance for more reasonable, decent and comfortable development.

Accordingly, our typically biased "afterimage" of the so-called "Culture"—such an image grossly distorted by the Market over time—might have started emphasizing the Market-inculcated *materialism* (absence of the *spiritual* concern), *individualism* (absence of the *social* concern), *progressivism* (absence of the *traditional* concern) and *egotism* (absence of the *mutual* concern), all which have reinforced one another and been accelerated by the "competitive" *antagonism*. Thus, most of our contemporary peoples and societies may have been largely inculcated and corrupted by the Market and the Big Market.

As a result, our contemporary peoples and societies cannot help but hurtle toward the incontinent direction of the "disparity-animosity spiral," endangering in perpetuity all humans and other ecological beings. The modern and contemporary value system, due to its grossly lopsided nature, has led our contemporaries to the incontinent material explosion and population explosion as well as to the destruction of human communities. Such incontinent direction, indeed, cannot be changed in the short term. If we humans earnestly want to overcome our probable "collective" suicide and survive into the future, it is about the time for us to start making wholehearted collaborative endeavors for the appropriate paradigm shift. Such a paradigm shift requires both local-and-global and personal-and-societal endeavors for the perpetual enrichment of the diverse holistic Cultures to make us survive in the dynamic world.

Multifaceted Value Enhancement for Balanced Development

Such a paradigm shift, for one thing, can be encouraged by the earnest collaborative endeavors of the respective people for personal-and-societal multifaceted value enhancement. To begin with, thought-frame enhancement can be pursued by means of collaborative endeavors of the social constituents for augmenting the values of intellectual and planning capacities, as well as for relaxing the existing constraints on human-capital formation and the planning time frame. Second, enhancement of humanities can be pursued by means of collaborative endeavors of the social constituents for augmenting the values of intellectual capacity and vital spiritual energy, as well as for relaxing the existing constraints on human-capital formation and human life span.

Third, lifestyle enhancement can be pursued by means of collaborative endeavors of the social constituents for augmenting the values of health care and sociocultural life, as well as for relaxing the existing constraints on human life span and societal capacity. Finally, common-goal enhancement can be pursued by means of collaborative endeavors of the social constituents for augmenting the values of common aspirations and long-term planning capacity, as well as for relaxing the existing constraints on infrastructural investment and planning time frame.

Thus, such multilateral value enhancement, assisting the thought-frame enhancement, enhancement of humanities, lifestyle enhancement and common-goal enhancement, may involve, over time, society-wide collaborative endeavors for personal and societal improvements of important and integral Culture-related values. Such society-wide endeavors may naturally be conducive to Holistic Culture Enrichment, by improving common aspirations and the communal value system, as well as by enhancing personal-and-societal thought-frames and capacities. The improved common values and goals, as well as enhanced thought-frames and capacities of the social constituents, may naturally enrich the Culture and simultaneously stimulate Comprehensive Human Development and Balanced Socioeconomic Development. Cultural enrichment may be largely incorporated into the personality, intellectuality, spirituality and thought-frames of the social constituents as well as into their general productive capacities and socioeconomic activities. Such simultaneous processes, by reinforcing the personal and societal capacities as well as the society-general and economy-specific future orientation, may provide the social constituents with the reliable sociocultural foundations for venturing into the unknown future.

Value-Real Interactions for Balanced Development

To rephrase the simultaneous processes as the complex sequences in a "virtuous circle," the reinforced *society-general future orientation* may coherently induce the future orientation of the economy-specific activities. Also, the reinforced *society-general future orientation* may, as a matter of course, increase the society's saving, investment and capital income simultaneously and equivalently for Balanced Socioeconomic Development. Such simultaneous increase in saving, investment and capital income may stimulate the synchronous processes of Comprehensive Human Development, Holistic Culture Enrichment and Balanced Socioeconomic Development, resulting in the on-going expansion of the all-encompassing aggregate value-added. Also, the increased investment may naturally enlarge the society's overall stock of capital to reinforce both the *economy-specific and society-general future orientation*.

In the meantime, the growing aggregate value-added may feed back to the growing saving, investment and capital income. The value-added expansion that entails Balanced Socioeconomic Development, propelling synchronously human development and Cultural enrichment, may naturally reinforce the *society-general future orientation*, to start a new spiral "virtuous circle." In this complex interaction between the society's Value Aspect and Real Aspect, the *future orientation of* the general public and economic entities may be further strengthened, eventually helping to generate human "self-preserving," "self-organizing" and "self-evolving" motivation (see Theoretical Appendix 2 for elaboration).

Local-Global Virtuous Circles for Integral Development

Such motivation, arising from the constantly reinforced *future orientation* of the general public, may usher in the "local" *trilateral virtuous circle* of the on-going Holistic Culture Enrichment (C), Comprehensive Human Development (H) and Balanced Socioeconomic Development (S), depicted as the *inner* triangular interactions in Figure E.1. This "local" process of *trilateral virtuous circle,* if emulated by an increasing number of societies across the world, may gradually strengthen the personal and societal motivation for global collaborations, inducing over time the "global" *trilateral virtuous circle* or the *outer* triangular interactions of Culture of Peace, Global Humanity and Sustainable Development. This *outer virtuous circle* may constitute, over time, both the cause and result of human qualities and capacities for the self-preservation, self-organization and self-evolution of the integral development of the prospective global community.

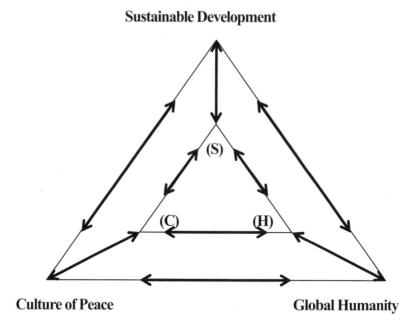

Sustainable Development

(S)

(C)   **(H)**

Culture of Peace   **Global Humanity**

Figure E.1   Local-global triangular linkage

Such human qualities and capacities, generated by means of the growing motivations for human survival as well as for sustainability of human communities, can be simultaneously encouraged and augmented by the New Enlightenment. This global movement is assumed to reinforce the motivation to appropriately enrich the diverse Cultures across the world in pursuit of Sustainable Development, while discouraging the Market-oriented crude mindset. The "self-preserving," "self-organizing" and "self-evolving" human qualities and capacities, thus enhanced, may naturally support the *paradigm shift* for the sound enrichment of the diverse Cultures across the world. This implies that the *paradigm shift* may acquire over time a force and drive of its own for Sustainable Development, supported by improved human qualities and capacities as well as by the worldwide New Enlightenment. Also, such human qualities and capacities as well as the New Enlightenment, by upholding human survival and sustainability as the top priority, may evolve at an accelerated speed and magnitude to aim at *conscious* global collaborations in perpetuity for simultaneous accomplishments of Sustainable Development, Culture of Peace and Global Humanity, for the integral development of the prospective global community.

The *conscious* global collaboration of individuals and collectives across the world, being firmly based on their constantly reinforced *general future orientation*, may aim specifically at developing a viable human future and sustainable global community. Such global collaboration may not only be conducive to the sound enrichment of the diverse Cultures but also induce person-to-person, people-to-people, society-to-society and Culture-to-Culture understanding and harmonious relationships. In addition, the *conscious* worldwide collaboration, encouraging self-organization, self-preservation and self-evolution of the respective societies, may usher in a prospective global community that is characterized by an "open general democracy" based on the politico-legal principle of Integrity in Diversity.

The Paradigm Shift and Diverse Sound Cultures

Feasible approaches based on such a worldwide collaboration can very well be focused on enhancing general awareness of the impending human predicament/catastrophe under the lopsided market fundamentalism (Market). To begin with, such approaches must aim at the emancipation of education from the modern shackles and the Market-oriented mindset to induce innovations particularly in Culture-enhancing education, employment, international trade and socioeconomic development. More urgently and earnestly, we must take stock of our respective Cultures, viewing them in the light of harmony and mutual respect without narrow-minded modern biases, prejudices and nationalism.

All the existing diverse Cultures may, over numerous generations, have accumulated their respective stocks of experience, knowledge, wisdom, values, mores, communicational skills and human relationships, among other things, for the sake of social harmony, subsistence and well-being in their given respective environments and geographical vantages. Thus, the respective Cultures can aptly guide both the individual and collective constituents of the respective societies how to interact harmoniously between social constituents and between different societies, as well as how to interact integrally and coherently with their respective environments, climates and resources. Also, such diverse Cultures can contribute for the sake of all peoples and societies to sharing most intrinsic and common human experiences, knowledge, wisdom, values and morality for the *development of a sustainable global community*.

Particularly in view of the simple diagram above (Figure E.1) referring to the interactive two-way and two-tier *trilateral virtuous circles*, it is apparent that we have a variety of actual/potential facets, angles and channels of approaches to starting *conscious collaborations* for the common good—the simultaneous accomplishments of Sustainable Development, Culture of Peace and Global Humanity for the integral development of the prospective global community. Given the formidable complexity of human societies worldwide, as well as the pervasive force of the Market in our *mindset*, however, we may focalize ourselves on the *paradigm shift*—the sound enrichment of our respective Cultures. Such a paradigm shift may find many appropriately diversified avenues toward the systemic accomplishments over time of the three important and mutually supportive global issues for the sake of a viable human future.

I will now introduce an illuminating flow chart (Figure E.2) produced for me by my colleague and friend, Professor Ayten Aydin of IIAS, Civil Engineer/Anthropologist and Former UN/FAO Senior Adviser, after her thorough reading of the early manuscript of this book. This diagram, I think, illuminates the gist of a general perspective that speaks for one of my analogies regarding the perpetual process of Sustainable Development.

Concluding this Epilogue, I would now like to quote the words of my deceased colleague and friend, Dr Robert John, which succinctly express the argument of this book. In his self-published compact book entitled *The Sage of San Diego Said Choose Quality and Reason* written under the pen name "Malcom Dalgliesh," he says, "A key to a positive future is the strengthening and evolution of Cultural norms that are consistent with a world view that best fits the way nature really works. It should provide a way to a future that we prefer." Also, he expresses his mind as if he were resonating with my inner voice:

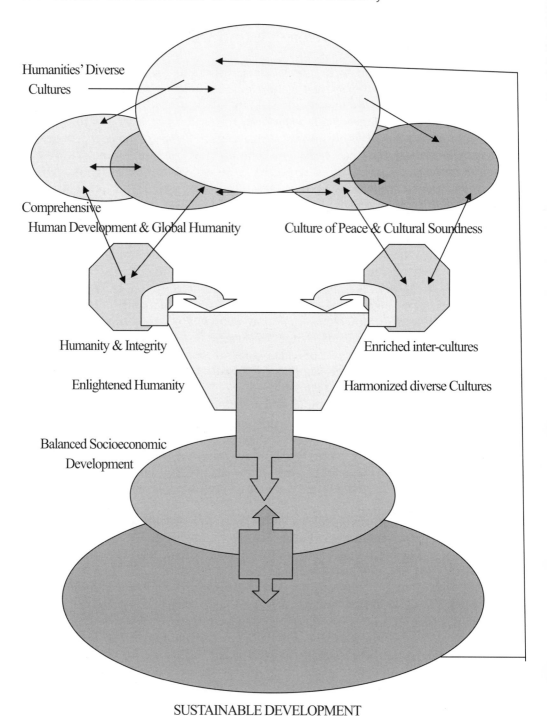

Humanities' Diverse Cultures

Comprehensive Human Development & Global Humanity

Culture of Peace & Cultural Soundness

Humanity & Integrity

Enriched inter-cultures

Enlightened Humanity

Harmonized diverse Cultures

Balanced Socioeconomic Development

SUSTAINABLE DEVELOPMENT

Figure E.2   Perpetual process of Sustainable Development

What Am I Doing Here?
I believe in putting into life at least as much
as one has taken out.
I respect the devotion of those who have preserved
for me the precious heritage of the past.
Without its stored wealth I would start with nothing.
I believe in the sacredness of duty to conserve
and renew our heritage and to preserve it
for my descendants.
I accept the challenge of the future,
realizing that its existence depends upon me.

Theoretical Appendices

Based on the following eight appendices I will elaborate on ideas relevant to our long-term integral theoretical framework. These ideas are based on the pivotal concepts and important premises and assumptions outlined in Chapter 10, as well as other relevant theoretical expositions in this book. In view of the complex subject matter I will try to offer a broad but adequately convincing picture of long-term socioeconomic activities relevant to Sustainable Development and the closely related important issues, leaving its precise formulation to pure-mathematicians. Thus, I do not pretend here to offer a "pure scientific" expression of long-term socioeconomic interactions and development. Rather, by adopting simple mathematical expressions, I will theoretically express a broad integral idea of intrinsic, general and normative socioeconomic interactions for an analogical and qualitative understanding of the complex activities.

Appendix 1 supplements the simple theoretical exposition in Chapter 10 by providing an elaboration on the present theoretical framework. Appendix 2 deals with our value premises in a nutshell and elaborates on the diagrammatic interactions between the society's Value Aspect and Real Aspects. Appendix 3 explains the mathematical derivation of the basic theoretical construct. Appendix 4 elaborates on the four processes (Growth, Maturation, Retrogression and Breakdown) on the Optimal Development Path (ODP). Appendix 5 diagrammatically illuminates the meaning of "long-term socioeconomic development" in terms of our basic theoretical construct. Appendix 6 discusses the derivation and the meaning of the Necessary and Sufficient Conditions for Balanced Socioeconomic Development. Appendix 7 illustrates the derivation of the framework for "thought-frame enhancement." Finally, Appendix 8 offers a discussion of Culture of Peace in terms of *Kendo* Spirit—a Japanese Cultural attribute.

Theoretical Appendix 1: Theoretical Framework—Basic Construct

BASIC RATIO AND SOCIOECONOMIC INTERACTIONS

The basic theoretical construct here is obtained by rearranging and simplifying Kenjiro Ara's interpretation of the Fisher-Ramsey saving function (Ramsey 1928). As shown in Appendix 3, I have arrived at the following equations (*approximations* to be more precise), by modifying our predecessors' premises in view of the long-term and socioeconomic applications, as well as in view of both demand-side and supply-side applications (Hiwaki 1979, 1998a):

$$T/r = C/V \tag{1}$$

$$T/r = 1 - (S/V) \tag{1.1}$$

$$T/r = 1 - (I/V) \tag{1.2}$$

$$T/r = W/V \tag{2}$$

$$T/r = 1 - (R/V) \tag{2.1}$$

The above expressions in terms of equations represent the approximations simplified for convenience with a possible justification. To begin with, each and all equations indicate the Value-Real Interactions between the left-hand variables (Value Aspect) and the right-hand ones (Real Aspect). The Value Aspect in the form of the Basic Ratio (T/r), being represented by the Trend Preference Rate (T: representing the long-term social discount rate or the long-term *society-general* time-preference) and the Trend Interest Rate (r: representing the long-term economic discount rate or the long-term *economy-specific* time-preference rate), is postulated to interact with the Real Aspect that is also expressed in the form of ratios consisting of the long-term socioeconomic variables. The relevant Real Aspect variables include the long-term aggregate consumption (C), saving (S), investment (I), labor income (W), capital income (R) and value-added (V).

The left-hand term of all equations (T/r) is assumed to take the initiative for interaction with the Real-Aspect ratios for Balanced Socioeconomic Development. Such Real Aspect ratios include the long-term consumption share (the consumption-value-added ratio: C/V), saving share (S/V), investment share (I/V), wage share (W/V) and profit share (R/V). Since C/V and W/V are equivalent by definition, and S/V, I/V and R/V are likewise equivalent, we may summarily express the basic construct *of* our theoretical framework as: T/r = A/V and likewise T/r = 1 − (B/V), where A and B represent, respectively (C, W) and (S, I, R).

The long-term socioeconomic framework evolves out of the pivotal Basic Ratio (T/r) that represents the society's Value Aspect. A decline in the Trend Preference Rate (T) indicates the reinforcement of the *society-general* future orientation induced by a change in the social value system. Such a change is induced by the Cultural dynamics encompassing economic, political, social, psychological, intellectual, educational, technological, institutional, moral, attitudinal, behavioral and other changes. For simplicity, such a change in the social value system that occupies the core of the Culture is assumed to represent a complex change. In contrast, a decline in the Trend Interest Rate (r) represents the reinforcement of the *economy-specific* future orientation, induced by the decline of the Trend Preference Rate (T). Roughly speaking, then, a decline in the Basic Ratio initiated by the decline of the Trend Preference Rate (T) may represent the Cultural enrichment that initiates the long-term interaction of social and economic phenomena to influence the right-hand real variables (Real Aspect) toward Balanced Socioeconomic Development.

As such, the Value Aspect interacts mutually with the Real Aspect that consists of various ratios of the long-term macroeconomic variables that include V, C, S, I, W and R. First, our long-term aggregate value-added (V) includes all the positive and productive activities in the society, both paid and unpaid, which may be calculated by market, shadow and/or psychic/emotional prices. Thus, our aggregate value-added (V) refers to all market transactions, barters, voluntary activities and all household productions of sustenance and cares. Second, the long-term aggregate consumption (C) includes all consumer expenditures except for the expenditures on human-capital formation over and above the standard minimum skills (acquired generally by compulsory education, for instance). Thus, our long-term consumption excludes the expenditures on formal education, training, self-learning and health-enhancing activities relevant to both mental and physical health.

Third, the long-term aggregate investment (I), therefore, includes such broad category of human-capital formation, as well as all the investments in plant and equipment, agricultural land, social infrastructure and residential facilities, to mention only the major items. Also, the long-term investment embodies the dynamic functions of transforming the long-term saving (S) into both human and material capitals, thus relating the on-going socioeconomic activities to those of the future, as well as balancing over time not only between the investment and saving but also between the aggregate demand and supply. Fourth, the long-term labor income (W) indicates the income accruing only to the "simple labor," which is *by definition* different among societies. The "simple labor" embodies only the standard-minimum skills of reading, writing and calculating and the standard minimum inheritance of the Cultural foundation, which are considered to be obtainable/accessible by the average social constituents.

Finally, the long-term capital income (R) refers to all the incomes accruing to the "*effective*" human capital, material capital and financial capital. The concept of "*effective*" human capital, being society-specific, goes beyond the popular definition of human capital (Becker 1964). Our concept of "*effective*" human capital covers a wide variety of human capacity that is over and above the standard minimum skills and the standard minimum Culture embodied in the society-specific "simple labor." Thus, such "*effective*" human capital consists of vocational and professional skills, intelligence, wisdom, knowledge, ingenuity, creativity, imagination, insights, foresight, benevolence, courage, public spirit, self-control, long-term perspectives, good health, communicational skills, linguistic and other Culture-related abilities, to mention only the major elements. Thus, the "*effective*" human capital is presumed "*effective*" largely specific to the relevant society. Within a society, such human capital exerts influence on all gainful and non-gainful production and also all other positive/constructive activities in consumption, saving, investment, technology development, waste management, health enhancement, self-learning, self-enlightenment, self-actualization, interpersonal relationship, political participation, voluntary activities, and so on.

FURTHER ELABORATION ON EQUATIONS AND VARIABLES

The first three mathematical expressions in the above—Equations (1), (1.1) and (1.2)—express the socioeconomic interactions of the Basic Ratio (T/r) with the long-term consumption-value-added ratio (C/V), saving-value-added ratio (S/V) and investment-value-added ratio (I/V), respectively. The socioeconomic variables, C, I, S and V, as seen from the above explanation, may differ significantly from the Keynesian "short-run" macroeconomic variables. The ratios of long-term real variables are postulated here to change by the initiation of the Basic Ratio (T/r). The concept of the long-term aggregate consumption (C), as mentioned above, indicates "pure" consumption that excludes almost all the socioeconomic activities for Comprehensive Human Development. Such human development, primarily consisting of formal and informal education, vocational-and-professional trainings, athletic-and-cultural enrichment, personal character building, health-enhancing and illness-preventing activities and researching-and-self-learning endeavors, is assumed to be enhanced by the long-term aggregate investment (I).

Thus, such aggregate investment (I), including human-capital formation as well as hard and soft investment in plant, equipment, agricultural land, social infrastructure and residential facilities, as mentioned above, excludes the material inventory investments which expediently facilitate only "short-run" ex-post equilibrium between aggregate saving and investment in the Keynesian framework. Such inventory investments are assumed here to largely average out to a trifle over time. For, the aggregate investment (I) is always equated with the aggregate saving (S), and the aggregate supply (V) with the aggregate demand (C+I) in the long-term framework. Such investment and saving as well as the supply and demand are assumed to share the same motivational force (the *society-general* future orientation or the Trend Preference Rate) that responds to a change in the social value system, which in turn reflects the Holistic Culture Enrichment.

Accordingly, a change in the Trend Preference Rate (T) may alter simultaneously both saving and investment to equilibrate over time. The investment (I), as indicated above, facilitates the saving (S) to be transformed into both human and material capitals to balance the aggregate demand and supply over time, as well as to link the socioeconomic activities of the present to those of the future. In other words, the equality of the socioeconomic variables S and I emphasizes the function of aggregate saving and investment to furnish a strong linkage between the demand and supply in the long term. It also emphasizes the importance of saving and investment in the process of socioeconomic development. The importance is particularly pronounced when human-capital formation (conducive to Comprehensive Human Development) enhances the Own Hands (people's future orientation and long-term perspectives). In other words, I am arguing that a sound human development (based on the sound Cultural enrichment), giving rise to an enhancement of personal and societal thought-frames and, hence, an improvement of the Own Hands, may propel Balanced Socioeconomic Development.

The aggregate value-added (V) includes all the positive and productive activities, both paid and unpaid. This implies that housekeeping, voluntary and barter activities, as well as other productive activities of a non-market variety that arise from the changes in socioeconomic values, lifestyles, institutions, attitudes, behaviors and human capacities should be accounted for, at least theoretically, in order to arrive at the aggregate value-added (V). As the society undergoes development and improvement, its values, human capital and lifestyles, among other things, may become inevitably diverse. Then, the theoretical value-added may tend to be much more at odds with the present statistical calculation that accounts only for the market-transacted final goods and services. Someday in the future someone may come up with an appropriate and concrete measurement, both qualitative and quantitative, of our highly abstract and complex concept of long-term aggregate value-added (V). In the meantime, we may utilize the concept as a theoretical entity in terms of "analogical" expression of such aggregate value-added.

The remaining theoretical expressions Equations (2) and (2.1) deal with W/V and R/V, which respectively represent the long-term income shares of labor and capital. These income shares correspond to their respective contributions to the aggregate value-added (V). These ratios (W/V and R/V) also correspond to the ratios (C/V and S/V), respectively. The socioeconomic variables, W and R, respectively, indicate the long-term incomes of labor and capital in real aggregate terms. The aggregate labor income (W), indicating the long-term income accruing to the "simple" labor that embodies only the standard minimum level of reading, writing and calculating skills and the standard minimum inheritance of the Cultural foundation obtainable/accessible by the people at large. Literally interpreted, the definition of "simple" labor depends mainly on the level of Comprehensive Human Development and Balanced Socioeconomic Development of each society, implying that the average productivity of "simple" labor may differ from one society to another.

The aggregate capital income (R) includes all capital income, the sum of interest, rent, dividend and income accruing to the *"effective"* human capital. In other words, the capital income consists of the one accruing to material/financial capital, as well as of the complex one accruing to the *"effective"* human capital. It is important to note that the income accruing to the *"effective"* human capital may include certain "psychic/emotional income" that arises from the *non-market* variety of mentally rewarding activities as part of housekeeping, voluntary and barter activities, as well as of self-learning, self-enlightenment, self-actualization, team achievement and societal accomplishment. Such mentally rewarding activities may largely depend on the "latitude" of the *"effective"* human capital available within each society.

Then, the aggregate investment (I) and saving (S), respectively, must include the sum equivalent to the "psychic/emotional income" (fulfillment, enjoyment and enthusiasm toward potential accomplishments in the future) for balancing among the aggregate capital income, the aggregate saving and the aggregate investment. Also, such *non-market* activities may often constitute learning experiences and, thus, contribute directly or indirectly to *"effective"* human-capital formation. At the same time, the *non-market* activities can generally represent the "latent" saving and investment (an implicit form of saving and investment) of the society in question, a constant increase of which may enhance human comfort, enjoyment and satisfaction. Then, it can be said that an increase of such "latent" saving and investment as well as of the "psychic/emotional income" is the most important aspect of Balanced Socioeconomic Development, Comprehensive Human Development and Holistic Culture Enrichment.

Owing to the same left-hand term (T/r) in all equations as well as to the same value of the aggregate value-added (V) in all equations and all denominator of the right-hand term, Equations (1.1), (1.2) and (2.1) all indicate exactly the same value. Accordingly, these equations together imply the following relationship: S = I = R. This expression, indicating the aggregate saving, investment and capital income, must be equivalent to one another to give rise to a *long-term equilibrium* of the socioeconomic system. In other words, the S = I = R represents the *long-term equilibrium condition* for Balanced Socioeconomic Development. It is explicit from the equilibrium condition that the aggregate investment (I) provides over time a linkage between the demand (through an improvement in socioeconomic needs) and the supply (through an improvement in socioeconomic productivity) of the society. Thus, the investment of the present framework inevitably contributes equivalently to the demand side and the supply side in the long-term process of Balanced Socioeconomic Development (see Appendix 5).

FURTHER ELABORATION ON TREND PREFERENCE RATE

Among the above long-term variables, the Trend Preference Rate (T) the long-term society-general "present time" preference may be most difficult to grasp. As an *analogical* variable, T reflects the socioeconomic dynamics that indicate the all-encompassing societal/cultural trend. Thus, a change in T represents, to a great extent, a change in the social value system consequential to the Cultural enrichment or degeneration. Phenomena specific to socioeconomic and environmental domains, such as changes in consumer tastes, human capital, technology, motivation to work, environmental impacts and resource constraints, are all considered to be relevant factors that have some influence upon T. Furthermore, phenomena that are customarily considered external to the economic domain, such as wars, civil strife, long-lasting economic depressions, drastic reforms in political system, new ideological and/or religious impacts, changes in social structure, and shifts in educational system and emphasis, are all assumed here as major factors that strongly affect T via changes in the social value system, reflecting either a Cultural enrichment or degeneration.

Conversely, we consider that any changes in T necessarily affect the thought-frame of people in general and, hence, their attitudes toward life, work, consumption, human-capital formation, paradigm in socioeconomic development, and environmental conditions, among other things. Thus, a change in T tends to reflect summarily a change in the social value system toward a further Cultural enrichment or degeneration. Apart from representing the changing people's values and attitudes in a dynamic society, T also facilitates a broad and dynamic linkage between economic and non-economic phenomena. Thus, T is not an easy concept to define *quantitatively*. Mathematically or rather *analogically*, however, T can be defined on the basis of Equation (1): $T/r = C/V$. We now rewrite the equation as: $T = r \cdot (C/V)$. In this expression, T is the product of r and C/V, both mathematical and *analogical* senses. Put differently, the Trend Interest Rate (r) multiplied by the long-term consumption-value-added ratio (C/V) suggests the Trend Preference Rate (T).

Also, T can be expressed in the form of *percentage change* as: $T = r + (C/V)$, where Italic expressions indicate the respective *percentage changes*. This *identity* suggests that a *percentage change* in the Trend Preference Rate (*T*) is equal to the sum of *percentage changes* in the Trend Interest Rate (*r*) and the consumption-value-added ratio (*C/V*). In other words, a change in the societal orientation to the future can be explained by the changes of two elements, namely, *r* and *C/V*. In other words, percentage decline indicated by the sum of *r* and *C/V* represents the magnitude of percentage decline in *T* (the magnitude of enhancement in the society-general orientation to the future). This suggests that the rate of change in the Trend Preference Rate (*T*) generally outweighs that of the Trend Interest Rate (*r*), indicating an important basis for the *lead-lag assumption* in the Basic Ratio (T/r).

Perhaps, a *caution* is in order at this juncture to avoid unnecessary confusion over a policy-related issue, which may arise by looking at the above equation and/or *identity*. We must emphasize that neither r (Trend Interest Rate) nor C/V (consumption share) indicates a policy variable amenable to short-run government manipulation for a possible influence on the value of T (Trend Preference Rate). In the present theoretical framework, it is T that declines first, for instance, along with an improvement in the social value system to influence and determine over time the value of r. I also envisage that a change in the consumption share (C/V) is consequential to a change in T. In an extreme exception, however, a government decision to go into all-out war against other nations may drastically change in a short time both the social value system and, hence, the Trend Preference Rate (T) at least for some unknown duration of time.

THE OPTIMAL DEVELOPMENT PATH AND LAO-TSU'S NATURALISM

The Optimal Development Path (ODP) is our normative/analogical expression of the Basic Ratio (T/r). Any given "Basic Ratio" may imply a long-term interaction between the Trend Preference Rate (T) and the Trend Interest Rate (r). An extra-long-term schedule of the Basic Ratio can be schematized as a "bow-like" curve to express the ODP. Such ODP portrays the changing interactions between the general societal trends of the people's future orientation (T) and the future orientation specific to the economic domain (r).

It is interesting to learn that an ancient Chinese thought on development/evolution had a close analogical resemblance in structure to the present idea of the ODP (Hiwaki 2002J). The *Taoist* idea of natural evolution can be discerned from the book *Lao-Tsu* by Mitsuji Fukunaga (Fukunaga 1997). According to Lao-Tsu, *Tao* (an all-embracing entelechy or the first all embracing principle) gives birth to the first *ki* (element/source of vitality or life energy), and this *ki*, in turn, gives birth to two *kies*—*Yin* (symbolizing femininity, passivity, darkness, wetness, and so on) and *Yang* (symbolizing masculinity, activity, brightness, dryness, and so on). These two *ki*(es) now jointly give birth to the third *ki* (balancing and integrative force), and this third *ki* gives birth to all creation.

Thus, the balancing and integrating force of *ki* maintains harmony in the process of all creation embracing both *Yin* and *Yang*. Such interpretation of development or generation of all creation in Taoism may correspond broadly with the diagrammatic expression (bow-like schedule) of the Basic Ratio (T/r) for the normative and analogical development on the Optimal Development Path (ODP) as shown in Figure A.1.

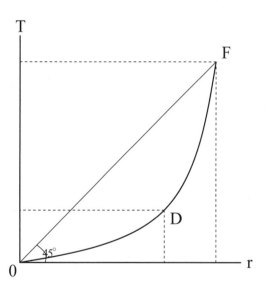

Figure A.1   Optimal Development Path

The first *ki* that *Tao* produces can be considered analogous to our 45-degree ray connecting the two extreme points Point O and Point F. Now, this original/initial *ki* dividing itself into two *ki*(es) *Yin* and *Yang* that are analogous to the horizontal axis (r) and the vertical axis (T). Next, *Yin* and *Yang* together, produces the third *ki* (the balancing and integrative *ki*), which can corresponds to the ODP. The analogical ODP gives rise to all production (all creation) over time in a harmonious long-term process of Balanced Socioeconomic Development. Then, Lao-Tsu's natural creation/evolution process resembles the long-term "normative" production process that is represented by the ODP on the basis of natural/harmonious interactions between the *society-general* and the *economy-specific* orientations to the future.

The above simplified interpretation of the Chinese naturalist philosophy may suggest the important aspect of natural balance in terms of *Yin* and *Yang*. In our analogical framework of Balanced Socioeconomic Development shown by the ODP, *Yin* is basically the Culture-oriented force and *Yang* the Civilization-oriented force. The implied analogical argument here is that the Culture-oriented force (T) needs to be reinforced constantly along with the perpetual sound enrichment of the relevant Culture (*Yin*) in order to accommodate and govern wisely the constantly expanding and thrusting force (r) of the Civilization (*Yang*) for maintaining a good balance in the socioeconomic development.

Theoretical Appendix 2: Value Premises and Value-Real Interactions

In this appendix I will first introduce our value premises and assumptions for the present theoretical framework. Then I will illustrate the core theoretical expression of the dynamic interactions between the Value Aspect and the Real Aspect in the form of a diagram. This diagrammatical expression of the Culture-based integral Value-Real interactions represents Balanced Socioeconomic Development. The present theoretical diagram, serving as a summary presentation of the development framework explained in Part 2, emphasizes the sound Cultural enrichment to culminate in Balanced Socioeconomic Development.

VALUE PREMISES AND ASSUMPTIONS

I will now summarily itemize the value premises and assumptions of the present theoretical framework of Sustainable Development (see Chapters 10 and 11), in order to facilitate a clear understanding of the analogical ideas. The following unique variety of value premises, together with the assumed *paradigm shift* (sound enrichment of the relevant Culture) discards and largely replaces the classical, neoclassical and Keynesian value premises and assumptions (Hiwaki 2009a):

1. *New definition of "human nature"*: Human social constituents cannot entirely preclude self-interest but can restrain it for common and public interest (or *mutual interest*).
2. *Long-term integral approach*: The long-term integral approach is taken to human socioeconomic behaviors and related phenomena.
3. *Balanced Socioeconomic Development*: The Balanced Socioeconomic Development at each national level is coherent with Sustainable Development.
4. *New temporal definition*: The "long term" indicates the long enough duration of time for a change in the social value system, while the "short term" refers to the duration without such change.
5. *Cultural value proxy*: The Trend Preference Rate as "Cultural value proxy" hints at the long-term *society-general* orientation to the future.

6. *Lead-lag assumption*: The Trend Preference Rate (T) leads the Trend Interest Rate (r) in the process of socioeconomic development.

7. *All-encompassing value-added*: The long-term aggregate value-added (V) includes all productive and positive activities, paid in the market or not.

8. *Human Development*: A perpetual generation of "effective" human capital over and above the basic skills is assumed *pivotal* for Sustainable Development.

9. *Optimal Development Path*: The ODP, derived from the long-term schedule of the Basic Ratio (T/r), indicates the processes of positive and negative socioeconomic development.

10. *Human needs and the Environment*: The theory addresses all the short-term and long-term material and spiritual needs based on Environment conservation.

11. *The third course of idea*: People's own invisible hands (the growing future orientation and long-term perspectives) equilibrate demand and supply as well as investment and saving.

12. *Long-term equilibrium conditions*: The equilibrium conditions of the long-term theoretical construct refer interchangeably to $S = I = R$ and $C = W$.

13. *Conditions of socioeconomic development*: The Necessary Condition indicates a continuous rise in the living standard, and the Sufficient Condition a continuous reinforcement of future orientation.

14. *Trilateral virtuous circle*: The theory generates a *trilateral virtuous circle* among sound Cultural enrichment, human development and socioeconomic development.

15. *New politico-legal principle*: The existing Unity in Diversity for the *closed* democracy is replaced by the new principle of Integrity in Diversity for an *open* democracy.

CULTURAL ENRICHMENT AND VALUE-REAL INTERACTIONS

I will now examine Holistic Culture Enrichment and Balanced Socioeconomic Development on the basis of interactions between the Value Aspect and the Real Aspect. The Value-Real interactions, which summarily represent the interactions relevant to the five basic equations, can allude to more concrete and simultaneous processes of Holistic Culture Enrichment and Balanced Socioeconomic Development. Such processes refer to both the Necessary and the Sufficient Conditions, albeit implicit (Theoretical Appendix 6). The basic construct of the theoretical framework can take the form of an interactive expression comprising both the Value Aspect (T/r) and the Real Aspect $(1 - B/V)$ as in the summary expression $T/r = 1 - (B/V)$, where B represents each and all of long-term saving (S), investment (I) and capital income (R) (Hiwaki 2002a, 2002b).

The summary expression of Value-Real Interactions indicates the dynamic interactions of the relevant variables for the on-going socioeconomic development. The Value Aspect (T/r) basically represents the expression that reflects the dynamics of the Culture, while the Real Aspect $(1 - (B/V))$ reflects the dynamics of real human activities for socioeconomic development. The most important and immediate effect on Balanced Socioeconomic Development, no doubt, involves Comprehensive Human Development that includes appropriately *cultured* intellectual-spiritual development, personal-character building, human-capital formation and thought-frame enhancement.

Such human development, to be natural and effective, must base itself inevitably on the relevant Culture. One cannot easily develop oneself without any Cultural foundation or totally detached from one's native Culture that provides the mother tongue, mores, spirits, knowledge, wisdom, ingenuity, among other things. Such a solid Cultural foundation may be inter-related with the other Cultures on the basis of dynamic human development. As a result, the Culture can acquire further stimulation to enrich itself, and the enriched Culture can, in turn, become a better basis for further human development and socioeconomic development. Such socioeconomic development may build the sound Cultural foundation for the harmonious societal growth and maturation. Thus, the positive interactions between the Value Aspect and the Real Aspect take the form of a multifaceted and synergistic "virtuous circle," which facilitates the perpetual interactions among Holistic Culture Enrichment, Comprehensive Human Development and Balanced Socioeconomic Development.

The "virtuous circle" of the Value-Real Interactions, which is shown in Figure A.2 (Hiwaki 1998a, 2005d), can be explained, as follows. An untiring endeavor for Cultural enrichment, bringing about a change in its value system, enhances the people's positive orientation to the future. This enhancement of the *"society-general" future orientation* is symbolically represented by a decline of the Trend Preference Rate (T), which is equivalent to a decline of the "present-time" preference. The resultant change in the social value system influences coherently the time frame of economic activities. Thus, the enhanced orientation to the future of the social constituents induces a somewhat lagged and coherent decline of the Trend Interest Rate (r) as shown by Arrow 1. The downward movement of the economy-specific time-preference rate (r) indicates the enhanced *"economy-specific" future orientation.*

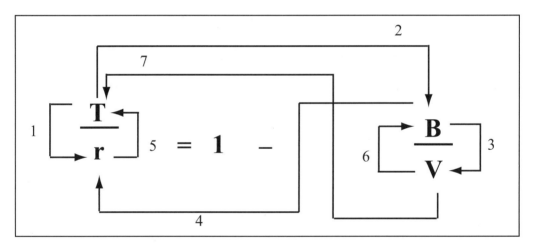

Figure A.2 Value-real interaction

In other words, the enhanced *"society-general" future orientation* indicates a decline of T and the lagged decline of r. Simultaneously, the enhanced *"society general" future orientation* may increase B, implying the systemic growth of the long-term aggregate saving (S), investment (I) and capital income (R), as shown by Arrow 2. The growing B may imply the growth of investment in the human-and-material capital (I). The investment growth stimulates the synchronous processes of human development, Cultural enrichment and socioeconomic development, expanding the long-term aggregate value-added (V), as shown by Arrow 3. Also, the increased investment may enlarge the stock of human and material capitals and induce the economy-specific orientation to the future, shifting the Trend Interest Tate (r) downward, as shown by Arrow 4. The declining Trend Interest Rate (r) may now influence the Trend Preference Rate (T) downward, as shown by Arrow 5.

In the meantime, the expanded value-added (V), indicating the socioeconomic development, may feed back to B, as implied by Arrow 6, to increase the saving, investment and capital income. Thus grown B may now enhance both the "economy-specific" and the "society-general" future orientation (as implied again by Arrows 4 and 5). Also, the expanded value-added (V) that, providing the justification as well as the means, may induce a further *trilateral virtuous circle* among Balanced Socioeconomic Development, Comprehensive Human Development and the Holistic Culture Enrichment. The implied dynamic Culture may reinforce the *long-term future orientation* of the social constituents, inducing a further decline of the Trend Preference Rate (T), as indicated by Arrow 7. This may start anew the Value-Real "virtuous circle," propelling a further socioeconomic development, human development and Cultural enrichment.

As seen from the Value-Real interactions, the Culture plays the *pivotal role* in both human development and socioeconomic development. This idea may suggest that the perpetual enrichment of the Culture is the most important precondition to the enhancement of mutual trust, reliability and interdependence as well as to the enhancement of social value system and general thought-frames, all of which together guarantee the overall invigoration of society and economy. The perpetual enrichment of the Culture, then, is crucial to the long-term government policy for preventing the Credibility Trap as well as for curing such a social malady. It may also imply that the "conscious" perpetual endeavor for the enrichment of the diverse Cultures all over the world may counterbalance the pervasive Market mindset in such a way as to induce a fair and viable market function for human survival and well-being.

Theoretical Appendix 3: Mathematical Derivation of Theoretical Construct

The basic construct of our framework owes much to F. Ramsey's mathematical formulation (Ramsey 1928, Ara 1966) containing Fisher's concept of time preference rate, as seen in the following:

$$S/Y = e\{(i\text{-}t)/i\}$$

This equation indicates that saving ratio (S/Y) is a function of interest rate (i) and time-preference rate (t), where the reciprocal of the constant (e) is the elasticity of marginal utility. I will derive our basic equations using a similar premise as the one adopted by Ramsey. In the following derivation process, however, we will modify Ramsey's steps for our *long-term, supply-side* and *socioeconomic* applications (Hiwaki 1979, 1998a).

The long-term demand-side equation (*approximation*) to be derived first is, as follows:

$$T/r = C/V$$

where T, r, C, and V stand for the Trend Preference Rate, the Trend Interest Rate, the long-term real aggregate consumption and the long-term real aggregate value-added, respectively. I will derive the above equation first by letting $U = U(c)$, where U stands for utility and c for real consumption.

The marginal utility is expressed as:

$$M = dU/dc$$

and the law of diminishing utility can be stated as:

$$dM/dc = (d/dc)(dU/dc) < 0$$

Now, let $e = -(dc/c)/(dM/M)$, where $1/e$ is the elasticity of marginal utility. I assume for simplicity that an average household is reasonably rational about consumption in the long term (or e being *approximate* unity), and rearrange the equation, as follows:

$$(c1-c0)/c0 = -(M1-M0)/M0 \tag{1d}$$

The law of equal marginal utility asserts that $M0(1+t0) = M1(1+i0)$, where t is the long-term time-preference rate and i is the corresponding long-term interest rate. By substituting this equation into Equation (1d), I obtain the following:

$$(c1-c0)/c0 = (i0-t0)/(1+i0) \tag{2d}$$

Next, I assume a constant growth rate of income, as well as a constant saving ratio. Then, the above equation becomes equivalent to the following:

$$(v1-v0)/v0 = (i0-t0)/(1+i0) \tag{3d}$$

Now, I define v1 as; $v1 = i0s0 + v0$, where v and s stand for long-term household income and saving, respectively. By substituting i0s0+v0 for v1 in Equation (3d), I obtain an equation for long-run saving ratio as; $s0/v0 = (i0-t0)/(i0+i0^2)$. Since $i0^2$ amounts to a trifle, I abstract it from the equation and derive the following simple equation (*approximation*):

$$t0/i0 = 1-(s0/v0) \tag{4d}$$

I now generalize Equation (4d) for an average household, as follows:

$$t/i = 1-(s/v)$$

where s/v represents the long-term saving ratio.

We then modify the generalized equation for a long-term socioeconomic relation, as follows:

$$T/r = 1-(S/V)$$

where T, r, S and V now stand for the Trend Time-Preference Rate, the Trend Interest Rate, the long-term real aggregate saving and the long-term real aggregate value-added of the relevant society. S/V denotes the long-term saving-value-added ratio.

Assuming S = I in the long term, I may alternatively express the above equation, as follows:

$$T/r = 1-(I/V)$$

where I is the long-term real aggregate investment and I/V is the long-term propensity to invest.

Assuming also that 1 = I/V+C/V, I arrive at the following equation:

$$T/r = C/V$$

where the Basic Ratio (or ratio of the Trend Preference Rate to the Trend Interest Rate) is set equal to the long-term consumption-value-added ratio. This is exactly the same equation (*approximation*) as stated in the outset.

The long-term supply-side equation (*approximation*) to be derived next is the following:

$$T/r = W/V$$

where W stands for the aggregate long-run income of "simple labor" in real terms (the income of "effective" human capital excluded). Now, the Basic Ratio is set equal to the long-term share of "simple labor" income (W/V). The derivation of this equation (*approximation*) is similar to that of the demand-side counterpart.

I now use a household utility function of real "simple labor" income, namely, $U = U(w)$, replacing the consumption utility function in the above. Then, the marginal utility of labor income is expressed as:

$$M = dU/dw$$

and the law of diminishing utility can be states as:

$$dM/dw = (d/dw)(dU/dw) < O$$

Let $e = -(dw/w)/(dM/M)$, where 1/e is the elasticity of marginal utility. I now assume for simplicity that an average household is reasonably rational about real labor income in the long term (or e being *approximate* unity) and rearrange this equation, as follows:

$$(w1-w0)/w0 = -(M1-M0)/M0 \qquad (1s)$$

Next, the law of marginal utility, namely, $M0(1+t0) = M1(1+r0)$, is substituted into Equation (1s), to obtain the following:

$$(w1-w0)/w0 = (i0-t0)/(1+i0) \qquad (2s)$$

Assuming a constant growth rate for income and a constant share of capital income, I may restate the above equation, as follows:

$$(v1-v0)/v0 = (i0-t0)/(1+i0) \qquad\qquad (3s)$$

which is equivalent to Equation (3d). Now, v1 is defined as; v1 = i0p0+v0, where p stands for the capital income (the income of human capital included) accruing to the capital stock owned by the average household. Here, we assume that the capital income is set entirely aside for reinvestment.

Skipping the derivation step leading to the equation (*approximation*) corresponding to Equation (4d), I now state only the result, as follows:

$$t0/i0 = 1-(p0/v0) \qquad\qquad (4s)$$

Now, I generalize Equation (4s) as:

$$t/i = 1-(p/v)$$

where p/v stands for the long-term share of capital income of an average household. I then modify the generalized equation (*approximation*) for a long-term socioeconomic relation, as follows:

$$T/r = 1-(R/V)$$

where R stands for the long-term real capital income and R/V for the long-term share of capital income. I may alternatively state this equation as; T/r = 1-(I/V), to indicate I = R = S which is the long-term equilibrium condition for a Balanced Socioeconomic Development.

By letting 1 = R/V+W/V, I now arrive at the following equation:

$$T/r = W/V$$

This formula equates the Basic Ratio to the long-term share of labor income. This equation is exactly the same as stated in the outset.

To sum up, the basic construct of our long-term socioeconomic framework consists of the following equations (*approximations*):

$$T/r = C/V \qquad\qquad (1)$$

$$T/r = 1-(S/V) \qquad\qquad (1.1)$$

$$T/r = 1-(I/V) \qquad\qquad (1.2)$$

$$T/r = W/V \qquad\qquad (2)$$

$$T/r = 1-(R/V) \qquad\qquad (2.1)$$

Theoretical Appendix 4: Four Processes on the Optimal Development Path

The analogical Optimal Development Path (ODP) is the theoretical and normative representation of Balanced Socioeconomic Development, which is drawn according to the assumption of *lead-lag* interactions between the Trend Preference Rate (T) and the Trend Interest Rate (r). As seen already, T represents the long-term Social Rate of Interest (SRI), or more broadly, the all-encompassing *society-general* future orientation, while r represents the long-term Economic Rate of Interest (ERI), or the *economy-specific* future orientation. The *lead-lag assumption* for the process on the ODP, with *no unique and universal point* to converge on over time, may provide a clue to the dynamic two-directional development, namely, the positive processes of Growth and Maturation and the negative processes of Retrogression and Breakdown (Hiwaki 1995b). One strong implication of the ODP is that the positive processes of Balanced Socioeconomic Development cannot be maintained without the constantly reinforced *future orientation* of the people in general. These four different processes can be classified into their corresponding dynamic patterns relevant to the gap (Social Premium for Development (SPD)) between T and r, namely, the patterns of changing "extra-profit rate" measured by the horizontal distance between any given point on the 45-degree ray and the corresponding point on the ODP.

THE GROWTH PROCESS AND EXPANDING PROFITABILITY

The first pattern, referred to as the "Growth Process" (F-D), is indicated in Figure A.3 by the ever growing "extra-profit rate" implied by the expanding SPD. This pattern is seen on our ODP from Point F to Point D or from the smallest SPD (no gap) to the largest SPD. The largest gap is shown by the SPD at Point D in the diagram, while the SRI and the ERI indicate the corresponding *social* and *economic* discount rates, respectively. A rapid expansion of economic activities based on a rather swift drop in the Trend Preference Rate (T) that is shown by the much shortened distance of the horizontally measured SRI may characterize the Growth Process. This process reflects the rapidly growing *society-general* future orientation and the people's untiring endeavors for the long-term betterment of their socioeconomic conditions. Declining T, representing the strengthened *society-general* future orientation, is tantamount to the simultaneous increase of society's long-term saving and investment, along with the concurrent rapid growth of the long-term aggregate value-added.

However, this process, when it begins, is like a "maiden voyage" or an unprecedented happening for any society. Therefore, any natural and legal persons in the relevant society, facing the unprecedented expansion of economic activities, may move on with little knowledge as to what the future may hold. Their path into the future over the long duration of time may be guided by the dynamic society-specific culture (Culture) and Comprehensive Human Development as well as by the reinforced *society-general* orientation to the future. Thus, the lenders of investment funds, on the one hand, may be highly conservative (risk-averse), at least in the beginning, and be inclined to protect themselves with an interest rate much higher than the risk justifies *ex post*. Owing to the scarcity of capital, however, such a high rate of interest may be justified by the on-going high "productivity" or the high "extra-profit rate" (represented by the SPD). Put differently, the lenders in an early growth phase may adjust their long-term interest rate downward only marginally over time and only after confirming a long-term "productivity gain" in the society.

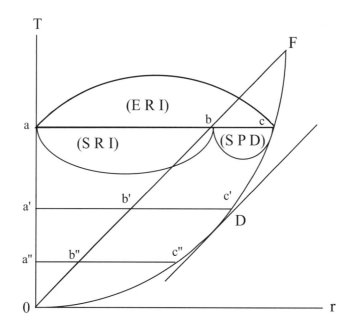

Figure A.3   Characteristics of the Optimal Development Path

On the other hand, the borrowers of investment funds—natural and legal persons contemplating a plant-and-equipment investment—also expect a rather high rate of return on their expanding capital stock, given the uncertainty regarding the magnitude of risk factor, as well as regarding the degree of potential "productivity gain." Their expected rate of return on the capital stock and their expected "extra-profit rate" (the rate of excess profit), however, may very well be justified by the society's declining average "impatience" (the declining SRI indicated by T), as well as by the high capital productivity (or the high ERI indicated by r). Such high expectations may not be limited to the lenders and the borrowers. The incumbent workers, as well as the prospective workers, may also expect a rather high long-term rate of return on their human-capital formation. Households that have increased their savings (providing funds through bank deposits), too, may claim a similarly high long-term interest rate to commensurate with their long-term "impatience" (time preference).

At the outset and in an early phase of the Growth Process, therefore, all the economic entities may expect rather high long-term rates of return with their respective economic roles, self-interest and possible misgivings about the future. This may imply that the expected high rates of return can be justified by the *lead-lag* declines between the Trend Preference Rate (T) and the Trend Interest Rate (r). Accordingly, it may also imply that the ERI declines *lagging* more and more behind the *lead* of the SRI, thus expanding gradually the gap between the Trend Preference Rate (T) and the Trend Interest Rate (r). The expanding gap ("extra-profit rate") may also reflect a rather difficult adjustment of the conflicting interests among the economic actors as well as between the economic actors and the general public. In short, the scarcity of capital in this early phase of the Growth Process may necessitate an enhanced *society-general* future orientation to induce an increasing "extra-profit rate."

As the high rate of economic expansion continues long enough to accumulate a much greater capital stock, as well as a new variety of experience, knowledge and success among the economic actors at large, however, the lenders (savers) and the borrowers (investors) may gradually become confident in the on-going economic trend and more optimistic about the future. They may also become more realistic about a steady decline of the Trend Interest Rate (r), which represents the reinforced *economy-specific* future orientation. Eventually, when the *growth-oriented* process of development reaches all the way to the climax at Point D on the ODP, the "extra-profit rate" (SPD) is maximized. This is the unique development point where T and r change together at the same rate. At this final point of the Growth Process, the rapid quantitative expansion may have utilized the mass-production methods, the economies of scale and the division of labor to the fullest extent.

THE MATURATION PROCESS AND NARROWING PROFITABILITY

The second pattern, where the gap (SPD) between the ERI and the SRI gradually narrows from its maximum at Point D (the Growth-Maturation turning point), indicates the process of socioeconomic maturation—the Maturation Process as in Figure A.3. This normative process of the present long-term framework is of the highest importance. It is the very process that may accumulate the momentum for Sustainable Development at national/societal level. Such a process begins at Point D and advances toward Point O. A further decline of the Trend Preference Rate (T) may now encounter increasing difficulty, owing to the fact that it has already fallen substantially (or the *society-general* future orientation has been reinforced substantially). The Trend Interest Rate (r), lagging always behind the Trend Preference Rate (T), may decline in a greater stride than T, owing mainly to the highly grown stock of capital in the meantime, which now induces a much strengthened *economy-specific* future orientation.

The Maturation Process is the process where the Trend Interest Rate (r) is catching up with the Trend Preference Rate (T) in order to induce the *social-economic* coherence and harmonious development. In order for T to decline further, the people must become even more positive about the future and acquire more long-term and broader perspectives, as well as a greater future-oriented motivation. In other words, they must now commit themselves to a *much more remote future* than before by nurturing longer-term and more harmonious/peaceful future goals and objectives by the accelerated accumulation of the broadly defined human capital based on Holistic Culture Enrichment. Such future orientation and longer-term perspectives may lead the national/societal contribution toward Sustainable Development.

This means that the people's socioeconomic values may have to change so much so that the people in general must become much longer-term oriented, as well as more seriously and realistically future-concerned. In addition, they must alter their own lifestyles and world views so much so that they can now derive their greater satisfaction based on much less self-seeking and much more public-interested (or mutual-interested) endeavors. Accordingly, they may now derive their greater satisfaction from much less *material* and much more *mental* (Cultural) sources, aiming at the satisfaction of much less short-term and much more long-term needs as well as at the satisfaction by much less *quantitative* and much more *qualitative* means. If such alterations will take place smoothly over time, the Maturation Process may become increasingly tangible and, perhaps, viable for the sound enrichment of Culture and the enhancement of the Environment and, hence, for Sustainable Development.

In this *quality-and-mentality* enhancing process, where the quality of production, consumption, education, health care, governance, lifestyle, natural environment, human capital, institutions, attitudes and behaviors, among other things, is fast improving, the share of "*effective*" human-capital formation in the aggregate investment and the total value-added may rise much faster than before. The similar expansion may prove to be true with the share of human-capital income (in comparison to "simple" labor income) in the aggregate household income. Thus, the social constituents may now obtain a greater enjoyment, comfort and satisfaction from both consumption and human-capital formation. Accordingly, individual persons as workers and consumers may strive much less for pecuniary and material gains and much more for spiritual fulfillment, aesthetic enjoyment and intellectual satisfaction in work life as well as in familial/social life. The increasing number of such natural persons may now show a growing interest in the ever diverse but harmoniously integrated human-capital formation as well as in the rapid improvement of the socioeducational environment appropriate for their expanding variety of needs, expectations and objectives in the age of Sustainable Development.

Moreover, they may now show a reinforced motivation for much broader and deeper cultivation of themselves, not only for their self-establishment, self-enlightenment and "self-actualization" (Gobble 1970), but also for discharging their responsibilities for themselves as well as for public purposes. Many natural persons may now try to identify themselves with the professions in the trans-Cultural, interdisciplinary, supra-national and global contexts, as well as with the professions in education, welfare and health care. They may strengthen simultaneously their Cultural identities, roles and relations in their respective families, local communities, nations and the prospective global community. In short, the demand for "*effective*" human capital (reflecting the enjoyment, comfort and satisfaction derived from human capacities, needs, goals and endeavors) and its supply (representing the endeavors for the growing variety of personal capacities, needs and goals) tend to influence each other and grow together rapidly in the Maturation Process.

Then, *what human capital denotes* may gradually change to encompass, in addition to the up-to-date vocational skills and professional requirements, the newly cultivated capacities for richer and harmonious intra-family, interperson, inter-generation, inter-Culture and international relations, as well as for much greater interest in education, welfare, health care, natural-and-social environment, cross-Cultural understanding, interdisciplinary explorations, international collaborations and global governance systems. Moreover, a wide range of less tangible personal abilities, such as self-command, prudence, decency, public concern, insights, foresight, imagination, ingenuity, creativity and long-term perspectives, among other things, may now grow in importance as the indispensable components of human capital and personal character.

These diverse and all-embracing human capacities may reinforce the concern for the balances in socioeconomic development, short-and-long-term needs and material-and-mental orientation. Along with such growing concern for the balances, both natural and legal persons may start being more strongly motivated to tackle the inevitable issue of Sustainable Development in their respective societies for generating the prospective global community, along with the synchronous issues of Culture of Peace and Global Humanity. Their growing motivation, supported by stepped-up human-capital formation and character building, may steadily expand their thought-frames to further the process of socioeconomic maturation. Such a dynamic process, therefore, has to be maintained by the tireless and perpetual personal and societal endeavors for Comprehensive

Human Development and Holistic Culture Enrichment. Also, such endeavors may have to reinforce the people's future orientation and long-term perspectives for Balanced Socioeconomic Development on the basis of the sound enrichment of the society-specific culture (Culture), as well as on the basis of the commitment to the common good and global purposes.

Also, it is important to count on the appropriate long-term government policy and sound market function, properly directed by the Own Hands (elaborated in Chapter 13), for the maintenance of public order as well as for the support of such personal and societal endeavors and commitments. An appropriate long-term public policy in the field of education, including diverse opportunities for continuing education and Cultural enrichment, may prove to be a potent support. Indeed, the continuation of its potency and future success will largely depend on the public policy's ability to broaden and balance the educational contents and opportunities for all, to expand the personal and societal thought-frames and to strengthen the socioeconomic value system favoring a harmonious lifestyle and fair distribution of income, as well as favoring Sustainable Development.

THE RETROGRESSION AND BREAKDOWN PROCESSES

The Retrogression Process

Even with the *society-general* endeavors accompanied by a long-term supportive government policy, the society may stray from the desirable course of socioeconomic development on the ODP, due to the "hangover" from the Growth Process: that is, the prolonged disregards of the "have-nots," the consequence of accumulated "policy failure," the long neglected "market failure" and the institutional exhaustion, even in the absence of devastating external economic impact, military conflict with another nation or global-scale warfare. Perhaps, an extreme structural distortion of the socioeconomy which still pervades in the early phase of the Maturation Process, can be the toughest foes against smooth progress into the socioeconomic maturation.

A possible process of the socioeconomic reversal, for instance, at Point a on the ODP in Figure A.4, may take one of the three general routes. The Retrogression Process (in-between Point O and Point D) on the normative development path is depicted by Route x, while Route y and Route z show the examples of *"derailed"* retrogression to the left and to the right of the ODP, respectively. The last possibility—Route z—however, may represent the most likely reaction in an actual retrogression, since the rise in the long-term interest rate may be exaggerated at least in the outset of the socioeconomic reversal. Perhaps, neither the Retrogression Process (in-between Point O and Point D) nor the Breakdown Process (in-between Point D and Point F) traces strictly the given ODP backward.

The Retrogression Process is generally characterized by declining long-term motivation to save and invest, consequential to the rising Trend Preference Rate (T) or the declining *society-general* future orientation. With the implied opaque future, the individual motivation to save may deteriorate mostly to a "defensive" or "rainy-day-oriented" one. This implies that the motivation to invest is also weakening by the effect of the rising T. Under the circumstances, financial institutions may become hesitant to lend long term, shifting their top priority to short-term lending, which may entail a rising interest rate in general with the dwindling long-term motivation

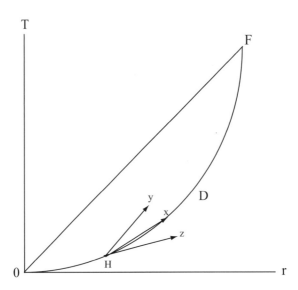

Figure A.4 Retrogression processes

to save. Owing to the already accumulated effects of Holistic Culture Enrichment and Comprehensive Human Development during the Maturation Process (O-D), a hysteric "money-breeds-money" and other types of speculation may not take place society-wide in the Retrogression Process.

The Breakdown Process

In the Breakdown Process (D-F), however, both natural and legal persons may start shying away from capital formation and may be strongly inclined to speculation for "short-run" gains. Such action also induces the rising short-term and long-term interest rates to induce over time a continuous rise in the Trend Interest Rate (r), indicating the declining *economy-specific* future orientation. When a fever for speculation prevails in a society, both natural and legal persons may show a strong preference to current accounts or other forms of short-term bank accounts and expect higher interest rates on their deposits, possibly causing both short-term and long-term interest rates to rise rapidly to push the Trend Interest Rate (r) upward eventually.

Under the circumstances, natural and legal persons alike may hope and attempt to make a fortune at a stroke and belittle the "sweat on the forehead." This may set the stage for a "bubble economy" causing a hysterical price hike in a wide variety of assets, such as stocks, land lots and objects of art and curios. Natural and legal persons may speculate also on foreign exchanges and a variety of commodities, participate in public lotteries, and bet on hose, boat and bicycle races, among other things. Along with these gambling activities, the inclination to "hard work" may fade away rapidly, and the existing social order and values may deteriorate or degenerate to selfish and/or anti-social variety.

Under such socioeconomic conditions a burst of the "bubble" may trigger off a financial panic and/or a serious depression. Such an economic downfall may rapidly decrease the gap ("extra-profit rate") between T and r. Put differently, the SRI is rising with the ERI, while the SRI is rising in a greater step than the ERI in the Breakdown Process. This may imply the shrinking SPD, accompanied by growing long-term *general-public* pessimism. The growing pessimism may constantly feed the negative force of "self-fulfilling prophecies" toward Point F (the "socioeconomic hell"), in the absence of strong and decisive countervailing remedies. In short, the *society-general* future orientation may rapidly wear off to induce an extreme social instability in the Breakdown Process.

Under the circumstances one corollary of the *derailed* Breakdown Process may occur, as a result of severe damage to the mutual trust of the social constituents and the centripetal force of the society, as well as to the holistic society-specific culture (Culture). This may mean the society falling into the Credibility Trap. In this case both personal and social vitalities of activities may degenerate rapidly, together with the rapid rise of *society-general present orientation* (a rapid increase in the Trend Preference Rate (T)). Given the extremely depressed personal and societal conditions with little hope for optimism, it is quite likely that saving and investment may decrease at an extreme pace beyond any rational explanation.

In the Breakdown Process, the long-term aggregate saving and investment may fall into a vicious circle: that is, the reduction in both saving and investment stimulates over time a rise in the Trend Interest Rate (r) and, in turn, a rise of the Trend Preference Rate (T) for a further reduction in saving and investment. In other words, as the socioeconomic activities degenerate to the position closer to Point F on the ODP, the people may become even more pessimistic. As the future hope wears off rapidly on their way to "socioeconomic hell," the people may become desperate and allow the social order to fall asunder. The disarray in social order may push further upward the Trend Preference Rate to start a vicious circle anew. Then, the economic activities may diminish in the absolute terms, and the society may fall into a situation where it is highly difficult to work out its salvation by its own efforts.

By the above lengthy discussion of four processes of socioeconomic development—Growth, Maturation, Retrogression and Breakdown—I have tried to convey that a society *does not* only *progress* but also *regress*, depending on the condition pertinent to the Basic Ratio (T/r) that largely represents the state of the existing dynamic Culture. In view of the four processes on the ODP, I am of the opinion that no modern, "modernized" and "modernizing" societies have already passed Point D and moved into the Maturation Process. It definitely requires the *paradigm shift* to advance into the Maturation Process. In other words, for society to move into that process it must sweep away the lopsided modern tenets and ideologies, such as materialism, scientism, expansionism, market fundamentalism, "law of the jungle," the sanction of personal and national self-interest, the enshrinement of private property and the "might-makes-right" ideology, among other things.

Theoretical Appendix 5: Diagrammatic Explanation of Theoretical Construct

The long-term theoretical framework for Balanced Socioeconomic Development primarily speaks for the long-term equilibrium condition (S = I = R) and the Necessary and Sufficient Conditions. The Basic Ratio is common to all the left-hand terms in the basic construct. In this Appendix, I will express the basic construct diagrammatically separated as the "demand-side" (expenditure-side) relations and the "supply-side" (distribution-side) relations, although the both sides are equivalent (Hiwaki 1993Ja, 1995b).

Now, the following equations (*approximation*) constitute the "demand-side" socioeconomic relations:

$$T/r = C/V \qquad\qquad (1)$$

$$T/r = 1 - (S/V) \qquad\qquad (1.1)$$

$$T/r = 1 - (I/V) \qquad\qquad (1.2)$$

The ratios C/V, S/V and I/V represent, respectively, the long-term shares of consumption, saving and investment in the aggregate value-added, where C, S, I, and V indicate the long-term aggregate consumption, saving, investment and value-added, respectively.

The remaining equations, together with Equation (1.2) above, constitute the "supply-side" socioeconomic relations:

$$T/r = W/V \qquad\qquad (2)$$

$$T/r = 1 - (R/V) \qquad\qquad (2.1)$$

$$T/r = 1 - (I/V) \qquad\qquad (1.2)$$

The two ratios, W/V and R/V, represent the long-term income shares of labor and capital, respectively, where W and R, respectively, indicate the labor income and the capital income.

The long-term investment share (I/V) is reinstated here as an important bridge between the "demand side" with the "supply side." This term can be treated as a *linkage* variable in the long-term socioeconomic interactions, for the long-term investment (I) transforms over time the saving (S) into the stock of capital. The linkage variable (I/V) also conduce to the *long-term demand-supply equilibrium* (S = I = R) in the process of Balanced Socioeconomic Development. The aggregate investment (I) with its growing share of human-capital formation over time is also postulated as the pivotal element that propels the *trilateral virtuous circle* among Comprehensive Human Development and Holistic Culture Enrichment with Balanced Socioeconomic Development.

The above "demand-side" and "supply-side" equations now constitute their "square-shaped" diagrams, respectively, in Figures A.5 and A.6. In Figure A.5, the Basic Ratio (T/r) is placed on the "upper vertical axis," while the investment share (I/V) is located on the "lower vertical axis." The consumption share (C/V) and the saving share (S/V) are placed, respectively, on the "right-hand horizontal axis" and the "left-hand horizontal axis." The 45-degree ray *rising diagonally* from the origin (O) indicates the equality of the Basic Ratio (T/r) with the consumption share (C/V), while the 45-degree ray *falling diagonally* from the origin shows the equality of the saving share (S/V) with the investment share (I/V), or S = I.

These two diagonal 45-degree rays connected at the origin forms a *straight diagonal shaft*, along which the "square-shaped" diagram of socioeconomic interactions is depicted to slide downward in the process of Balanced Socioeconomic Development. Parallel

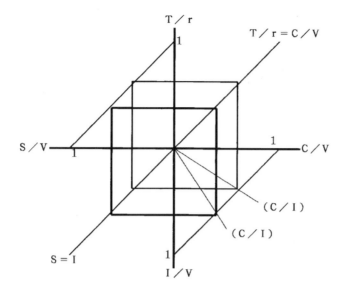

Figure A.5 Demand-side development

to the 45-degree shaft, there are two diagonal lines: one line connecting the points of unity respective to both T/r and S/V in the second quadrant and another connecting the points of unity respective to both C/V and I/V in the fourth quadrant. Along the latter diagonal line, the consumption-investment ratio (C/I) is depicted to move downward in the process of Balanced Socioeconomic Development.

Now, the Trend Preference Rate (T) begins to decline with the enhanced *society-general future-orientation*. This decline is followed, with a time-lag, by a coherent decline of the Trend Interest Rate (r). Accordingly, the Basic Ratio (T/r) and the consumption share (C/V) begin simultaneously to move downward along the *straight diagonal shaft*. These downward movements stimulate over time the growth in the saving share (S/V) and the investment share (I/V), simultaneously. These changes in C/V, S/V and I/V, triggered by the decline in the Basic Ratio (T/r), are depicted by a slide downward of the "square-shaped" diagram along the *diagonal straight shaft*, indicating Balanced Socioeconomic Development. Likewise, the decline of the Basic Ratio (T/r) can be seen as reflected on the slide downward of the "consumption-investment" ratio (C/I) along the parallel diagonal line in the fourth quadrant.

As seen also in Figure A.6, the Basic Ratio (T/r) is placed on the "upper vertical axis," and the investment share (I/V) on the "lower vertical axis." Now, the long-term labor-income share (W/V) is shown on the "right-hand horizontal axis" and the capital-income share (R/V) on the "left-hand horizontal axis." The 45-degree ray *rising diagonally* from the origin (O) indicates the equality of the T/r with W/V in the first quadrant, while the 45-degree ray in the third quadrant *falling diagonally* from the origin indicates the equality of the capital-income share (R/V) with the investment-income share (I/V), or R = I. This equality (R = I) and the above-mentioned equality (S = I) in Figure A.5, together, comprise the *long-term equilibrium condition* (S = I = R). The two 45-degree straight lines combined at the origin represent the *straight diagonal shaft*, along which the "square-

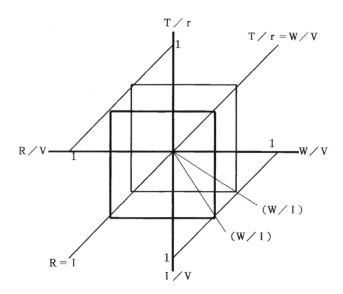

Figure A.6   Supply-side development

shaped" diagram of socioeconomic interactions slides down, indicating the process of Balanced Socioeconomic Development.

Parallel to the *straight diagonal shaft*, there are two diagonal lines: the one connecting the points of unity respective to both T/r and R/V and another connecting the points of unity respective to both W/V and I/V. Along the latter diagonal line in the fourth quadrant, the "wage-investment" ratio (W/I) slides downward. This change in the wage-investment ratio, implying a long-term coordinated change between the long-term labor income (W) and the long-term investment (I), also implies the process of Balanced Socioeconomic Development.

The above two diagrams (Figure A.5 and Figure A.6), together, may amply provide the implications of the Necessary and Sufficient Conditions relevant to Balanced Socioeconomic Development. Such implications will be taken up in Appendix 6.

Theoretical Appendix 6: The Necessary and Sufficient Conditions

Based on the above-mentioned theoretical expressions, Balanced Socioeconomic Development can be explained by two fundamental conditions or the Necessary and the Sufficient Conditions (Hiwaki 1993Ja, 1998a). Such conditions can be derived from Equation (1): T/r = C/V. Now, the equation is changed into the following expression after dividing thorough by the left-hand term (T/r):

$$1 = (C/V) \bullet 1/(T/r)$$

The term 1/(T/r), being equal to 1/(C/V) by definition, can be interpreted here as the "long-term multiplier" for the determination of the aggregate value-added (V). For simplicity, Q is now used to replace the term $1/(T/r)$ in the above expression, namely, $1 = (C/V) \cdot Q$. Multiplying both sides of this expression by V, I now obtain the equation to determine the long-term aggregate value-added, as follows:

$$V = C \bullet Q$$

This expression can also be translated into the following identity (*Italic* expression) that shows the *percentage changes* in all the variables. *Italic V* indicates the rate of Balanced Socioeconomic Development:

$$V = C + Q$$

Similarly, by manipulating Equation (2) or $T/r = W/V$, I obtain the following identity of *percentage changes*:

$$V = W + Q$$

Now, assuming a population change over time, it is more appropriate to express the rate of Balanced Socioeconomic Development in terms of the per-capita rate. In this case both of the equations ($V = C \cdot Q$ and $V = W \cdot Q$) have to be divided through by the population (N), as follows, in which V/N, C/N and W/N mean respectively per-capita value-added, per-capita consumption and per-capita wage income:

$$V/N = (C/N) \cdot Q$$

$$V/N = (W/N) \cdot Q$$

The respective equations can be expressed as $v = c \cdot Q$ and $v = w \cdot Q$ (for per-capita value-added) in the respective short-hand forms. Now the generalized identities of *percentage changes* can be stated, respectively, as follows:

$$v = c + Q$$

$$v = w + Q$$

The above two *italicized* identities of *percentage changes* indicate the per-capita rate of Balanced Socioeconomic Development. In other words, the socioeconomic development per capita can be explained by either the sum of the "per-capita consumption growth rate" and the growth rate of the "long-term multiplier," or the sum of the "per-capita wage growth rate" and the growth rate of the "long-term multiplier."

Also, the *italicized* identities can be used to explain both the Necessary and the Sufficient conditions for Balanced Socioeconomic Development. The terms c and w, referring to the respective increases in the per-capita consumption (c) and the per-capita labor income (w), indicate the Necessary Condition. The Necessary Condition represents the long-term improvement of people's living standard.

The term Q, referring to a change in the "long-term multiplier," indicates the Sufficient Condition for Balanced Socioeconomic Development. The Sufficient Condition represents the long-term enhancement of the *society-general future orientation* (decline in T). As indicated above, the term Q is the abbreviation of the term $1/(T/r)$. Since the Trend Preference Rate (T) must decline ahead of the Trend Interest Rate (r), in accordance with our *lead-lag assumption*, Q may gradually increase along with Balanced Socioeconomic Development.

It is important to note that the Sufficient Condition for Balanced Socioeconomic Development represents the dynamics of the Value Aspect. The Sufficient Condition also prescribes the nature of the Necessary Condition in such a way as the growth in consumption being characterized by a continuous shift from the *short-term* focus to the *short-and-long-term* balance, from the *quantity* bias to the *quality* orientation, and from the *material* centeredness to the *personal-spiritual-intellectual* (or Cultural) emphasis in the process of Balanced Socioeconomic Development.

Likewise, the long-term growth in "simple" labor income is prescribed by the Sufficient Condition. Such income may reflect the on-going improvement in personality, spirituality, intellectuality and productivity of the people in general. Hence, the Sufficient Condition may also reflect the on-going improvement of the standard minimum knowledge/skills and the standard minimum Cultural incorporation into "simple" labor. In this manner, the Sufficient Condition may reflect the general improvement of living standard as well as the Cultural enrichment over time. Then, the Necessary and the Sufficient Conditions, together, imply the long-term *trilateral virtuous circle* among Balanced Socioeconomic Development, Comprehensive Human Development and Holistic Culture Enrichment.

To sum up, the long-term theoretical framework requires both a continuous rise in the *living standard* (Necessary Condition) and a continuous reinforcement in the long-term *society-general future orientation* (Sufficient Condition) for Balanced Socioeconomic Development. A constant satisfaction of both the Necessary and Sufficient Conditions of Balanced Socioeconomic Development may, therefore, suggest the importance of the accelerated increase in human-capital formation as well as of the continuous endeavor for personal-character building, spiritual development and human-capacity improvement on the basis of the growing long-term orientation to the future. Such acceleration and continuity of multifaceted human development pertinent to the people at large must be based, by necessity, on the sound enrichment of the Culture. In other words, the Necessary and Sufficient Conditions may suggest that Balanced Socioeconomic Development depends primarily on Comprehensive Human Development that is constantly encouraged by Holistic Culture Enrichment.

Theoretical Appendix 7: A Framework for Thought-Frame Enhancement

Enhancement of the people's thought-frame ("thought-frame enhancement") can now be discussed through a diagrammatic approach based on the basic long-term theoretical construct. A diagrammatic derivation of the *built-in mechanism* for "thought-frame enhancement" is depicted in Figure A.7 (Hiwaki 1996a). The first quadrant, showing the Trend Preference Rate (T) on the vertical axis and the Trend Interest Rate (r) on the horizontal axis, depicts the Optimal Development Path (ODP: "bow-shaped" curve). In other words, this quadrant portrays the long-term schedule of the Basic Ratio (T/r), which indicates synergistic interactions of T with r. In principle, T leads r, but they influence each other to form the ODP, a bi-directional representation of the normative socioeconomic development.

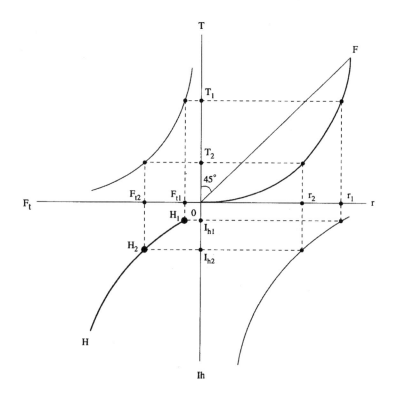

Figure A.7 Derivation of Curve H

The second quadrant depicts an *intuitive* downward sloping curve convex to the origin, which represents straightforward synergistic interactions between the Trend Preference Rate (T) and the people's *conscious future* time horizon (F_t). A decline of T indicates that the people are placing a greater value to the "future" relative to the "present" to broaden the scope of planning for the future. An expansion of the *conscious future* time horizon for planning, in turn, reinforces the decline in the long-term *society-general* time-preference rate (T), which also indicates the reinforced future orientation. Throughout such synergistic interactions, the people's time frame, especially the "future" in their time frame, tends to expand over time.

A similarly straightforward relation is *intuitively* depicted in the fourth quadrant, where the Trend Interest Rate (r) synergistically interacts with the human-capital formation (I_h). The long-term interactions of these variables are such that a decline in the long-term interest rate (or a decline in the long-term cost of capital formation) stimulates the investment in human capital, while an increase in the stock of human capital reduces the long-term interest rate (the long-term rate of return on human capital). I may express these synergistic interactions by an *intuitive* curve convex to the origin.

The above various interactions, together, lead to further synergistic interactions in the third quadrant that portrays Curve H to indicate the enhancement schedule of people's thought-frame in time and space. This quadrant, showing the people's *conscious future* time horizon (F_t) on the horizontal axis and the broadly defined human-capital formation (I_h) on the "lower vertical axis," depicts Curve H upside down. This diagram, therefore, demonstrates the theoretical derivation of Curve H directly from the long-term theoretical framework. The "thought-frame enhancement" is a highly complex phenomenon based on the compounded synergistic interactions of long-term nature.

I will now explain step by step the derivation relevant to Curve H in Figure A.7. Now, starting from T_1 (Trend Preference Rate) on the "upper vertical axis," the corresponding Trend Interest Rate is represented by r_1 on the horizontal axis in the first quadrant. The corresponding people's *conscious future* time horizon is shown by F_{t1} on the horizontal axis in the second quadrant. The amount of human-capital formation at the given long-term interest rate r_1 is represented by I_{h1} on the "lower vertical axis." Then, I_{h1} and F_{t1}, together, indicate a point—Point H_1—on Curve H in the third quadrant. Another random position on the "upper vertical axis" such as T_2 finds the corresponding r_2 and F_{t2} on the horizontal axes, as well as I_{h2} on the "lower vertical axis." Now, I_{h2} and F_{t2}, together, indicate Point H_2 on Curve H in the third quadrant. Repeating the same process, we can trace the entire schedule of Curve H that implies the extra-long-term process of thought-frame enhancement.

Theoretical Appendix 8: Peace and Harmony—Japanese Style

As a representation of Japanese Culture and the related human development, in this appendix I will discuss the teachings of *Kendo* (the Way of the Sword) that may contribute also to a Culture of Peace (Hiwaki 1999a, 2002J). Historically speaking, the physical, moral and spiritual strains of warriors during more than a century of war-torn Japan (1467–1600) led to the nascent warrior ethics to gradually generate the art of living combined with the discipline for peace-and-harmony-oriented character building. This character building development, indeed, had many twists and turns, leaving room for a variety of interpretations of *Kendo* and *Bushido* (the Way of the Warrior). One important heritage of the warrior ethics that blossomed during the long *Tokugawa Peace* (1600–1868), however, is today's view of *Kendo* as an element for training the mind and body. Those seeing *Kendo* in terms of human development may argue that the greater the achievement in *Kendo* the greater the appreciation of life and peace. *Kendo's* approach toward peace and harmony is briefly investigated in the following as a possible breakthrough for the dilemma of war or peace.

Referring to "peace," we usually think of "war" as alternative and unknowingly perceive the issue often in the dilemma of war or peace. This setting of the issue may suggest discontinuity of war and peace. War and peace, however, can be perceived as continuous, similar to the mental continuum between animosity and harmony of individuals with each other. This mental aspect is stressed in the teachings of *Kendo*, for mind and body are considered inseparable in the training of *Kendo*. Every action has an effect on every mental activity, and every mental activity affects every action (Suino 1996). Thus, one's keeping amity or enmity with another may depend on their physical and mental interactions.

The founding fathers of *Kendo*, drawing from numerous *Kenjutsu kata* (formal attack and parrying exercises) of traditional Japanese fencing schools, selected three *kata* at the beginning of the twentieth century, particularly for educational consideration, to emphasize the importance of earnest training for appreciation of life and for consideration toward each other (Inoue 1997). Such emphasis by means of *kata* deals with appropriate character building: The higher the level of training accomplished, the greater the appreciation of life and peace. A seemingly paradoxical view regarding the states of harmony and animosity is summed up in the *kata* approach to *Kendo*. *Kendo* with its own physical, moral and spiritual implications shares a characteristic common to all sports with sportsmanship, on the one hand, and distinguishes itself from the latter, on the other, by going far beyond the issue of competition and seeking cultural refinement and spiritual serenity.

A BRIEF HISTORY OF KENDO

Kendo is a relatively recent term that implies spiritual discipline as well as fencing technique (Hazard 1983). As recently as in 1919, Hiromichi Nishikubo, the then Vice Chairman of *Dai Nippon Butokukai* (All Japan Martial Virtue Society) and the President of the College of *Bujutsu*, renamed *Kenjutsu* (the Art of the Sword) as *Kendo* (the Way of the Sword). The naming and purpose of *Kendo*, as part of *Budo* (the general term referring to the Japanese martial arts) has had a history of many twists and turns (Nakamura 1994). The prevailing view of *Kendo*, however, indicates that the training in *kata* must go far beyond acquiring the techniques of attacking and parrying so as to seek embodiment of justice, benevolence and courage.

Referring to the very beginning of fencing techniques, we must go all the way back in history to the time of the *Sui* Dynasty (589–618) or the early *Tang* Dynasty (618–907) in China, when Japanese imperial missions to China might have brought back to Japan the Chinese art of using the single-edged, straight-blade sword. In ninth century Japan, however, combat on horseback led to the use of a longer curved blade, and the increased length made it necessary to abandon the one-handed Chinese style of sword fighting for a two-handed style (Hazard 1983). The cultivation of sword skills (*Kenjutsu*) flourished, especially after the ascension to power of martial aristocrats in the period between the twelfth and sixteenth centuries.

With the establishment of secluded nationwide peace by the *Tokugawa Shogunate* (*Tokugawa Peace*) in the early seventeenth century, *Kenjutsu* went into a decline; its skill was no longer essential for survival, and the moral and spiritual elements became predominant, drawing on Confucius, Shinto and Buddhism, especially Zen (Tomiki 1992, Hazard 1983). In this context, *Kenjutsu* began to relate itself to *Bushido* (the Way of the Warrior). According to the much misunderstood book entitled *BUSHIDO* by Inazo Nitobe, "*Bushido* means literally Military-Knight-Ways which fighting nobles should observe in their daily life as well as in their vocation, in a word, the 'Precepts of Knighthood', the *noblesse oblige* of the warrior class" (Nitobe 1998).

Spanning more than 260 years, the *Edo* period (*Tokugawa Peace*) was an age in which much of what are now considered "Japanese traditions" in the realms of art and culture was nurtured and flourished (Ozawa 1997). During this period *Kenjutsu* became an element for training the mind and body. Immediately following the *Meiji Restoration* (1868), in which the Emperor was restored to the throne after almost 700 years of military rule, the practice of *Kenjutsu*, seen then as an undesirable relic of the warrior class, declined again temporarily. Before long, however, a new policy of *fukoku-kyohei* (literally, national wealth for military strength) led to a heightened national awareness, and it was in this climate that *Kendo* began once again to attract attention as a method of building strong character (Tomiki 1992, Ozawa 1997).

The Second World War ended with the Japanese defeat in 1945, and the Occupation authorities banned *Kendo*. Soon after the end of the Occupation, however, the All Japan Kendo Federation was established in 1952 to resume *Kendo*, and has since acquired a new reputation as an educational sport, and its practice in school and society has become as popular as the practice of *Judo*. Like Judo, but to a lesser degree, the scope of Kendo in terms of cultural, moral and spiritual aspects has, however, suffered. Many now train in Kendo as purely physical education or as merely a competitive sport.

KENDO KATA AND THE CULTURE OF PEACE

As the All Japan Martial Virtue Society was formed in 1895, it became necessary to unify numerous *kata* developed by some 200 *Kenjutsu* schools in *Tokugawa Peace* (Mitsuhashi 1972). The society's unified and standardized *Kenjutsu kata* came into being in 1906, and, then, *Dai Nippon Kendo Kata* (abbreviated as *kata* here) was established in 1912, as *Kendo* became part of regular high school curricula. Seven *kata* for long sword and three for short sword were selected for educational purposes, but the first three long-sword *kata* came to be considered especially important for educational consideration. My discussion in this section will mainly follow the exposition of the mental aspect by Yoshihiko Inoue (Inoue 1997).

Referring to the statement of Hiromichi Nakayama (a member of the committee that laid down *kata*) to the effect that the principal objective of *Budo* amounts to the very embodiment of justice, benevolence and courage, Inoue relates these virtues respectively to the lessons of the first, second and third *kata*. Both the first and second *kata* are supposed to represent the necessary learning and cultivation of forms and motions as well as their respective mental attitudes toward justice and benevolence, while the third *kata* is for the quest and endeavor to acquire the virtue of great courage that emphasizes peace and harmony, implying the core value of society-specific culture (Culture).

The *kata* exercise is carried out between the person assuming the role of teacher (*uchidachi*) and the one the role of student (*shidachi*) in the training of all *kata*. The first *kata* exercise begins with *jodan-no-kamae* (the "overhead" posture: holding the respective swords overhead). As the teacher executes a frontal attack with an indomitable fighting spirit, the student parries and deliver a frontal strike. In this *kata* exercise, both the teacher and the student attack each other from the "overhead" posture, implying a clash of justice against justice. Thus, the first *kata* is meant to teach that one defeats the other with the difference of relative skill cultivation that corresponds to the laws of nature. The first lesson in Kendo means training for self-acquirement of the physical motion and mental attitude, as well as cultivation for self-manifestation of justice. In addition to this self-manifestation, the first *kata* teaches the importance of repentance for the killing. In real combat, the loser dies, and the winner who survives is required to repent the killing. This mental attitude in part represents the assertion of *zanshin* pose—the positive follow-through of strike that entails repentance as well as mental and physical alertness.

Such mental attitude leads to the second *kata* exercise. The second exercise begins with *chudan-no-kamae* (the "middle" posture: holding the respective swords in front). This "middle" posture is the most basic posture good for both attack and defense in *Kendo* exercise. Now, the teacher executes an attack on the right forearm of the student. Parrying the attack, the student delivers a strike to the teacher's right forearm, and asserts a positive follow-through with dignity. We should note that the student could deliver a frontal attack to kill his opponent, but he commits himself only to strike the forearm. In other words, the student learns in this *kata* exercise to take away only the opponent's combat capability, rather than taking his very life, the value of which is immeasurable. Since it is exceptionally difficult to acquire such spirit of benevolence, the second *kata* demands the virtue that naturally emanates benevolence to all the surrounding people. According to Inazo Nitobe, the benevolence of a *samurai* (warrior), recognizing due regards to justice, is not a blind impulse. His benevolence does not remain merely a certain state of mind, but it is backed with power to save or kill (Nitobe 1998).

The lesson of second *kata*, therefore, refers to a much higher accomplishment than the case of first *kata* that demands only the virtue of justice. According to the Confucian doctrine, the man of benevolence always has courage. The lesson of higher accomplishment leads to the third *kata* or to the cultivation of great courage. Now, both the student and the teacher begin with *gedan-no-kamae* (the "low" posture: holding the respective swords downwards) and, then, move naturally to the "middle" posture in the spirit of mutual combat. The teacher, watching for an opportunity to act, delivers a thrust to the student's solar plexus. Against the weakening inward thrust of the teacher, the student now counterthrusts toward the teacher's chest. As the teacher pushes the student's sword to the left, the student steps forward in the spirit of thrust and proceeds pressing in on the opponent with dignity. Then, with small quick steps the student proceeds further, raising the point of the sword to the center of the teacher's face and asserts positive follow-through with dignity.

The lesson of the third *kata* exercise indicates the idea of peace and harmony. The lesson, in addition to the highest accomplishment of mental maturity and sword technique, demands great courage to resist the temptation of thrusting at once in fear that the opponent may attack in desperation. Figuratively speaking, great courage sends forth a soothing atmosphere to calm the opponent's violent temper. Also, such courage may teach the opponent the importance of life as well as the purpose of life. Still more, great courage may let the opponent learn to appreciate truly his indispensable and fragile life and to live in harmony with the other. In this manner, the third *kata* teaches the importance of peace and harmony, and asserts the value that is closely related to a Culture of Peace or the core value of a Sound Culture.

In conclusion, let me warn the reader that, by the above exposition, I do not intend to assert that *Kendo* is a *panacea* or that *Kendo* leads to a Culture of Peace. In spite of the excellent teachings of *Kendo*, the "modern" Japanese have fought the Sino-Japanese War, the Russo-Japanese War, the First World War and the Second World War. Whatever good teachings we may receive from histories and Cultures, we do not seem to have made the best use of them, seeking new, easy, transient and, often ending up with, unwise solutions to an old and common problem, rather than *consciously* taking stock of our long-accumulated experiences and wisdom. It is about time to reconsider such mentality and attitude, for we are not as wise as we may think, without the backing of the precious heritage—the accumulated wealth—of the past. I am of the opinion that peace and harmony should be *cultivated* within every person, with earnest and unflagging endeavors of all people on the basis of inherited respective Cultures. No lasting peace can be achieved without the dynamic and harmonious interactions of all people, firmly supported by the harmony-respecting values of diverse Sound Cultures.

Bibliography

General

Allen, R.L. 1993. *Irving Fisher—A Biography*. Cambridge, MA: Blackwell.

Andonian, G. 2001. The three caves of European identity: from critical to creative thinking. *Consciousness, Literature and the Arts* [Online]. Available at: http://www.aber.ac.uk/tfts/journal/march2001/bioandonian.html [accessed: April 5, 2001].

Ariki, S. 1986. Post-war industrial policy in Japan. *Rivista Internazionale di Scienze Economiche e Commerciali*, 33(5), 425–445.

Arndt, H.W. 1987. *Economic Development: The History of an Idea*. Chicago: The University of Chicago Press.

Aydin, A. 2003. Healing the planet with a friendly cooperation with ecosystems: a process towards achieving sustainable life on earth, in *Sustainable Development and Global Community—Volume IV*, edited by G.E. Lasker and K. Hiwaki. Canada: IIAS, 7–12.

Aydin, A. 2004. Dialogue between outer and inner sensory impressions, in *Personal-Spiritual Development in the World of Cultural Diversity—Volume I*, edited by G.E. Lasker and K. Hiwaki. Canada: IIAS, 7–12.

Azariadis, C. 1975. Implicit contracts and unemployment equilibria. *Journal of Political Economy*, 83(6), 1183–1202.

Balasa, B. and Noland, M. 1988. *Japan in the World Economy*. Washington DC: Institute for International Economics.

Ballon, R.J. and Tomita, I. 1988. *The Financial Behavior of Japanese Corporation*. Tokyo: Kodansha International.

Becker, G.S. 1964. *Human Capital: A Theoretical and Empirical Analysis, with Special Reference to Education*. New York: NBER.

Beneditti, E. and Solaris, S. 1996. Evolutionary system and long run economics. *Human Systems Management*, 15(2), 125–134.

Birkhn, H. 1999. *Kelten/Celts: Images of Their Culture*. Wien: Verlag der Osterreichischen Akademie der Wissenschaften.

Boltho, A. 1975. *Japan: An Economic Survey 1953–1973*. Oxford: Oxford University Press.

Brekilian, Y. 1993. *Mytologie Celtique* (Japanese translation by H. Tanaka and K. Yamamura in 1998; *Keruto Shinwa no Sekai*).Tokyo: Chuo Koron-sha.

Bronfenbrenner, M. 1950. Four positions on Japanese finance. *Journal of Political Economy*, LVIII(4), 281–288.

Bronfenbrenner, M. 1979. *Macroeconomic Alternatives*. Illinois: AHM Publishing Corporation.

Bronfenbrenner, M. and Yasuba, Y. 1987. Economic welfare, in *The Political Economy of Japan: Volume 1: The Domestic Transformation,* edited by K. Yamamura and Y. Yasuba. Stanford, CA: Stanford University Press

Canterbery, E.R 1980. *The Making of Economics*. California: Wadsworth Publishing Co.

Caves, R.E. 1982. *Multinational Enterprise and Economic Analysis*. Cambridge: Cambridge University Press.

China (Hainan) Reform Development Research Center. 2000. *Blue Book of the Chinese Society: Analysis and Forecast of the Chinese Society*. Hainan: Social Sciences Documentation Publishing House.

China (Hainan) Reform Development Research Center. 2003. *Blue Book of the Chinese Society: Analysis and Forecast of the Chinese Society*. Hainan: Social Sciences Documentation Publishing House.

Chinese Academy of Science. 1998. *Employment and Development*. Liaoning: Liaoning People's Press.

Chuo Daigaku Jinbun-kagaku Kenkyu-sho. 1996. *Keruto: Sei to Shi no Henyo* (literally, *The Celts: Transfiguration of Life and Death*). Tokyo: Chuo Daigaku Press.

Chuo Daigaku Jinbun-kagaku Kenkyu-sho. 2001. *Keruto Fukko* (literally, *Celtic Revival*). Tokyo: Chuo Daigaku Press.

Clark, R. 1987. *The Japanese Company*. Tokyo: Charles E. Tuttle Company.

Cunliffe, B. 1997. *The Ancient Celts*. London: Penguin Books.

Czinkota, M.R. and Woronoff, J. 1986. *Japan's Market: The Distribution System*. New York: Praeger.

Dalgliesh, M. no date. *The Sage of San Diego Said Choose Quality and Reason*. La Jolla, California and New York: A New Enlightenment.

Daly, H.E. and Cobb Jr., J.B. 1994. *For the Common Good: Redirecting the Economy toward Community, the Environment, and a Sustainable Future*. Boston: Beacon Press.

Dam, van A. 1982. *Waste Not, Want Not: Approaching The 21st Century: Global Problems And Human Choices: Proceedings of the Club of Rome Symposium in Tokyo* 1982 (The Japan Committee of The Club of Rome).

Davies, J. 2000. *The Celts*. London: Cassell and Co.

Davies, N. 1996. *Europe: A History*. Oxford: Oxford University Press.

Delaney, F. 1991. *Legends of the Celts*. London: Grafton.

Diamond, J. 1997. *Guns, Germs and Steel: The Fates of Human Societies*. New York: W.W. Norton and Company.

Dornbusch, R. and Fischer, S. 1978. *Macroeconomics*. New York: McGraw-Hill Book Company.

Douglas, P.H. 1948. Are there laws of production? *American Economic Review*, 38(1), 1–41.

Eatwell, J., Milgate, M. and Newman, P. (ed.) 1991. *The World of Economics*. London: Macmillan Press.

El-Agraa, A.M. 1988. *Japan's Trade Frictions: Realities or Misconceptions?* London: Macmillan Press.

Ellis, P.B. 1998. *The Ancient World of the Celts*. London: Constable.

Ellisworth, P.T. 1964. *The International Economy* (Third Edition). New York: The Macmillan Company.

Ellwood, C.A. 1938. *A History of Social Philosophy*. New York: Prentice-Hall, Inc.

Eluere, C. 1993. *The Celts—First Masters of Europe*. London: Thames and Hudson.

Engel, F. and Marx, K. 1955. *The Communist Manifesto*. London: Appleton-Century-Crofts.

Fisher, I. 1912. *Elementary Principles of Economics*. New York: The Macmillan Company.

Fisher, I. 1930. *The Theory of Interest*. New York: The Macmillan Company.

Fukunaga, M. 1997. *Roshi* (literally, *Lao-Tse*). Tokyo: Asahi Shinbun-sha.

Galbreith, J.K. 1971. *Economics, Peace and Laughter*. Boston: Houghton Mifflin Co.

Galbreith, J.K. 1973. *Economics and The Public Purposes*. Boston: Houghton Mifflin Co.

Gobble, F.G. 1970. *The Third Force: The Psychology of Abraham Maslow*. New York: Grossman Publishers.

Gordon, D.F. 1974. A neo-classcal theory of Keynesian unemployment. *Economic Enquiry*, 12(4), 431–459.

Graham, W. 2005. Collaborative consciousness and sustainable societies, in *Sustainable Development and Global Community—Volume VI*, edited by G.E. Lasker and K. Hiwaki. Canada: IIAS, 7–14.

Greider, W. 1997. *One World, Ready or Not*. New York: Simon and Schuster.

Haberler von, G. 1950. *The Theory of International Trade*. New York: The Macmillan Company.

Hanami, T. 1979. *Labor Relations in Japan Today*. Tokyo: Kodansha International.

Harris, P.R. and Moran, R.T. 1979. *Managing Cultural Differences*. Texas: Gul Publishing Co.

Hashimoto, J. 1989. Kigyo keiei to roshi kankei (literally, Corporate administration and labor-management relations), in *Sekai Keizai IV: Nippon—Momoku-teki Seicho no Kiketsu* (literally, *The World Economy IV: Japan—Consequences of Reckless Growth*), edited by K. Baba. Tokyo: Ochanomizu Shobo.

Haywood, J. 2001. *The Historical Atlas of the Celtic World*. London: Thames and Hudson.

Hazard, B.H. 1983. Kendo, in *Kodansha Encyclopedia of Japan*. Tokyo: Kodansha.

Heckscher, E. 1950. The effect of foreign trade on the distribution of income, in *Reading in the Theory of International Trade*, selected by the Committee of the American Economic Association. Rechard Irwin, Inc.

Heller, H.R. 1973. *International Trade: Theory and Empirical Evidence*. New Jersey: Prentice-Hall, Inc.

Henderson, J.M. and Quandt, R.E. 1971. *Micro-Economic Theory: A Mathematical Approach* (Second Edition). New York: McGraw-Hill.

Herm, G. 1975. *Die Kelten* (Japanese translation by K. Seki in 1999; *Kerutojin*). Tokyo: Kawade Shobo Shinsha.

Higgins, B. 1968. *Economic Development: Problems, Principles and Policies*. New York: W.W. Norton and Company, Inc.

Hodder, J.E. and Tschoegl, A.E. 1990. Some aspects of Japanese corporate finance, in *Japanese Capital Market*, edited by E.J. Elton and M.J. Gruber. New York: Harper and Row.

Holbrook, S.H. 1953. *The Age of the Moguls: The Story of the Robber Barons and the Great Tycoons*. New York: Doubleday and Company, Inc.

Hollander, S. 1992. *Classical Economics*. Toronto: Basil Blackwell.

Hosoya, C. and Okuma. H. 1980. EC to Nippon (literally, EC and Japan), *Oshu kyodotai (EC) no kenkyuusho: seiji rikigaku no bunseki* (literally, *Studies on the European Community: Analyses of the Political Dynamics*), edited by C. Hosoya and Y. Minami. Tokyo: Shinyu-do.

Hu, A.G. (ed.) 2002. The upcoming 20 years' road of China. *Southern Weekend*, November 16.

Hutchison, T. 1994. *The Uses and Abuses of Economics*. London: Routledge.

Inamori, K. 2007. *Jinsei-no-Odo: Saigo Nanshuu no Oshie ni Manabu* (literally, *Royal Road to Life: Learning from the Teachings of Saigo Nanshu*). Tokyo: Nikkei BP-sha.

Inoue, Y. 1997. *Nippon Kendo Kata no Ichi Kosatsu* (literally, *A Study on Nippon Kendou Kata*). Tokyo: Nisshin Insatsu-sho.

James, S. 1995. *Exploring the World of Celts*. London: Thomas and Hudson Ltd.

Keynes, J.M. 1936. *The General Theory of Employment, Interest, and Money*. New York: Harcourt, Brace and World, Inc.

Kodama, M. 1987. Nippon to EC no boeki mondai (literally, Trade issues between Japan and the EC), in *EC—Oshu Togo no Genzai* (literally, *The EC—the Present Stage of the European Integration*), edited by T. Manamaru. Osaka: Sogen-sha.

Kodansha. 1983. *Kodansha Encyclopedia of Japan Volume 2*. Tokyo: Kodansha.

Koizumi, T. 1994. *Japanese Creativity and Sustainable Development: Proceedings of Kyoto Conference on Japanese Studies*, October 17–22.

Kokuritsu Shakaihosho-Jinkoumondai Kenkyusho [KSJK]. 2005. *Shakaihoshou Tokei Nenpo* (literally, *Annual Report of Social Security*). Tokyo: Jinkomondai Kenkyuusho.

Komiya, R. and Ito, M. 1988. Japan's international trade and trade policy, in *The Political Economy of Japan: Volume 2: The Changing International Context*, edited by T. Inoguchi and D.I. Okimoto. Stanford, CA: Stanford University Press.

Kosai, Y. 1988. Reconstruction period, in *Industrial Policy in Japan*, edited by R. Komiya, M. Okuno and K. Suzumura; Tokyo: Academic Press.

Landes, D.S. 1998. *The Wealth and Poverty of Nations* (Japanese translation by H. Takenaka in 2000; *Kyokoku-ron*). Tokyo: Mikasa Shobo.

Landreth, H. 1976. *History of Economic Theory: Scope, Method and Content*. Hopewell, NJ: Houghton Mifflin Company.

Lasker, G.E. 1998. Developing collaborative consciousness: methodological issues, in *Strategies for Peace*, edited by G.E. Lasker and V. Lomeiko, Canada: IIAS, 135–141.

Lasker, G.E. 2002. Human development: socio-political control and global dictatorship, in *Advances in Sociocybernetics and Human Development—Volume X*, edited by G,E. Lasker. Canada: IIAS, 53–61.

Lasker, G.E. and Hiwaki, K. (ed.) 2000. *Sustainable Development and Global Community—Volume I*. Canada: The International Institute for Advanced Studies in Systems Research and Cybernetics (IIAS).

Lasker, G.E. and Hiwaki, K. (ed.) 2001. *Sustainable Development and Global Community—Volume II*. Canada: IIAS.

Lasker, G.E. and Hiwaki, K. (ed.) 2002. *Sustainable Development and Global Community—Volume III*. Canada: IIAS.

Lasker, G.E. and Hiwaki, K. (ed.) 2003. *Sustainable Development and Global Community—Volume IV*. Canada: IIAS.

Lasker, G.E. and Hiwaki, K. (ed.) 2004. *Sustainable Development and Global Community—Volume V*. Canada: IIAS.

Lasker, G.E. and Hiwaki, K (ed.) 2004. *Personal and Spiritual Development in the World of Cultural Diversity—Volume I*. Canada: IIAS.

Lasker, G.E. and Hiwaki, K. (ed.) 2005. *Sustainable Development and Global Community—Volume VI*. Canada: IIAS.

Lasker, G.E. and Hiwaki, K. (ed.) 2005. *Personal and Spiritual Development in the World of Cultural Diversity—Volume II*. Canada: IIAS.

Lasker, G.E. and Hiwaki, K. (ed.) 2006. *Sustainable Development and Global Community—Volume VII*. Canada: IIAS.

Lasker, G.E. and Hiwaki, K. (ed.) 2006. *Personal and Spiritual Development in the World of Cultural Diversity—Volume III*. Canada: IIAS.

Lasker, G.E. and Hiwaki, K. (ed.) 2007. *Sustainable Development and Global Community—Volume VIII*. Canada: IIAS.

Lasker, G.E. and Hiwaki, K. (ed.) 2007. *Personal and Spiritual Development in the World of Cultural Diversity—Volume IV*. Canada: IIAS.

Lasker, G.E. and Hiwaki, K. (ed.) 2008. *Sustainable Development and Global Community—Volume IX*. Canada: IIAS.

Lasker, G.E. and Hiwaki, K. (ed.) 2008. *Personal and Spiritual Development in the World of Cultural Diversity—Volume V*. Canada: IIAS.

Lasker, G.E. and Hiwaki, K. (ed.) 2009. *Sustainable Development and Global Community—Volume X*. Canada: IIAS.

Lasker, G.E. and Hiwaki, K. (ed.) 2009. *Personal and Spiritual Development in the World of Cultural Diversity—Volume VI*. Canada: IIAS.

Learner, A.P. 1970. *The Economics of Control: Principles of Walfare Economics*. New York: Augustus M. Kelly Publishers.

Lekachman, R. 1959. *A History of Economic Ideas*. New York: Harper and Row.

Li, T.W. (ed.) 1998. *The Chinese Livelihood Report*. Jincheng: Jincheng Publishing House.

Marshall, A. 1959. *Principles of Economics*, London: Macmillan.

Mayor, F. 1997. The human right to peace: declaration by the director general of UNESCO, in *A Design for Peace*, edited by G.E. Lasker and V. Lomeiko. Canada: IIAS.

Meade, J.E. 1966. *The Trade and Welfare*. Oxford: Oxford University Press.

Meadows, D.H. and Randers, J. 1972. *The Limit to Growth*. New York: Universe Book.

Meadows, D.H., Meadows, L.D. and Randers, J. 1992. *Beyond the Limit*. Post Mills, Vermont: Chelsea Green Publishing Company.

Meier, G.M. 1980. *International Economics: The Theory of Policy*. Oxford: Oxford University Press.

Minabe, S. 1986. Nippon-teki keiei to hikakuyui riron (literally, the Japanese business management and the theory of comparative Aadvantage), *Hiroshima Daigaku Keizai Ronso*. Hiroshima: Hiroshima Daigaku.

Mitchell, W.C. 1941. *Business Cycles and Their Causes*. Berkeley, CA: University of California Press.

Mitsuhashi, S. 1972. *Kendo*. Tokyo: Taishuukan Shoten.

Modigliani, F. and Brumberg, R. 1954. Utility analysis and the consumption function, in *Post Keynesian Economics*, edited by K.K. Krihara. New Jersey: Rutgers University Press.

Morishima, M. 1995. *Shiso to shiteno Kindai Keizaigaku* (literally, *Modern Economics as an Idea*). Tokyo: Iwanami-Shinsho.

Myrdal, G. 1960. *Beyond the Welfare State*. New Haven: Yale University Press.

Myrdal, G. 1972. *Against the Stream: Critical Essays on Economics*. New York: Random House.

Nakamura, T. 1994. *Kendo Jiten: Gijutsu to Bunka noRekishi* (literally, *Kendo Dictionary: The History of Techniques and Culture*). Tokyo: Shimazu Shobo.

Nakanishi, T. 2004. *Kokumin-no Bunmei-shi* (literally, *The History of National Civilization*). Tokyo: Sankei Shinbun-sha.

Nakayama, I. 1975. *Industrialization and Labor-Management Relations in Japan*. Tokyo: The Japan Institute of Labor.

Nihon Keizai Shinbun (daily newspaper). 2004a. News, June 26, November 9 and December 11, 2004.

Nihon Keizai Shinbun. 2004b. News, December 7.

Nihon Keizai Shinbun. 2008. News, December 26.

Nishibe, S. 2000. *Kokumin no Dotoku* (literally, *Morality of the Nation*). Tokyo: Fuyosha.

Nishikawa, J. 2000. *Ningen-no tameno Keizaigaku* (literally, *Economics for the Humanity*). Tokyo: Iwanami Shoten.

Nitobe, I. 1998. *Bushido*. Tokyo: Kodansha International.

Okada, T. 1995. *Shakai Fukushi-gaku: Ippan Riron no Keifu* (literally, *Social Welfare: A Genealogy of General Theory*). Osaka.

Okada, T. 1997. From "welfare state" to "welfare world". *Japanese Journal of Social Services*, l, 1–5.

Orwell, G. 1949. *1984*. New York: The New American Library.

Ozawa, H. 1997. *Kendo: The Definitive Guide*. Tokyo: Kodansha International.

Peccei, A. 1982. *Approaching the 21st Century: Global Problems and Human Choices: Proceedings of The Club of Rome Symposium in Tokyo 1982*, The Japan Committee of The Club of Rome.

Perlmutter, H. 1982. *Building the Symbiotic Societal Enterprise: A Social Architecture for the Future: Proceedings of The Club of Rome Symposium in Tokyo 1982*, The Japan Committee of The Club of Rome.

Pittway, R.H., Sicherman, N.W. and Yamada, T. 1990. The market for corporate control, the level of agency costs, and corporate collectivism in Japanese mergers, in *Japanese Capital Market*, edited by E.J. Elton and M.J. Gruber. New York: Harper and Row.

Powell, T.G.E. 1981. *The Celts*. London: Thames and Hudson.

Ramsey, F. 1928. A mathematical theory of saving. *Economic Journal*, December 1928, 543–559.

Randall, J.H. 1976. *The Making of the Modern Mind* (50th aniversary edition). New York: Columbia University Press.

Reynolds, L.G., Masters, S.H. and Moser, C.H. (ed.) 1978. Readings in *Labor Economics and Labor Relations*. Englewood Cliffs, NJ: Prentice-Hall.

Roessler, O.E. 2003. The science of human rights, in *Sustainable Development and Global Community—Volume IV*, edited by G.E. Lasker and K. Hiwaki. Canada: IIAS.

Roessler, O., Lasker, G.E. and Hiwaki, K. 2007. A cosmic synthesis, in *Personal and Spiritual Development in the World of Cultural Diversity—Volume IV*, edited by G.E. Lasker and K. Hiwaki. Canada: IIAS.

Schumpeter, J. 1951. *The Theory of Economic Development*. Cambridge, MA: Harvard University Press.

Schumpeter, J. 1954. *History of Economic Analysis*. Oxford: Oxford University Press.

Sen, A. 1992. *Inequality Reexamined*. Cambridge, MA: Harvard University Press.

Sen, A. 1999. *Development as Freedom*. New York: Alfred A. Knopte.

Shiga, I. 2003. *Roshi no Shin-kaishaku* (literally, *New Interpretation of Lao-Tsu*). Tokyo: Taishukan Shoten.

Shinohara, M. 1982. *Industrial Growth, Trade, and Dynamic Patterns in the Japanese Economy*. Tokyo: University of Tokyo Press.

Shinohara, M. 1987. *Nippon Keizai Kogi* (literally, *Lectures on the Japanese Economy*). Tokyo: Toyokeizai Shinpo-sha.

Smith, A. 1937. *An Inquiry into the Nature and Causes of the Wealth of Nations*. New York: The Modern Library.

Soros, G. 1998. *The Crisis of Global Capitalism*. New York: Public Affairs.

Spencer, M.H. 1974. *Contemporary Economics*. New York: Worth Publishers, Inc.

Stern, R.M. 1973. *The Balance of Payments: Theory and Economic Policy*. Chicago: Aldine Publishing Company.

Stigliz, J.E. 2002. *Globalization and Its Discontents*. New York: W.W. Norton and Company.

Suino, N. 1996. *Arts of Strength, Arts of Serenity*. New York: Weatherhill.

Suzuki, Y. (ed.) 1987. *The Japanese Financial System*. Oxford: Clarendon Press.

Symonides, J. 1999. Building a culture of peace, in *Culture of Peace*, edited by G.E. Lasker and V. Lomeiko. Canada: IIAS.

Tanaka, K. 2002. *Shotoku Taishi: Nihon Tetsugaku Kotohajime* (literally, *Prince Shotoku: A first Attempt on the Philosophy of Japan*). Tokyo: Toshi Shuppann.

Thurow, L.C. 1996. *The Future of Capitalism*. New York: William Marrow and Co.

Tiedemann, A.E. (ed.) 1974. *An Introduction to Japanese Civilization*. New York: Columbia University Press.

Tokunaga, H. 2005. *Yokoi Shonan: Ishin-no Aojashin-wo Egaita Otoko* (literally, *Yokoi Shonan: The Man Blueprinted the Restoration*). Tokyo: Shincho-sha.

Tomiki, K. 1992. *Budo-ron* (literally, *Theories of Budo*). Tokyo: Taishuukan Shoten.

Tomiyasu, N. 1973. *Shushinkoyo to Nenko-Joretsu* (literally, *The Lifetime Employment and the Seniority-based Wage and Promotion*). Tokyo: Rodo-Hogaku Shuppan.

Tsuda, M. 1994. *Nippon-no Keiei Bunka: 21Seiki-no Soshiki to Hito* (literally, *Japanese Management Culture: Organization and Man in the 21st Century*). Tokyo: Mineruba Shobo.

Tsuruoka, M. 1999. *Zusetsu Keruto no Rekishi* (literally, *Illustrated History of the Celts*). Tokyo: Kawade Shobo.

Uchino, T. 1983. *Japan's Postwar Economy: An Insider's View of its History and its Future*. Tokyo: Kodansha International.

Umesao, T. 1997. Nihon towa Nanika (literally, *What is Japan?: The Formation and Development of the Modern Japanese Civilization*). Tokyo: Nippon Hosokyokai.

UNDP. 1994. *Human Development Report 1994*. New York: United Nations.

UNDP. 1999. *Human Development Report 1999*. New York: United Nations.

UNDP. 2005. *Human Development Report 2005*. New York: United Nations.

United Nations. 1998. Toward a culture of peace, in *Strategies for Peace*, edited by G.E. Lasker and V. Lomeiko. Canada: IIAS.

Urabe, K. 1978. *Nippon-teki Keiei wo Kangaeru* (literally, *A Thought on the Japanese-style Business Administration*). Tokyo: Chuo-Keizai-sha.

Weizsacker, von R. 1990. Address at the Opening Ceremony of 41st Academic Year of the College of Europe, Bruges, Belgium, September 24.

White, B. 1911. *The Book of Daniel Drew: A Glimpse of the Fisk-Gould-Tweed Regime from the Inside*. New York: Doubleday, Page and Company.

Wojciechowski, J.A. 2003. Who Are We, and Where Are We Heading?, in *Advances in Sociocybernetics and Human Development—Volume VI*, edited by G.E. Lasker. Canada: IIAS.

World Commission on Environment and Development (WCED) 1987. *Our Common Future*. Oxford: Oxford University Press.

Wu, J.C. 2002. *China's Strategy*. Guan Ming: Guan Ming Daily Press.

Yamada, Y., Koizumi, A., Shinohara, M., Miyazawa, and Ara, K. 1966. *New Dictionary of the Modern Economics* (in Japanese). Tokyo: Kobunsha.

Yang, Y.Y. 1997. *China's Problems*. Today's China Press.

Yoshimura, T. 2004. *Shotoku Taishi* (literally, *Prince Shotoku*). Tokyo: Iwanami Shinsho.

Yushkiavitshus, H. 1995. *Does Democratization Help Economic Development?: Keynote Address at the International Conference on Interdisciplinary Research*, Karlovy Vary, Czech Republic, August 10–14, 1995.

Author's Work in English

1979. *Some Analytical Aspects of the Japanese "Lifetime Employment" system* (PhD Dissertation). The City University of New York (microfilmed 1979), 1–248.

1990. The stable long-term employment system of Japan: a microeconomic perspective. *Human Systems Management*, 9(1), 15–28.

1991. The stable long-term employment system and the postwar economy of Japan. *Human Systems Management,* 10(2), 107–139.

1992. View from Japan: asymmetries in the evolving European-Japanese dialogue, in *Toward Political Union*, edited by R. Rummel. Boulder: Westview Press, 227–238.

1995a. General—as opposed to Orwellian—socioeconomic development, in *The 2nd Orwellian Symposium*, edited by George E. Lasker. Canada: The International Institute for Advanced Studies in Systems Research and Cybernetics (IIAS), 51–55.

1995b. Prelude to the global management of human systems, in *Advances in Human Development— Volume I*, edited by G.E. Lasker. Canada: IIAS, 59–63.

1995c. Sustainable socioeconomic development, in *Advances in Human Development—Volume II*, edited by G.E. Lasker. Canada: IIAS, 58–63.

1995d. People's own invisible hands and evolution of high concern, in *Advances in Human Development—Volume II*, edited by G.E. Lasker. Canada: IIAS, 68–73.

1996a. People's own invisible hands for sustainable socioeconomic development, in *The Study of International Relations*, edited by the Graduate School of International Relations, Tokyo International University. Saitama, Japan: Tokyo International University. 9, 1–18.

1996b. Human development and Sustainable Development: consequences of the Japanese general education, in *Advances in Education—Volume II*, edited by G.E. Lasker. Canada: IIAS, 10–16.

1997. Society of longevity and Sustainable Development: a positive perspective, in *Advances in Sociocybernetics and Human Development—Volume IV*, edited by G.E. Lasker. Canada: IIAS, 41–46.

1998a. Sustainable development: framework for a general theory. *Human Systems Management*, 17(4), 267–279.

1998b. *Development Theory of Interest or Interest Theory of Development?*: Proceedings of the 15th International Congress on Cybernetics (Congress of the Association Internationale de Cybernetique), Namur, Belgium, August 24–28, 1998, 598–603.

1998c. Culture of peace, Sustainable Development and society of longevity: a theoretical perspective, *Strategies for Peace*, edited by G.E. Lasker and V. Lomeiko. Canada: IIAS, 62–66.

1999a. A breakthrough in the dilemma of war or peace: the teachings of Kendo, in *Culture of Peace*, edited by G.E. Lasker and V. Lomeiko. Canada: IIAS, 107–112.

1999b. Culture of peace and long-run theory of employment, in *Culture of Peace*, edited by G.E. Lasker and V. Lomeiko. Canada: IIAS, 143–147.

1999c. *Japan in Distress: Economic or Societal Malfunction?*: Proceedings of the 11th International Congress of Cybernetics and Systems, edited by R. Vallee and J. Rose (Brunel University, Uxbridge UK) August 23–27, 1999, 131–133.

2000a. Thought-frame enhancement for peace consciousness, in *Quest for Peace*, edited by G.E. Lasker, A. Aydin and H. Schwarzlander, Canada: IIAS, 61–65.

2000b. A long-run approach to international trade for Sustainable Development, in *Sustainable Development and Global Community—Volume I*, edited by G.E. Lasker and K. Hiwaki. Canada: IIAS, 25–30.

2000c. *Small-Firm Strategy in the Computer Age—A Culture-Oriented Approach: Proceedings of the 8th Annual International Conference on Business and Economic Development in Central and Eastern Europe: Implications for Economic Integration into Wider Europe* (Technological University of Brno, Czech Republic) September 7–9, 2000, 291–302.

2000d. *An Essential Role of Education for Our Market-Driven Computer Age*: Proceedings (CD) of the Seventh Conference of the International Society for the Study of European Ideas (University of Bergen, Norway) August 14–18, 2000.

2001a. Thought-frame enhancement for the age of digitized globalization. *Consciousness, Literature and the Arts* [online], 2(1), 1–13 [online]. Available at: http://www.aber.ac.uk/tfts/jounal/march2001/biohiwaki.html [accessed: May 4, 2001].

2001b. A culture-enhancing theory of flourishing employment (Editorial Feature Article). *The Journal of the BWW Society*, 1(2), 1–14.

2001c. Sustainable development: essentials for an integrated approach, in *Sustainable Development and Global Community—Volume II*, edited by G.E. Lasker and K. Hiwaki. Canada: IIAS, 7–12.

2001d. Celtic civilization and modern economics, in *Advances in Sociocybernetics and Human Development—Volume IX*, edited by G.E. Lasker. Canada: IIAS, 95–99.

2002a. Sustainable development and a culture-integrated theory of international trade (Editorial Feature Article). *The Journal of The BWW Society*, 2(1), 2–18.

2002b. *Education, Thought Frame, and Important Issues of the 21st Century: Proceedings (CD) of the 8th Conference of the International Society for the Study of European Ideas* [ISSEI 2002] (University of Wales, Aberystwyth, Wales, UK) July 22–27, 2002.

2002c. Why does Sustainable Development require enrichment of cultures worldwide? in *Sustainable Development and Global Community—Volume III*, edited by G.E. Lasker and K. Hiwaki. Canada: IIAS, 13–8.

2002d. Celts and diverse human cultures, in *Advances in Sociocybernetics and Human Development—Volume X*, edited by G.E. Lasker. Canada: IIAS, 107–111.

2002e. *Cultural Enrichment and Diversity for the Advancement of Positive Global Solutions: Proceedings of the 1st International Congress of the BWW Society* (Saint Germain-en-Laye, France) August 4–8, 2002.

2003a. Innovative education for important issues under globalization. *Consciousness, Literature and the Arts*, 4(1), 1–14 [Online]. Available at: http://www/aber/ac/uk/tfts/journal/archive/hiwaki2.html [accessed August 14, 2003].

2003b. Sustainable development: functional guideline for a multi-dimensional approach, in *Sustainable Development and Global Community—Volume IV*, edited by G.E. Lasker and K. Hiwaki. Canada: IIAS, 1–6.

2003c. Celtic and Roman patterns of aggression recurring as mingled in the modern world, in *Advances in Sociocybernetics and Human Development—Volume XI*, edited by G.E. Lasker. Canada: IIAS, 79–83.

2003d. *A Devastated Culture and Non-Credibility Trap: A Theoretical Approach: Keynote Address as the Honorary Chairman of the 2nd International Congress of the BWW Society* (Malaga, Spain) August 3–7, 2003.

2004a. Personal-spiritual development and new enlightenment, in *Personal and Spiritual Development in the World of Cultural Diversity—Volume I*, edited by G.E. Lasker and K. Hiwaki. Canada: IIAS, 1–6.

2004b. Wheels for Sustainable Development, in *Sustainable Development and Global Community—Volume V*, edited by G.E. Lasker and K. Hiwaki. Canada: IIAS, 1–6.

2004c. *Big Brother or Big Market: How Can We Escape the Dilemma?: Keynote Address of the 3rd Orwellian Symposium* (organized by G.E. Lasker): (the 16th International Conference on Systems Research, Informatics and Cybernetics, Baden-Baden, Germany) July 29–August 5, 2004.

2005a. *Global or Insular: A Conflicting Reality: Keynote Address to the Symposium on Dream Globe Where the Sorrow and Joy are Shared* (the 17th International Conference on Systems Research, Informatics and Cybernetics, Baden-Baden, Germany) August 1–7, 2005.

2005b. *Sustainable Societies Require Wholesome Cultures as Immune Systems: Keynote Address to the Collaborative Inquiry into Processes for Creating Sustainable Societies* (the 17th International Conference on Systems Research, Informatics and Cybernetics, Baden-Baden, Germany) August 1–7, 2005.

2005c. Cultural enrichment and personal maturation, in *Personal and Spiritual Development in the World of Cultural Diversity—Volume II*, edited by G.E. Lasker and K. Hiwaki. Canada: IIAS, 1–5.

2005d. Culture-hinged campaigns for Sustainable Development, in *Sustainable Development and Global Community—Volume VI*, edited by G.E. Lasker and K. Hiwaki. Canada: IIAS, 1–5.

2005e. *Deadly Paradoxes of the Contemporary World: A World View Keynote Address at the 2nd International Symposium on Strategic Planning for the Future: Visions and Challenges* (Francensbad, Czech Republic) August 8–10, 2005.

2006a. Credibility Trap: Japan today and China tomorrow. (written with Junie Tong). *Human Systems Management*, 25(l), 31–50.

2006b. Developing Creativity: A Sound Culture for Sound Creativity: *Proceedings (CD) of the 10th Conference of International Society for the Study of European Ideas* [ISSEI 2006] (the University of Malta, Malta) July 24–29, 2006.

2006c. Integrity or progress: life or death?, in *Personal and Spiritual Development in the World of Cultural Diversity—Volume III,* edited by G.E. Lasker and K. Hiwaki. Canada: IIAS,1–6.

2006d. Sustainable development and worldwide "social cost", in *Sustainable Development and Global Community—Volume VII,* edited by G.E. Lasker and K. Hiwaki. Canada: IIAS, 1–5.

2007a. Economic globalization as against Sustainable Development, in *Sustainable Development and Global Community—Volume VIII,* edited by G.E. Lasker and K. Hiwaki. Canada: IIAS, 1–5.

2007b. Democracy for our insular planet, in *Personal and Spiritual Development in the World of Cultural Diversity—Volume IV,* edited by G.E. Lasker and K. Hiwaki. Canada: IIAS, 1–5.

2008a. Sustainable development: local-global linkage, in *Sustainable Development and Global Community—Volume IX,* edited by G.E. Lasker and K. Hiwaki. Canada: IIAS, 1–5.

2008b. Sound culture and wisdom complex, in *Personal and Spiritual Development in the World of Cultural Diversity—Volume V,* edited by G.E. Lasker and K. Hiwaki. Canada: IIAS, 1–8.

2009a. Sustainable development: a general theory in a nutshell, in *Sustainable Development and Global Community—Volume X,* edited by G.E. Lasker and K. Hiwaki. Canada: IIAS, 1–5.

2009b. "Integrity in diversity" for an "open" democracy, in *Personal and Spiritual Development in the World of Cultural Diversity—Volume XI,* edited by G.E. Lasker and K. Hiwaki. Canada: IIAS, 1–5.

Author's Work in Japanese

1982J. Nippon-teki sutagufureshion (literally, A Japanese stagflation), *Journal of the International College of Commerce and Economics* (25), 79–89.

1983J. Boeki Masatsu no Nippon-teki Enin (literally, A fundamental Japanese factor behind the prevailing trade conflicts), *Journal of the International College of Commerce and Economics* (27), 95–103.

1985J. Nippon-teki kigyo chikuseki: roshi kyodotai no jiko-zoshoku kino (literally, Corporate accumulation "Japanese style": self-proliferation of the communal firm), *Journal of the International College of Commerce and Economics* (edited by the Department of International Studies and Human Relations) (32), 15–44.

1986Ja. Shiron: Nippon-teki shihon shijo: kodo seichouke ni okeru roshi kyodotai no shihon chotatsu mekanisumu (literally, A "Japanese phenomenon" in capital market: the communal firm's capitalization mechanism), *Journal of the International College of Commerce and Economics* (edited by the Department of International Studies and Human Relations) (33), 31–39.

1986Jb. *Shiron: Chouki Antei-teki Koyo-seido to Hikaku–yui Kozo no Henka* (literally, *The Long-term Stable Employment System and Changes in the Structure of Japanese Comparative Advantage*): *Proceedings of the 37th Japanese Association of International Economics*, 81–89.

1987Ja. Nippon-teki kojin chochiku (I): shokasetsu no seiri to mondai teiki (literally, Personal aving "Japanese style" (I): prelude to a new hypothesis), *Journal of Tokyo International University* (edited by the Department of International Studies and Human Relations) (35), 143–154.

1987Jb. Nippon-teki kojin chochiku (II): chochiku ippan riron wo mezasu kyoyu-shiyu zaisan kasetsuno teisho (literally, Personal saving "Japanese style" (II): proposition of "common-and-private" properties hypothesis in an attempt for a general theory of personal saving), *Journal of Tokyo International University* (edited by the Department of International Studies and Human Relations) (36), 39–54.

1990J. Nippon-teki kojin chochiku (III): kyoyu-shiyu zaisan kasetsu no seichika to Nippon tokutei no kokoromi (literally, Personal saving "Japanese style" (III): refinement and application of the common-and-private properties hypothesis to the Japanese economy), *Journal of Tokyo International University* (edited by the Department of International Studies and Human Relations) (41), 65–76.

1993Ja. Chikyu keizai no jizoku-kano na hatten: choki makuro-keizai wakugumi ni yoru ippan riron no kokoromi (literally, Sustainable Development of the global economy: a general theory based on a long-term macroeconomic framework), *Journal of Tokyo International University* (edited by the School of International Studies and Human Relations) (48), 1–5.

1993Jb. *Sekai Keizai no Juyo Kadai to Nippon Keizai no Seisaku Sentakushi—choki Makuro-keizai Wakugumi no Teisho wo Kanete* (literally, *Important Issues of the World Economy and Policy Choices of the Japanese Economy: Based on the Proposed Theoretical Framework for Long-term Macroeconomics*): *Proceedings of the 44th Japanese Association of International Economics*, 216–222.

1994Ja. Nippon-gata keizai shisutemu ni taisuru choki-bunseki-teki shiza—saisei-ki ni okeru seicho mekanizumu (literally, A long-term analytical view of the Japanese economic system: An inquiry into the growth mechanism during the golden age), *Journal of Tokyo International University* (edited by the School of International Studies and Human Relations) (49), 15–37.

1994Jb. Nippon-gata keizai shisutemu ni taisuru choki-bunseki-teki shiza: choki makuro-keizai wakugumi ni okeru apurochi (literally, A long-term analytical view of the Japanese economic system: socio-macroeconomic approach), *Journal of Tokyo International University* (edited by the School of International Relations) (50), 29–6.

1995Ja. Shakai · keizai hatten to Nippon no kyoiku mondai (literally, Socioeconomic Development and Japan's Educational Issue), *Kaihatsu Kyouiku* (published by Kaihatsu Kyouiku Kyogikai) (30), 31–46.

1995Jb. Chikyu shakai no jizoku-kano na hatten to Nippon-EU kyoryoku wo kangaeru (literally, Sustainable development of the global community and indispensable Japan-EU cooperation), *Journal of Tokyo International University* (edited by the School of International Relations) (52), 1–30.

2002J. Heiwa bunka to jizoku-kano na hatten: Kendo seishin kara no sekkin (literally, Culture of peace and Sustainable Development: an approach from the Kendo spirit and teaching), *Journal of Tokyo International University* (edited by the School of International Relations) (59), 1–17.

2004J. Shakai-tokutei bunka to shijo genri-shugi: sekai-teki juyo kadai heno hokatsu-teki apurochi (literally, Society-specific cultures and market fundamentalism: a comprehensive approach to the important issues worldwide), in *Atarashii Kyodotai heno Mosaku to Kigyo Rinri* (iterally, *A New grope for Community and Corporate Ethics*), edited by Tokyo Kokusai Daigaku-Kokusai Koryu Kenkyuusho (22), 17–46.

2005J. Jizoku-kano na hatten to setsuna-teki na shijo genri-shugi: hokatsu-teki kaiketsu no arikata towa (literally, Sustainable development and market fundamentalism: A Comprehensive Approach to Solution). *Journal of Tokyo International University* (edited by the School of International Relations) (62), 1–33.

Index